WHOLENESS AND HOLINESS

MEDICINE, DISEASE, PURITY, AND THE LEVITICAL PRIESTHOOD

Michael A. Glasby

WIPF & STOCK · Eugene, Oregon

Wipf and Stock Publishers
199 W 8th Ave, Suite 3
Eugene, OR 97401

Wholeness and Holiness
Medicine, Disease, Purity, and the Levitical Priesthood
By Glasby, Micahel
Copyright©2017 Apostolos
ISBN 13: 978-1-5326-6913-2
Publication date 9/16/2018
Previously published by Apostolos, 2017

More Books from Apostolos

Romans: Hope for the Nations

The Emergence of Pentecostalism in Wales

New Exodus in Hebrews

The Role of the Holy Spirit in Biblical Hermeneutics

A Comprehensive Reference Dictionary of Linguistics

For details of all our publications visit www.apostolos-publishing.com

CONTENTS

INTRODUCTION: WHOLENESS, HOLINESS AND HEALTHCARE 9

Hermeneutics of This Study 10

Medical Exegesis 12

Reception History 13

Wholeness and Holiness as Parameters of the Investigation 13
    Wholeness 13
    Holiness 14

THE LEVITICAL TEXTS AND ASSOCIATED MATERIAL 16

The Biblical Book of Leviticus 16

Jewish Material From Later Times and a Later Worldview 34
    The Talmud 35
    Leviticus Rabbah 36
    The Dead Sea Scrolls: A Later Viewpoint 36

WHOLENESS AND HEALTHCARE IN THE ANCIENT NEAR EAST 38
    Disease and Illness 38

Influences From Other Cultures of the Ancient Near East 39
    Egypt 40
    Mesopotamia 44
    Greece 49
    Arabia 50

Healthcare in Ancient Israel Outside the Priestly Society 52

A Unique Example of an Israelite Physician from a Later Period 53

Magic and Manticism 57

Botanical Medicine in Ancient Syria–Palestine 63

WHOLENESS AND HEALTHCARE IN THE PRIESTLY SOCIETY OF ISRAEL 67

Priestly Ideology and Ritual 67
    The Priestly Weltanschauung 67
    Priestly Duties 69
    The Priestly Concept of Ritual 70

Medicine in the Priestly Society 72
    Medical Language in the Hebrew Bible 73

PURITY AND IMPURITY IN THE PRIESTLY SOCIETY OF ANCIENT ISRAEL 83
    The Priestly View of Purity and Impurity 84
    Terminology 85
    Impurity and Defilement 86
    Ideas of Ritual Impurity and Moral Impurity 86
    [Im]Purity and [Un]Holiness 88
    Sin 91

Modern Views of Biblical Impurity 94
    Douglas: A Sociological Approach. 94
    Neusner: A Working Hypothesis. 96
    Neusner's Idea of Cultic Purity/Impurity 97
    Milgrom: An Exhaustive Analysis 100
    Frymer-Kensky: A Classification of Impurity. 104
    Wright: Permitted and Prohibited Impurities 109
    Jenson: A Holiness Spectrum 111
    Klawans: Ritual and Moral Impurity, Revised 112

THE "LEPROSY" PROBLEM 121

Background 122

Hansen's Disease 124
    Aetiology 125
    Diagnosis 125

Epidemiology 126
Pathology 127
Physical Symptoms and Signs 127
Treatment 128

Elephantiasis Graecorum 128

"Leprosy" or צרעת in the Hebrew Bible 133
Etymology of צרעת 134
Other Hebrew Words to Describe "Leprosy" 136
Cognate Languages of the Ancient Near East 136

צרעת — Semantics or Semiology? 140

Archaeological Evidence from the First Century 141

צרעת A MEDICAL EXEGESIS OF LEVITICUS CHAPTER 13 143

The Nature of צרעת 143

A Medical Exegesis of Leviticus Chapter 13 144
13:1 Introductory Command 144
13:2–17 Symptoms and Signs 144
13:7–46 Further Symptoms and Signs 150

The Leviticus Rabbah and צרעת 160

צרעת In the Dead Sea Scrolls 164

זוב GENITAL EFFLUXIONS: A MEDICAL EXEGESIS OF LEVITICUS CHAPTER 15 171

Structure of Leviticus Chapter 15 173

A Medical Exegesis of Leviticus 15 175

The Leviticus Rabbah & Genital Discharges 197

BLEMISH, DEFORMITY & DISABILITY 199

Terminology and Logometrics 199

Negative Imagery and Disability 201

Beauty and Ugliness in the Hebrew Bible 204

A Neuro-Biological Approach to Blemish 207

Mortal Flesh as a Symbol of Defilement 211

Blemishes in the Hebrew Bible 212
    Classification of Blemishes in the Hebrew Bible 213
    The Emphasis on Sexual Function and Dysfunction 221
    Mental Disability 224
    Blemished Individuals in Israelite Society 227

CONTAGION 229

Nosologies of the Ancient Near East 230

A Comparative Approach 230
    Egypt 231
    Mesopotamia 231
    Arabia 235
    Greece and Rome 236

Ancient Syria-Palestine 237
    Lieber's View of Contagion 238

Contagion as Symbolism and Metaphor 239

צרעת AND UN-WHOLENESS 245

Evidence From the Language of the Texts 246
    Language and Thought in the Hebrew Bible 246
    Context Logometrics 248
    Doctors and Physicians 249
    זוב 252
    צרעת 253
    צרעת—Evidence from the Hebrew Bible 256

What צרעת Might Have Been if it Were a Disease 257
    Elephantiasis Graecorum 258
    Vitiligo—Leucoderma 258
    Scabies 258
    Favus 258
    Pellagra 259
    Leishmaniasis 259
    Chronic Psoriasis 259
    The Treponematoses 260
    Lieber's Medical View of צרעת 261

צרעת AND UN-HOLINESS 265

Baden's and Moss's View — צרעת and Sin 265

Impurity and Holiness: the Influence of Deuteronomy 269
    Levitical Dynamic-Holiness and Deuteronomic Static-Holiness 270

צרעת in Biblical Passages Beyond the Torah 275

The Case of Ancient Israel 279

HEALTHCARE, WHOLENESS, AND HOLINESS: SYNERGY OR TENSION? 285

Healthcare ↔ Wholeness ↔ Holiness 285
    Healthcare ↔ Wholeness 285
    Wholeness ↔ Holiness 286
    Healthcare ↔ Holiness 288

BIBLIOGRAPHY 293

SELECTED INDEX 294

Chapter 1

INTRODUCTION: WHOLENESS, HOLINESS AND HEALTHCARE

It is generally accepted that the *Levitical Purity Laws* of ancient Israel were established and maintained as measures against defilement of sacred objects and places. This book investigates the extent to which they were also intended to be seen as public health measures contributing to the wellbeing of individuals and society—for although the biblical book of Leviticus has often been described as the "Earliest textbook of medical hygiene", it is no doubt pertinent for us to ask whether such an appellation accurately reflects the intentions of the priests or if it is simply the result of modern opinion formed (perhaps inappropriately) through an accumulation of later redaction and exegesis.

Gorman[1] has made the point that scholarship relating to the Levitical priesthood has concentrated upon textual analysis with inadequate concern for the conceptual, ideological, and theological aspects of the priestly cult. If the purity laws are to be seen as based largely upon ritual, this is an omission requiring remedy. Equally, it may be said that the medical aspects of the purity laws, if they existed at all, might have been emphasized by an overzealous desire to interpret them in terms of modern medical and scientific understanding. A central objective of the present work, therefore, is to investigate the relationship between the Levitical priestly wholenesss ↔ holiness paradigm for ritual purity and the development of medical practice in ancient Israel. In so doing it must concern itself, above all, with evaluating the Levitical textual material to establish whether the priestly *Weltanschauung* provided a substrate permitting the development of a rudimentary form of public healthcare, or was simply concerned with the establishment and maintenance of sacramental hygiene. In order to do this, it will be necessary for us to consider a number of points:

(1) The priestly world view and the place of ritual within it.
(2) The extent to which medicine/healthcare as we understand it today, had developed in the Ancient Near East (ANE) in general and in particular in ancient Israel.
(3) The nature of purity/impurity as seen by the Levitical priesthood.
(4) The nature and provenance of the available textual material.
(5) Those diseases/quasi-diseases and forms of blemish seen by the priests as causing ritual impurity.

---

[1] Frank H. Gorman, *The Ideology of Ritual: Space, Time and Status in the Priestly Theology* (Sheffield: JSOT Press, 1990).

(6) The transmissibility of risk to people, society and sacred objects by the contagious nature of such conditions.

As a working hypothesis, the following are proposed:

(1) That in the worldview of the Levitical priesthood, holiness was established and maintained through ritual purity.
(2) That ritual purity in individuals depended upon their organic integrity—wholeness. That wholeness was manifested in terms of bodily appearance and reproductive capacity and, to a lesser extent, by the absence of blemish.
(3) That wholeness, and therefore ritual purity, was compromised by violation of these categories.
(4) That the most serious of these violations, צרעת and זוב were characterized by their being contagious.
(5) That both צרעת and זוב had features in common with, but were not wholly identifiable as, diseases known today.
(6) That the priestly countermeasures—sacramental hygiene—taken against these infractions of wholeness were aimed solely at the preservation of holiness and should not be interpreted as rudimentary public health medicine.
(7) That their later adoption into the field of medical care was fortunate but unintentional.

HERMENEUTICS OF THIS STUDY

From the above it may be supposed that *wholeness* and *holiness* are the *parameters* governing all of the *variables* to be considered in this investigation. It is necessary, therefore, to begin with an attempt to put these into an appropriate context.

The most tangible and available resource for a study of this kind is textual material.[2] It is has been said by Jenson[3] that no theological or historical study of textual material can be totally disinterested, and that the difficulty in attempting to overcome this intrinsic problem has led to an embarrassing plethora of diverse approaches. Of these, Jenson cites the following:

(1) Lexical—key words.
(2) Thematic—important ideas.
(3) Comparative—other ANE contexts.
(4) Historical—in Israelite and related civilizations.
(5) Kerygmatic—entailing a message for a specific community.
(6) Canonical—a finalized theological text aimed at a specific community.

---

2 See chapter 2 for a full consideration.
3 Philip Peter Jenson, *Graded Holiness: A Key to the Priestly Conception of the World* (Sheffield: JSOT, 1992), 212.

(7) Apologetic—explanatory especially for later civilizations.
(8) Dimensional—ordering of a cult in space, society, action time etc.

Jenson supposes that because each of these approaches asks a specific question, each is *ipso facto* limited in terms of the conclusions which can be reached: this is almost certainly the case. In the present work, it is necessary to go a step further and attempt to investigate the relationship between the priestly worldview and priestly activity in ancient Israel to see if this included any medical practice—which I shall conveniently (albeit inelegantly) term *healthcare*.[4] The central question is whether the priestly worldview encompassed any sort of medical thinking and whether the priests had any *sense* that their practices might have had a role beyond the preservation of the purity of sacred objects and sites.

The difficulty in answering this question is that it is not intellectually legitimate to extrapolate from a priestly worldview in ancient Israel to a medical worldview in modern times. Even if the priestly worldview encompassed "medical thought" we have no legitimate reason to suppose that it necessarily operated in any modern sense. These strictures will severely curtail any conventional deductive scientific method. Textual evidence, considered alongside historical material may be interpreted in a medical context only as far as this is possible without entraining the pitfalls enumerated below. It is, nevertheless important to address Jenson's categories 1, 2, 3, 4 and (in respect of the priestly worldview) 8, in order to cover appropriate aspects of the problem. The plan is therefore, to combine review and analysis and to avoid unjustified speculation. This will necessarily involve a survey of the state of medicine in the Ancient Near East with particular emphasis on Syria-Palestine and a consideration of what this subsequently became. This is not intended to be a "reception historical" approach but simply a means of testing the intention behind earlier practices. The ideology of the Levitical priests and the nature of their rituals will also be considered. Analysis will involve a lexical, semantic, and etymological approach to important words and their usage concerned with health, wholeness, and holiness, using the technique of *context logometrics*. In addition, the nature of those conditions that appear to be *category violaters* of the wholeness↔holiness relationship and which in modern thought *may be* true diseases, will be considered by *medical exegesis*. The central role of צרעת and זוב as substrates for priestly activity, what these were and what they were seen to be under the priestly worldview, is the focal point of this study. There are certain difficulties that one might expect to encounter in reaching for this goal. An author with an experimental scientific background is bound to feel most comfortable with an approach that involves deductive reasoning. Inductive reasoning must, nevertheless be employed in

---

4 Defined in the OED as: "health care orig. U.S., care for the general health of a person, community." For present purposes it is not intended that a more specific definition should be considered.

dealing with material from ancient times where incontrovertible, independently verifiable, and detailed factual evidence is unlikely to be available. Inductive reasoning is very helpful if care is taken to keep as close as possible to the textual material and to avoid speculation and anachronism, the latter especially where medical matters are concerned.[5] In a study of this nature there are two areas where it is especially important to be vigilant for these pitfalls, they are the use of medical exegesis and unintended lapses into reception history.

MEDICAL EXEGESIS

Chapters 13 and 15 of the book of Leviticus appear *prima facie* to be of medical interest and it is important to consider how far it is intellectually permissible to conclude that the Levitical usage of certain medical-sounding words (especially the elusive weasel-words צרעת and זוב), signified a true a medical context or simply referred to a generic moral or spiritual but not pathological uncleanness.

The making of any such distinction, risks the projection of modern ideas and definitions on to ancient events. The priestly practices may appear to be both diagnostic and preventive, but nowhere in the text is it specifically implied that priests operated as physicians or any sort of therapeutic agent. The idea that their worldview encompassed any sort of "medical sense" may be no more, therefore, than a presumption by later readers.

Those who, like the present author, were school children in the 1950s were, on the whole, discouraged from reading Leviticus for fear of awkward questions that might embarrass parents and teachers. Attention was preferentially directed to the more wholesome narrative passages of the Old Testament. Nevertheless, it was fashionable, at that time, to make the very positive assertion that the Levitical text was the "first textbook of hygiene". A modern alternative viewpoint is that priests "invented hygiene" by default. This is *post hoc* analysis and begs the question: "By their 'hygienic' measure what were they trying to protect?'" It is important in trying to answer this question, that any approach does not risk inappropriate thinking such as anachronism and *hyperdiagnosis*: the tendency to over-interpret the medical data available in ancient texts in a modern way. *Medical exegesis* must combine a degree of legitimate medical and historical interpretation with a semantic/etymological/linguistic approach and wherever possible, avoid hindsight. It was a failure to apply such principles in an informed and self-critical way that led to the confusion of צרעת with leprosy by the early translators of the Hebrew Bible and Septuagint into English.[6]

---

5 Any reasoning may, however, prove difficult given the inexactitude of the relevant information and the "pietic licence" that often pervades later biblical writings and writings about biblical writings. The considerable imbalance between the greater mass of biblical and the lesser mass of secular material that has persisted to modern times may skew the making of rational judgements with any realistic degree of probability.
6 See M. Glasby, "What was Biblical Leprosy?" (MTh thesis, University of Edinburgh, 2011) and M. Glasby, "Wholeness and Holiness: Synergy or Tension? Medicine, Disease and the Purity Laws of Ancient Israel" (PhD thesis, University of Edinburgh, 2015).

RECEPTION HISTORY

Historical material used in this study is no less at risk from a potential source of error that parallels *hyperdiagnosis*. This is *reception history,* a relatively recent and controversial approach to history. It concentrates preferentially on meanings that have been imputed to historical events by tracing the ways in which participants, observers, historians, and other retrospective interpreters have attempted to make sense of events, not only as they occurred but also over the time that has elapsed since.[7] The intention is supposedly to make these events more meaningful for the present.

The problem with reception history is that retrospective interpretation risks both colouration and harmonization either by emphasis of what the ultimate recipients (e.g. faith communities) believe to be important and/or by the presentation of exhaustive collections of others' interpretations. There is a subtle distinction, therefore, between *reception history* and the scholarly *review* of others' work. Where for example, a survey is made of alternative forms of contemporaneous healthcare in the Ancient Near East, it may be difficult to avoid the criticism of reception history. However, presentation of multiple examples is surely legitimate where the objective (chapter 3) is to emphasize how one particular culture stands out from others because of its uncharacteristically involving a tightly-knit priesthood and well-developed cosmic, social, and cultic *Lebensformen*.

WHOLENESS AND HOLINESS AS PARAMETERS OF THE INVESTIGATION

As I have already stated, the two central parameters of the present study are *wholeness* and *holiness* as perceived in the worldview of the Levitical priesthood. This worldview is more fully considered in chapter 4, but the two parametric working definitions must be formulated at the outset.

Wholeness

The worldview of the Levitical priesthood was religious, concerned with the structure of the cosmos and also with the appropriate way to live in the created world. Self-awareness for individuals in such a society and their resultant acting upon that self-awareness, was mediated in priestly society through *ritual*. Ritual was always symbolic and directed ultimately at the avoidance of chaos and at maintenance of the social order demanded by the priestly *Weltanschauung*. In order to participate fully and effectively in ritual, the individual must be free of anything that might compromise his wholeness. Wholeness is, therefore, a necessary qualification for ritual purity in the individual and as such contributes

---

[7] Hans Robert Jauss, *Aesthetic Experience and Literary Hermeneutics* (Minneapolis: University of Minnesota Press, 1982); Hans Robert Jauss and Timothy Bahti, *Toward an Aesthetic of Reception* (Minneapolis: University of Minnesota Press, 1982).

to the maintenance of order on the larger social and cosmic scales. In the Hebrew Bible, there is no clear definition of wholeness. Leviticus more customarily dwells on its antithesis, "impurity", and so un-wholeness is more available as subject matter for investigation. *Prima facie*, in the Levitical text three major factors appear to be operational as infractions of wholeness. These are: disfigurement of the (visible) body surface; compromise of reproductive capacity; and to a lesser extent, the presence of blemish. The relationship of these factors is complex and penetration into the density of this relationship is a major aim of this work. Although the same organic precipitating factors (צרעת, זוב and מום) operate universally, two somewhat different models of the symbolic nature of wholeness have been proposed by later authors.

(1) Anthropological/Sociological model—absence of any antitypicality of appearance (visible body parts) or compromise of reproductive function.
(2) Taxonomical model—a maintained state of sacramental hygiene.

In either case wholeness is the organic cause and manifestation of ritual purity and at the root of its positive symbolism. Here in both cases, wholeness is seen as a *categorical determinant* of ritual purity and a prerequisite for its symbolic place in the attainment of holiness.

The anthropological/sociological model is based somewhat upon the idea of *taboo* with *wholeness* and *un-wholeness* seen as *type* and *antitype*.

The taxonomical model, preferred by most ancient and modern Jewish authors, although recognizing the same causative factors (צרעת, זוב and מום), has focussed less upon the aetiology of impurity than upon its scope. As a result, categories of impurity (major and minor, metaphorical) have been postulated and from this classification corresponding antidotal categories of ritual necessary for expiation, have been formulated.

Holiness

A general definition of the word from the OED is: "The quality of being holy; spiritual perfection or purity; sanctity, saintliness; sacredness." This is unsatisfactory for present purposes as it is too general. The priest-mediated society of ancient Israel had as a fundamental consequence of its established tripartite[8] order, the immanence of Yahweh in the holy shrine, which was (ultimately) at the heart of the nation. This indwelling may be thought of as the primary constitutive element of the priestly world order and this is holiness in its priestly form. It was put at risk by a loss of ritual purity in individuals whose wholeness was compromised. It was the priests' job to preserve holiness by

---

8 The three parts were cosmic, social, and cultic—see chapter 4.

guarding sacred objects and places, diagnosing loss of personal wholeness in individuals[9] and taking appropriate action through the enactment of restoration rituals so that the order of creation might be preserved.

---

9 And of course, objects and even buildings that might become afflicted by צרעת.

Chapter 2

THE LEVITICAL TEXTS AND ASSOCIATED MATERIAL

The Levitical writings embody laws relating to the practicalities of Israelite life. The most important of these is, of course, the biblical book of Leviticus which, in contrast to the preceding and succeeding biblical books, contains instructions about life-style rather than narrative. For Leviticus, the avoidance of sin is paramount because its presence disrupts the harmony between God and his chosen people. The avoidance of sin entails, *inter alia*, the maintenance of purity and this is ultimately the responsibility of the priesthood. The book of Leviticus is self-contained and deals with the formulation and enactment of laws of behaviour, food-hygiene, and especially sexual matters. Two conditions (possibly diseases) צרעת and זוב, are the subject each of a chapter of the book and the specific nature of these conditions and the way they were regarded within the priestly worldview is a central objective of any study of the notion of purity/impurity. As might be expected, a very considerable body of interpretative literature that deals with similar subject matter has grown up surrounding the book of Leviticus and for this reason has been termed collectively the *Levitical writings*. This in particular includes the Leviticus Rabbah,[10] a homiletic midrash thought to have been written, or more likely redacted out of older texts, in the 5th century and there is "Levitical" material concerned with healthcare matters to be found in the Dead Sea Scrolls.[11] By far the greatest volume of interpretative, *secondary* Levitical literature is, however, to be found in the Talmud.[12]

THE BIBLICAL BOOK OF LEVITICUS

Liber Leviticus or ἡ βιβλιον των λευιτιων in the Septuagint (LXX), is the third book of the *Torah* (*Pentateuch*).[13] While its Hebrew title ספר ויקרא suggests instructions to Moses about the covenant between God and Israel, these Latin and Greek appellations more accurately imply its destination in defining laws

---

[10] Jacob Neusner, "Studying Synoptic Texts Synoptically the Case of Leviticus Rabbah," *PAAJR* 53 (1986): 111–45; Jacob Neusner and Alan J. Avery-Peck. *Encyclopaedia of Midrash: Biblical Interpretation in Formative Judaism*. 2 vols. (Leiden: Brill, 2005); Burton L. Visotzky, *Golden Bells and Pomegranates: Studies in Midrash Leviticus Rabbah* (Tübingen: Mohr Siebeck, 2003).
[11] M. Flint, P. Abegg and E. Ulrich, *The Dead Sea Scrolls Bible* (Edinburgh: T&T Clark, 1999); E. Ulrich, *The Biblical Qumran Scrolls*, ed. H. M. Barstad et al. (Leiden; Boston, MA: Brill, 2010); F. G. Martinez and E. J. C. Tigchelaar, *The Dead Sea Scrolls. Study Edition* 2. (Leiden; Boston, MA: Brill, 1998).
[12] John Joseph Collins and Daniel C. Harlow, *The Eerdmans Dictionary of Early Judaism* (Grand Rapids, MI: Eerdmans, 2010); Charlotte Elisheva Fonrobert and Martin S. Jaffee, *The Cambridge Companion to the Talmud and Rabbinic Literature* (Cambridge; New York: Cambridge University Press, 2007); H. L. Strack, Gunter Stemberger, and Markus N. A. Bockmuehl, *Introduction to the Talmud and Midrash*. (Einleitung in Talmud und Midrasch). English Edition (Minneapolis: Fortress, 1996).
[13] Michael David Coogan, *The Oxford Encyclopedia of the Books of the Bible*, 2vols. (New York: Oxford University Press, 2011).

and rituals for the obedience and use of priests[14] and Levites.[15] The instructions to Moses and Aaron are, to a large extent, couched in the form of divine speeches, in some cases presented in the first person, but more usually in the third person. Because of this distinction and other more minor differences, it is generally agreed that the book in its final form contains two units,[16] the smaller of which (chapters 17–26) has been termed the *Holiness Code* (H). H was originally thought to be unique to the book of Leviticus but recent authors have identified small islands of H text embedded in other biblical books (see below). This H material lies in contradistinction to chapters 1–16 and 27, which are generally referred to as the *Priestly Material*[17] (P) of which a great deal more is to be found elsewhere in the biblical books of Genesis, Exodus, and Numbers. This corresponds to what has traditionally been regarded as the P source of the *Documentary Hypothesis*[18] which, since its promulgation in 1885, has enjoyed an oscillating popularity dependent on the scholarly fashions of the day.[19] The problem has been well reviewed by Propp and by Kratz.[20] The important point for the exegete is that the H and P material show linguistic and stylistic similarities and differences that sometimes help and sometimes confuse in identifying their dates, origins, and purpose.[21]

All linguistic studies of ancient texts risk wreckage by entrapment in a circular argument. Linguistic (and stylistic) variation is a function of time, or at least "the times", and if we are uncertain about these variables, we may not legitimately use any one to predict another. We should choose, as evidence permits, one measurable quantity to be the *independent variable* against which all other, *dependent variables*, are assayed.

From the earliest days of Levitical studies, it has been important to establish the dates of P and H relative to one another. However, this subject remains one of controversy among scholars. Wellhausen originally postulated a late date for P of around 500 BCE. He surmised that the P source emanated from exiled Aaronid priests in Babylon who would have been familiar with J and E and JE[22] material. They set out to produce a formalized working edition with additions of a

---

14 And, though not *prima facie*, for transmission to the chosen people. The rabbinic name for Leviticus is, תּוֹרַת כֹּהֲנִים
15 Levites are, in fact, represented more specifically in the book of Numbers.
16 For want of a better name: their nature is the subject of discussion and must not be prejudged.
17 Sometimes the Priestly Code.
18 Julius Wellhausen, *Prolegomena To the History of Israel* (Edinburgh: Black, 1885).
19 Antony F. Campbell and Mark A. O'Brien, *Sources of the Pentateuch: Texts, Introductions, Annotations* (Minneapolis: Fortress, 1993); R. E. Friedman, *The Bible with Sources Revealed* (San Francisco: Harper Collins, 2003); Martin Noth, *A History of Pentateuchal Traditions* (Chico, CA: Scholars Press, 1981); Martin Noth, *The History of Israel* (London: Xpress Reprints, 1996).
20 William H. C. Propp, "The Priestly Source Recovered Intact?" *VT* 46, no. 4 (1996): 458–78. R. G. Kratz, "The Growth of the Old Testament," in *The Oxford Handbook of Biblical Studies*, ed. J. W. Rogerson and Judith Lieu. (Oxford: Oxford University Press, 2006), 459–88.
21 Ian Young, Robert Rezetko, and Martin Ehrensvärd, *Linguistic Dating of Biblical Texts*, Vol. 2 (London; Oakville, CT: Equinox, 2008), 144.
22 The combined and redacted form of J and E, which is supposed to have been produced around the time of the fall of the Northern Kingdom in 722 BCE.

halakhic or legalistic[23] nature. Wellhausen reached his conclusion largely because the P material makes no mention of the Prophets nor do the Prophets refer to specific P events. He concluded that P was, therefore, from a time after the Prophets and, by a similar inductive process, that references to the Tabernacle in P were metaphors for the Temple which had been established by the time in question. These views have, today, come to be regarded as without foundation and have been largely discarded on the likely grounds that the priests might well have wished to avoid any mention of Prophets in an attempt to emphasize and improve their own position and importance. As something of a reaction to the "late P" hypothesis, authors such as Wenham,[24] have even suggested that some of the J narrative drew upon an earlier P source, but this seems unlikely and remains an atypical and perhaps idiosyncratic viewpoint.

Later scholars noted that the authors of P were almost certainly acquainted with aspects of JE but, where they used JE material in their writings, the Hebrew language took on a later form. It was, therefore, argued that if the author(s) of P knew JE, this defines a *terminus a quo* for P around the time of the fall of the northern kingdom of Israel in 722 BCE.

Yehezkel Kaufmann[25] has argued for a date of P after 722 BCE, but before the reign of Josiah.[26] Kaufmann believes P's role to have been central in the establishment of Judaism and notes that the idea of *cultic centralization* everywhere pervades the P text making it Jewish parænetic, or even Jewish proto-dogma rather than historical narrative. This is a very important observation in relation to the Levitical material. Lane[27] has noted that, "Leviticus is a book of repetitions and technical terms, with only the briefest of narrative elements … and comparatively little in the way of sustained discourse. … [This] gives a good chance to observe a translator at work and to detect … his cast of mind." This is a good summary of Leviticus, though not necessarily of all the P material in the Torah. The strictly legalistic nature of P is less evident in, for example, Genesis and Exodus but nevertheless, if one adheres to the idea of form criticism and the Documentary Hypothesis, P is probably the easiest textual form to identify.

Post-Babylonian prophets like Ezekiel[28] quote directly from P and imply that as the temple was constructed to have the same dimensions as the tabernacle it was likely that the latter was to be either housed separately within or incorporated into the fabric of the temple (Ezek 41:1). The implication is, therefore, that P was available for quotation or redaction at the time of the Babylonian exile.

---

23 Since priestliness and the interpretation of the law were regarded as the same thing.
24 G. J. Wenham, "The Priority of P," *VT* 19, no. 2 (1999): 240–58.
25 Y. Kaufmann, *The Religion of Israel* (London: George Allen & Unwin Ltd, 1961).
26 649–609 BCE; and therefore also before D.
27 D. J. Lane, "The Best Words in the Best Order: Some Comments on the "Syriacing" of Leviticus," *VT* 39, no. 4 (1989): 468–79.
28 Ezek 1:1–2 suggests that having begun as a prophet in Judah in his thirtieth year which was the fifth year of King Jehoiachin's exile: he was probably born around 622 BCE.

Haran[29] has said of the P source, "Anyone who moves this source back to pre-exilic times, imposes on himself the obligation to write biblical history practically anew." In saying this, he is agreeing with Wellhausen's original view and with Kaufmann that P is not an historical retrospective like J/E/JE but a specific, defining characteristic of burgeoning Judaism. However, he does not agree with Kaufmann's view that P originated at the time of Hezekiah nor with the view that it is post-Ezekielian and so, as some have suggested, influenced by the law-code of Ezekiel (Ezek 40–48). Haran strives to reconcile three seemingly conflicting observations: first, the clear dependence of P on J/E/JE; secondly the fact that any evidence for P is undetectable in the pre-exilic period; and thirdly, that P cannot be satisfactorily explained as a product of post-exilic times. To achieve a reconciliation of these disparities, Haran supposes that there must have been a gap in time between P's original formulation and/or composition, which he presumes began in Hezekiah's reign, and the production of a "fair copy" or "publication version" at a later date. This view has been supported by the work of Hurwitz[30] which has approached the question purely from a consideration of the language. Arriving thus by two different routes has given force to this argument which is now generally accepted as the most likely pedigree for P. Helpful though this may be in understanding the development of the text, it does not supply any unequivocal dates for either origin or redaction.

As is so often the case, fashions change with old arguments rehearsed and new arguments aired. In expectation of the recurrence of such controversy, the best we can do in setting a *terminus ad quem* for P is to suppose that it was completed by the end of the exile. There is thus a space of approximately 200 years during which P might have been composed and redacted so as to achieve its final state. During this period, we must suppose that changes in history, language, and written style all occurred *pari passu* with changes in the worldview of the priestly authors. A graphical attempt to summarize this situation is as follows. It is an attempt by the present author at a conflation of the various theories and explanations that are currently on offer and no claim of authority is made for it. The origin of P cannot be more accurately defined than to say that it most probably occurred at one time or in stages in the period between the two dates for P shown here.

---

[29] Mehahem Haran, "Behind the Scenes of History: Determining the Date of the Priestly Source," *JBL* 100, no. 3 (1981): 321–33.
[30] A. Hurwitz, "Dating the Priestly Source in Light of the Historical Study of Biblical Hebrew a Century after Wellhausen," *ZAW* 100 (1988): 88–99; A. Hurwitz, *A Linguistic Study of the Relationship between the Priestly Source and the Book of Ezekiel*, CRB Vol. 20 (Paris: Gabala, 1982).

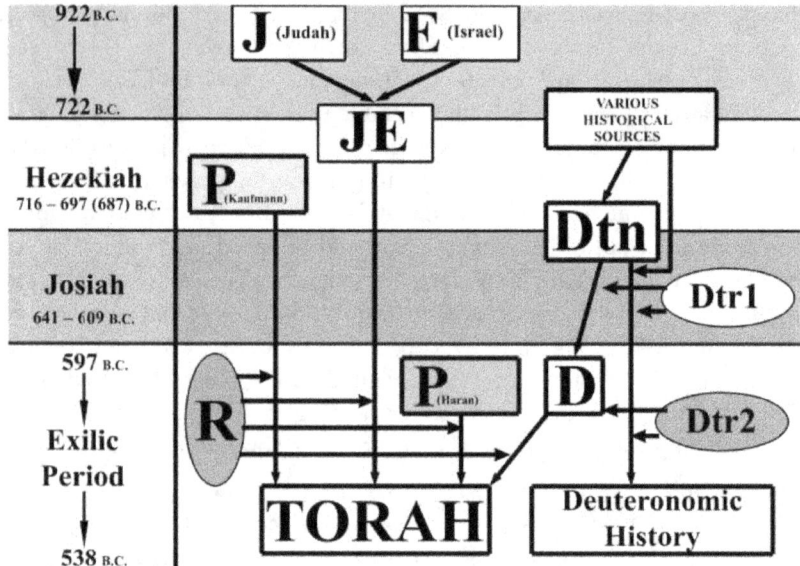

Plan of the Documentary Hypothesis
(With alternative dates of origin of P)

In the diagram:

- J = Jahwist
- E = Elohist
- JE = combined/redacted, (J+E)
- D = Deuteronomic source
- P = Priestly source
- Dtn = Source of Deuteronomistic History
- Dtr1 & Dtr2 = Deuteronomistic redactors
- R = a congeries of general redactors.

A final but important point in the matter of P material in Leviticus is to note the P-Leviticus standpoint on purity and impurity (טמא/טהור).[31] Their worldview steeped in the establishment and maintenance of ritual meant that purity (טהור) was quite simply the absence of impurity[32] (טמא), which was invisible but real

---

31 See chapter 5 for a fuller description.
32 Ritual impurity was not always or necessarily the result of sin, and in such cases carried no moral stigma. See chapters 4, 5 and 12.

and able to affect, and be communicable among, both persons and objects. The Levitical view was that the sanctuary/tabernacle somehow was constantly at risk of attracting ritual impurity to itself, and the build-up therein of this undesirable quality ultimately threatened the continuing presence of Yahweh within the sanctuary: indeed, impurity actively drove Yahweh out. It was thus the foremost duty of the priest to cleanse individuals and objects of impurity and thus preserve the presence of the deity within an appropriately sanitized holy place. The book of Leviticus was the "instruction manual" for priests in respect of this.

As indicated in chapters 4 and 5, the P view of purity was, therefore, that it was an imperative that had to be maintained in order to protect Yahweh, who is holy, from all threats of impurity. Holiness, in the priestly view, was a property of the deity but one which can also be attributed to persons, places, and objects particularly associated with (or reserved for) Yahweh. The sanctuary is an obvious example. We can, therefore see that in the priestly worldview and in the P writings, holiness means *holiness attained through ritual*. The book of Leviticus, however, also contains the contrasting view in its H material where the idea of *theological holiness* emerges. If we are to suppose that H belongs to a different time from P, we may also suppose a different or changed body of priests and/or a different or changed worldview. Theological (H) holiness was, in contrast to ritual holiness, available to all the Israelites, for them to earn and attain by their appropriate adherence to the commandments of Yahweh and therefore, to the priestly laws and ordinances. *H holiness* does not, *ipso facto*, confer *P holiness* upon the masses: the priests, therefore, by this mechanism, retained for themselves the many rights and privileges which they were accustomed to enjoy. If this is the case, we must add to our list of possibilities a two-tiered system in which priests and people operated different codes of behaviour. Whatever the case, H material stands in clear distinction to P material as to content and this distinction naturally leads us to question the relative dating of H and P. We must ask, *"Which came first?"* The view that H is earlier than P was championed by, among others, Yehezkel Kaufmann[33] and Samuel Rolles Driver;[34] but it is probably fair to say that current fashion favours a later date for H: though there remains dispute over what that date may be. It is worth rehearsing the arguments for the various cases.

Kaufmann bases his conclusions largely on the absence, within H, of any mention of the cultic centralization so prominent in P, and upon the prohibition of sacrifice and worship in *high places*. However, it is always wise to remember the adage that, *"Absence of evidence is not necessarily evidence of absence"*. Kaufmann's inference is that the authorship of H must have pre-dated Hezekiah's attempts to "clean-up" polytheistic practices in order to restore

---

33 Kaufmann, *The Religion of Israel.*
34 S. R. Driver, *An Introduction to the Literature of the Old Testament* (New York: Charles Scribner's Sons, 1897; repr. 1909 and 1916).

unquestioning monolatry. If this is correct, it would thereby have also pre-dated P which Kaufmann, as we have seen, places within Hezekiah's reign, citing the following as evidence for this:

הוא הסיר את־הבמות ושבר את־המצבת וכרת את־האשרה וכתת נחש הנחשת אשר־עשה משה כי עד־הימים ההמה היו בני־ישראל מקטרים לו ויקרא־לו נחשתן

> He removed the high places, and brake the pillars, and cut down the Asherah: And he brake in pieces the brasen serpent that Moses had made; for unto those days the children of Israel did burn incense to it; and he called it Nehushtan. (2 Kgs 18:4)

Indeed, the only reference to *high places* in the Holiness Code indicates that *high-places* were popular, fully operational and deserving of divine destruction:

והשמדתי את־במתיכם והכרתי את־חמניכם ונתתי את־פגריכם על־פגרי גלוליכם וגעלה נפשי אתכם

> And I will destroy your high places, and cut down your sun-images, and cast your carcases upon the carcases of your idols; and my soul shall abhor you. (Lev 26:30)

Driver's argument is more literary; he writes at some length on Lev 17–26 which he calls the *Law of Holiness*.[35] This, he identifies as distinct from P by the "presence of a foreign element" manifested both in style and phraseology and by the presence of motive clauses. He considers that this points to an early and independent collection of laws which were edited at some later date and then added into the P material.

The editing consisted largely of re-phrasing the laws in a more appropriately hortatory style.[36] Therefore Driver, with Kaufmann, opts for H's having existed before P and, importantly, having been seen as worthy of incorporation into P. Driver makes no attempt to identify the agent of these changes as being either the author of P or a later redactor(s), or both.

The contrary argument for H's having been written after P owes its popularity mainly to the work of Israel Knohl[37] and, perhaps more significantly, to the fact that his ideas were embraced—hesitatingly at first—by Jacob Milgrom. Knohl's is a well-argued thesis: his central point is that H was written as both an explicatory and a horatory message for non-members of a "priestly club", the Israelite population as a whole. Furthermore, Knohl rejects the Driver-Kaufmann view when he makes the observation that the very literary

---

35 The term *Das Heiligkeitsgesets* was coined by Klostermann in 1877.
36 If, as has been suggested, the reason for this was to extend the laws relating to holiness beyond the priestly/levitical group to the entire population of Israel, one might even say this was 'popularizing'.
37 I. Knohl, *The Sanctuary of Silence* (Minneapolis: Fortress, 1995).

characteristics these authors identify as H material are, on wider searching,[38] to be found elsewhere in the Hebrew Bible. Knohl believes H shows a broader and more inclusive awareness of the non-Priestly sources in the Torah (J, E and D), in contrast to the seemingly limited awareness that gives rise to the isolationist viewpoint of P. In particular, incorporation of material from the E and D sources appears to have been used to revise P.[39] Such characteristics embody not only language and style but also doctrinal, ritual and legal matters. There is, however, in the H material, almost nothing to be said of quasi-medical matters such as occupy so much space in the P material of Leviticus. An exception is the single following verse which, quite efficiently summarizes those lengthy P discourses and may have been regarded by the author(s) of H as adequate in this respect:

איש איש מזרע אהרן והוא צרוע או זב בקדשים לא יאכל עד אשר יטהר והנגע בכל־טמא־
נפש או איש אשר־תצא ממנו שכבת־זרע

What man soever of the seed of Aaron is a leper, or hath an issue; he shall not eat of the holy things, until he be clean. And whoso toucheth any thing that is unclean by the dead, or a man whose seed goeth from him; (Lev 22:4)

It seems curious, even so, that if H is an attempt, as Knohl claims, to "bring P to the people" it does not contain any greater encouragement for preventive measures, self-diagnosis, or even self treatment for such afflictions as צרעת and זוב than this single proscriptive sentence.

Knohl sees H as being more practical than P; for where P concentrates on ritual and offers no practical advice about, for example, social and agricultural matters, H brings together laws relating to the temple, to sacrifice, and to legal, social, and particularly agricultural aspects of life: it exists, therefore, surely not so much for priestly consumption and ritualistic ingemination, but rather, as a means of maintaining priestly control over the populace.

Where Wellhausen argued for H's antedating P by acting as a sort of paraenetic bridge between the older J/E/JE/D material and P, Knohl offers the diametrically opposite argument—that a consideration of the established, un-redacted P reveals a need for the inclusion and publication of guidance beyond the esoteric and purely ritualistic and aimed at a wider audience than the priesthood. Moreover, taking this view along with his observation of H-like material elsewhere in the *Torah*,[40] Knohl postulates the existence of a *Holiness School* (HS), a subset[41] of the *Priestly School* (PS). Knohl's view may be summarized thus:

---

38 One must remember that the means of searching, using for example computers, is a quite different thing today from what it was in Driver's time.
39 Coogan, *Encyclopedia of the Books of the Bible*, 574.
40 Perhaps this should extend to the Hexateuch. See C. A. Simpson, *The Early Traditions of Israel* (Oxford: Oxford University Press, 1948).
41 But nevertheless quite separate.

Priestly School (PS) → Priestly source (P) → Priestly Torah (PT)

Holiness School (HS) → Holiness Source (H) → Holiness Code (H)

Both schools probably originated among priests, but whereas P differentiated and reserved its views on dogma, doctrine, and ritual as being inappropriate for the masses, H sought to promulgate and integrate them with popular customs and traditions in order to emphasize the holiness of the entire nation and especially of the land. Knohl suggests that HS may even have been redactors of the *Torah* and it was they who incorporated, *inter alia*, the H material. If this were the case, he postulates *a terminus ad quem* for H late in Hezekiah's reign, (*c.* 741–686/7 BCE), but of course, after the completion of P.[42] The evidence he cites for this is the treatment by H of matters such as the incursion of idolatrous practices into Israel, soothsaying, ejection of tenant farmers for enslavement by the wealthy, the general separation of morality from the cult, and, in particular, Molech-worship.[43] All of these things Knohl notes as having been recorded during the reign of Hezekiah's father Ahaz (734–728 BCE) and in the early part of Hezekiah's reign (728–686/7 BCE). Knohl is thus in agreement with Driver and Kaufmann as to *era* but in disagreement as to *order* regarding the origins of P and H. We should not forget, however, Haran's[44] suggestion of a gap between authorship and publication; but Knohl's hypothesis about the dates and relationship of H and P has been supported in a well-argued article by Hess[45] which is also a review of Milgrom's contribution. It should be noted also that Knohl's hypothesis does not rule out a further, later redaction of P, H or P+H.

It must have been comforting for Knohl to receive Jacob Milgrom's endorsement of his views.[46] Milgrom says of the H material in comparing it with P: "Two critical changes occur: ritual impurity becomes moral impurity; and the domain of the sacred expands, embracing the entire land, not just the sanctuary, and all of Israel, not just the priesthood".[47] If we are looking for a summary of H's purpose, this remains the best, although the word "becomes" remains problematic. It seems unlikely that Milgrom means "turns into" by this. This would only be possible if the entire priestly worldview had changed. None of the authors considered in chapter 5 has contemplated this view. Milgrom never appears to have implied any conflation or dynamic between the two forms of impurity and this is the view taken subsequently by a majority of commentators. Milgrom's final position is the suggestion that H sets out to define the rules by

---

42 That is not to say that a later redaction of the combined P and H did not also take place.
43 N. H. Snaith, "The Cult of Molech," *VT* 16, no. 1 (1966): 123–24.
44 Haran, "Behind the Scenes of History."
45 R. S. Hess, "A Reassessment of the Priestly and Cultic and Legal Texts," *JLR* 17, no. 1/2 (2002): 375–91.
46 In fact he devoted a chapter of his book to this: Knohl, *The Sanctuary of Silence*, Excursus 5.
47 J. Milgrom, *Leviticus: A Continental Commentary* (Minneapolis: Fortress, 2004), 175.

which Israel is to isolate itself from the *nations* and so develop its own *imitatio Dei* which will eventually become a model for a universal *imitatio Dei*.[48]

Recently, this view has encountered a challenge from David Wright who, while broadly agreeing with the Knohl–Milgrom hypothesis, dates the Holiness School later, to the time of the exile, with some even later updating in the early post-exilic period. Wright considers the major function of the *Holiness Code* was to amplify the Priestly *Torah* by *including the land*, (הארץ), as a potential *locus of pollution*, where the pollution is necessarily caused by sin. However, in an article[49] which, in so many respects, minutely differentiates H and P, he is irritatingly vague[50] about the precise grounds upon which he chooses to place H at this late date.

If we consider those linguistic and stylistic characteristics that allow us to differentiate H from P, the most comprehensive listings are from Driver[51] followed closely by Knohl.[52] They are the two major protagonists in the argument but, whereas *prima facie*, Driver approaches the problem from a purely linguistic viewpoint, Knohl tends to favour an analysis based upon style. We should not be hasty in criticizing either without understanding that between them time had elapsed, research methods improved, and attitudes changed. At the centre of both approaches lies √קדש and its very specific meaning (or, more accurately, range of meanings) in Jewish Scripture.[53] The differences appear to be less to do with vocabulary and grammar than with the *usage* of particular words, phrases, and formulae. Driver[54] provides a list of those words and phrases he identifies in Leviticus as specifically characteristic of H whereas Knohl[55] makes a very clear distinction between words and phrases characteristic of HS and PT but sees them both as extending *beyond* Leviticus. Driver's work has been the subject of an extensive critique by Paton[56] and he has enlarged upon this in his own, *The Original Form of Leviticus*.[57] This extensive work is,

---

48 Milgrom, *Leviticus: A Continental Commentary*, 180.
49 D. P. Wright, "Holiness in Leviticus and Beyond," *Interpretation* 53, no. 4 (1999): 351–64.
50 In a footnote, all he says is that he differs from foregoing authors by dating the Holiness School to the exile.
51 Driver, *Introduction*, 49–50.
52 Knohl, *The Sanctuary of Silence*, 106–110.
53 M. Douglas, "Purity and Danger: An Analysis of Concepts of Pollution and Taboo," in D. J. A. Clines, ed. *Dictionary of Classical Hebrew*, 9 vols. (Sheffield: Phoenix, 2010); Knohl, *The Sanctuary of Silence;* S. Mandelkern, *Veteris Testamenti Concordantiae Hebraicae atque Chaldaicae*, ed. F. Margolin, 2 vols. (Gratz: Akademische Druck U. Verlagsanstalt, 1896); J. Milgrom, *Leviticus: A New Translation with Introduction and Commentary*, Anchor Bible 3 vols. (New York: Doubleday, 1991); J. P. Peters, "The Hebrew Idea of Holiness," *Biblical World* 14, no. 5 (1899): 344–55; Marcel Poorthuis and Joshua Schwartz, *Purity and Holiness: the Heritage of Leviticus* (Leiden; Boston: Brill, 2000); Eyal Regev, "Priestly Dynamic Holiness and Deuteronomic Static Holiness," *VT* 51, no. 2 (2001): 243–61.
54 Driver, *Introduction*, 49–50.
55 Knohl, *The Sanctuary of Silence*, 106.
56 Lewis B. Paton, "Notes on Driver's Leviticus," *JBL* 14, no. 1/2 (1895): 48–56.
57 L. B. Paton, "The Original Form of Leviticus xxiii., xxv," *JBL* 18, no. 1/2 (1899): 35–60; L. B. Paton, "The Original Form of Leviticus xvii.-xix," *JBL* 16, no. 1/2 (1897): 31–77; L. B. Paton, "The Original Form of Leviticus xxi., xxii," *JBL* 17, no. 2 (1898): 149–75.

however, mainly exegetical and is not in conflict with Driver over either the dating or the nature of the *Holiness Code.*

Driver would have compiled his analysis from a painstaking direct examination of the texts with the aid of a concordance such as that of Solomon Mandelkern.⁵⁸ Today, searches can be carried out more efficiently, more extensively and with greater speed and rigor using biblical software such as *Bibleworks* or *Accordance*⁵⁹ and this advancement in methods has not been without very considerable effects on interpretation.

While Driver, writes extensively on *The Priestly Narrative of the Hexateuch,*⁶⁰ he concerns himself primarily with differentiating J, E, P and D. H, he regards as a subset of P, and lists twenty phrases characteristic and in his view *diagnostic* of H. It is not within the scope of this study to examine them all, but two examples suffice to show how they may be used by researchers in different ways. If we consider the first of these phrases: אני יהוה אלהיכם (an injunction), Driver says that this form occurs "nearly fifty times".⁶¹ We find, for the entire Hebrew Bible, if we look for matching cases *by biblical book,* (for convenience dividing Leviticus into H and P), the following distribution:

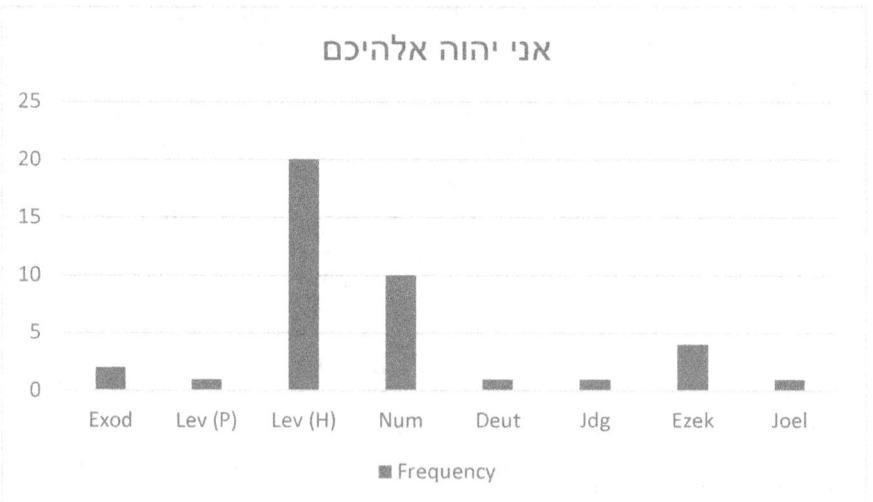

The above phrase occurs 50% more times in H than in any of the other books where it is to be found and it is because of this excess that Driver believes it is characteristic of H. He is curiously silent about the ten instances of the phrase in Numbers but makes much of the similarities he finds with Ezekiel whom he calls the "Priestly Prophet". In particular, Driver notes Ezekiel's "affinities with P and even more strikingly with H" and argues that H was a fundamental

---

58 Mandelkern, *Veteris Testamenti.*
59 Bibleworks, "Software for Biblical Exegesis and Research." Accordance, "Bible Software."
60 Driver, *Introduction,* 126–159. See also: Simpson, *The Early Traditions of Israel.*
61 In fact 40 times in the entire Hebrew Bible.

Pentateuchal Code which subsequently became incorporated, *mutatis mutandis,* elsewhere:

H → P → Ezekiel

or alternatively

H → $\Sigma_?^P$ → Ezekiel

Haran,[62] criticizes such orthodox research where P has been regarded as a post-Ezekelian work, influenced by the law-code of Ezekiel (Ezek 40–48)[63] and developed thence as the embodiment of Judaism. Haran's view is that P is, much earlier and, displays "far more perfection and originality than Ezek 40–48, to such an extent that Ezekiel's code looks merely as an epigonic outgrowth of the priestly school."[64] P is thus *not* supposed to be a product of the Second Temple Period and is likely to have pre-dated H, in which case H's characteristic phraseology is a *de novo* event, so:

P ± (Ezekiel) → H

Driver, is postulating that the phrase אני יהוה אלהיכם, by its overwhelming predominance in Leviticus (H), is a defining characteristic of H and the non-Levitical and P-Levitical instances of the phrase are so few as to be, effectively, random events.

However, a quite different picture appears if we re-plot the graph to show the distribution of the phrase אני יהוה אלהיכם within the Hebrew Bible by chapter.

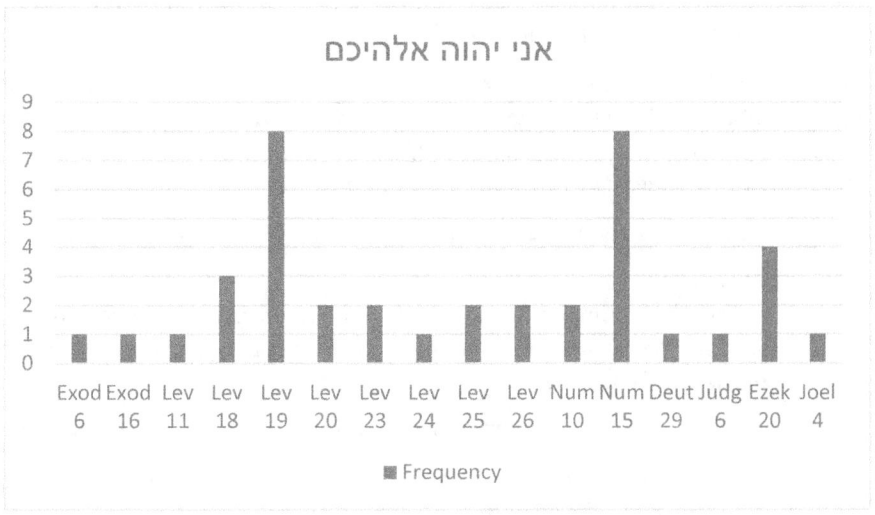

---

62 Haran, "Behind the Scenes."
63 So much so that Ezekiel is sometimes depicted as "the spiritual father of Judaism."
64 See also A. Hurwitz, "A Linguistic Study."

This graph is unconvincing as evidence that the phrase is H-specific but might be in accord with Knohl's idea of a Holiness School favouring certain phrases used *pro rata* among books containing HS material. It comes as no surprise, given the nature of the intensely similar content of Lev 19 and Num 15 that these two chapters score highly for matches. Elsewhere, the traditional H material compared with other chapters contains this phrase in the ratio of at least 2:1 which hardly defines a *Sitz im Leben*.

A second, interesting phrase, which Driver regards as characteristic of H includes the well-known "setting face against and cutting off" formula. Examples of the two key phrases quoted by Driver are: ונתתִּי פני בנפש,[65] and והכרתִּי אתה מקרב עמה.[66] Driver's point is that only in the H material and in the single verse of Ezek 14:8 do the verbs carry the first person common singular pronominal suffix.

> ושמתִּי אני את־פני באיש ההוא ובמשפחתו והכרתִּי אתו ואת כל־הזנים אחריו לזנות אחרי המלך מקרב עמם:
>
> then I will set my face against that man, and against his family, and will cut him off, and all that go a whoring after him, to commit whoredom with Molech, from among their people. (Lev 20:5)

> ונתתִּי פני באיש ההוא והשמתיהו לאות ולמשלים והרתיו מתוך עמי וידעתם כי־אני יהוה:
>
> and I will set my face against that man, and will make him an astonishment, for a sign and a proverb, and I will cut him off from the midst of my people; and ye shall know that I am the Lord. (Ezek 14:8)

Yahweh is saying "*I will* set *my* face/*I will* cut him off" and thereby making a highly emphatic and personal statement. Elsewhere, Driver says, these phrases which are diagnostic characteristics of P, are always rendered in the passive, (*nif'al*) *he/she/it/they* shall *be cut off*, for example:

> זכר אשר לא־ימול את־בשר ערלתו ונכרתה הנפש ההוא מעמיה את־בריתי הפר
>
> And the uncircumcised male who is not circumcised in the flesh of his foreskin, that soul shall be cut off from his people; he hath broken my covenant. (Gen 17:14)

> איש אשר ירקח כמהו ואשר יתן ממנו על־זר ונכרַת מעמיו
>
> Whosoever compoundeth any like it, or whosoever putteth any of it upon a stranger, he shall be cut off from his people. (Exod 30:33)

---

65 Lev 17:10; 20:5, 6; 26:17.
66 Lev 17:10; 20:3, 5, 6.

The Levitical Texts and Associated Material

והנפש אשר־תאכל בשר מזבח השלמים אשר ליהוה וטמאתו עליו ונכרתה הפש ההוא מעמיה

> but the soul that eateth of the flesh of the sacrifice of peace offerings, that pertain unto the Lord, having his uncleanness upon him, that soul shall be cut off from his people. (Lev 7:20)[67]

If H uses the first person active and P uses the passive voice, it becomes necessary for Driver to explain why Ezekiel follows H and not P, given that he believes H to be earlier than P and Ezekiel to be P material. His explanation falls back upon the idea of a *Law Code*, of which H was (Driver claims), an early example, predating P, but usefully incorporated into it, along with Ezekiel—a late addition to P—so that both used established characteristics of H for purposes of emphasis. This would seem a more plausible argument than that used by Driver to justify his conclusions about the first of the supposedly characterizing phrases; but it cannot obtain if we believe H to be later than P. It seems more likely that the authors of H, as Milgrom has suggested,[68] were trying, in a spasm of social conscience perhaps, to extend their Law Code—the inchoate P—from being esoteric and relevant to a purely priestly/levite minority audience into the broader auditorium of the Israelite people in general. Nothing, therefore, might have been considered more appropriate and motivating than a first-person exhortation from the mouth of the deity himself.

Knohl[69] describes the PT material in the Hexteuch[70] as having a "schematic, measured and restrained" style throughout: by which he means including narrative passages. Where laws are formulated or stated, he finds scrupulous attention given to the choice of words and phrases and cites as an important example the distinction made between purity laws and sacrificial laws by the using of different nouns/pronouns for the subject of the sentence. So, in purity laws, the subject is always either איש (or אשה) whereas in sacrificial laws it is נפש. Knohl, agrees with Driver, that the use of the *nif'al* in the *cutting off formula* is diagnostic of PT and in contrast to HS.

Knohl makes two further and important assertions about style: that "Hortatory motive clauses are completely absent from PT laws" and "There are no points of contact at all between PT language and JE language". Even more significantly, Knohl suggests that because scholars formerly believed H to have pre-dated P and to have been assimilated into it, they consequently found, within H, no evidence of any literary creativity. Knohl believes this is unfair and that HS, though undoubtedly lacking PT's precision of rhythm and fastidious use of language, does offer certain identifiable, characteristic stylistic features. These,

---

67 See also Lev 7:21, 25, 27.
68 Milgrom, *Leviticus: A Continental Commentary*; Milgrom, *Leviticus: A New Translation*.
69 Knohl, *The Sanctuary of Silence*.
70 See also: Simpson, *The Early Traditions of Israel*.

he believes, are closer to JE than P and consequently, within HS, moralizing passages and attempts at ideological justification may be found. Moreover, HS is inconsistent in distinguishing, as P does, between איש and נפש (Knohl suggests almost to the point of carelessness).

In Leviticus, Knohl, like Milgrom, concentrates upon the *differences* between what he sees as HS and PT material rather than simply attempting to define their characteristics as Driver does. Of course, this immediately extends the scope of the argument by asking questions about the *reasons* for these differences. The result is certainly more convincing when sampled in the light of modern exegetical, linguistic and stylistic tastes. An example is Knohl's re-thinking of the business of אני in Driver's first phrase above. Knohl, like Driver, accepts this pronoun as emphatic but believes that if one considers the P/PT/HS sources together and extending beyond Leviticus, one can demonstrate a temporal relationship with the revelation of the Holy Name (Exod 3:13 *et seq*).

ויאמר אלהים אל־משה אהיה אשר אהיה ויאמר כה תאמר לבני ישראל אהיה שלחני אליכם

> And God said unto Moses, I am that I am: and he said, Thus shalt thou say unto the children of Israel, I am hath sent me unto you. (Exod 3:14)

In P/PT אני is used very sparingly and only in Yahweh's conversation with Moses; never in his addresses to the congregation of Israel. After the revelation of the *Holy Name* (Exod 3:14), it is *never* used again. This is in contrast to the HS material where, as already noted, אני is more widely used especially in addressing the congregation of Israel. The importance of Knohl's observation over Driver's is that the latter did not believe that examples of H-sounding language outside Lev 17–27 were anything more than coincidental. Knohl, in contrast, sees the whole of the HS material, scattered throughout the *Torah* and indeed the *Hexateuch* as super-added *propaganda*,[71] aimed beyond the esoteric and formulaic style of the priestly cadre at the Israelite people as a whole.

As Knohl remarks, these different forms of divine speech used by the two schools express their different theological viewpoints. This may be further illustrated by their different usages of the word for (the) tabernacle המשכן/משכן. In HS this appears in the construct state juxtaposed to the name of God (or appropriate pronoun) and, therefore, indicating *possession* of the sacrifices, for example in the phrase: ונתתי משכני בתוככם (Lev 26:11).

The tabernacle and sacrifice therein is Yahweh's and also Yahweh's gift to the Israelite people—a symbol of his dwelling amongst them. No such inclusivity is implied in P/PT material where משכן appears always without possessives and Yahweh is never described as dwelling (שכן) among his people. Statutes and

---

71 Used non-pejoratively, in its original sense as a neuter plural gerundive.

ordinances relating to the tabernacle in respect of its construction and use are, in P/PT, addressed to Moses alone and not, as in H/HS, to the people.

A final example by which Knohl differentiates PT from HS is that the latter represented a more human, all-embracing, and egalitarian ethic than that embraced by priests and Levites. HS frequently ascribes to the Israelite and to the resident alien (sojourner) equality before the Lord whereas P/PT is manifestly less generous to the resident alien. This may be seen in the following verse from Lev 19:34:

כאזרח מכם יהיה לכם הגר הגר אתכם ואהבת לו כמוך כי־גרים הייתם בארץ מצרים אני יהוה אלהיכם

> The stranger that sojourneth with you shall be unto you as the homeborn among you, and thou shalt love him as thyself; for ye were strangers in the land of Egypt: I am the Lord your God. (Lev 19:34)

There are many recorded instances of phrases and styles that have led authors to differentiate between H and P and those discussed here are but a few. It is probably fair to say that the work of Driver and Knohl illustrates the two principal opposing viewpoints in the argument. While they are clearly in disagreement about, for example, the dates and sequence of P and H, one must ask how much that may be a function of the respective times at which their accounts were written and therefore of the different methods of research that were available to them. If we accept that because of this, the later view—that H followed P as Knohl,[72] Haran,[73] and Wright[74] have suggested—is more likely, then it is possible to see that Driver and Knohl are not so far apart in their appreciation of what the Holiness Code was *about*. Both authors see it as hortatory for the people; an extension of the Torah from an introspective priestly worldview into the province of the whole Congregation of Israel and even beyond that to the sojourners.[75] It is *practical, user-friendly, advertising, parænetic, propaganda, understandable, acceptable* and *believable*—a step away from esoteric priestly, ritualistic law-making and control—towards a practical Jewish doctrine. The H material extends Leviticus beyond a rubric to a manifesto for the land and all its people, as a blueprint for establishing their *imitatio Dei*.[76]

With all of the above in mind, we must ask, in the context of the present study, why then did H pay so little attention to צרעת and to זוב? As a crude illustration of the P/H differential for these conditions we may do a simple *Bibleworks*

---

[72] Knohl, *The Sanctuary of Silence*.
[73] Haran, "Behind the Scenes."
[74] Wright, "Holiness in Leviticus and Beyond."
[75] Dare we say: "Ad captandum vulgus"?
[76] There may be here a parallel to the covenantal nomism of Pauline scholars. Cf. E. P. Sanders, *Paul and Palestinian Judaism: A Comparison of Patterns of Religion* (London: SCM, 1977); E. P. Sanders, *Judaism: Practice and Belief, 63 BCE–66 CE* (London Philadelphia, PA: SCM; Trinity Press International, 1994).

search⁷⁷ in English for the *lep** morpheme within the P and H components of Leviticus. English is chosen to embody all variants of the *lep** morpheme such as *leprosy*, *leper*, *leprous* etc. with no regard to precise meaning. In the ERV⁷⁸ there are 31 "hits" for *lep** of which only 1 is in H material (Lev 22:4), and this verse is clearly a summary of material already presented much more extensively in P:

איש איש מזרע אהרן והוא צרוע או זב בקדשים לא יאכל עד אשר יטהר והנגע בכל־טמא־נפש או איש אשר־תצא ממנו שכבת־זרע

> What man so-ever of the seed of Aaron is a leper, or hath an issue; he shall not eat of the holy things, until he be clean. And whoso toucheth any thing that is unclean by the dead, or a man whose seed goeth from him (Lev 22:4)

Likewise, if we search Leviticus for the word *issue*⁷⁹ and exclude inappropriate usages of this word, we find it used 19 times (ERV) in the book as a whole but only once in H—again at 22:4. Observations made after simple analyses such as this, have been widely used to reinforce the notion that P was for priests while H was for the ordinary people who did not need to know much about the specific nature of צרעת and זוב. A favourite alternative explanation is that the priests and Levites were operating a "closed shop" on all rituals and especially on purity/impurity regulation(s) and secondarily on certain medical matters—a monopoly of knowledge always guarantees a monopoly of control. However, this view is not substantiated, or at least becomes unnecessary, if we accept Milgrom's reasoning for the differences between Lev 13:1 and 15:2.⁸⁰ Milgrom notes that both of these chapters open with the following identical verse:

וידבר יהוה אל־משה ואל־אהרן לאמר

> And the Lord spake unto Moses and unto Aaron, saying, (Lev 13:1 & 15:1)

Moses and Aaron are, we must suppose, being used as metaphors for the entire priesthood,⁸¹ now and in the future. Whereas it is to them alone, in chapters 13 and 14 that instructions are given for dealing with צרעת; in chapter 15:2 relating to זוב, there is the important further instruction that Moses and Aaron must inform the children of Israel:

דברו אל־בני ישראל ואמרתם אלהם איש איש כי יהיה זב מבשרו זובו טמא הוא

---

77 Bibleworks, "Software for Biblical Exegesis and Research."
78 P:H = ERV 30:1; KJV 30:1; RSV 31:1; NRSV 29:1. In each case the variability is in P and the single instance in H is invariable 22:4. The ERV, for reasons outlined in Appendix 1, seems most appropriate for this task.
79 Searching is more difficult here as the newer translations prefer the word "discharge". Today, "issue" has become, almost, "the universal noun"!
80 See also chapters 6, 7, and 8.
81 Lev 13:2 makes this clear by invoking their successors.

Speak unto the children of Israel, and say unto them, When any man hath an issue out of his flesh, because of his issue he is unclean. (Lev 15:2)

In other words, the priests are to pass on at least some information about genital discharges to the people themselves—these latter should be *actively* on the lookout.[82] Milgrom[83] accounts for this difference by supposing that while צרעת would surely be apparent to all onlookers, a genital discharge would be concealed by clothing and by modesty. Why Milgrom should attribute a lesser degree of observational effort and wit to those with genital discharges than to the rest of the population is unclear. Perhaps the reasoning is that shame and fear would discourage them from seeking treatment—a problem still found, all too often, today. Milgrom, nevertheless, is suggesting that the זוב sufferer needs more information in order for him to initiate appropriate precautionary and therapeutic measures.[84] This is a difficult argument to accept—it seems absurd to suppose that an individual should fail to notice the symptoms of a skin disease and even more absurd that this should have to wait for its recognition until sufficiently developed to become a public spectacle. Admittedly, many of the contenders for צרעת affect the head[85] and looking-glasses would have been unusual; reflections could be observed in water and these conditions also affect the extremities. In the early stages of these diseases it is likely that they would be more apparent to the sufferer than to his associates. Also, it is difficult to understand why, if both conditions ultimately need referral to the priest, the need to do this should not be equally urgent. Milgrom, therefore, appears to be making a distinction on the highly dubious grounds that, if one has contracted צרעת, one's associates are likely to notice it first and so active vigilance is unimportant!

There were almost certainly constraints placed by the conventions of the day, upon what parts of the body could and could not be exposed within the limits of decency.[86] We have to view this, of course in the context of the dress-code for

---

[82] If this is correct, one must applaud the priests for advocating self-examination.
[83] Milgrom, *Leviticus: A New Translation*; Milgrom, *Leviticus: A Continental Commentary*.
[84] Admittedly, genital discharges may be less noticeable especially early on in females for obvious anatomical reasons. However the opposite is true for circumcised males compared with uncircumcised males.
[85] See chapter 6.
[86] We are not informed in the Scriptures what these might be. However in the much later Leviticus Rabbah (qv infra), we find two passages that are suggestive of the fact that constraints did operate. First, on the anatomical level. See: Leviticus Rabbah 15:8 extracts below:
> How [much of a person's body] is [to be visible at] an examination for leprosy? In the case of a man, as [much as one digs, is visible] when one digs, and as when one plucks olives; as when one digs, for [the examination of] the privy parts, and as when one plucks olives, for [the examination of] the arm-pit. In the case of a woman, as [much as is visible] when she is preparing bread, and as when she is suckling her child; [as when she is preparing bread, for the examination of the privy parts, and as when she is suckling her child] for the examination under the breasts....

34

male and female Israelites at the time and also in the context of the priest himself having acquired the affliction.[87]

By any rational argument, early referral to the priest could be thought to be an important anti-contagion measure and so one might think that widespread public awareness would be advantageous; and what better medium by which to distribute this information than H? Why then was anti-contagion awareness or at least diagnostic indicators for early referral to the priesthood, not given greater pride of place in H which, if after all, it was intended to make the general public more aware of impurity/purity and other priestly matters and thus more able to interact with their priests?

While the Hebrew Bible leaves us unable to answer this question, we are left in no doubt about the enthusiasm later generations had for interpreting the Levitical writings on צרעת and on זוב. We should not, in the context of the present study, expect to encounter much new information about צרעת and on זוב. This is a shame because these works of interpretation were produced over a lengthy period of time in which, elsewhere, great medical advances were being made.

Jewish Material From Later Times and a Later Worldview

There is a great deal of largely interpretative material to be found in later Jewish literature. These texts cannot be compared directly with Biblical texts on account of the different worldviews that would have been prevalent in later times. The argument here, however, is the same as that applied in chapter 1: as long as the appropriate hermeneutical caveats about reception history are in place, it is helpful to see the whole evolutionary process in order to understand its early phases.

---

[87] We also find in the Leviticus Rabbah 15:8, evidence for the priests' closed shop where the diagnosis of צרעת was concerned:
> We have learnt in the Mishnah[87]: One is entitled to examine for [and pronounce on] any leprosy except his own leprosy. R. Meir said: Not even for the leprosy of one's relatives.

This appears to be in conflict with the Scriptures where diagnosis of "leprosy" is exclusively for the priests. The situation is not helped by a piece of rationalization (or even sophistry) which is typical of the convoluted argumentation seen in the rabbinical writings:
> Who then examined the leprosy of Miriam? If you should say it was Moses who examined, why, a non-priest may not examine for leprosy. If you should say it was Aaron who examined her, why, a relative may not examine for leprosy. [The answer is]: The Holy One, blessed be He, said: "I am a priest, I shut her up and I shall declare her clean." This is indicated by what is written, And the Lord said, "Let her be shut up without the camp seven days, and after that she shall be brought in again" ... and the people journeyed not till Miriam was brought in again (Num XII, 14 f.). Since it is the case that the people [halted and journeyed] with the Shechinah, it follows that the Shechinah waited for her [i.e. Miriam].
>
> R. Levi said in the name of R. Hama b. R. Hanina: Moses was much grieved on account of this matter, saying: "Is it in accordance with the dignity of my brother Aaron that he should have to examine for leprosy?" Said the Holy One, blessed be He, to him: "Does he not [by way of recompense] have the benefit of the twenty-four gifts [which are the prescribed perquisites] of the priesthood?" The proverb says: "He who eats of the palm's heart will be beaten with the stick of the dried up palm."

This does nothing to clarify the situation.

The Talmud

It might be thought, given the very extensive nature of the Talmud[88] that it would be particularly helpful in the quest to differentiate true medical practice as it developed from early ritual concerning צרעת and זוב: this turns out not to be the case. While admittedly extensive—indeed exhaustingly so—on these topics, the information in the Talmud is disappointingly familiar and repetitive and consists mainly of many and varied rabbinical opinions as to the interpretation of what has already been said in the Hebrew Bible. There are a very few new and original allusions in the Talmud to medical matters; notable perhaps is the prescription found at *Shabbath 110a* for treating the זב or זבה in such a way that the latter does not become barren. Generally, the Talmud faithfully preserves the *Weltanschauung* of the Levitical priesthood [89] the rabbis appear to have been less concerned with passing on *propositional knowledge* or insight than *procedural knowledge* in the very greatest of detail.

יראת יהוה ראשית דעת חכמה ומוסר אוילים בזו

> The fear of the Lord is the beginning of knowledge: but the foolish despise wisdom and instruction. (Prov 1:7)

For the purpose of the present study, therefore, the very considerable mass of literature embodied in the Talmud is mentioned only to say that it has little to offer. In contrast other late material indicates that by the time of its writing when the influence of the priesthood had waned or was defunct, a somewhat more physiological approach was being taken.

---

88 The Talmud is a work of interpretation for the Jewish faith written by a succession of rabbis over a considerable time encompassing the Tannaite and Amorite and later Geonic rabbinical periods. It is concerned with history, law, ethics, religious customs, philosophy and the Jewish way of life generally. It comprises two parts, the Mishnah (2nd century CE) and the Gemara (5th century CE) and has a supplement, the Tosefta. It is, as it were, an interpretation within an interpretation. See: D. W. Halivni, *The Formation of the Babylonian Talmud*, trans. J. L. Rubenstein (New York: Oxford University Press, 2013); Fonrobert and Jaffee, *The Cambridge Companion;* Strack, Stemberger, and Bockmuehl, Introduction to the *Talmud and Midrash.*
This work, designed first to state and then to upgrade the Mishnah by means of interpretative notes—the Gemara—took place in two locations that were centres of Jewish scholarship at the time. Thus came about the Palestinian Talmud (Talmud Yerushalmi) and the later Babylonian Talmud (Talmud Bavli). The latter is both more complete and more extensive and it is the Babylonian Talmud that is most often referred to. Within this work the Mishnah is written in Mishnaic Hebrew and the Gemara is written in Jewish Babylonian Aramaic. See: W. B. Stevenson, *Grammar of Palestinian Jewish Aramaic*, Vol. 2 (Oxford: Clarendon, 1962); M. Sokoloff, *A Dictionary of Jewish Babylonian Aramaic of the Talmudic and Geonic Periods* (Ramat-Gan, Israel; Baltimore, MA; London: Bar Ilan University Press; Johns Hopkins Press, 2002); M. Sokoloff, *A Dictionary of Jewish Palestinian Aramaic of the Byzantine Period*, 2nd ed. (Ramat-Gat, Israel; Baltimore; London: Bar Ilan University Press; Johns Hopkins University Press, 2002); M. Sokoloff, *A Dictionary of Judean Aramaic* (Ramat-Gat, Israel: Bar Ilan University Press, 2003); Caspar Levias, *A Grammar of the Aramaic Idiom contained in the Babylonian Talmud. With Constant Reference to Gaonic Literature* (Cincinnati: Bloch Publishing & Printing Co., 1896). M. Jastrow, *Dictionary of the Targumim, the Talmud Babli and Yerushalmi and the Midrashic Literature* (Peabody, MA: Hendrickson, 2006).
89 For example, an electronic search using the lep* morpheme results in 1415 "hits" and a search using zab* in 691 "hits". Soncino, *The Soncino Classics Collection: Judaic Texts; Talmud, Mishnah, Midrash Rabbah and Zohar in Hebrew, Aramaic and English* (Chicago, IL: Davka Corporation and Soncino Press, 2009).

Leviticus Rabbah

It is unsurprising that the *Leviticus Rabbah*,[90] for the most part, reiterates the Levitical viewpoint. An electronic search[91] of the *Leviticus Rabbah* discloses 133 pericopes containing the *lep** morpheme. The *zab** morpheme does not appear but *issue* used in the context of effluxion delivers 25 "hits" none of which offers any insight beyond what is to be found in Leviticus itself.

The *Leviticus Rabbah* is significantly more helpful in the matter of צרעת, where it offers the most—perhaps the only—pathophysiological consideration of this condition to be encountered in early Jewish literature. It seems appropriate, however, to deal with this at the end of Chapter 7, (*qv infra*). It is, important to remember that the *Weltanschauungen* of the Levitical priesthood and the later rabbis cannot be assumed to have been the same. However, this evidence strongly suggests that by the time of the Leviticus Rabbah, it was thought necessary to try to formulate some sort of physiological explanation for צרעת. It seems likely that in arriving at such a formulation, earlier ideas of the word's meaning would have been taken into account.

The Dead Sea Scrolls: A Later Viewpoint

The same argument may be applied in the case of the Dead Sea Scrolls. In the Qumran fragment 4Q272, there is an allusion to the fact that an intact circulation is necessary for good health whereas a bad spirit blocks the circulation of the blood and causes צרעת. It should be noted that the word "circulation" is not meant in this context to indicate a circulation in the Harveian sense. It would have been well noted that serious cuts resulted in the ejection of blood with some force and this is probably all that is meant.

[ו]הגיד נמלא דם ורוח החיים עולה וי[ורדת בו נרפא מן]1.

[הנ]גע זה [משפט הצ]רע[ת לב]ני אהרון [להבדיל ל]2.

1. [And] the artery is filled with blood and the spirit of life pulsates up and d[own in it, the plague is healed.]

---

90 The Leviticus Rabbah is often called the V/Wayikrah Rabbah. Much of the early midrash of Jewish biblical exegesis was transmitted orally but eventually a written midrash emerged alongside the Talmud. The Midrash Rabbah (Great Midrash) covers the Torah, Esther, Song of Songs, Ruth, Lamentations and Qoheleth and thus includes the Leviticus Rabbah. The Midrash Rabbah is a collection of homilies and exegetical discourses on particular subjects. Both major forms of midrashim are represented: halakhic midrash which is concerned with the law; and aggadic midrash, concerned with non-legal exegesis. The Leviticus Rabbah is among the most developed and well-edited of the homiletic aggadic midrashim. It dates from the 4th–5th centuries ce and embodies the teachings of Jewish sages accumulated and modified over four centuries. The elements of midrash presenting a commentary, view or story are called derashoth and the homiletical elements are called pethichoth. From the 4th and 5th centuries, a pethichah was included in an aggadic midrashim as an introductory paragraph. Ostrer, refers to the Leviticus Rabbah—and to midrashim generally—as an 'allegorical commentary': B. S. Ostrer, "Leprosy: Medical Views of Leviticus Rabba." *Early Science and Medicine* 7, no. 2 (2002): 138–54 [154].
91 Soncino, *The Soncino Classics Collection*.

2. This is the [rule of ṣa]raʿa[t for the s]ons of Aaron [to separate] (4Q272 (4QD-g) 1ii:1–2)

This fragment, part of the *Damascus Document*, is concerned with Community Rules. Even here, with such physiological advancements as a rudimentary awareness of the circulation of the blood, "leprosy" is still seen as an infringement of the *status quo* for religious purity.

Chapter 3

WHOLENESS AND HEALTHCARE IN THE ANCIENT NEAR EAST

All societies are confronted by disease and illness and are obliged to develop appropriate strategies in order to respond. These responses have recently acquired for themselves the collective and useful—though inelegant—name *healthcare*. Healthcare confronts *disease* and *illness* which technically are different[92] and it is important to understand this difference when reviewing practices and attitudes in the healthcare of different societies and civilizations over generations.

Disease and Illness

Disease is the malfunctioning of biological processes as a result of a congeries of causative factors. It is principally the transition in a biological system from the *physiological* to the *pathological*.[93] The precise nature of any disease is the summated effect of the causative agent(s) on the body/mind, its pathological *sequelae,* and the ability of the patient to resist and recover or succumb. Disease is manifested by *symptoms* that the patient reports, and *signs* that are observed or elicited by others. The specific nature of a disease is altered absolutely only by genetic mutation; its effects may be altered relatively by neglect, treatment and the passage of time. Over historical time, the apparent nature of diseases has changed with better understanding, experimental research, and with the application of scientific principles. In some cases, this has, gratifyingly, resulted in more effective treatment.

Illness is the psychosocial experience and the meaning of perceived disease. It is *not,* therefore, independent of the affected subject as disease is. Its definition is, accordingly, more fluid than that of disease and depends upon the society in which it occurs. So, for example, if we are thinking about צרעת, we may suppose that its physical nature as a *disease*[94] will not have changed dramatically over the years, whereas its perception as *illness* may be expected to have varied among societies and over time.[95]

Good modern medical practice must, ideally, be directed both at the disease and the illness. However, this distinction has not necessarily been made by past

---

92 In current usage a taste for imprecision, cliché, and "Humpty Dumpty hermeneutics" has led, to a convergence of their meanings. See: Lewis Carroll, *Through the Looking Glass* (London: The Folio Society, 1962), 75, where Humpty Dumpty says, 'When I use a word, it means just what I choose it to mean—neither more nor less.'
93 Within the term biological must be understood the idea of psychological malfunction also.
94 Whatever that was and, indeed, if it was a single disease.
95 Compare, Biblical צרעת; Elephantiasis Graecorum of Hellenic and Roman times; "leprosy" of the medieval period and modern "Hansen's disease".

generations and cultures. If anything, in the past (and especially in ancient times) greater attention was given to illness than to disease. This may have been particularly true where there were religious or cultic perceptions of the causation. Although illness is a less clearly defined term than disease, its nature may be easier to understand when dealing with ancient texts because an accurate vocabulary to describe disease was either absent or un[der]developed at the time. Because of this it is always dangerous—though tempting—to try to make precise diagnoses from biblical symptomatology. This is the so-called *hyperdiagnostic* approach whose very significant limitations have taken far too long to be recognized in scholarship.

The study of medical practice in ancient Israel is to some extent a subtractive process. There is a considerable dearth of medical literature compared with the relative wealth of such material from Egypt or Mesopotamia. Where authors wishing to investigate the relationship of medical and biblical material have used the Bible, they have perhaps too often ignored alternative sources so that associations have been drawn from too restricted a pool'. It has been said frequently that the biblical priestly code embodies the best hygienic principles of any ancient civilization. However, all too often this relationship has been posited without due regard for the intensely ritualistic and cultic nature demanded by the priestly worldview, making it all too easy to view the situation through the lens of modern medicine. It is in fact, almost impossible to find clear evidence from the texts for any sort of "healthcare edifice", and so one is forced to consider the possibility that the priests only interested themselves in conditions that they believed had important ritual cultic significance and that they did so without any understanding of their biological or medical context. Of course, in any and every society, a wide range of diseases and injuries are prevalent and common (some unavoidably fatal but others not), and ancient Israel would be no exception. So who in ancient Israel would have dealt with these: where and how?

INFLUENCES FROM OTHER CULTURES OF THE ANCIENT NEAR EAST

Egypt and Mesopotamia were the two civilizations adjacent to ancient Syria-Palestine and it might be expected that there would have been cultural diffusion of medical techniqes among civilizations. Whereas medical practice in Egypt and Mesopotamia is well documented, we have little textual evidence concerning healthcare in Israel and the medical literature of later Hellenic and Arabian civilizations shows no sign of medical antecedents from Israel but significant medical antecedents in Egypt and Mesopotamia.

In all societies and cultures, the development of medical healthcare practice has been a lengthy, evolutionary process. A perusal of the Bible suggests that the everyday medicine of ancient Syria-Palestine was either not well developed or not well reported. In considering how, if at all, medical practice in ancient Syria-

Palestine developed, we must carefully examine external influences and these fall roughly into two categories. First, those cultures dating from an earlier period and with an established medical tradition of their own: namely Egypt and Mesopotamia. Both of these appear to have had, (each in its own way), well-developed medical traditions and, because of their geographical proximity, might be expected to have influenced Israel. By post-exilic times, Greek (Hellenic) medicine was emerging and would have been at least a potentially significant influence. As a result of the work of Hippocrates (*c.* 460–370 BCE) and through the time of Alexander (356–323 BCE) and into the Roman Period, Greek medicine became very highly developed and was widely exported. All of these influences operated coincidentally with the final redactions of biblical books. By the time of the *Mishnah* and the *Talmud*, a further variable in the form of Arabian medicine was emerging and it is through this medium that much ancient material pertaining to medical matters has been preserved, though possibly redacted. Arabian medicine both complemented and challenged Greek (and Roman) medicine so that they all must be considered together as significantly contributing to the foundation and evolution of modern, Western medicine.[96]

The two civilizations, Egypt and Mesopotamia, that pre-dated that of Syria-Palestine both had well-developed medical traditions and both were highly polytheistic civilizations. Unlike Israel, neither Egypt nor Mesopotamia moved towards monolatry or monotheism and this difference may have had a crucial impact on the degree to which their practices became absorbed into a burgeoning Israelite culture.

Egypt

It would be a mistake to suppose, as many have, that Egyptian medicine consisted of little more than *post mortem* practices. It is true that in a culture where the after-life was central and all-important, preparation for it necessitated the development and perfection of embalming. The Egyptians were, as we well know, particularly good at this, but much of their apparent success was due to the preserving qualities of the land and its warm, dry climate—as has been shown to be the case also for the preservation of papyri. The name most associated with ancient Egyptian medicine is *Imhotep*, vizier to the pharaoh *Djoser* of the Third Dynasty (*c.* 2650–2560 BCE) of the Old Kingdom (2700–2200 BCE). Imhotep is described as having been a skilled physician in respect of living patients and is sometimes claimed to be the founder of Egyptian medicine.[97] However, there is no textual evidence from these early times and the present day

---

[96] J. V. Kinnier-Wilson, "Medicine in the Land and Times of the Old Testament," in *Studies in the Period of David and Solomon and Other Essays*, ed. T Ishida (Winona, IN: Eisenbrauns, 1982). Plinio Prioreschi, *A History of Medicine*, 2 vols. (Omaha, NE: Horatius Press, 1996).
[97] Prioreschi, *A History of Medicine*.

view of Egyptian medicine is compounded largely from two sources: the one, a small number of nevertheless very informative papyri; the other, speculative accounts by writers from later civilizations, notably Hippocrates, (*c.* 460–370 BCE)[98] and Herodotus, (*c.* 484–425 BCE).[99]

The Greeks held Egypt in great regard and recognized that its achievements were largely due to the presence and exploitation of the Nile. It was an emphatically riparian civilization then, and remains so today. Herodotus described Egypt as: δῶρον τοῦ ποταμοῦ and even Homer believed the land of Egypt to be a great source of botanical medicines and a place where every man was, to some extent, skilled in the art of the physician. Egypt, for Homer, is the place that:

> τῇ πλεῖστα φέρει ζείδωρος ἄρουρα
> φάρμακα, πολλὰ μὲν ἐσθλὰ μεμιγμενα πολλὰ δὲ λυγρά·
> ἰητρος δὲ ἕκαστος ἐπισταμενος περὶ πάντων ἀνθπώπων.
>
> Bears the greatest store of drugs,
> many that are healing when mixed
> and many that are baneful;
> there, every man is a physician.
> (Homer *Odyssey* IV 229–232)[100]

Kinnier-Wilson,[101] has identified two kinds of doctor in ancient Egypt. The first was the *ḥry-ḥȝb*,[102] (literally, *carrier of the ritual book*): with *ritual* referring to magic. These doctors were, therefore, magicians, exorcists, and sorcerers.[103] In contrast, members of the second group, the *synw*[104] were, to a degree, practical physicians and surgeons in the modern sense. Both physician/surgeon and embalmer would be versed in botany and in minor surgical procedures along with the dissection necessary for embalming.[105]

Avalos,[106] has set great store by the *locus of healthcare* by which he means the place where healer and patient interact. This can be the home, the temple, outside the encampment, in the wilderness etc. The implication is that, from a consideration of the *locus*, some idea can be obtained as to the way healthcare was perceived as being a domestic matter or one of divine propitiation. In the

---

98 Hippocrates et al., *Hippocrates*, 10 vols. (Cambridge, MA; London: Harvard University Press; William Heinemann, 1923–2012).
99 Herodotus, *The Persian Wars*, trans. A. D. Godley, 4vols. (Cambridge MA: Harvard University Press, 1999).
100 Homer, *The Odyssey*, trans. George Dimock and A. T. Murray, 2vols. (Cambridge, MA: Harvard University Press, 2002).
101 Kinnier-Wilson, "Medicine in the Land," 338.
102 E. A. Budge, *Egyptian Hieroglyphic Dictionary*, 2 vols. (New York: Dover, 1920), 849a. Note that as the nature of Egyptian vowels remains uncertain it is customary to vocalize with 'e's except for the glottal stops which use 'a's. Thus ḥry-ḥȝb becomes 'heri-ha'ab' and synw is spoken as seynu.
103 Equivalent to the Mesopotamian ašipu[m], see below.
104 Budge, *Egyptian Hieroglyphic Dictionary*, 605b, and equivalent to the Mesopotamian asû.
105 Bill B. Baumann, "The Botanical Aspects of Ancient Egyptian Embalming and Burial," *Eco Botany* 14, no. 1 (1960): 84–104.
106 Hector Avalos, *Illness and Health Care in the Ancient Near East: The Role of the Temple in Greece, Mesopotamia, and Israel* (Atlanta: Scholars Press, 1995).

case of the Egyptians, the *locus* was clearly the home, making healthcare a purely domestic matter.

Present-day knowledge of Egyptian medicine comes from two sources, *paleopathology* and *papyrology*. The former has been less helpful than might be expected, largely because of the processing and the removal of organs prior to mummification. The preservation of the internal organs in canopic jars was not of a high standard compared with mummification and little of interpretative value remains from this practice today. Dermatological and musculo-skeletal evidence has emerged from the examination of mummies in some cases and from the use of modern techniques such as magnetic resonance imaging and computerized tomographic examination. These techniques have proved particularly helpful in establishing in ancient remains the presence of bone diseases and fractures that have healed and it is clear from such studies that surgical measures such as traction and splinting of fractures were known and used routinely.[107]

There are about a dozen *medical papyri* from Egypt.[108] They describe mostly magical spells and recipes but two stand out and are of considerable size and importance. These are the *Ebers Papyrus* and the *Edwin Smith Papyrus*. Neither has any religious or cultic content and both appear to be very serious, purely medical textbooks. The *Ebers Papyrus*,[109] has been dated to approximately 1550 BCE: it is extensive as it contains 877 sections. There is a detailed pharmacopœia involving not merely botanical remedies but also prescriptions using animal and mineral substances. There follow sections easily identifiable as gastroenterology, minor surgery, urology, gynaecology, dermatology, ophthalmology, otorhinolaryngology, neurology and cardiology; there is also advice on diagnosis, hair-care, cosmetics, and domestic hygiene. All of these are, of course, rudimentary by present-day standards but it is important to recognize that the systematic development of medicine into an art and science was already taking place. One small section is devoted to the gods of Egypt. They are not in any way seen as the authors of disease and illness which itself, in turn, is not seen as punishment for sin or for anything else. The involvement of the Egyptian gods is purely as divine reinforcement of the potency of earthly remedies. Of these, some are specifically attributed to a particular god, for example a headache cure purporting to have been invented by Isis. However, it was never supposed that the remedy would be effective, on its own, without the divine component.[110]

---

[107] This is not entirely surprising. By the time of Hippocrates, fracture treatment by external fixation had reached a degree of refinement not far short of the present time. Hippocrates et al., *Hippocrates*.
[108] Kinnier-Wilson, "Medicine in the Land," 342.
[109] C. P. Bryan, *The Papyrus Ebers* (Chesapeake, NY: E.C.A. Associates, African Heritage Classical Research Studies Series, 1990).
[110] Its inclusion was, most probably, no more than the modern expedient of employing so-called celebrities to promote the sale of branded goods.

A significant medical theme of the *Ebers Papyrus* is that illness often results from the retention of excess food within the body.[111] Consequently, remedies for purgation and emetics figure prominently among the prescriptions. The descriptions of a few conditions are sufficiently detailed to allow a clear diagnosis and it is interesting to note that these are diseases that are still indigenous to, and prevalent in, Egypt: they are nematode infestation (*ḥfȝ.t*), tapeworm (*pnd*) and, more seriously, trachoma (*nḥȝ.t*), and schistosomiasis (*ʿȝ*).[112] The *Ebers Papyrus* is a truly scientifically orientated piece of work and points clearly to a well-developed medical tradition which, we must assume, went hand in hand with more dubious practices such as magic, divination, and sorcery.

The *Edwin Smith Papyrus* is a lengthy exposition on mainly surgical topics and it has been hailed as the *fons et origo* of surgery, whilst the *Ebers Papyrus* holds a corresponding place in physic. It is incomplete and, being arranged anatomically beginning at the head, it is missing any discussion of some structures below the lumbar region. Unsurprisingly, the interest and concern [near obsession?] shown by so many ancient civilizations towards the genitalia is well represented throughout the text. The *Edwin Smith Papyrus* was translated and produced in a critical edition by Breasted in 1930.[113] Its scope as a surgical treatise is very much limited to the treatment of wounds and fractures. Pillars of treatment that remain in place today can be identified in the text. Some examples are the cleansing of wounds, reduction and immobilization of fractures by traction and/or splinting, and suturing. There is no invocation of the Egyptian gods in what is strictly a surgical textbook.

Neither the *Ebers Papyrus* nor the *Edwin Smith Papyrus* is at all concerned with embalming. These show us that the Egyptian civilization had a well-developed system of healthcare for living patients and that it was in a state of evolution and separate from mortuary techniques. The *locus* of healthcare was undoubtedly the home, but we remain uncertain as to the precise relationship between the *ḥry-ḥȝb* and the *synw*. It is unclear under what circumstances either would be "called-out", whether they worked in harmony or conflict and whether they enjoyed an equivalent social standing.

The extent to which Egyptian medical practice may have influenced the Syria-Palestinian civilization remains an open question. It depends ultimately upon one's beliefs regarding the exodus. It is hard to understand why, if the exodus took place as described in the Hebrew Bible, there is so little evidence for the adoption of Egyptian medical techniques by the Israelites. There are several possibilities for why this might have been so. One possibility is that it simply

---

111 This became a central pillar of medical practice in many societies and persisted in some degree, up until the nineteenth century. It was not a diagnosis customarily made by the Israelite priesthood.
112 See chapter 7
113 J. H. Breasted, *The Edwin Smith Surgical Papyrus: Facsimile, Hieroglyphic Transliteration and Translation* (Chicago, IL: University of Chicago Press, 1930).

did not fit into the priestly ideology. Egyptian medical practices *may* have been transported to Israel but there been neglected or suppressed. Alternatively, as seems more likely, if the exodus was a minor affair or if it did not occur at all, then it is quite plausible that Egyptian medical influence in Syria-Palestine would have been minimal or non-existent.

Mesopotamia

While the exodus remains a matter for doubt, there is no such unclarity about the Assyrian invasion of Israel (722 BCE) or the Babylonian exile (587–538 BCE) both of which provided ample opportunity for the interaction of Mesopotamian and Israelite (medical) cultures. Times of war and strife have traditionally been associated with advances in medical care and this remains, very much, the case today, with the most striking examples having occurred in the twentieth century.

The most recent and comprehensive study of medicine in ancient Mesopotamia is that of Geller,[114] though this study is somewhat restricted to the Neo-Assyrian (935–612 BCE), Neo-Babylonian (626–539 BCE) and Persian (539–332 BCE) periods. For a detailed account of earlier times, back to the Sumerian period, one must consult Prioreschi, Kinnier-Wilson, Van de Mieroop, and Mykytiuk.[115]

The Mesopotamian civilizations, like the Egyptian, were dependent upon rivers, but whereas the seasonal hydrological behaviour of the Nile was relatively predictable, the Tigris and Euphrates were erratic so that the riparian settlements experienced an irregular oscillation from drought to flooding.[116] There are no extant images of Mesopotamian doctors and the oldest reference we have is the cylinder-seal of the physician *Ur-lugal-edinna*[117] now in the Louvre. *Ur-lugal-edinna* was an *asûm* which, Kinnier-Wilson informs us, was the equivalent of the Egyptian *synw*. It appears that in the Sumerian period, this was the only kind of physician to be found. The *āšipu*[118] (Egyptian ≡ *ḥry-ḥ3b*), did not emerge until Old-Babylonian times. They were diviners and specialists in incantations and spells. The *asû*, by contrast, were entirely practical doctors

---

114 M. J. Geller, *Ancient Babylonian Medicine: Theory and Practice* (Oxford: Wiley-Blackwell, 2010).
115 Prioreschi, *A History of Medicine*; J. V. Kinnier-Wilson, "Diseases of Babylon: An Examination of Selected Texts," *JRoy Soc Med* 89 (1996): 135–40; Kinnier-Wilson, "Medicine in the Land and Times of the Old Testament"; Marc Van de Mieroop, *A History of the Ancient Near East, ca. 3000–323 B.C.* (Oxford: Blackwell, 2007); Lawrence J. Mykytiuk, *Identifying Biblical Persons in Northwest Semitic Inscriptions of 1200–539 BCE*, no 12 (Atlanta: Society of Biblical Literature, 2004).
116 The incidental advantage of this to Babylo-Assyriologists is that, because mud was plentiful, it became the vehicle for the written word. A wealth of baked mud tablets bearing cuneiform writing exists. Some tablets bear medical information but much is still un-translated and it remains to be seen how much more information may, one day, emerge. The politico-religious vicissitudes of modern Middle-Eastern civilizations makes this goal seem still a long way off.
117 He is delightfully represented on the seal by his personal symbol as a physician—a forceps.
118 Nominative singular āšipum and the singular of asû is asûm in Old Babylonian which is the usual paradigm for Akkadian grammar books. However, later usage from Assyrian to Neo-Babylonian times often formed the nominative singular in '-u' like the nominative plural. John Huehnergard, *A Grammar of Akkadian*, 2nd ed. (Winona Lake, IN: Eisenbrauns, 2005); Douglas B. Miller and R. Mark Shipp, *An Akkadian Handbook: Paradigms, Helps, Glossary, Logograms, and Sign List* (Winona Lake, IN: Eisenbrauns, 1996).

and it seems likely that in the early Mesopotamian period the healthcare over which they presided was a purely domestic matter with the *locus* being the home which *asû* would visit as and when they were needed.

The Egyptian and Mesopotamian terminologies may be compared thus:[119]

EGYPT		MESOPOTAMIA	
ḥry-ḥ₃b	𓉔𓂋𓏭𓎛𓃀𓏛	āšipu(m)	𒈡𒈦𒈨
synw	𓋴𓏌𓏤𓅱𓀗	asû(m)	𒀀𒍪

Medicine in Mesopotamia almost certainly, over time, developed a greater theological component than that in ancient Egypt. This was especially the case once the *āšipu* became established as an alternative, or at least an additional, medical force in society. Some *āšipu* became associated with specific gods and therefore operated out of their temples. By the end of the *Old-Babylonian Period* and into the *Assyrian Period*, there was a multiplicity of gods and the *āšipu* were likely to have been seen as being able to read from the symptoms and signs of diseases the hand of divine involvement or even of divine punishment. If nothing else, this appears to have given rise to a rudimentary form of diagnosis based upon a *protasis–apodosis* algorithm directed at the patient.[120] Relevant cuneiform inscriptions from this time frequently contain the words *qātum* (construct, *qāt/šu* = 𒋗) meaning "the hand" and *DINGIR* (*DN* = 𒀭), a determinative,[121] for "deity" in Akkadian, so that "*qāt DN*" (𒋗𒀭)or "hand of god" appears both as the instrument of disease and as the instrument of healing.[122] Sometimes, the hands of specific gods are implicated as in *qāt Ishtar* or *qāt Shamash* and some diseases were seen as having been brought about, not by deities, but by demons (*qāt eṭimmi*; literally the "hand of ghosts"). The expression *qāt DN* appears to have been a generic term for disease but there were undoubtedly, also specific pathological terms in use. For example, we have the

---

119 Budge, *Egyptian Hieroglyphic Dictionary*; Gardiner, *Egyptian Grammar*; R. Labat and F. Malbran-Labat, *Manuel d'Épigraphie Akkadienne: Signes Syllabaire Idéogrammes*, ed. Paul Geuthner (Paris: Geuthner S.A., 1988); R. Borger, *Mesopotamisches Zeichenlexikon* (Münster: Ugarit-Verlag, 2004).
120 This technique, is still very much in use and today is described as 'taking a medical history'.
121 Therefore written UPPERCASE or as a superscript.
122 Borger, *Mesopotamisches Zeichenlexikon*. Labat and Malbran-Labat, *Manuel d'Épigraphie Akkadienne*.

term *šeʾu* meaning "cysts", *pūṣu*, spots and *nuqdū*, "nodules". The latter two are of particular interest as they appear in an *omen text* from the Old Babylonian period describing a skin disease (perhaps "leprosy"/צרעת) and indicating that this affliction resulted in rejection, not only by one's fellows, but, more importantly, by the deity.[123]

DIŠ LÚ pa-ga-ar ši-ru-šu pu-ṣa-amku-ul-lu-u[m]-ma

If the flesh of a man shows white spots and

ù nu-uq-di i-ta-ad du

is dotted with nodules

LÚ šu-ú i-ti i-lí-šu sà-ki-ib

this man is rejected by his deity

i-ti a-ul [u-t]i sà-ki-ib

(and) rejected by mankind.

An important dermatological condition is often to be found recorded in Akkadian inscriptions on boundary stones. This is *saḫaršuppû*,[124] probably derived from the Sumerian *saḫar-šub-ba*. Some authors, perhaps with well-developed eyes of faith, see from variants of this word a degree of phonetic similarity to צרעת. This disease appears to have been so serious that sufferers were prohibited from entering settlements and the boundary stones were erected to inform passers-by and to prohibit this.[125] It appears also that this affliction could be imposed as a punishment by disaffected divine beings. There is a notable example of this in the *Vassal Treaty of Esarhaddon* where *saḫar-šub-ba-e* appears amid a torrent of maledictions, from a pantheon of gods, and invoked in response to particular infractions of the treaty.

---

123 F. Köcher and A. L. Oppenheim, "The Old Babylonian Omen Text VAT 7525," *AfO* 18 (1957): 62–77.
124 Von Soden gives the following recorded variants: saḫar-šub-ba-e, saḫar-šup-pú, saḫar-šub-bû, saḫar-tu, saḫaru, saḫḫaru. W. von Soden and B. Meissner, *Akkadisches Handwörterbuch*, Vol. 2 (Wiesbaden: Otto Harrassowitz, 1965), 1005.
125 Kinnier-Wilson, "Medicine in the Land," 355. K-W suggests that saḫaršuppû was, most probably, scurvy.

Wholeness and Healthcare in The Ancient Near East

420

419 [dXXX n]a-an-nar [AN-e U KI-ti SAHAR.SUB.BA-e]

419 [May Sin], the brightness of heaven and earth, clothe you with

420 [ii-h4al-iip-ki-n [ma IGI DINGIR.MES U LUGAL e-rab-ku-nu a-a iq-bi]

420 [a leprosy; [may he forbid your entering into the presence of the gods]

421 [ki-]ma sir-ri-me MAS.DA [ia EDIN ru-np-d]a

42I [or king (saying): "Roam the desert] like the wild-ass (and) the gazelle."

There are too few translations of this treaty for extensive textual criticism but that above, from Wiseman,[126] is part of a study carried out with sedulous and scholarly attention to detail. Wiseman is cautions in implicating *saḥar-šub-ba-e* as leprosy and rehearses all the usual *caveats*. However, he thinks the similarities to צרעת are too obvious to be ignored. Whatever *saḥar-šub-ba-e*/צרעת may have been, the important point is that skin diseases such as this were seen in Mesopotamia, quite clearly as divine punishment. In dealing with this the *āšipu* operated in a fully polytheistic milieu that involved all the gods and godlets of Assyrian society. Unlike Israel where there was a single set of rituals defined and operated within the priestly worldview, in Mesopotamia a pantheon of gods was to be found, alongside a panoply of rituals.

Nevertheless, we may be already beginning to see similarities with the Levitical view of skin diseases and the emphasis on treatment by segregation from normal society rather than by any effort to heal. While Mesopotamian civilization appears to have regarded *leprosy/saḥar-šub-ba-e*/צרעת as very serious, it is interesting to note that it appears not to have paid the same attention to genital discharges that we see in the Levitical canon. This is surprising in view of the fact that schistosomiasis, so common in the Nile valley and endemic in Egypt,

---

126 D. J. Wiseman, "The Vassal-Treaties of Esarhaddon," *BISI* 20, no. 1 (1958): i–99.

was also widely recognized on the flood-plains of the Tigris and the Euphrates and remains so today. The Akkadian word *mūṣu* appears to have been used to describe both haematuria and bladder calculi and both of these are pathognomonic for infection by *S. haematobium*.[127]

While the primary locus of healthcare in Mesopotamia was undoubtedly the home we must note also that a secondary locus—at least as a temporary measure—was the river. This was because the river was the place where rituals were performed. With the rise in importance of the *āšipu*, this temporary site became more frequently used though it is clear from inscriptions, that the *āšipu* invariably visited their patients at home in the first instance and even maintained a form of follow-up by way of home visits. In contrast to what we find later, in both Israelite and Greek medical practice, there is no textual evidence from Mesopotamia to suggest that patients were ever encouraged to visit the temple when they were ill.[128]

In summary, therefore, Mesopotamia had a medical theology wherein two key factors operated. The first was that illness was regarded, throughout Mesopotamian civilization, as not merely affecting the patient, but also as an attack on the entire household. This partly explains the logic of the home as the *locus* for healthcare for whatever sin or impurity might have caused the illness, it was most likely to have originated or been compounded by events in the home. It is interesting to speculate upon whether an extension of this idea resulted in the Levitical view that צרעת could infect fabrics and buildings. The second key factor was that, as the influence of the *āšipu* increased, ultimately, the large variety and number of divine beings who could inflict sickness upon humankind and/or subsequently control it, grew in parallel. Propitiation of the correct agency(-ies) was, theoretically the treatment for a disease and identification of the causative god was a central part of the *āšipu*'s job as "*theognostician*". Because of this multifactorial divine aetiology, there was no opportunity for the development of a unified system of temple-mediated healthcare, nor any real place for a single generic healing deity as his/her role could never be sufficiently specific. This diversity doubtless kept the *āšipu* in work but was of little substantive help either for patient care or public health.

This somewhat unhelpful situation was perhaps offset by the work of the *asû*. We know from textual evidence that there was also a well defined realist viewpoint in operation and that as a result, rudimentary approaches to aetiology, diagnosis, and prognosis were beginning to emerge. While the *āšipu* worked to assign the appropriate *qāt DN* to the symptoms and signs and so arrive at a *theognosis*, the *asû* would be able to administer temporizing measures based on botanical or chemical treatments, or minor surgical procedures such at blood-

---

127 See chapter 7.
128 Avalos, *Illness and Health Care in the Ancient Near East*, 172-3.

letting or cupping. This dualistic approach satisfied both ritualistic and propitiatory needs and provided some practical measures that developed, over time, into therapeutic regimina.

Greece

Greek medicine, although it overlapped the Second Temple period, obviously cannot have directly influenced the genesis and evolution of the much earlier medicine of ancient Syria-Palestine which, for the purposes of the present study, has been termed *biblical medicine*. However, Greek medicine ultimately made such an impact on society in the whole of the Ancient World that it very likely influenced the redactors of earlier Semitic material and so it may have changed the textual evidence available to us today.

The literature on Greek medicine is vast.[129] For present purposes, we can divide Greek medicine into three phases. There was an early phase which centred on the temple cult of Aesculapius (*aka* Asclepius) and which, in many respects, incorporated features of Egyptian and Mesopotamian medical practice. The second phase is that of Hippocratic medicine of which there is an extensive surviving literature.[130] The third phase of Greek medicine was based on Hippocratic medicine but modernized and extended by the works of later physicians who were often working in the Roman Empire.[131] It is particularly important to note that the development of the latter two phases of Greek medicine took place hand in hand with both the evolution of Greek philosophy and the rise of Rome. This adds a new dimension to the medical thought of writers of that period. In Rome, medical practice became almost exclusively the province of expatriate Greeks. Galen studied under Greek teachers and would have been instructed, not only in the works of Hippocrates, but also in the philosophies of the Platonic, Peripatetic, Stoic, and Epicurean Schools and the biological writings of Aristotle and Pliny. He travelled widely around Greece and visited Egypt.

The latter two phases of Greek medicine also drew upon Greek philosophy and the early dawning of Greek scientific thought, and so embodied the notion of παιδεία which derived from the Greek idea that education should begin in childhood and include both body and mind. Just as both were important in Greek philosophy for the normal relationship of body and soul, both were also thought to become deranged by disease and so to a varying degree, medical

---

129 Prioreschi has devoted the whole of Volume 2, (673 pages) of his *History of Medicine* entirely to the Greeks. It would be *ultra vires* in the present work to attempt anything more than the briefest summary.
130 Not least the complete works of Hippocrates of Kos (c. 460–370 BCE) which runs to ten volumes in the Loeb edition and of which so much remains relevant to this day.
131 Foremost among these was Galen of Pergamum (129/30–215/6 CE), a Roman of Greek ethnicity. In particular see: Galen, *Method of Medicine*, trans. Ian Johnston and G. H. R. Horsley, 3 vols. (Cambridge, MA; London: Harvard University Press, 2011); Galen, *On Diseases and Symptoms,* trans. I. Johnston (Cambridge: Cambridge University Press, 2006).

treatment for the first time became aimed at both of these components. As time passed, the idea of the professional physician/surgeon emerged and medical treatment became dislocated from Aesculapian temples so that the *locus* of healthcare moved, much later in Greece than elsewhere, into the home. Nevertheless, Greek medicine never abandoned its philosophical elements nor the notion of παιδεία in relation to medical education which, for the first time, was seen as an entity in its own right. Hippocrates clearly believed that the physician's role embodied wisdom as well as factual knowledge when he averred, ἰητρός φιλόσοφος ἰσύθεος ("a thinking doctor is like a god").[132]

The pre-Hippocratic phase of Greek medicine has come to be called *Aesculapian medicine* on account of its having been operated within the cult of Aesculapius and practised in Aesculapian temples—the *locus* of healthcare at that time. Early Greek medicine, in contrast to that in Egypt and Mesopotamia, placed divine beings at its centre from the very beginning. According to Homer, Aesculapius was the son of Apollo; he began life as a mortal but became a demigod and eventually a god. His two sons Podalirus and Machaon feature in the *Iliad* as physicians/surgeons during the siege of Troy. Physicians are also mentioned by Hesiod and by Pindar (*c.* 518–438 BCE).[133] It is only from early writings such as these that the origins of Greek naturalistic medicine have been placed, by convention, in the 6th century BCE and centred around the cult of Asculapius.[134] Within this culture, disease was *never* considered to be a defilement of the body nor any kind of *impurity* and so it *never* prevented attendance by the sick at sacred places. Thus, the temples of Asclepius and the dwelling places of an assortment of gods, demigods, and even heroes became, from the earliest times, the Greek *locus* of healthcare. However, the Greek temples, and those that operated out of them, bore no resemblance to the Levitical priesthood, and there are no clear parallels to be drawn between the role of the temple which was the undoubted *locus* in Greek medical practice and the *tent-of-meeting/sanctuary or tabernacle,* (משכן/מקדש/מועד אהל) which served as the *locus* in ancient Syria-Palestine and the Hebrew Bible, before the building of the temple in Jerusalem.

Arabia

Arabian medicine impinged upon that of ancient Syria-Palestine in rather the same way as Greek medicine and that is to say indirectly, for its only possible effect would have been upon redactors of earlier writings and upon later Jewish and other commentators. Nevertheless, the effects of Arabian medicine, both on later Jewish medicine and world-wide, were very considerable. Arabian medicine began and flourished in the *Islamic Golden Age* which began in the Umayyad

---

132 Here in Hippocrates' Ionic dialect. For the Attic purist this would be, ἰατρός φιλόσοφος ἰσόθεος.
133 Pythiae III.
134 Prioreschi, *A History of Medicine*; Avalos, *Illness and Health Care in the Ancient Near East*.

Caliphate (661–750 CE) and extended throughout the Abbasid Caliphate (750–1258 CE). During this period, the capital was moved from Damascus to Baghdad and there developed, over time, a rigorous dependency on the Qur'ān, (القرآن) and upon the recorded homiletic pronouncement(s) of the Prophet, (ḥadīth, حديث). In contrast to more recent times, this imposed no stricture; scientific exploration burgeoned and medicine underwent a great surge of development so that from just after the fall of the Roman Empire until the Renaissance of Western culture in the 15th century, the Islamic world dominated science and medicine.[135] The Jewish diaspora, especially in countries where Arab influence was present (e.g. Spain), benefitted from and contributed significantly to this age of scientific progress.[136] Particularly strong was ophthalmological medicine which was of particular interest to the Arabs probably because trachoma (التراخوما) was (and remains), endemic in Arabia. The Arabian physicians were also particularly distinguished in the practice of pharmacy, which was growing to include chemistry as well as botany, and many Arabic medicinal terms such as *drug, syrup, alcohol, alkali*, have migrated and been preserved in Western languages. Arabian medicine also gave rise to the establishment of formal medical training and qualifications and the testing by examination of aspirants thereto.

While none of these later hapenings could have had a direct influence upon the subject of the present study, it is important nevertheless to learn to what extent these later developments influenced commentators on the Biblical texts and reportage generally. It is always difficult to put oneself in the place of an ancient and not to interpret through the lens of later developments. Any study of Israelite medicine must perforce be a speculative process because so little textual information has come down to us, and where it has, it may have been heavily redacted.

---

135 Many texts from Greek medicine lost to the Western World in the Dark Ages were preserved only by having been translated into Arabic. At the Renaissance, they were re-translated into Latin and so Greek medical thought was preserved and augmented through the offices of Islamic physicians.
136 This can be seen from the works of, for example, Avicenna and Maimonides. It became quite difficult to distinguish between Jewish and Muslim contributions towards Arabian medicine. Many Jews knew Arabic and wrote in that language but Judeo-Arabic—the Arabic language written in Hebrew script—was much favoured also by Jewish writers. At later times, Hebrew proper was used but the mixture of languages has imposed a burden upon modern scholarship which has led to difficulty. See: Moses Maimonides and Gerrit Bos, *Medical Aphorisms. Treatises 10–15: A Parallel Arabic-English Edition* (Provo, UT: Brigham Young University Press, 2010); Moses Maimonides and Gerrit (Ed) Bos, *Medical Aphorisms. Treatises 1–5: A Parallel Arabic-English Edition*, 2 vols. (Provo, UT: Brigham Young University Press, 2004); Moses Maimonides and Gerrit (Ed) Bos, *Medical Aphorisms. Treatises 6–9: A Parallel Arabic-English Edition*, 2 vols. (Provo, UT: Brigham Young University Press, 2007). Elinor Lieber, "Asaf's 'Book of Medicines': A Hebrew Encyclopedia of Greek and Jewish Medicine, Possibly Compiled in Byzantium on an Indian Model," *DOPs* 38 (1984): 233-49. One of the best collections of medical manuscripts in all these forms is from the Cairo Genizah now in the Library of Cambridge University. H. D. Isaacs, ed., *Medical and Para-medical Manuscripts in the Cambridge Genizah Collections*. Vol. 11 of Cambridge University Library Genizah Series, ed. S. C. Reif (Cambridge: Cambridge University Press, 1994). A Shivtiel and F Niessen, eds., *Arabic and Judaeo-arabic Manuscripts in the Cambridge Genizah Collections*. Vol. 14 of Cambridge University Library Genizah Series, ed. S. C. Reif, 1 Vol. (Cambridge: Cambridge University Press, 2006).

Healthcare in Ancient Israel Outside the Priestly Society

It has been a widely, and perhaps unfairly, held view that ancient Israel was relatively backward in both the art and science of medicine when compared with its neighbours Egypt and Mesopotamia. Several explanations have been put forward to explain this apparent difference. For example, it has been suggested that the progression from magic and mantic through botanical medicine to scientific medical thought was stifled by the progression towards monotheism, and that the subsuming of therapeutic practices into the province of the priest and the temple was such that the professions of physic and surgery never developed.[137] A more likely explanation might be the disparity between the mass of religious and secular literature that has survived.[138] A considerable majority of authors addressing this subject have written from a Second Temple viewpoint; unsurprisingly, as a comparative wealth of both textual and other evidence is more plentiful from this period than from pre-exilic times. This stance assumes a Yahwistic milieu whereas early medical influences coming from Egypt and Mesopotamia undoubtedly had a polytheistic background which remained a significant element into Hellenic/Greek medicine. We have no clear evidence as to how and at what rate this polytheism became attenuated as it became incorporated into Israelite society. Knowledge of the true date of the writing of the Levitical P and H material becomes vitally important in addressing this problem.[139] If one argues from first principles, it is axiomatic that minor survivable medical conditions and injuries existed in ancient Syria-Palestine and were likely to have been treated by someone. The question is, therefore, whether these events were simply not interesting enough to be included in Scripture whose purpose was not, after all, historical reportage or narrative beyond that necessary for the establishment and inculcation of an extended creation myth. Equally were they irrelevant in the priestly *Weltanschauung* and code of religious law and ritual considered desirable for a developing society? An account of the treatment of minor ailments and injuries hardly gels with such lofty purpose. A side effect of this might have been the priesthood's reserving for itself a powerful and extensive element of control within the developing society. However, although we may suppose the existence of minor healthcare held no interest for the priests and merited no place in their worldview, we have no evidence to make us suppose that they actively opposed it.[140]

---

[137] If one's reading on the subject is confined to the Bible, this *prima facie* conclusion is entirely understandable. See, Maurice Bear Gordon, "Medicine Among the Ancient Hebrews," *Isis* 33, no. 4 (1941): 454–85. Edward Neufeld, "Hygiene Conditions in Ancient Israel (Iron Age)," *BibArch* 34, no. 2 (1971): 42–66. Roderick Saxey, "A Physician's Reflections on Old Testament Medicine," *Dlge* 17, no. 3 (1984): 122–28. Charles Weiss, "Medicine in the Bible," *Sci Mth* 50, no. 3 (1940): 266–71.
[138] If indeed any secular literature ever existed.
[139] See chapter 2.
[140] For similar reasons we cannot know whether the ordinary people liked or disliked priests or if they respected or feared them. Recourse to the doctrine of *oderint dum metuant* has, however, always been popular with those having power as a method of control.

Secular healthcare in ancient Israel, as far as it went, is likely to have embodied those activities which were common to healthcare in coeval cultures. These are magic and botanical medicine and the rise of the apothecary. We have little idea of how, and how far, such activities were utilized as modes of healthcare by ordinary people but it is probably safe to suppose that the work of magicians and apothecaries existed, at least initially, to much the same degree in Israel as in other Mediterranean civilizations. We are, therefore, looking for reasons why these remained unrecorded for posterity. They may have been ignored or suppressed or may have gone unrecorded simply as a result of the illiteracy of its practitioners.

A Unique Example of an Israelite Physician from a Later Period

It was not until the time of the Talmud[141] that Hebrew writings began to indicate the beginnings of rudimentary science. However, with the passage of time, a tolerance appears to have developed towards those outside the priesthood who practised medicine. By the 2nd century BCE, at the time when the Wisdom of Jesus ben Sira appeared in the Septuagint, physicians and their art appear to have become better thought of:

¹ τίμα ἰατρὸν πρὸς τὰς χρείας αὐτοῦ τιμαῖς αὐτοῦ καὶ γὰρ αὐτὸν ἔκτισεν κύριος

² παρὰ γὰρ ὑψίστου ἐστὶν ἴασις καὶ παρὰ βασιλέως λήμψεται δόμα

³ ἐπιστήμη ἰατροῦ ἀνυψώσει κεφαλὴν αὐτοῦ καὶ ἔναντι μεγιστάνων θαυμασθήσεται

⁴ κύριος ἔκτισεν ἐκ γῆς φάρμακα καὶ ἀνὴρ φρόνιμος οὐ προσοχθιεῖ αὐτοῖς

⁵ οὐκ ἀπὸ ξύλου ἐγλυκάνθη ὕδωρ εἰς τὸ γνωσθῆναι τὴν ἰσχὺν αὐτοῦ

⁶ καὶ αὐτὸς ἔδωκεν ἀνθρώποις ἐπιστήμην ἐνδοξάζεσθαι ἐν τοῖς θαυμασίοις αὐτοῦ

⁷ ἐν αὐτοῖς ἐθεράπευσεν καὶ ἦρεν τὸν πόνον αὐτοῦ μυρεψὸς ἐν τούτοις ποιήσει μεῖγμα

⁸ καὶ οὐ μὴ συντελεσθῇ ἔργα αὐτοῦ καὶ εἰρήνη παρ' αὐτοῦ ἐστιν ἐπὶ προσώπου τῆς γῆς

⁹ τέκνον ἐν ἀρρωστήματί σου μὴ παράβλεπε ἀλλ' εὖξαι κυρίῳ καὶ αὐτὸς ἰάσεταί σε

¹⁰ ἀπόστησον πλημμέλειαν καὶ εὔθυνον χεῖρας καὶ ἀπὸ πάσης ἁμαρτίας καθάρισον καρδίαν

¹¹ δὸς εὐωδίαν καὶ μνημόσυνον σεμιδάλεως καὶ λίπανον προσφορὰν ὡς μὴ ὑπάρχων

¹² καὶ ἰατρῷ δὸς τόπον καὶ γὰρ αὐτὸν ἔκτισεν κύριος καὶ μὴ ἀποστήτω σου καὶ γὰρ αὐτοῦ χρεία

¹³ ἔστιν καιρὸς ὅτε καὶ ἐν χερσὶν αὐτῶν εὐοδία

---

141 Halivni, *The Formation of the Babylonian Talmud*, trans. J. L. Rubenstein.

¹⁴ καὶ γὰρ αὐτοὶ κυρίου δεηθήσονται ἵνα εὐοδώσῃ αὐτοῖς ἀνάπαυσιν καὶ ἴασιν χάριν ἐμβιώσεως
¹⁵ ὁ ἁμαρτάνων ἔναντι τοῦ ποιήσαντος αὐτὸν ἐμπέσοι εἰς χεῖρας ἰατροῦ

¹ Honor the physician with the honor due him, according to your need of him, for the Lord created him;
² for healing comes from the Most High, and he will receive a gift from the king.
³ The skill of the physician lifts up his head, and in the presence of great men he is admired.
⁴ The Lord created medicines from the earth, and a sensible man will not despise them.
⁵ Was not water made sweet with a tree in order that his power might be known?
⁶ And he gave skill to men that he might be glorified in his marvelous works.
⁷ By them he heals and takes away pain;
⁸ the pharmacist makes of them a compound. His works will never be finished; and from him health is upon the face of the earth.
⁹ My son, when you are sick do not be negligent, but pray to the Lord, and he will heal you.
¹⁰ Give up your faults and direct your hands aright, and cleanse your heart from all sin.
¹¹ Offer a sweet-smelling sacrifice, and a memorial portion of fine flour, and pour oil on your offering, as much as you can afford.
¹² And give the physician his place, for the Lord created him; let him not leave you, for there is need of him.
¹³ There is a time when success lies in the hands of physicians,
¹⁴ for they too will pray to the Lord that he should grant them success in diagnosis and in healing, for the sake of preserving life.
¹⁵ He who sins before his Maker, may he fall into the care of a physician.

It seems worthwhile to quote all of this rather long eulogy (Sira 38:1–15) as it is so untypical of the Hebrew Bible and associated writings. That is perhaps unsurprising given that it is the account written in Greek by Ben Sira *nepos* that appears in the Septuagint. The original text of Jesus Ben Sira was written in Palestine, in Hebrew and is traditionally dated as 175–200 BCE. The translation and redaction into Greek by Ben Sira *nepos*, that appears in the Septuagint, was written approximately two generations later. It almost certainly reflects a milieu quite different from that of Palestine and different again from the pre-exilic times of the Levitical *Grundlage*. Given that uncorroborated, unitary examples invoke the old legal adage "*unus testis, nullus testis*" ("one witness is no witness"), it is impossible to draw firm conclusions from these writings by any deductive process. However, arguing inductively, it seems unlikely that a single author and his translator would create the idea of doctors and their work *ex aethere*. If this is correct, it is highly suggestive of the fact that physicians existed at this time. As we no longer have the complete original Hebrew text of Jesus Ben Sira[142] it is impossible to know if and how terms appearing in the Greek were rendered by Ben Sira in the original. For example, the word μυρεψὸς,[143] almost universally translated into English as pharmacist, must be supposed to be Ben Sira *nepos*'s rendering of his grandfather's word רקח,[144] which is usually translated as "apothecary". Strictly, the two are different so it is unclear whether this represents an historical change between versions or simply a lack of attention to detail or Ben Sira *nepos*'s loose translation. It is likely that apothecaries were a common ancestor to both physicians and pharmacists, though by the time of Ben Sira *nepos*, at least in Hellinic culture, the two were separately identifiable. More importantly we have no knowledge as to whether the writing of Jesus Ben Sira and Ben Sira *nepos* were unique or one such text among many, now lost. Much as the idea might appeal, it would unsafe to describe the text of either version as a counteracting parænesis against negative views about physicians. This idea comes largely form Collins[145] who has dated the Greek text of Ben Sira *nepos* somewhat later (*c.* 117 BCE) than the traditional view; and what remains of the Jesus Ben Sira's Hebrew original, he dates to sometime in the first quarter of the second century BCE. He supposes that since the book purports to be an accumulation of wisdom, it is unlikely to have been written by a young man. As with Proverbs, Collins supposes an Egyptian influence upon the genre which embodies observations and prohibitions along with comparisons. He notes, perhaps importantly for the present context, that:

> One of the hallmarks of the biblical wisdom tradition, as found in Proverbs, Ecclesiastes, and Job, is a lack of reference to the distinctive traditions of Israel. The concern is with humanity as such, not with the special status of one people ... Ben Sira breaks with the tradition of biblical wisdom by devoting extensive attention to the history of Israel. This history is not presented, however as the history of the acts of God or even as sequential narrative. Instead it is cast as the praise of famous men who stand as examples for future generations.

In this encomiastical genre, besides famous men, Ben Sira tackles professions such as those of the physician and the scribe. This all makes one doubt that there is any scope for justifiable backward extrapolation to the society of the Levitical purity laws. The germ of what is said would surely have derived from Jesus Ben Sira himself, but on balance it seems likely that Ben Sira *nepos* conflated his

---

142 Fragments exist in the Cairo Geniza which, it has been suggested amount to 68% of the text.
143 ὁ μυρεψὸς, (μύρον, ἕψω). Properly one who boils and prepares unguents, perfumer. H. G. Liddell and R. Scott, *Greek English Lexicon* (Oxford: Oxford University Press, 1940).
144 See chapter 11.
145 J. J. Collins, "Ecclesiasticus, or the Wisdom of Jesus Son of Sirach," in *The Oxford Bible Commentary*, ed. John Barton and John Muddiman (Oxford: Oxford University Press, 2001).

grandfather's ideas with his own observations and so was commenting on the *mores* of a later civilization, beyond even that of the Second Temple period. It must be remembered also that Ben Sira *nepos* may well have encountered Greek medicine and its central concept of παιδεία.

It is in chapter 38 of Ben Sira that we learn about physicians. Collins draws a comparison between Ben Sira and the Hebrew Bible when he says "Physicians are rarely mentioned and regarded as unreliable". The justification for this stance he finds in quotations such as 2 Chron 16:12,

> ויחלא אסא בשנת שלושים ותשע למלכותו ברגליו עד־למעלה חליו וגם־בחליו לא־
> דרש את־יהוה כי ברפאים

> And in the thirty and ninth year of his reign Asa was diseased in his feet; his disease was exceeding great: yet in his disease he sought not to the Lord, but to the physicians.

a mistaken strategy, with a fatal outcome for Asa as it turned out, (16:13):

> וישכב אסא עם־אבתיו וימת בשנת ארבעים ואחת למלכו

> And Asa slept with his fathers, and died in the one and fortieth year of his reign.

One might argue that Collins's choice of Chronicles is not properly representative of the Hebrew Bible as a whole. The dates of Chronicles and Ben Sira are not very far apart in time, both being products of a late period.

Collins[146] makes the entirely plausible suggestion that Ben Sira *nepos* had seen the results of the well-established medical traditions of Greece and Egypt and felt the need of a counteracting paraenesis aimed at the negative view of physicians that he supposed had been habitually taken in Israel. To avoid the problem that disease and its cure were dispensed solely by the hand of God, Ben Sira tactfully suggests (38:4) that the healing powers of God are secondarily mediated through physicians working with, for example, botanical remedies.[147] Such remedies by this time, would have been well tested and established in Greek Medical practice[148] and it would have been impossible to deny their existence and efficacy. Nevertheless, Ben Sira still cannot completely detach himself from the idea that illness is due to sin (38:10), and so predictably advocates the offering of sacrifices (38:11) to cleanse impurity before a physician can act. The physician himself is driven by divine will (38:14) and so heals, as it were, by proxy. The physician in Israel remains, in the end, no more than the instrument through which Yahweh operates. The Greek text of Ben Sira *nepos* undoubtedly proves to be helpful in a consideration of the hypothetical problem

---

146 Collins, "Ecclesiasticus, or the Wisdom of Jesus Son of Sirach," in *The Oxford Bible Commentary*, 691.
147 He does not imply any such mediated powers of divination, or magic.
148 Hippocrates et al., *Hippocrates*.

of having, under Yahwism, an omniscient and omnipotent deity who is seen to dispense and to alleviate disease so that both the positive and negative aspects of healthcare were, doctrinally-speaking, exclusively in the hands of the deity.

> τίμα ἰατρὸν πρὸς τὰς χρείας αὐτοῦ τιμαῖς αὐτοῦ καὶ γὰρ αὐτὸν ἔκτισεν κύριος παρὰ γὰρ ὑψίστου ἐστὶν ἴασις καὶ παρὰ βασιλέως λήμψεται δόμα

> Honour physicians for their services, for the Lord created them; for their gift of healing comes from the Most High, and they are rewarded by the king. (Ben Sira nepos 38:1–2)

In this verse Ben Sira *nepos* cleverly attributes the practicalities of the physician's art, along with its pecuniary rewards, to the deity from whom ultimately they emanate as a gift, delegated to physicians. As seen above, this is an enduring proposition in the Abrahamic religions, but there is no evidence that such a formula was ever applied in Leviticus. There, responsibility and credit were vested entirely in the deity who was πρῶτον κινοῦν ἀκίνητον ("first unmoved mover"). Ben Sira's formula has proved, nevertheless, useful and enduring and, in more fundamentalistic faiths, his idea continues to prove indispensable as a means of circumventing the difficulty in overcoming the doctrinal and dogmatic assertion that there is no possibility of events (including healthcare) occurring in our world which are independent of the will of a single omnipotent deity.

Magic and Manticism

Magic, divination and demonology have been traditionally viewed as being separate from, and even as perversions of, science, logic, and religion. Unsurprisingly, among Christian Western civilizations, they have not been a popular substrate for academic and scholarly interest and there is a relatively sparse literature. An excellent starting-point is Toorn's compendious account.[149] It was never in the [Western] Church's interest to allow such subjects to become popular with the common people and we have all grown up familiar with stories of the triumph of the righteous over magic and evil. Magicians or sorcerers, (חרטם) appear in Exodus where they are portrayed in a bad light as evil, yet incompetent, instruments of Pharoah. Nevertheless, it is likely that in most, if not all, ancient civilizations, much use was made of magicians and diviners and undoubtedly by Roman times, haruspication and especially hepatoscopy, were as commonplace as the modern weather forecast. They had become an essential part of a polytheistic civilization. We are indebted to Thomas Witton Davies, (1851–1923),[150] Baptist minister, Semitic scholar, and Professor of Hebrew at

---

149 K. van der Toorn, Bob Becking and Pieter Willem van der Horst, *Dictionary of Deities and Demons in the Bible* (DDD) (Leiden: Brill, 1995).
150 For reasons that are unclear, in his early publications he uses the spelling Wytton Davies. T. Wytton Davies, "Bible Leprosy," *ONTS* 11, no. 3 (1890): 142–52. The present author was acquainted with his son the Venerable Carlyle Witton Davies who always insisted upon the "-i" spelling.

Bangor University (1905–21), for his interest in this subject. Despite a distinguished career as a teacher, he published very little: his most noted work, however, was on magic among the Hebrews and this book has remained a corner-stone of scholarship on this subject.[151]

Witton Davies follows the traditional view that magic/sorcery was the practice of using secret or hidden powers to manipulate individuals or events. Divination was the art of reading signs in order to foretell the future. This view has been challenged by Jeffers as simplistic, on the grounds that it presupposes a sequential evolution of ideas that has not been formally demonstrated and which takes no account of any *ontology* or *cosmogony,* and so of any *Weltanschauung* proper to the various participants.[152] She accepts, however, that after Witton Davies's mantle at Bangor fell upon Islwyn Blythin, he, and so the "Bangor School", took an increasingly holistic approach to the idea of magic in order to incorporate the *cosmology* appropriate to whatever civilization was under consideration.[153] It will be necessary to return to and expand this approach in chapter 4 in respect of the Levitical priesthood and the cosmology underlying their rituals.[154] The following table is an attempt to summarize these viewpoints.

	Magic	Divination	Demonology
Witton-Davies	Man's attempt at intercourse with spiritual and supernatural beings and to influence them for benefit	Man's attempt to obtain from the spiritual world super-normal or superhuman knowledge [of the future]	The belief that there exist evil spirits responsible for the misfortunes that assail men
Blythin & Jeffers	A self-contained system of rationality through which men realize their independence from the behaviour of natural phenomena	The ability to relate the parts (i.e. signs) of a cosmic framework to the whole	

---

151 Thomas Witton Davies, *Magic, Divination, and Demonology Among the Hebrews and their Neighbours: Including an Examination of Biblical References and of the Biblical Terms* (London; Leipzig: James Clarke & Co.; M. Spirgatis: 1898).
152 Ann Jeffers, *Magic and Divination in Ancient Palestine and Syria* (Leiden: Brill, 1996), 2.
153 Islwyn Blythin, "Magic and Methodology," *Numen* 17, no. 1 (1970): 45–59.
154 Frank H. Gorman, *The Ideology of Ritual: Space, Time and Status in the Priestly Theology* (Sheffield: JSOT Press, 1990).

In the light of an absence of non-biblical material from Israel on this subject, we may take for our starting point instances where the Bible mentions magic. Witton Davies has, most helpfully, compiled a list of Hebrew words for, and which relate to, magic.[155] These words may be used in analytical software such as *Bibleworks* and *Accordance*[156] to identify all instances of their usage in the canon. Witton Davies further relates these words to other Semitic languages, notably Akkadian and Arabic, and their occurrence in those languages. Witton Davies's thesis—which, if correct, is of signal importance—is to show that many of the words used in a cultic or religious sense in the Hebrew Bible may have been derived from earlier usages in the sphere of magic; the implication being that aspects of priestly ritual may also have derived from earlier profane practices. A good example is the idea that the serpent is associated in many ancient civilizations with evil, misfortune and unhappiness: serpents were implicated frequently in divination. The Hebrew for serpent is נחש and Witton Davies suggests that the word לחש, to "whisper" or to "hiss" found in later Rabbinic Hebrew and in Aramaic, may be a dialectical variant or a confusion of the two liquids נ and ל which both may fall-out in *Pe nun* verbs. He further cites the parallel from Arabic of لَحَسَ (lāḥăsă), meaning "lick" in the metaphorical sense of "licked by the serpent's tongue" and therefore "cursed", with نَحَسَ (năḥăsă), meaning "jinx": the "l" (ل) and "n" (ن) consonants are transposed without losing the overall sense of misfortune. Witton Davies is, presumably, implying that לחש may be used as a *denominative* with a meaning invoking notions of a serpent or of "serpentine evil" or "misfortune through serpentine malevolence and guile". This use of the serpent was a common metaphor throughout the ancient world, indeed Ecclesiastes (10:11) makes a pun of the two Hebrew words לחש and נחש in the context of a snake and a snake-charm(er).[157]

> אם־ישך הנחש בלוא־לחש ואין יתרון לבעל הלשון
>
> If the serpent bite before it be charmed, then is there no advantage in the charmer. (Eccl 10:11)

And Jeremiah (8:17) uses the two words together in a similar way but as a threat of divine punishment:

> כי הנני משלח בכם נחשים צפענים אשר אין־להם לחש ונשכו אתכם נאם־יהוה
>
> For, behold, I will send serpents, basilisks, among you, which will not be charmed; and they shall bite you, saith the Lord. (Jer 8:17)

---

155 Thomas Witton Davies, *Old Testament Words for Magic or in Relation to It* (London; Leipzig: James Clarke & Co; M. Spirgatis, 1898).
156 Bibleworks, "Software for Biblical Exegesis and Research." Accordance, "Bible Software."
157 But note the use of Hermes's messenger's rod (κηρύκειον) eventually became identified with the Rod of Asclepius entwined with a single snake, in Greek and later in Roman medical iconography. In more recent times the caduceus, with two entwined snakes appears to have usurped this role.

In both cases the serpent has been retained from early superstition and is being used metaphorically or symbolically in Yahwistic religion.

Jeffers has written extensively on diviners, magicians, and other such specialists using an etymological study of their titles and job-descriptions to understand their function in society.[158] She takes as her starting point two verses of Deuteronomy (18:10–11) in which she finds nine such categories listed:

> לא־ימצא בך מעביר בנו־ובתו באש קסם קסמים מעונן ומנחש ומכשף
>
> There shall not be found with thee any one that maketh his son or his daughter to pass through the fire, one that useth divination, one that practiseth augury, or an enchanter, or a sorcerer,
>
> וחבר חבר ושאל אוב וידעני ודרש אל־המתים
>
> or a charmer, or a consulter with a familiar spirit, or a wizard, or a necromancer. (Deut 18:10–11)

Jeffers's view is that if one consults both canonical and non-canonical textual material more carefully, this emerges as too simple a classification. She divides the magicians into two major categories. The first category, *undisputed cases*, consisted of skilled individuals who offered their services as it were professionally, while the second category consisted of *disputed cases* where the data is insufficient to ascribe a magical or divinatory role to these individuals in any professional sense. Within the first group, Jeffers identifies eighteen different classes of individual and within the second group eight. Their definitions have been arrived at by a consideration of the occurrence of these Hebrew nouns in the Hebrew Bible and other available non-canonical texts. The differences are summarized in the table below.

---

158 Jeffers, *Magic and Divination in Ancient Palestine and Syria*, 25–124.

Wholeness and Healthcare in The Ancient Near East

UNDISPUTED	HEBREW TITLE	DESCRIPTION
1	איש אלהים	Man of God
2	אשפין	Professional Exorcists
3	גזרין	Sacrificial Diviners/Dream Analysts
4	חבר	A Spell Binder
5	חוזה	A Court Seer
6	חכמם	Professional Wise Magicians
7	חרתמים	Miracle Performers/Dream Interpreters
8	חרשים	Medicine Men
9	כהן	Oracular Functions of Priest
10	כשדים	Dream Interpreters of Nebuchadrezzar
11	לוי	Oracular Attendant & Healer
12	(מ)כשף	Magician/Semitic Herbalist
13	מלחשים	Enchanter, snake charmer
14	מנחש	One who Observes Omens
15	מעוננים	Soothsayers
16	נביא	Prophet Channel of Gods Power
17	קסמים	Those who Obtain an Oracle by Drawing Lots
18	ראה	A Seer

DISPUTED		
1	פועלי עון	Evildoers
2	אריאל	An Oracle Attendant
3	טפסר	Astrologer
4	מנזרים	Diviners
5	נקד	Sheep-tender or Hepatoscopist
6	סחרים	Those who Ensnare
7	רשעים	Wicked Ones
8	רכלים	Magicians or Traders

Certain of these titles and descriptions correspond to those in Deut 18:9–10 and others, notably חרשים and כשפים(מ) deserve, in the light of the present study, further exploration for they are, seemingly, the likely ancestors of apothecaries and herbalists. It is noteworthy that these two categories are not proscribed in the above verses from Deuteronomy. Jeffers[159] finds a commonality of her classification derived from the Hebrew Bible, Caananite, Ugaritic, and Assyrio-Babylonian cultures and so postulates a *Semitic mentality* which allows for no clear distinctions having been made between science, religion, and magic. It is important to stress that this conclusion is arrived at from inspection of what textual evidence we have and from a semantic analysis of the respective languages of these cultures. Since there is no evidence to be had from non-textual/linguistic sources and since languages evolve at quite a rapid rate, we have to accept a substantial degree of entropy in any systematic survey of this nature. Such a philological approach is limited by the availability of surviving literary and linguistic material.

It seems likely that the secular practice of magic and divination was taking place in Levitical times but it was kept out of the Scriptures either because it was thought irrelevant or a bad influence. Curses, vows, and predictions, in a religious context, form a considerable part of the narrative of the Hebrew Bible but it may be that the (priestly) authors of the Scriptures maintained, in their dealings with lay individuals, a relationship akin to that often seen today between orthodox medical practitioners and those practising various kinds of alternative medicine.

---

[159] Jeffers, *Magic and Divination in Ancient Palestine and Syria*, 16.

Botanical Medicine in Ancient Syria–Palestine

Botanical or herbal medicine has a long history. One can speculate that it grew out of the need of a foraging, prehistoric man to recognize which plants were good to eat and which were poisonous. It is known that in Sumerian and Babylo-Assyrian cultures, plants had been used as perfumes, incense, and cosmetics as early as 3000 BCE. It is not difficult to suppose that from such familiarity came the observation that some plants might also have therapeutic value if applied locally or even taken enterally.[160] Eventually, herbs were combined to form flavourings, perfumes, dyes, and medicines and so arose the need to lay-up stores of fresh and dried plants for future and out-of-season use. From such beginnings came the art of the apothecary.[161]

The earliest literature describing the therapeutic qualities of plants is from the time of Aristotle,[162] who himself made a significant contribution to botanical writing. Later authors such as Pliny further contributed to botanical knowledge and by the Middle Ages, the role of the apothecary was well established and important, especially in the monasteries, where the resources for maintaining a *physick-garden* and the appropriate books could be found and skills developed and passed on. In ancient times in Egypt, botanical preparations were used for the embalming of cadavers. Herodotus describes this in some detail and the subject has been extensively investigated and reviewed by Baumann[163] who lists the plants that were used and available on the Nile flood-plain at that time. It is almost certain that these would have been available to Egyptian proto-apothecaries as well as to the embalmers and it is interesting to look up the history of their use in medical, culinary, and cosmetic practices over time.[164] Plants are mentioned in the Bible and their appearances there have been reviewed extensively by Zohary.[165] In his book Zohary, who is both a linguist and botanist, considers every *plant pericope* of the Hebrew Bible, LXX, Vulgate and Targum Onkelos. This is a fascinating book which, besides discussing the pharmacological aspects of the plants, considers also the climate and vegetation of different regions, crop cultivation, and the herbs used in cooking, incense, and perfume. Zohary identifies the biblical plants mainly by the use of comparative linguistics of the Semitic languages, though reference to the Septuagint and Vulgate has also been helpful. In particular, among Semitic languages, Arabic has changed relatively little over time and so, in the naming

---

160 And later, of course, parenterally.
161 ἀποτιθέναι = to lay-up; ἀποθήκη = storehouse. The Worshipful Society of Apothecaries, (of which the present author is a Liveryman), is one of the oldest and most respected Livery Companies in the City of London.
162 Wilfrid Blunt and Sandra Raphael, *The Illustrated Herbal* (New York: Thames and Hudson, 1994).
163 Herodotus, *The Persian Wars*, trans. Godley; A. D. Baumann, "The Botanical Aspects of Ancient Egyptian Embalming and Burial."
164 Maud Grieve and C. F. Leyel, *A Modern Herbal: The Medicinal, Culinary, Cosmetic and Economic Properties, Cultivation and Folklore of Herbs, Grasses, Fungi, Shrubs and Trees with all their Modern Scientific Uses* (London: Tiger Books International, 1998).
165 M. Zohary, *Plants of the Bible* (Cambridge: Cambridge University Press, 1982).

of plants, cognates with Hebrew and Aramaic can be found with relative ease. Unfortunately, the same cannot be said for Akkadian. The English translators of the Bible were unhelpfully imaginative in this respect and took outrageous liberties over their translations, perhaps with an overzealous view to Anglicizing them. Thus chestnut, hazel, and heather have appeared in exotic guise although they are not indigenous to the biblical lands. Worse, however, is the wide-ranging inconsistency of the English translators who have employed inappropriate terms such as "briar", "bramble", "thorn", and "thistle" in a wholly indiscriminate manner.

Despite all of this, Zohary makes the all-important point that nowhere in the Bible is *healing* by plants specifically mentioned.[166] He is, nevertheless, adamant that herbal remedies would have been commonplace, numerous, and used in a highly specific way to treat specific conditions. The reason for their non-inclusion in the Scripture, he offers, is the same as that proposed for the non-inclusion of secular magic: namely that it could lead to polytheism and idolatry. The ultimate healer was Yahweh, (Ps 41:4), and so in cases of illness, the proper remedy was prayer.

יהוה יסעדנו על־ערש דוי כל־משכבו הפכת בחליו

> The Lord will support him upon the couch of languishing: thou makest all his bed in his sickness. (Ps 41:4)

Today, approximately one hundred plants have been identified as being used for medicinal purposes by the modern Bedouin.[167] Moreover, the climatic conditions and therefore the native vegetation of the region have hardly changed over millennia and so this seems a good place to start. Zohary points out that of these plants still in use today, the following, all native to the region, may be identified by comparative linguistic analysis as being of medicinal use and specifically mentioned in the Bible:[168] *hemlock, henbane, mandrake, aloe, white wormwood, mallow, castor oil bean, cassia, laudanum, laurel, vine, olive, fig,*

---

166 Rachel and Leah (Gen 30:14) make the pharmacological error of using mandrake (דּוּדָאִים) *Mandragora officinarum*, which belongs to the nightshade family (Solanaceae) as a means of promoting fertility. Mandrake in fact, contains deliriant hallucinogenic tropane alkaloids such as atropine, scopolamine, apoatropine, and hyoscyamine. Ginseng has a pedigree in folklore as an aphrodisiac and an appearance similar to mandrake. It is possible that it is ginseng that is being implicated. In Song of Songs (7:13) mandrake appears again as a source of fragrance along with henna (כֹּפֶר) *Lawsonia inermis* as a cosmetic dye. Brenner has suggested that 'A number of the plants mentioned in the Song of Songs were used by women in the ancient Mediterranean world as contraceptives and abortifacients. These include pomegranates (רמון), wine (ענב), myrrh (מור), spikenard (נרד) and cinnamon (קנמון)'. Athalya Brenner, *The Intercourse of Knowledge: On Gendering Desire and 'Sexuality' in the Hebrew Bible*, Biblical Interpretation Series, Vol. 26 (Leiden: Brill, 1997), 190. However it is not always possible to to make positive identifications of these plants from the Hebrew texts. Moreover it is doubtful if an appropriate concentration of their active principles would be obtainable in the domestic environment.
167 Naomi Feinbrun and Michael Zohary, *Flora of the Land of Israel* (Jerusalem: Weizmann Science Press, 1956); Naomi Feinbrun-Dothan and Michael Zohary, *Flora Palaestina* (Jerusalem: Israel Academy of Sciences and Humanities, 1981); Daniel Zohary and Maria Hopf, *Domestication of Plants in the Old World* (Oxford: Oxford University Press, 1999); Michael Zohary, *The Flora of Iraq and its Phytogeographical Subdivision: Baghdad*. Iraq Ministry of Economics. Directorate-General of Agriculture. Bulletin. no. 31. 1946.
168 Zohary, gives chapter and verse for each of these and several more: Zohary, *Plants of the Bible*. Isaiah has the largest botanical vocabulary.

almond, pomegranate, wild gourd, hyssop, acacia, cedar, terebinth,[169] *myrrh, (Commiphora myrrha), frankincense, (Boswellia sacra), balm, myrtle, tamarisk, tragacanth,*[170] *storax, ginger-grass, caper, garlic, cinnamon, turmeric, cumin, spikenard, and saffron.*

Some of these are, of course poisonous and feature thus in biblical narratives. It is significant also to note the high frequency of laxatives among all these worts and it seems likely that the Egyptian idea of relating illness to the congestive effect of the retention of foodstuffs may also have been popular in ancient Israel. Zohary's list of Biblical plants—after allowing for the Akkadian—bears a significant relationship to a *Materia Medica* of Assyrian royal families, documented by Thompson,[171] and it seems entirely likely that, given the similarity of terrain and climate, the (hypothetical) physick-gardens of Syria-Palestine, Egypt, and Mesopotamia might be expected to have shown a correspondence of native flora. Although Thompson's *Herbal* is specifically derived from material relating to Assyrian royalty, he postulates that the remedies it contains could equally be expected to have been used by ordinary people as the plants were wild and not cultivated in physic gardens. We cannot be sure of this but, as with much from Mesopotamia, as a rule it was only royalty that figured in the Cuneiform tablets that have been preserved and translated; the *plebes* were unlikely to have been the objects of much scribal effort.

It seems probable that botanical medicine was, in the Ancient Near East, *the* predominant form of secular medical practice; or, at any rate, the form of medical practice that would have produced positive results and even, perhaps, saved lives. It should be noted, in passing, that some plants also served religious functions or were objects of awe. In the former category fruit and seeds were used as offerings, especially at harvest times (the festivals of *Pesaḥ, Shavuoth* and *Sukkoth*) and incense was used in the tabernacle. Great trees, groves, and woodlands were variously objects of veneration among ancient peoples and woods as places of worship are mentioned specifically in Deut 12:2 and 16:21 and in 2 Kgs 16:4 and 17:10, in relation to Josiah's centralizing reforms.

As a working hypothesis therefore, we must assume that, without some form of healthcare, the day-to-day activities of ordinary people would have been sorely incommoded; even so whatever *was* operational was thought of insufficient significance to be recorded by the priestly authors. The evolution of botanical medicine by the hand of a developing cohort of apothecaries might be expected to have overtaken the less effective remedies of the magicians. But human beings, even today, are apt to prefer tradition to innovation, and folklore to science, when they have been appropriately indoctrinated. It is quite probable

---

169 אֵלוֹן מוֹרֶה, usually translated into English as "oak" as in the "oak of Moreh" (Gen 12:6); it is clearly not oak.
170 Probably the gum of Gen 37:25 RSV. Gum tragacanth is still used in confectionary.
171 R. Campbell Thompson, *A Dictionary of Assyrian Botany* (London: British Academy, 1949).

that in the day-to-day running of Israelite civilization both of these systems of healthcare were in operation.

The simplest notion of *wholeness* that we would understand today is good health: the absence of disease and illness. In the priestly society of ancient Israel, the notion of wholeness appears to have been quite different because it was governed by a worldview that operated through ritual. In adjacent civilizations in the ANE, wholeness appears to have been often regarded more simply as normal good health and, as a result, we have evidence that healthcare there was of a more practical nature, though it was not, of course, necessarily successful. All this took place in a highly polytheistic environment where certain gods were specifically seen as operating in the sphere of health. The purpose of the present chapter has been to present a factual review of evolving healthcare in these adjacent civilizations for comparison in the chapter that follows with practices under the umbrella of the priestly *Weltanschauung*. No apology is made for the inclusion of material relating to periods later than that of the Levitical priests. A consideration of what a rudimentary system grew into invariably sheds light on the evolutionary mechanism, and in many instances we owe a debt to later civilizations for the transmission of information from earlier times and places. It is now necessary for us to specifically consider the priestly worldview, with its attendant rituals, and the *wholeness* ↔ *holiness* relationship which is embodied in Leviticus.

Chapter 4

WHOLENESS AND HEALTHCARE IN THE PRIESTLY SOCIETY OF ISRAEL

If *wholeness* was the prerequisite of *holiness* in ancient Israel, its definition and operation would have been established and maintained within an ideology proper to those who carried out these tasks, namely the priesthood. Such an ideology would have existed within a specific and unique worldview. From the evidence that we have, it is apparent that a central pillar of this priestly *Weltanschauung* was ritual and so it must be supposed that the enactment of ritual occupied a central place among the priestly duties and activities pertaining to *wholeness* and *holiness* and *ipso facto* to *purity* and *impurity*. In order to understand such associations, it is essential to consider the nature of priestly ideology and the nature of priestly ritual.

Priestly Ideology and Ritual

The Levitical priesthood operated in such a way as to connect the divinity with the people of Israel through the medium of ritual. In this way they transmitted the cosmic order of creation into the social and cultic order of the Israelite people. How these factors interacted is central to the way in which the priests saw and managed wholeness and holiness and the effects of impurity.

The Priestly Weltanschauung

Worldview is the socio-cultural context within which ritual operates. As the entirety of evidential material on this subject is textual, we can only arrive at definitions of worldview by an indirect means. Most simply, worldview has been seen as the way in which a given society attempts to impose structure on the world and upon human existence and behaviour within the world. Worldview has been described by Turner[172] as a dynamic concept embodying three elements:

1. A body of knowledge that serves to identify, categorize and organize the cosmos.
2. A set of meanings related to the structure of the world that locates human existence and gives it meaning within the cosmos.

---

[172] Victor W. Turner and Richard Schechner, *The Anthropology of Performance* (New York: PAJ Publications, 1986), 76.

3. A system of conduct (praxis) that directs proper and appropriate actions within a specific world of meaning. Ritual is an essential component of this praxis.

Consequently, it may be supposed that a particular view of the world order is necessary to define and enact a particular system of conduct. In the case of the Levitical priesthood, the particular worldview was religious and its central tenet was that the world order was created by Yahweh. The priests themselves became intermediaries between Yahweh and society and their rituals were an enactment of their obligation to bring order to human existence on Yahweh's behalf. This idea of order was extended to embody Yahweh's dwelling among the Israelites in their holy shrine(s), and in their given land. Any violation of this dynamic relationship between creation and cult would be seen as both implausible and impossible within the worldview/ideology because its integrity was essential to maintain the Yahweh-enabled transition from chaos to cosmos.

From the priestly writings—especially Leviticus—it can be seen that there were two potential threats to this sort of order: they were *defilement* and *sin*.[173] These specifically threatened the three components of created order seen by the priests. These components were, *cosmic, social,* and *cultic:* they were interrelated and interacted with one another. A further secondary aspect of the priestly worldview was that the establishment of order by Yahweh was mediated through *speech*. It was, therefore through the medium, first of Yahweh's and secondarily the priests' speech that the cosmological, societal, and cultic elements of order were formulated, merged, and enacted. Societal and cultic orders were themselves further regarded as subsets of the cosmological order, and this gave rise to a hierarchy within the divinely created order such that:

- Cosmological order → a system of identification.
- Social order → a system of meaning and value.
- Cultic order → a system of praxis.

Gorman[174] proposes that the conceptual notion that binds these three orders together is that of "order through separation". By this he means the establishment of *boundaries* between *categories* of created things. Once again, as already encountered in Douglas's interpretation of wholeness, we see the enthusiasm shown widely in the ancient world for categories (and their violation). This is nowhere more clearly expressed in the context of the present work than in Leviticus 10:10:

ולהבדיל בין הקדש ובין החל ובין הטמא ובין הטהור:

---

173 See chapter 12.
174 Gorman, *The Ideology of Ritual.*

and that ye may put difference between the holy and the common, and between the unclean and the clean; (Lev 10:10)

Within priestly ritual (see below) these categories were themselves identified and compartmentalized in terms of *space, time,* and *status*. These sub-categories operated parametrically in terms of separation so that:

- Space → the separation of the holy of holies from all other places.
- Time → the separation of the Sabbath from all other days.
- Status → the separation of the priests from all other persons.

We may conclude from this that the central pillar of the priestly worldview was that order could be established and maintained through the sedulous observation of categorization, i.e. the recognition and observance of boundaries. It was sin and defilement that could confuse these distinctions and so obfuscate the boundaries and categories and compromise world order itself.

Priestly Duties

Within the priestly *Weltanschauung* as laid out above, the priest would be required to carry out specific duties to maintain the separations demanded by the idea of *order through catagorization*. Foremost among these would have been the need to make distinctions between the holy and non-holy and the clean and the unclean. The texts pertaining to this process are notable for their inclusion of √בדל , *hiph'il* = הִבְדִּיל = *distinguish*. This triage was directed at the preservation of sacred space particularly and required a diagnostic ability not dissimilar to that of the physician—both are roughly based on a system of questioning using a *protasis* ↔ *apodosis* algorithm. It is possible that it is because of this observation that so much effort has been spent on trying to show a "hygienic" and/or "medical" role for Leviticus.

והזרתם את־בני־ישראל מטמאתם ולא ימתו בטמאתם בטמאם את־משכני אשר בתוכם:

> Thus shall ye separate the children of Israel from their uncleanness; that they die not in their uncleanness, when they defile my tabernacle that is in the midst of them. (Lev 15:31)

In maintaining ritual societal and cultic order in the world, the priests would have seen themselves as keeping in contact and interacting dynamically with the divinely created cosmic order and so with Yahweh. This activity was aimed ultimately at preserving the central pillar of their worldview and thereby ensuring Yahweh's continued dwelling in the tabernacle and in the land.

If one accepts this idea of a priestly worldview aimed at the establishment of a set of categories necessary to preserve world order, it is difficult to see in such a worldview any place for medicine as we think of it today.

The Priestly Concept of Ritual

Definitions of Ritual

There are many definitions of ritual to be found in the extensive literature of anthropology. These range from the general to the highly specific. For present purposes, where there is a specific concern with the Levitical priestly society, a composite definition from the writings of Turner and Gorman seems appropriate.[175] Thus, "Ritual may be defined as a social act that takes place in a specific and dynamic socio-cultural context [worldview]." And so, "Ritual acts may be secular, sacred, private or communal and are about symbols, and meaning through which the ritual is conceptualized constructed and enacted."[176] Rituals that are related in form or purpose may be considered as a *ritual system* as in the case of priestly rituals where they effectively represent the complex performance of symbolic acts.

Gorman has emphasized the fact that "Priestly rituals come to us in texts without any observable social context ... this demands a methodological shift from a text oriented analysis to a socio-cultural analysis".[177] Since the only substantive evidence we have *is* textual—from the Hebrew Bible—he accepts, therefore, that his approach must be largely theoretical and believes that, "Models provide a framework for interpretation." This logic and methodology, in the absence of anything better, has been widely adopted today by workers in the field and has led to the following ideas.

Purpose of Ritual

Turner has said that:

> Ritual is social drama.... One may well ask why it is that liminal situations and roles are almost everywhere attributed with magico-religious properties, or why these should so often be regarded as dangerous, inauspicious, or polluting to persons, objects events and relationships that have not been ritually incorporated into the liminal contest. My view is briefly that from the perspectival viewpoint of those concerns with the maintenance of "structure" all sustained manifestations of *communitas* must appear as dangerous and anarchical and have to be hedged around with proscriptions, prohibitions and conditions.[178]

---

[175] V. Turner, *The Ritual Process: Structure and Anti-structure* (Picataway, NJ: Transaction Rutgers, 1969); Gorman, *The Ideology of Ritual*.
[176] Where a specific purpose can be ascribed to a ritual, it may also be called a rite.
[177] Gorman, *The Ideology of Ritual*, 13.
[178] V. Turner, *The Ritual Process*, 108–9.

This seemingly mildly paranoid view of Turner's is appropriate because it emphasizes the dependence of human nature upon a perception that structure and order will be maintained, coupled with fear lest it be not. Such a dualistic tendency within the human psyche extends far beyond the concepts of purity and impurity. In the current context it is seen to be, not just at the centre of Douglas's idea of wholeness, but entailed to some degree by all of the other ideas of purity and impurity to be discussed in the next chapter.[179]

The Nature of Priestly Ritual

Gorman has suggested that in the priestly society where rituals were aimed at the preservation of the cosmic order under the priestly worldview, the following categories of ritual were in operation:

Types of Ritual

1. Preventative rituals—to obviate threat of social disruption.
2. Rites of passage—to alter the status of the individual or society.
3. Founding rituals—to bring into being a state, institution or situation.
4. Maintenance rituals—to preserve/maintain the established order.
5. Restoration rituals—to restore the broken order of creation.

Category 5 is of importance as this would include purification rituals for צרעת and זוב.

As mentioned above, the priestly worldview demanded that ritual be sub-categorized into elements of *space*, *time*, and *status*.

Ritual Space

Ritual space has real dimensions and is a clearly defined type of social space. Examples are the map of the tabernacle/temple, the inclusion/exclusion of lepers in respect of the camp, and clean and unclean places. All of these spaces have physical boundaries that can be transgressed *pari passu* with the violation of the spatial categories that they represent and the holiness that is entailed. For example, the specific architectural geometry of the tabernacle encompasses different categories of space dependent on the depth of penetration in relation to the כפרת and commensurate with different grades of holiness.

Ritual Time

Ritual time is seen from both a qualitative and a quantitative viewpoint. There is the time—on the calendar—at which other specific rituals must take place, the time to be taken for the enaction of a specific ritual and the cycle of time during

---

179 See also: Sigmund Freud, Angela Richards, James Strachey, and Alan Tyson. *The Psychopathology of Everyday Life*, Pelican Freud Library, Vol. 5 (Harmondsworth: Penguin, 1975).

which specific rituals are scheduled to take place. It was through the idea of ritual time that the priests identified meaningful experience for the created order. For example, founding rituals might be expected to be associated with specific times, sacrifices with recurring specified times, and there would be undefined times where unexpected disorder occurred and required an appropriate restoration ritual to be instituted. It is interesting to note the importance of the number seven in defining rituals associated with time. This is particularly the case in relation to quarantine periods prescribed by the priests in cases of צרעת where in reality, such a short period would be wholly inadequate for virtually all known infectious diseases. The supposition is that the number seven reflects the number of days taken for the creation and that this time-span has been projected upon rituals so that the social and cultic (praxis) aspects of the ritual reflect the cosmic.

Ritual Status

The priestly ritual process often entails a declaration by the priest of the status of the individual or object involved. This is particularly the case in communal rituals such as the Day of Atonement ritual where the scapegoat assumes the status of those shedding their guilt. Ritual status, furthermore, can be seen to have included the status of all three components of the priestly *Weltanschauung*: *cosmos, society,* and *cult*. As such it offers a mechanism by which persons and objects, especially sacred objects, may have their status defined and, if necessary, re-formulated within the cosmic order. It is likely that the priesthood saw status as indicating the separation of categories for the proper maintenance of cosmic, social, and cultural bounderies. In particular this would be the holy status of sacred places and the set-apart status of the priests themselves.

From a theological point of view, ritual may be considered to have operated for the priests as a direct means of interaction with Yahweh and his created order.

MEDICINE IN THE PRIESTLY SOCIETY

Israelite healthcare and the theology it entailed, was not monolithic. The sentiment of Deut 28:28 admittedly displays patently utopian undertones such that we are left in no doubt that unrighteousness causes illness and righteousness is the pathway to good health.[180]

---

[180] In contrast to this view from the Torah, the Ketuvim take a more realistic approach and in Job—who is righteous and ill—Yahweh uses illness more subtly and for reasons beyond the comprehension of the patient. Job (13:4) appears to have had little faith in physicians and was not easily fooled by their arts:
ואולם אתם טפלי־שקר רפאי אלל כלכם | ὑμεῖς δέ ἐστε ἰατροὶ ἄδικοι καὶ ἰαταὶ κακῶν πάντες | ERV→ But ye are forgers of lies, ye are all physicians of no value. | NETS→ But you are injurious physicians and wrongful healers, all of you. For Job, an entirely modern view is found to prevail: psychological support from family and friends is an essential part of healthcare. J Kahn and H Solomon, *Job's Illness: Loss, Grief and Integration. A Psychological Interpretation.* (London: Gaskell/Royal College of Psychiatrists, 1986).

As Israelite healthcare developed, there were significant changes. Most notable was a shift of the assurance of immortality from the individual to the population as a whole, as a result of accepting Yahweh's omnipresence, omniscience, and omnipotence as underpinning the Yahwistic principles implicit in the Covenant Psalm:[181]

כרתי ברית לבחירי נשבעתי לדוד עבדי

> I have made a covenant with my chosen, I have sworn unto David my servant; (Ps 89:4)

עד־עולם אכין זרעך ובניתי לדר־ודור כסאך סלה

> Thy seed will I establish forever, and build up thy throne to all generations. [Selah] (Ps 89:5)

This embodies a shared responsibility such that dependence upon Yahweh was conditional upon maintaining a state of righteousness and thereby ensuring good health. Breach of this responsibility resulted in affliction. It became the duty of the individual to adhere to his part in the covenant and so help to ensure the health of the community and population as a whole. A parallel responsibility for the priests was to disseminate this idea by propaganda and the maintenance of ritual and to deal with any compromise or infraction of this arrangement that might occur.

Medical Language in the Hebrew Bible

We may ask what medical facts are evident in the Bible. A good place to start is with the trilateral Hebrew root √רפא (*rp'*) which has the sense of "to *heal, repair* or *make whole*".[182] This root is unattested in Akkadian but the cognate Arabic word for *repair* or *unite* is رفَى (*rafaa*),[183] and the root also appears in Aramaic as רפי.[184] In addition, the feminine noun ארוכה is sometimes used as the substantive *health* for example in Jer 8:22 (see below). In Jer 30:17 and 33:6 we find the noun and verb juxtaposed as *health* and *heal/cure*:

כי אעלה ארכה לך וממכותיך ארפאך נאם־יהוה...

> For I will restore health unto thee, and I will heal thee of thy wounds, saith the Lord (Jer 30:17)

הנני מעלה־לה ארכה ומרפא ורפאתים...

---

181 Psalms 89:4–5 in the Hebrew Bible, LXX and Vulgate but vv. 3–4 in English Bibles
182 Clines, ed., *Dictionary of Classical Hebrew*, Vol. VII, 533–535. G. J. Botterweck, H. Ringgren, and H. J. Fabry, *Theological Dictionary of the Old Testament* (hereafter TDOT), Vol. VII (Grand Rapids, MI: Eerdmans, 1995), 593–602. In the Hebrew Bible this root appears, in this context, 67 times—Qal 38, niph'al 17, pi'el 9, hithpa'el 3 and also 19 times as a participle (marpē', מרפא).
183 Although the usual Arabic word for 'healing' is الشفاء. Lane, *Arabic-English Lexicon*.
184 Sokoloff, *A Dictionary of Jewish Babylonian Aramaic*; Sokoloff, *A Dictionary of Judean Aramaic*; Sokoloff, *A Dictionary of Jewish Palestinian Aramaic*; Jastrow, *Dictionary of the Targumim*.

> I will bring it health and cure, and I will cure them; (Jer 33:6)

The association of *healing* with *wholeness* is well established in Semitic languages and extends in Hebrew beyond the simple curing of diseases to the healing of wounds and to the curing of psychological illness or madness.[185] Physicians in the Bible were sometimes sought out and put to use. The *Qal* participle רפָא was used to describe them, as in Jeremiah's plea:

הצרי אין בגלעד אם־רפא אין שם כי מדוע לא עלתה ארכת בת־עמי

> Is there no balm in Gilead? Is there no physician there? Why then is not the health of the daughter of my people recovered? (Jer 8:22)

Clearly, there were physicians in Gilead of a sort who dispensed balm and were sufficiently widely known about that the infirm consulted them there to seek their help. Nevertheless, Jeremiah appears to have had little faith in their ability,

עלי גלעד וקחי צרי בתולת בת־מצרים לשוא (הרביתי) [הרבית] רפאות תעלה אין לך

> Go up into Gilead, and take balm, O virgin daughter of Egypt: in vain dost thou use many medicines; there is no healing for thee. (Jer 46:11)

In a strictly Yahwistic society, healing ultimately became the province of the deity—as indeed did the infliction of disease and illness. Philo summarizes this rather well, when he describes Yahweh as τὸν μόνον ἰατρὸν ψυχῆς ἀρρωστημάτων[186]—*the only physician for the diseases of the soul*. For Philo, Yahweh's was a healing monopoly.

However, a more thorough reading of the Scriptures discloses what might be seen as a conflict with this view. Gordon,[187] understands Exod 21:18–19 to confer upon mortals the *right* to practice medicine:

וכי־יריבן אנשים והכה־איש את־רעהו באבן או באגרף ולא ימות ונפל למשכב

> And if men contend, and one smiteth the other with a stone, or with his fist, and he die not, but keep his bed:

אם־יקום והתהלך בחוץ על־משענתו ונקה המכה רק שבתו יתן ורפא ירפא

> if he rise again, and walk abroad upon his staff, then shall he that smote him be quit: only he shall pay for the loss of his time, and shall cause him to be <u>thoroughly healed</u>. (Exod 21:18–19)

And we should note the emphasis on *thorough healing* conveyed by the use of the *pi'el* binyan *and* the *pi'el* infinitive absolute. It is, nevertheless, difficult to see this as an instruction to go out and practise medicine, especially in the light

---

185 Clines, ed., *Dictionary of Classical Hebrew*, Vol. VII, 534.
186 De sacrificiis Abelis et Caini 1:70.
187 Gordon, "Medicine among the Ancient Hebrews."

of Yahweh's healing monopoly. Gordon, in 1941, made an extensive study of almost everything that might conceivably be thought medical in the Bible.[188] His paper was, at the time, considered to be ground-breaking but today it would be seen as oversimplified. It suffers from having made no effort to go beyond the traditional concepts of ancient Israelite civilization and look into the worldview of the priesthood who were the interface between Yahweh and the proletariat. Nevertheless, it is a useful collecting-together of the medical material in the Bible and offers a platform for further study.

In accounting for the importance of Yahweh's healing monopoly, Gordon has made the initially rather attractive suggestion that there is documentary evidence for the Hebrews' belief that disease was a divine dispensation. He believes this to come from as early and as lithographic a source as the *Lachish ii* letter where, in the defective line 5, it says: ע בדה יבכר יהוה את א

His translation of this line is "[his servant.] May Yahweh afflict those", but it is difficult to see how he arrives at this meaning. It all depends on the meaning of יבכר. The Hebrew √בכר usually means to "be early" or to "treat preferentially" or to "bring about quickly."[189] Gibson[190] clearly prefers this idea of "earliness" as he translates the phrase, "[his servant.] Let Yahweh send an early sign"; but he acknowledges the alternative possibility of יעכר "Let Yahweh discomfit" on the grounds that in the Paleo-Hebrew inscription it is difficult to be sure that the word is not from √עכר = to discomfit. Clines, supports this view or at least recognizes the uncertainty.[191] Aḥituv, perhaps with the advantage of more recent evidence and scholarship, takes an entirely different view and prefers to vocalize the line thus: [192] עַבְדֹּה יְבַכֵּר יהוה אֶת אֲדֹנִי

He then translates it as: "[his servant.] May Yahweh make known to my lord". Aḥituv agrees with Clines that the meaning of יבכר is to confer something quickly or preferentially and he, therefore, choses to say "make known" although there is no verb of *knowing* in the clause. This is a translation based solely on context: he does not mention the alternative possibility of עכר.

Whichever translation we prefer, there is little real support for Gordon's hypothesis. It would have been nice to have had such an ancient justification for Yahweh's monopolizing healthcare but the explanation that this came about gradually, and as a consequence of the ultimate decline of polytheism, is much more likely.

---

188 Gordon op cit.
189 Clines, ed., *Dictionary of Classical Hebrew*.
190 John C. L. Gibson, *Textbook of Syrian Semitic Inscriptions*, Syrian Semitic Inscriptions (Oxford: Clarendon, 1971).
191 Clines, ed., *Dictionary of Classical Hebrew*, Vol. 2, 173.
192 Shmuel Aḥituv, *Echoes from the Past: Hebrew and Cognate Inscriptions from the Biblical Period* (Jerusalem: Carta, 2008).

Much of Gordon's paper is devoted to recording medical events that occur in the Bible. Where Gordon attempts to answer the questions *why?* and *how?* he invariably falls foul of *hyperdiagnosis*.[193] However where he simply presents illustrative examples, he provides a useful compendium of medicine at the time. Some of these examples are worthy of consideration here.

1. Cause of Death

Old age is the commonest recorded cause of death in the Bible. Longevity was wildly over-emphasized and so meaningless. Otherwise, few causes of death are recorded. 2 Chron 21:15 probably describes a form of dysentery and the amoebic form is known to be prevalent in the Near East.

Lieber[194] has suggested that Uzziah's death (2 Chron 26:21) was from Hansen's disease. She does not, however equate this with צרעת in general and regards Uzziah's as a unique case.[195]

2. Hygiene

Hygienic ablution is closely connected with the maintenance of ritual purity. In chapters 7 and 8 these measures are discussed in relation to צרעת and זוב. Either whole body washing or washing of the hands and feet was prescribed for ritual purification. The מקוה is still in use today for this purpose.

3. Barrenness

This was an important consideration in ancient Israel where childlessness was considered a major social disadvantage and stigma. The Hebrew adjective for "barren" is עקר (Greek: στεῖρα), and derives from √עקר meaning *uproot*[196] which reflects the state of misfortune supposed to be visited upon those not blessed with progeny. Ancient Israelite society was a very tribalistic and materialistic society where the presence of numerous [male] children and kinsmen was seen as a measure of prosperity both present and future. A specific duty of children was to be present to perform the funeral rites of their parents and without children these rites could not be fulfilled adequately and souls could not be at rest.

---

193 The present author must declare guilt in this respect inasmuch as he has offered an explanation for Jacob's "groin strain" in Gen 32:24-33. Glasby, "An Assessment of the Predictive Value of Laboratory Studies in the Management of Peripheral Nerve Injuries", MD thesis, University of Edinburgh, 2005, Appendix 1.
194 E. Lieber, "Old Testament 'Leprosy', Contagion and Sin," in *Contagion, Perspectives in Pre-modern Societies*, ed. L. I. Wujastyk and D. Conrad (Aldershot: Ashgate, 2000).
195 This view is doubted by the present author on the grounds that this would imply that Hansen's disease existed in Israel before the time it is thought to have been imported by Alexander's troops returning from the Indus valley (c. 333 BCE). Admittedly, this might have been possible but if so, this is the only reported case of צרעת's being fatal. In any case Hansen's disease does not really fit the symptoms as it is usually drawn-out and chronic rather than acutely fatal. Glasby, "What was Biblical Leprosy?".
196 Clines, ed., *Dictionary of Classical Hebrew*, Vol. VI, 543b.

There are several stories in the Bible of barren women who eventually bear children as the result of divine providence. No medical cause of infertility was ever mentioned or contemplated: barrenness and its reversal were entirely at the dispensation of Yahweh.

4. Obstetrics

Some of the most accurate medical accounts of the Hebrew Bible are in the field of obstetrics. By their very commonness, obstetrical procedures would have been familiar to ordinary people. We come across twins (תאומים) in the story of Tamar (Gen 38:27–30) and breech-delivery in the story of Rachel who died as a consequence (Gen 35:16–17).[197] The *lanugo* is described in relation to the birth of Esau. We are told in Exod 1:15–16 that midwives such as *Shiphrah* and *Puah* used a *birthstool* (אבנים) as an aid to delivery;[198] however this does not appear to have been invariably the case as a number of passages suggest that the mother gave birth not squatting but in a semi-erect position with the midwife squatting before her. The child was delivered, it is thought, onto the knees of the midwife and this process has appeared in metaphorical usage in a number of instances in the Hebrew Bible, perhaps most memorably Job 3:12:

מדוע קדמוני ברכים ומה־שדים כי אינק

> Why did the knees receive me? Or why the breasts, that I should suck? (Job 3:12)

Puerperal fever caused by *Streptococcus pyogenes* would have been common and most probably fatal then and, indeed up to the 20th century, it was a common cause of maternal septicaemic death in the *post-partum* period.[199]

5. Infant Mortality and Stillbirth

Both were, undoubtedly, highly prevalent throughout the Ancient World. Poor nutrition, poor hygiene, infection, and undeveloped obstetric practice would have been major contributors. Failure to thrive among neonates would have been commonplace and failure of lactation among mothers would have, in the absence of an available wet-nurse, almost certainly have resulted in infant death.

6. Anatomy

A number of anatomical terms appear in the Hebrew Bible though not necessarily used in a strictly anatomical or medical sense. As might be expected,

---

197 The terminology is confusing. In the story of Tamar the baby "breaks out" and is named after this "breach" (פרץ) sic. Rachel's case, by contrast is, in obstetrical terms a "breech delivery" meaning that the part of the child destined to wear "breeches" presents first and may be difficult to deliver. The advent of obstetrical forceps improved this prospect but breech-presentation remains associated with risk. This is made clear by the fact that the midwife was able to tell the sex of the child early on in the delivery before its head presented.
198 Such contraptions persisted right up to the 20th century. This word is also attested as a potter's wheel and a euphemism for the female and male genitals.
199 Cf. Jane Seymour, wife of Henry VIII.

the majority of these describe visible parts of the body (hand, finger, thumb, breast etc.) or anatomical structures used in sacrifices as in Exod 29:17. Many occurrences are in poetry and employ anatomical terms in a metaphorical sense in, for example, Job 16:13 and 21:24 or in Ps 69:4. Notable examples of Hebrew anatomical terminology are given in the table below:

ANATOMICAL	HEBREW WORD	BIBLICAL TEXT
Abdominal muscles	שרירי בטנו	Job 40:16
Blood [? = soul]	דם	Gen 9:4ff.
Bone [= self, strength]	גרם / עצם	Gen 2:23ff.; Prov 25:15
Bowels	מעה	Gen 15:4ff.
Brain/mind [= heart]	לב (Aram = לבב)	Daniel 4:13ff.
Breast (female)	שד [dual = שדים]	Song 4:5
Caul	יתרת	Exod 29:13, 22
Flesh	בשר	Gen 17:11ff.
Foreskin	ערלה	Gen 17:11ff.
Gall	מררה	Job 16:13
Heart	לב	Exod 7:3ff.
Hip joint [?]	כף הירך	Gen 32:32
Kidney	כליה	Exod 29:13, 22
Liver	כבד	Exod 29:13, 22
Loins / hips	מתנים	Job 40:16
Marrow	מח	Job 21:24
Omental fat	חלב מכסה הקרב	Exod 29:22
Pericardium	סגור לבם	Hos 13:8
Peri-renal fat	חלב	Exod 29:13, 22
Sinew [??nerve]	גיד	Job 40:17 (Gen 32:32)
Throat	גרון	Ps 64:9
Tooth	שן	Lev 24:20ff.
Vagina	חר	Song 5:4
Womb	בטן/רחם	Exod 13:15; Job 1:21

7. Wounds

Wounds must have been commonplace in every ancient civilization, not just from war but from everyday activities such as chopping wood or masonry. Where the wound was not exsanguinating or otherwise fatal, the most likely risk was that of septicaemia. Although the wound may have occurred accidentally, the septic consequences were, nevertheless, seen as divine punishment for foolishness and carelessness.

הבאישו נמקו חבורתי מפני אולתי

My wounds stink and are corrupt, because of my foolishness. (Ps 38:6)

One of the very few passages in the Hebrew Bible that gives any inkling of practical medical treatment—presumably by relatives, bystanders or by secular medical practitioners—is to be found in Isa 1:5-6 and relates to wounds.

על מה תכו עוד תוסיפו סרה כל־ראש לחלי וכל־לבב דוי

Why will ye be still stricken, that ye revolt more and more? the whole head is sick, and the whole heart faint.

מכף־רגל ועד־ראש אין־בו מתם פצע וחבורה ומכה טריה לא־זרו ולא חבשו ולא רככה בשמן

From the sole of the foot even unto the head there is no soundness in it; but wounds, and bruises, and festering sores: they have not been closed, neither bound up, neither mollified with oil. (Isa 1:5-6)

Olive oil, besides acting as an emollient, would perhaps have reduced the local effects of aerobic bacteria and binding, by applying pressure, would stem bleeding. As a simple measure, this treatment—apart from taking little or no account of cleanliness and sterility—has much in common with the modern first-line treatment of wounds. If the patient did not bleed to death or develop sepsis, such treatment would have been effective and one must suppose that it was used with great frequency in minor domestic accidents.

8. Boils

This subject is considered at considerable length in Chapter 7 in relation to צרעת; and the medical vocabulary employed by the Hebrew Bible to describe skin lesions is considerably bigger than that available for other medical conditions.[200] Undoubtedly, the ancients paid particular attention to dermatological conditions presumably on account of their obviously disfiguring nature.[201] There are very few references to conditions that are simply painful without being visible to add shame to the sufferer's misery. Apart from זוב which belonged in the priestly sphere, we only have the famous verse from Deut 28:27 which is thought to describe *inter alia*, haemorrhoids.

---

[200] Glasby, "What was Biblical Leprosy?".
[201] See chapter 7.

יככה יהוה בשחין מצרים (ובעפלים) [ובטחרים] ובגרב ובחרס אשר לא־תוכל
להרפא

> The Lord shall smite thee with the boil of Egypt, and with the emerods, and with the scurvy, and with the itch, whereof thou canst not be healed. (Deut 28:27)

This verse, besides being wonderfully descriptive, raises a number of questions. The term שחין is widely used to mean an *inflamed spot*. It occurs in Lev 13 in reference to צרעת but here it is being used quite differently to refer to the *boil of Egypt* which was almost certainly acute cutaneous *leishmaniasis*.[202] This disease is common, disfiguring but transiently so and usually resolves spontaneously in 3–12 months. In contrast, within this verse stands חרס which "cannot be healed". This statement has usually been interpreted as meaning that חרס was fatal but that it cannot be cured does not necessarily imply this. This word is not used for צרעת and so may have referred to an enduring or recurrent dermatological condition such as scabies or psoriasis.

9. Infestations

Unsurprisingly, infestations would have been common in ancient Israel. Food hygiene would have been rudimentary particularly in respect of the water used for food preparation and for washing. Many helminthic infestations are caused by worms that have a stage of their life-cycle in either stagnant or running water. Guinea worm and a number of other intestinal worms; both platyhelminth and nematode, are today still very common in the Middle East. It has been suggested that the avoidance of the pork tape-worm (*Taenia solium*) was the reason for which the Israelites were forbidden from eating pork, though it would be surprising if this connection could have been made at such an early date.

10. Surgical Procedures

Circumcision[203] which was mandatory (Gen 17:10–11), and castration which was forbidden (Deut 23:2), are the only surgical procedures mentioned in the Hebrew Bible. The precise technique for the former is nowhere mentioned but was even then probably more technically advanced than that used as an emergency measure by Zipporah (Exod 4:25).

11. Pharmacology

Botanical medicine and early chemistry have been discussed above.

---

202 We can suppose this because the name has persisted in various forms such as: Baghdad boil, Oriental sore, Aleppo boil, Delhi boil.
203 See also chapter 9.

12. Insanity

Instances of mental dysfunction abound in the Hebrew Bible.[204] The concept of the brain did not exist and mental function of a conscious nature was usually ascribed to the heart. "Bewilderment of the heart" appears in Deut 28:28 along with madness proper, שגעון. As usual, these were dispensations from Yahweh in punishment of waywardness:

יככה יהוה בשגעון ובעורון ובתמהון לבב

> The Lord shall smite thee with madness, and with blindness, and with astonishment of heart. (Deut 28:28)

13. Ophthalmology

By the time of the *Mishnah* and the *Talmud*, ophthalmic medicine was relatively well developed and is widely discussed in these works. This was not the case, however, in earlier writings and the Hebrew Bible makes no reference to ophthalmology. We know, however, that trachoma was (and still is) rampantly endemic in the Near East and that the Egyptians made much of diseases of the eye. One might suppose, therefore, that these conditions were common in Syria-Palestine and known to the Hebrew secular medical practitioners. Acquired gonorrhoeal infection of the eye and particularly congenital *Ophthalmia neonatorum* were widespread in ancient times.

Blindness was also common and due to a variety of causes, most frequently trachoma. The Hebrew terminology, סנורים (e.g. Gen 19:11), and עורון (Zech 12:4) is vague about the precise causes of the blindness. Senile cataract must have been the foremost contender.[205]

14. Communicable Diseases

If we restrict our sources to biblical texts, only two diseases, צרעת and זוב, qualify for consideration under this heading. It is noteworthy that only these two conditions are mentioned in the Levitical writings wherein none of the above categories 1–13 appear as significant.[206] Gordon also notes the important point that the progress of צרעת if it were Hansen's disease (and most other infectious dermatoses) most certainly could not have been tracked by the priests in seven-day intervals as is suggested by a reading of Leviticus.[207] There is little evidence to suggest the priests were interested in therapeutic measures. Regarding quarantine, Gordon[207] has pointed out, "This isolation of 'lepers' demanded by the Old Testament is of less importance as a hygienic measure than it is as an

---

204 See chapter 9.
205 M. A. Glasby, "New Testament Diagnoses," 122, no. 2 (2010): 98. J. K. Howard, *Medicine, Miracle and Myth in the New Testament* (Eugene, OR: Wipf and Stock, 2010).
206 Although categories 2 and 8 are relevant.
207 Gordon, "Medicine among the Ancient Hebrews," 484

influencing factor on medical history" and indeed, on the wielding of power by successive theocracies and church hierarchies.

From these few biblical examples, it can be seen that the earliest medical events were purely observational. For example, Jacob's injury (Gen 32:32) is described in the Hebrew, purely in anatomical terms relating to what might have been visible to Jacob himself or at least to a confidante. Because, in a Yahwistic society, the cause and relief of disease was seen as a matter for Yahweh alone, it was not for priests to speculate about aetiology. The dearth of any recorded data makes one suppose that practitioners of secular healthcare were not party to priestly deliberations and were unlikely either to be educated or motivated sufficiently to make textual recordings of their ideas and activities.

We must conclude that in Israel as in Egypt and Mesopotamia, what medical practice existed was essentially supernaturalistic. The activities of the priests were restricted to the two communicable diseases, צרעת and זוב, which, one feels obliged to conclude, they did not regard as diseases or illness in the modern sense. They were exclusively concerned with the impact of these conditions on the maintenance of the *wholeness* ↔ *holiness* equilibrium.

Priestly ritual furnishes the means by which society can maintain its order and re-establish that order if it has been compromised. In any society ritual must operate within a particular worldview that encompasses cosmic, societal, and cultic elements proper to that society. For the Levitical priests, their worldview set the parameters for their priestly rituals and priestly duties. Rituals are the social acts that are operational within a particular worldview. Priestly rituals can be categorized into five broad classes. Each operates in the spheres of space, time, and status in relation both to those enacting and to those in receipt of the rituals.

In contrast to the purely ritualistic activities of the Levitical priests, it is possible to identify within the Hebrew Bible some clearly medical material. This appears to have no obvious interaction with the ritualistic activities and worldview of the priesthood. It seems likely that this represents simple narrative relating to occasions where medical events were identifiable in their own right. Such incidences never involve צרעת and/or זוב which appear to have been regarded exclusively as in the ritualistic province of the priesthood and not as pathophysiological phenomena. While צרעת and זוב imperilled the idea of ritual purity, other purely medical conditions did not.

It is now necessary to consider more carefully the nature of the *purity-impurity* relationship within the priestly milieu in order to understand their role in the synergy or tension between wholeness and holiness.

Chapter 5

PURITY AND IMPURITY IN THE PRIESTLY SOCIETY OF ANCIENT ISRAEL

Arriving at useful, working definitions of purity and impurity as seen in biblical times, and particularly within the Levitical priestly *Weltanschauung*, is a difficult task. The relevant literature is extensive and many different approaches have been used. A good starting place might be to to examine the reasons for the inclusion of צרעת and זוב—those clearest of all infractions of ritual purity—in the *purity laws* and to ask if, in the priestly milieu, these were envisaged as illness and disease, or if they were seen purely as imperilling *sacramental wholeness* and *holiness*. The nature of biblical purity has been approached by different authors in markedly different ways. Time and place are important factors: we might, for example, expect to find differing views of purity and impurity in Levitical times, exilic times, the Second Temple period, the Qumran society, in rabbinical times and, of course, in any writings deriving or redacted at any of these times. It is vitally important, therefore, to try to confine conclusions exclusively to historical, textual, and even "medical" material from within the priestly worldview and to distinguish original writings from later additions and redactions. That is not to say that a consideration of later developments and evolutionary processes is not valuable (if reception history is avoided) in shedding light on the evolutionary process. Major modern authors such as Neusner, Milgrom, Douglas, Frymer-Kensky, Klawans, and Jenson have all contributed substantially to the debate on impurity, but each has employed a particular approach and attributed a different weighting to the specifics of צרעת and זוב so that each of these viewpoints may be usefully considered and evaluated here.

The tension between being *pure* (טהור) and being *impure* (טמא) must, for present purposes, be seen first and foremost as a creature of the priestly milieu.[208] The majority of authors have tended to examine the purity laws in a Second Temple context, taking this as a starting point and working backwards and forwards in time. It is difficult to see a logic in this approach, though an explanation might be that this period has attracted a greater mass of scholarship than any other in biblical studies. The problem that particularly faces students new to this field is that, whereas there is an undoubted mass of opinion and literature, this has not always been a critical mass, and it is nigh impossible to extract a single, convincing, explanatory thread running through the impurity-

---

[208] The priestly contribution to the Hebrew Bible has itself been divided into P and H material and there still exists a healthy debate about the value of such categorization, whether P or H holds primacy and what the *terminus a quo* and *terminus ad quem* for each might be. This is discussed at greater length in chapter 2.

purity tension. In particular the application of an informed medical viewpoint to the problem has been infrequent and the resulting exegesis unsatisfactory.

A key point is the question of when and how Israel established itself as a specifically Yahwistic society. By Second Temple times it may be supposed that the dynamic between polytheism and monotheism was moving towards the latter under the influence of the priestly worldview. This argument has been extended by some authors to suggest that the genesis of any systematic medical practice in Israel would have challenged priestly monopoly and so the priesthood was sedulous in keeping to itself the diagnosis and treatment of carefully selected, prevalent diseases. This argument breaks down, however, when one is thinking about pre-exilic times when it is almost certain that there was persisting polytheism *pari passu* with the emergence of a specifically Yahwistic culture and that priest-operated sanctuaries were widespread in the land up to the time of Josiah's centralization. There is argument to this day about the extent of this, and the situation is rendered impossible to resolve because of the uncertainties about the time and authorship of the relevant texts. Whether there was active suppression of medical and scientific development by the priests fearing it might lead to polytheism and idolatry remains to be seen. It is important to remember that even if the priests opposed the development of medicine and science, this does not mean that they were also interested in it.

The Priestly View of Purity and Impurity

Within the priestly *Weltanschauung* where ritual was paramount, it was one of the foremost duties of the priest to *distinguish* (בדל √, *hiph'il* = הִבְדִּיל) between what was ritually unclean, (impure, defiled) and what was clean (pure, undefiled). This was because ritual (cultic) uncleanliness could not be reconciled in any way with the holiness of Yahweh.

ולהבדיל בין הקדש ובין החל ובין הטמא ובין הטהור

> and that ye may put difference between the holy and the common, and between the unclean and the clean; (Lev 10:10)

Material things that conferred impurity were certain animals and groups of animals, צרעת, זוב, sexual aberrations, especially among other races, death, and some activities associated with alien cults. However, nowhere in the Hebrew Bible do we find any convincing attempt to explain precisely *why* these particular things conferred uncleanliness whilst other things did not—it appears they simply broke ritual and that was enough. Unsurprisingly, this has led to wide (and sometimes wild) speculation on the matter by exegetes over many years. It is possible that death, in a rather broad sense, may have been a common factor inasmuch as a sense of "deadness" could (at a stretch) be imagined for all of the defiling proscriptions. For example, *dermopaths*²⁰⁹ were kept separate like corpses, and live, ritually clean animals were the only ones permitted to be used for sacrifices, offerings of first-fruits, and for food. A genital discharge, it has been suggested,²¹⁰ was seen as the potential life that, because it remained unrealized, became transmogrified to equate with death and thereby uncleanness.²¹¹ There is an interesting parallel here with the notion that dirt is simply *matter in the wrong place*.²¹²

As noted above, the precise nature of either of the components of the טהור↔טמא relationship remain *definienda* throughout the entire Hebrew Bible. It is unclear whether this is because it was assumed by its authors that these terms would be universally understood or because their definition(s) represented an inconvenient task that was better avoided. For any attempt at a definition, we have to rely on later interpreters and therefore, of course, second-hand opinions: these have been many and various. A significant component of this second-level commentary comprises a vast rabbinical hermeneutic evolving over a considerable time. We are, thus, in the (arguably) fortunate position of being able to use twenty-first century scholarship and technology as a means of distilling the fruits of many authors' and many centuries' exegesis.

Terminology

Old Testament *purity* is significantly different from the *purity* (ἁγνότης/ἁγνεία) of the New Testament, where the word is more often than not used in the sense of "chastity". Editions of the Bible in English vary enormously in their usage of the relevant words and so must be viewed, in the present quest, with especial caution.²¹³ A search²¹⁴ for the lexeme *purity* in English translations of the whole Bible yields only three citings (2 Cor 11:3, 1 Tim 4:12, 1 Tim 5:2), all in the New Testament.²¹⁵ In contrast, the lexeme *impurity* yields nine examples, all in Leviticus, and all referring to menstruation. There is, quite clearly, no implied antithesis between these two lexemes. In contrast, if we search for the lexeme *unclean* we get 35 "hits" in the New Testament and 176 "hits" in the Old Testament of which 112 are in Leviticus. From this we may suppose the Levitical view of what is, as a rule, in English commentaries called *impurity*, and used to translate the Hebrew word טמא, may be, perhaps, better represented by the term

---

209 A neologism, used for convenience here to conceal ignorance about humans afflicted with צרעת.
210 See chapter 8
211 However this view fails in the case of sexual intercourse and parturition which were self-evidently life-producing but nevertheless regarded as unclean.
212 Cf. V. Turner, *The Ritual Process: Structure and Anti-structure* (Picataway, NJ: Transaction Rutgers, 1969); Douglas, *Purity and Danger: An Analysis of Concepts of Pollution and Taboo*.
213 Although far from universally popular, the English Revised Version (ERV) of 1885 has much to recommend it as it is more linguistically accurate than the KJV and embodies a more literal translation of the Hebrew words than later versions (e.g. the RSV) which offer (perhaps) a more theologically-orientated interpretation.
214 Bibleworks, "Software for Biblical Exegesis and Research."
215 However pure occurs 1213 times but mainly in expressions such as pure gold. One exception is Ezra 6:20.

uncleanness/uncleanliness. Its antonym, (strictly *antithet) pure/clean*, at least in respect of ritual purity, is almost always טהור. The etymologies, semantic fields, and usages of these adjectives and related verbal forms has been considered by Clines[216] and in even greater detail by Botterweck et al.[217] The latter group of authors looked extensively at cognates from Akkadian, Ugaritic, and Arabic to underline their exegesis.

Impurity and Defilement

It is important to know if these two terms are used synonymously in the Hebrew Bible. The former implies a persisting state and the latter an active process. Does defilement therefore, necessarily confer impurity and is this always the case? The translators of the Bible into English appear to have reserved "impurity" for the New Testament and used it to translate the Greek words μίασμα or μόλυσμα but not the Hebrew טמא; the Septuagint uses the adjective ἀκάθαρτος to mean *defiled*. Nevertheless, defilement appears in the Hebrew Bible to be the process by which impurity is acquired and this is true of both ritual and moral impurity (see below). Therefore, the question becomes "what causes defilement?" In the case of moral impurity, the answer is "sin", and it is relatively easy to understand this association in the context of most societies that may be envisaged. In the case of ritual impurity, the answer must take account specifically of the ritual-based priestly worldview within which the defiling influences are clearly demarcated but poorly explained. In particular, priestly ritual looks to two contagious and severely defiling influences: צרעת and זוב, but tells us all too little about how they defile.

Ideas of Ritual Impurity and Moral Impurity

Within the *Torah*, we may clearly distinguish two different kinds of purity/impurity. Although the P material in Leviticus more or less exclusively deals with ritual impurity, the H material and much else in the *Torah* is concerned with moral impurity. To explain either it is necessary to consider both. Most of the textual material that might be considered as the *purity laws* is concentrated in (P and H) Leviticus but there are verses in Genesis, Exodus, and Numbers that deal with these topics in a similar way.[218] If we subscribe to the *Documentary Hypothesis*, all those parts that were influenced by the P and H, as opposed to the D, authors appear to treat purity/impurity in a like manner so that within the Levitical corpus, the differentiation into *ritual purity/impurity* and *moral purity/impurity* is clearly made. Both are seen as *defilement,* though in English translations, as we have already noted, the word *impurity* rarely

---

216 Clines, ed., *Dictionary of Classical Hebrew*, Vol. III, 342, 368.
217 *TDOT,* Vol. V, 87–296; 330–342.
218 The situation concerning Deuteronomy is rather different and will be dealt with in chapter 11.

appears; it is restricted in its use and gives way to the much more common expression, *uncleanness*. The sense of *defilement*, though unstated, nevertheless emerges because the emphasis is almost always upon what begets and constitutes *impurity* rather than *purity*. Leviticus is, essentially, a very negative text: it is about the mechanisms and consequences of *transgression* rather than the acquisition of grace.[219] Both ritual impurity and moral impurity entail defilement:[220] in the case of ritual impurity, through contagion—a process that can be entirely passive[221]—and in the case of moral impurity, through sin. Sin as the antithesis of moral purity was, in practical terms, mostly the eating of forbidden foods, idolatry, malicious bloodshed, and violation of sexual prohibitions and hence must have entailed both an active and a personal element. There is no textual indication, for example, that moral impurity brought on by sinful acts might cross over into ritual impurity. Surprisingly, this appears to be so even for cases of זוב with apparently venereal origins. Some authors prefer to equate moral impurity with sin *per se*,[222] others see it as the *consequences* of sin such that divine displeasure at sin may lead to such contagious afflictions as צרעת and זוב, which are, strictly, forms of ritual impurity.

A dualistic nature of impurity was central to the view taken by David Hoffmann around the middle of the twentieth century. Hofmann acquired his ideas from texts using purely syntactical study-methods. He made the observation in the Levitical text, that those instances of the word טמא that were followed by a preposition, exhibited a bimodal distribution.[223] Hoffman thus recognized two forms of impurity which were identifiable, each by its conjoined preposition, as being able to stand in opposition *either* to *purity*, by which he meant ritual purity, or to *holiness*. The first case was identifiable by the attachment of the inseparable preposition -ל to signify the object or instrument of the impurity [hypothetical example *X*-ל טמא]:

ויהי אנשים אשר היו טמאים לנפש אדם

And there were certain men, who were unclean by the dead body of a man (Num 9:6)

This arrangement represented bodily defilement (טומא הגויות). The second case was characterized by the preposition,-ב [as in *X*-ב טמא]. Here it is attached to the object of the impurity and it represented the defilement of something (טומאת הקדושות) that was sacred or holy. Furthermore, Hoffmann divided up bodily

---

219 Though it is not to be suggested that such an acquisition was not a specific goal for the Levitical priesthood.
220 Making this differentiation, of course, hinges upon when we believe the P and the H material were first produced. There is considerable dispute over this: see chapter 4.
221 At least in respect of the sufferer; see chapter 8. The active agent here is the divinity, showing his displeasure.
222 Though how this may be defined remains a matter for speculation. Probably not St Augustine's "original sin". See chapter 11.
223 David Hoffmann, *Tsevi Har-Shefer, and Aharon Liberman, Sefer va-Yikra Meforash*, 2 vols. (Yerushalayim: Mosad ha-Rav Kook, 1963), 1:236.

defilement[224] into three levels of seriousness. Each of these involved a transferable contagion but was reversible through a process of purification defined in Scripture and carried out at the behest of, and by, the priests. Hoffman's three levels of bodily defilement resulted from contact with or, in the cases of diseases, the acquisition of:

1. Death of humans (Num 19) and certain animal carcasses (Lev 11:24–40; 22:5).
2. צרעת (Lev 13, 14), זוב (Lev 15) and childbirth (Lev 12).
3. Ritual objects conferring impurity e.g. scapegoat (Lev16:26), burnt or sin-offering (Lev 16:27–28), ashes and water used in sacrifices (Num 19:7–10).

Hoffmann's somewhat rigid textually-based system for defining impurity has fallen from favour today but must be seen as the first attempt at a classification based entirely on textual sources. In this respect it stimulated a lasting curiosity among scholars that has led to a very considerable amount of later work in a similar vein: especially that of Milgrom[15] whose highly analytical style constitutes a substantial development of that of Hoffmann, but is intrinsically similar.[225]

For present purposes, since the integrity of *ritual impurity* depended upon *wholeness*, we wish to investigate and understand the question of whether *wholeness* itself depended upon *health*. In other words, did priestly duties involve active *healthcare*? In what follows, no specific distinctions will be made between the terms *impurity, uncleanness, uncleanliness,* and *defilement* when they are used to translate the Hebrew word טמא as this word was used in the Hebrew Bible.

[Im]Purity and [Un]Holiness

It is important not to confuse טהור with קדש; uncleanliness was always seen as unholy but cleanliness was not necessarily holiness.[226]

---

224 Hoffmann, *Tsevi Har-Shefer,* 1:212–213.
225 Jacob Milgrom, "Two kinds of hatta't," *VT* 26, no. 3 (1976): 333-37; Milgrom, *Leviticus: A New Translation;* Milgrom, *Leviticus: A Continental Commentary.*
226 See Isa 35:8. There is but a single situation where holiness and uncleanliness appear to interact and this is described in the Mishnah where Holy Scriptures are said to defile the hands: כל כתבי הקודש מטמין את הידים (Yadayim 3:5). Traditionally, this has been construed as meaning that the Scriptures are so very holy that even the hands of otherwise "clean" individuals must be unclean by comparison. However, a more recent view of this is that holy Scriptures confer a "sacred contagion" by virtue of their association with the ark of the covenant which was seen as a cultic object, a palladium and repository for holy things. To touch it evoked the lethal wrath of God—2 Sam 6:6-7. Presumably this was extended to the holy texts it contained and to texts subsequently derived from them. See: T. H. Lim, "The Defilement of the Hands as a Principle Determining the Holiness of Scriptures," *JThS* 61, no. Pr 2 (2010): 501–15.

Purity and Impurity in the Priestly Society of Ancient Israel 89

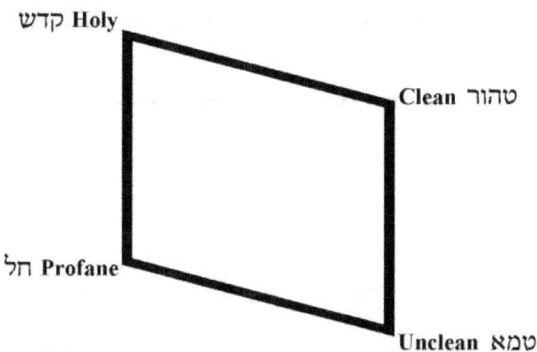

Lev 10:10 implicates two pairs of words in opposition: *holy* and *profane* (where profane = common), against *clean* and *unclean*. We have already seen that the latter pair may be equated with *pure* and *impure*. Barr[227] has proposed a two-dimensional relationship for these four words, in the shape of a rhombus.

The choice of the rhombic geometry is supposed to imply a tighter and more well-defined relationship of the word pairs in the (truly) vertical dimension than in the (displaced) "horizontal" dimension.

Jenson has introduced the concept of a purely lexical *holiness spectrum* as central to his concept of *graded holiness* and so peculiar to the P texts.[228] Jenson's spectrum embodies the same four words: *holy* (קדש), *profane* (חל), *clean* (טהר), *unclean* (טמא), which he calls the "holiness word group". Unlike Barr, he sees a dynamic relationship in which the four terms at the corners of Barr's rhombus, besides defining status, additionally define the transitions between these four states. Thus, a temporal dimension is added. Wenham[229] has proposed a simple diagrammatic scheme to portray Jenson's spectrum. The transitions are indicated by arrows.

---

[227] J. Barr, *Semantics and Biblical Theology, a Contribution to the Discussion*, Vetus Testamentum Supplement 22 (Leiden: Brill, 1972).
[228] Jenson, *Graded Holiness*.
[229] Gordon J. Wenham, *The Book of Leviticus* (Grand Rapids, MI: Eerdmans, 1979).

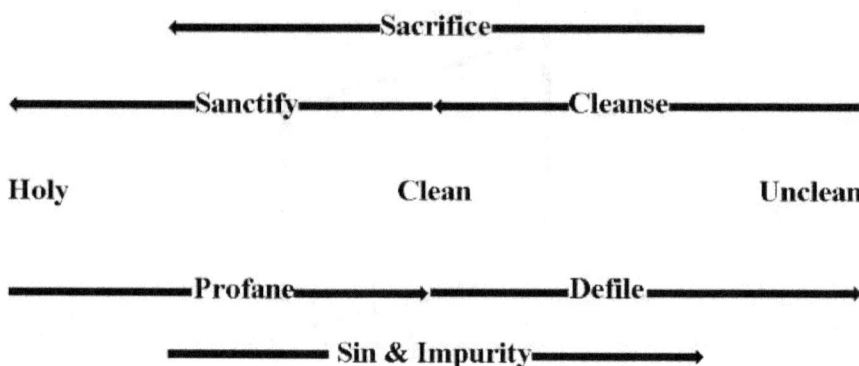

The scheme does not imply any linear proportionality in the steps between states and does not, therefore, adequately represent the temporal dimension or embody true vector quantities. However, it is a good diagrammatic model for illustrating the active causative and restorative factors *(sin* and *sacrifice)* that must be brought into play in order to move between the various states.

The rabbis were always enthusiastic about classification, and it is worth noting, in passing, that a scheme for categorizing impurity and its severity was eventually bound to emerge. This happened, of course, much later than the Levitical writings but it involved the notion of *major impurity* and *minor impurity* which although not formally classified are implied in the more constrained milieu of biblical texts. Danby, in his translation of the Mishnah,[230] summarizes the rabbinic *Rules of Uncleanness* as formally laid down in the *Eliyahu Rabbah*, a commentary on the *Tahoroth* by Elijah, who was the Gaon of Wilna (1720–97). This Appendix runs to twenty-three substantial paragraphs which may be crudely summarized in the following table.

---

[230] Danby, *The Mishnah*, 800.

Cause	Hebrew	Translation
Contact with corpse	אב אבות הטומאה	father of fathers of impurity
Major impurity (Contagious)	אב הטומאה	father of impurity
Minor Impurity (Non-contagious)	טומאה	impurity
Secondary effect of major impurity (by contagion)	ילד טומאה	child of impurity

This is really no more than a formalized and slightly expanded re-statement of what may be deduced from a careful reading of the text of Leviticus. The notion of a *family of impurities* probably has no more significance than its being a convenient way of formulating a hierarchy. Ricoeur in his work *The Symbolism of Evil*[231] notes the divergence in meaning between defilement and sin. The former is phenomenological whereas the latter is historical but in the Bible and associated works a transition of one to the other is frequently observable.

Sin

Especially in the light of its association with moral impurity, it is expedient to make a brief *excursus* into the specific nature of sin as encountered in the Hebrew Bible and associated texts.[232] At the risk of being judged simplistic, one may note that the word "sin" (חטאת/ἁμαρτία), in these contexts is almost invariably used as a trope, and most often as a metaphor. There are two

---

[231] Paul Ricœur, *The Symbolism of Evil*, trans. E Buchanan (Boston: Beacon, 1969), 47.
[232] Achieving brevity in reviewing the extensive subject-matter on this topic in the Hebrew Bible and New Testament, along with the considerably more extensive body of thinking and writing from theologians and philosophers of subsequent generations, is no easy task.

metaphors that were used for sin and a time-dependent dichotomy in their usage has arisen. In the Hebrew Bible, the common metaphor for sin is that of either a *weight/burden* or of a *stain*. In either case this must be borne by the afflicted individual(s), or by society, or by a *scapegoat* conveniently appointed to bear their collective burden or stain. For example:

ונשא השעיר עליו את־כל־עונתם אל־ארץ גזרה ושלח את־השעיר במדבר

> And the goat shall bear upon him all their iniquities unto a solitary land: and he shall let go the goat in the wilderness. (Lev 16:22)

In the Hebrew Bible the *weight* metaphor occurs six times more often than the *stain* metaphor. In the latter case, the idea is that the stain can be eradicated by washing or bathing as in:

(הרבה) [הרב] כבסני מעוני ומחטאתי טהרני

> Wash me throughly from mine iniquity, and cleanse me from my sin. (Ps 51:4 HB; LXX = 50:4; ERV = 51:2)

Anderson has studied extensively the language used in this metaphor.[233] He takes the view that the noun for sin, which in both of the above instances is עון, does not determine the *metaphorical unit*. Rather, Anderson believes, it is the verb for the *removal* of the sin that fulfils this role. There are three verbs commonly found in this context: √נשא (108 times), √סלח (17 times), and √כפר (6 times).[234] Ricoeur has argued backwards from this position that these mechanisms for the removal of sin necessarily entail the notion that sin was being viewed by Israelite priestly culture as a concrete entity with "mass and weight".[235] It is by way of the covenant with God that arrangements for the alleviation of this weight are made so that it may be transferred to the goat and sent away into oblivion.

The alternative metaphor is thought to represent the evolution in both language and thought that came about as the First-Temple Period and exile gave way to the period of Persian rule (538–333 BCE) and the Second Temple period, and thereafter, in the writings of the rabbis, the Dead Sea Scrolls and the New Testament. Here, the metaphor changes from the *burden/stain* idea to one about *debt* and its *repayment*. Anderson[236] has linked this change in metaphorical usage to the influence of the Imperial dialect of the Aramaic language which had become the *lingua franca* of the Persian Empire. An example quoted by Anderson is:

---

233 Gary A. Anderson, *Sin: A History* (New Haven, CT; London: Yale University Press, 2009).
234 For the extensive range of meanings attested by these verbs see: Clines, ed., *Dictionary of Classical Hebrew* and *TDOT*.
235 Ricœur, *The Symbolism of Evil*, 81. Ricœur is unclear as to whether "weight" is simply mass multiplied by the Constant of Gravitation, or whether he is imputing some higher distinction to these physical terms.
236 Anderson, *Sin: A History*, 6, 27–39.

להן מלכא מלכי ישפר (עליך) [עלך] (וחטיך) [וחטאך] בצדקה פרק ועויתך במחן
ענין הן תהוא ארכה לשלותך

> Wherefore, O king, let my counsel be acceptable unto thee, and break off thy sins by righteousness, and thine iniquities by shewing mercy to the poor; if there may be a lengthening of thy tranquillity. (Dan 4:24, LXX & ERV = 4:27)

Nebuchadnezzar can, according to Daniel, redeem his sin by giving alms to the poor.

The important verb is פְּרֻק (Aramaic *pe'al* imperative 2nd person masculine singular of √פרק = wipe away, remove[237]); this verb is also used in the sense of "redeem" and "buy out of slavery". Anderson points out that if one compares texts from the Hebrew Bible with the equivalent Targums one finds that the *weight* idea of the Hebrew gives way to the *debt* idea of the Aramaic so that, in Lev 5:1, where the Hebrew reads,

ונפש כי־תחטא ושמעה קול אלה והוא עד או ראה או ידע אם־לוא יגיד ונשא עונו

> And if any one sin, in that he heareth the voice of adjuration, he being a witness, whether he hath seen or known, if he do not utter it, then he shall bear his iniquity: (Lev 5:1)

The Aramaic reads,

מומתא והוא סהיד או חזא או ידע אם לא יחוי ויקביל חוביה   מומי ואנש ארי יחוב וישמע קל

The Aramaic noun חוב, in the Imperial Aramaic of the book of Daniel, has the specific meaning *debt* or *obligation*, so that the expression, (ונשא עונו), "he shall bear the weight of his sin" there becomes "he shall take on a debt" (ויקביל חוביה).

By the time of the New Testament, the idea of sin as debt was ubiquitous and the idea of sin as a burden no longer found favour. Anderson[238] has suggested that, when Ricoeur remarked that these metaphors were important because they stimulated thinking, he meant that they formed the semantic framework for the many extensive narratives[239] on subjects like forgiveness and punishment. These stories, in turn led to the ethical and philosophical views we hold today about these subjects and the processes by which we can atone for them. The concept of sin in whatever form was, and remains, so central to all biblical literature that it is often difficult to separate it from other aspects of religious philosophy. In particular there has been a degree of confusion regarding the place of sin in the priestly worldview and its ritual enactment. It is, however, important that such

---

237 Jastrow, *Dictionary of the Targumim*, 1239.
238 Anderson, *Sin: A History*, 38.
239 For example, the exile might be seen as the consequence of Israel's spiritual indebtedness.

a distinction is made and this will be considered again in chapters 11 and 12 in relation to that primary defiling agent, צרעת, in priestly ideology.

MODERN VIEWS OF BIBLICAL IMPURITY

It would be impossible to do justice even to twentieth and twenty-first century writings on the subject of Levitical and Second Temple purity and impurity in the space available here. However, if consideration is carefully restricted to the question in hand, namely the role of צרעת and זוב as determinants of unwholeness and impurity, and the critique furthermore restricted to ideas from the twentieth and twenty-first centuries, there immediately appears a group of authors each one of whom merits individual consideration. None of these has taken a specifically medical exegetical view of the biblical material but each has dealt with its consequences and formulated a viewpoint of impurity as a generality.

Here follows a brief summary of the approaches to biblical impurity from a selection of important twentieth-century authors. The epithets appended to their names reflect, entirely, the views of the present author.

Douglas: A Sociological Approach.

The earliest, and perhaps the most controversial of the recent authors to consider the question of Biblical impurity was Mary Douglas (1921–2007), a British Roman Catholic social anthropologist with a particular interest in symbolism within cultures. Her seminal work in respect of impurity was published in 1966[240] but she made a further two contributions on the specific subject of Leviticus three decades later, whereby she significantly revised her former approach.[241] Much of this revision resulted from Jacob Milgrom's having largely discredited Douglas's interpretation of certain aspects of Levitical dogma: in particular the dietary laws. Nevertheless, as a behavioural study, Douglas's work has much to commend it as it implicates *impurity* as society's explanation for the distaste and fear aroused in the human psyche by *anomalous* people, objects or situations.[242] Anomalies that are manifested to society-at-large in a visual way figure particularly prominently in Douglas's systematic analysis and one might suppose that, in ancient civilizations, such anomalies would *have been the widely apparent in daily life.* Douglas's formal statement of her viewpoint was therefore, that "Human beings tend to reject things that fall outside certain categories dictated by their society." This has acquired for itself the appellation *category violation.* Of prime importance, in this context is the notion of unwholeness and/or *blemish*[243] which Douglas sees as an intensely

---

240 Douglas, *Purity and Danger.*
241 Douglas, "The Forbidden Animals in Leviticus."; Douglas, *Leviticus as Literature.*
242 This is the "Dirt is simply matter in the wrong place," idea; see above.
243 For more on this subject see chapter 7.

powerful "socio-symbolic taboo". Thus, (especially visible) blemishes and related phenomena confer impurity upon individuals by a process of setting them apart. Different societies achieve this in different ways that develop to become customs and practices specifically associated with impurity.[244] Such physical causation must, by definition, be either congenital or acquired, and though the latter case can be easily extrapolated to be the wages of sin (or divine displeasure), it is difficult for us in today's social climate to see why congenitally afflicted individuals should have been so heavily stigmatized and marginalized. Nevertheless, we well recognize today that in bygone societies, the sins of the fathers were, to a very great degree, held to account for the afflictions and misfortunes of their children. Douglas and Turner both take the view that socio-symbolic taboos of this kind have been a function of all societies at all times. Douglas strongly refuted the idea of the Levitical purity laws having been formulated specifically and absolutely as a hygienic measure rather than to fulfil the ideological needs of a ritual-driven society. She is adamant that, *mutatis mutandis*, these taboos persist into modern society: "are our ideas hygienic where theirs are symbolic? Not a bit of it ... the difference between pollution and behaviour in one part of the world and another is only a matter of detail".[245] Modern society has tempered this equivalence because it has knowledge and experience of hygiene and of bacteriology: consequently, this particular taboo, although it persists, has become dislocated from religious practice and consigned to *healthcare* by modernist thought. Douglas extended the simple equation *dirt = matter in the wrong place* to mean *defilement/impurity = purity in the wrong place* where *wrong place* implies *category violation*—anything outside the socially-defined compass of a specific society. This is, therefore, a symbolic system of impurity which, because it influences and/or controls behaviour, fulfils a function for society as a whole and thereby defines its morality. Within this definition, Douglas takes the view that "A polluting person is always in the wrong"[246] and it is, above all, this somewhat dogmatic statement that led later to substantial criticism of her views, especially by Neusner and Milgrom. Central to the argument is the unanswered question of whether by *matter* Douglas meant all matter or merely those objects, people, and situations already seen as anomalous/impure. Douglas appears not to have been paying attention to the difference between ritual impurity and moral impurity and was simply considering the former as a largely undefined subset of the latter. Both Neusner and Milgrom (see below), nevertheless, based their own ideas of impurity loosely on Douglas but made significantly more of this distinction. Douglas herself, influenced by the ideas of Milgrom especially, latterly revised

---

244 This viewpoint has been strongly supported by the extensive anthropological work of Victor Turner, see: V. Turner, *The Ritual Process: Structure and Anti-structure* (Picataway, NJ: Transaction Rutgers, 1969).
245 Douglas, *Purity and Danger*, 43.
246 Douglas, *Purity and Danger*, 140: where "always" presumably meant "de facto" and "de jure".

her work[247] with an emphasis on Leviticus and Numbers. She came to the conclusion that the universality of her earlier ideas simply could not apply in the case of the laws of Judaism. This was a complete re-appraisal of the notion of ritual impurity as being specific to the Israelite system, and this re-appraisal and its consequences have been carefully and critically considered by Klawans.[248] Undoubtedly, Douglas seems to have missed the point about ritual impurity but this should not diminish her overall contribution. Douglas's anthropological analysis placed the purity laws firmly within a socio-symbolic framework which she found to be present, *aliquantum,* within all societies. She underestimated, however, the extent to which super-added influences might alter the basic symbolism and in particular she underestimated this effect in a priest-dominated Israelite society. In fairness to Douglas, and in the context of the present study, it should be emphasized that she based her arguments particularly on dietary practices and taboos relating to congenital blemishes and not upon צרעת or זב. In fact, the word "leprosy" does not appear at all in the index to her book, *Purity and Danger.*

Despite this, Douglas and Turner represent the anthropological viewpoint regarding purity/impurity and it is from them that we can most readily formulate an idea of *wholeness* as a working definition for the present study where it must be seen in relation to our understanding of the priestly ideology. The authors that follow stand apart from Douglas in that their appreciation of the purity/impurity relationship is largely taxonomical and directed at formal categorization of effect rather than cause. All appear, nevertheless to be based to some degree—perhaps in some cases tacitly—upon the Douglas/Turner anthropological model of category violation as the causative agent of impurity-through-unwholeness.

Neusner: A Working Hypothesis.

Jacob Neusner (b. 1932), the American Jewish scholar, is particularly noted for his analytical work on the rabbinic period, the Mishnah, and the Talmud. He has written extensively between 1973 and 2005 on the subject of purity/impurity. This work necessarily also encompasses the biblical and Second Temple periods.[249] An important thread running through this work is Neusner's assertion that later developments relating to purity and impurity within Jewish culture were all founded upon a biblical legacy, this being largely the P texts of Leviticus and Numbers. Purity and impurity, in Neusner's opinion, are primarily

---

247 Douglas, "The Forbidden Animals in Leviticus"; Douglas, *Leviticus as Literature.*
248 Jonathan Klawans, *Impurity and Sin in Ancient Judaism* (Oxford: Oxford University Press, 2000), 18–19.
249 Jacob Neusner, *The Idea of Purity in Ancient Judaism*, Vol. 1 (Leiden: Brill, 1973); Jacob Neusner, "The Idea of Purity in Ancient Judaism," *JAAR* 43, no. 1 (1975): 15-26. Jacob Neusner and Alan J. Avery-Peck, *Encyclopaedia of Midrash: Biblical Interpretation in Formative Judaism*, 2 vols. (Leiden: Brill, 2005).

cultic matters but secondarily may have functioned in the priestly environment as metaphorical exemplars for moral and religious behaviour.

Above all, it is important to understand that Neusner's analysis of purity/impurity is derived wholly from a study of textual sources. Where he is concerned with purity/impurity in the biblical period, it should be noted that Neusner considers the Book of Leviticus as a single unit of priestly law: as such he makes no distinction between P and H.[250]

Neusner's Idea of Cultic Purity/Impurity

By his use of the terms *cult* and *cultic purity*, Neusner is thinking primarily in a Second Temple context and so is particularly concerned with the *Temple Cult*, by which he means the establishment of a philosophy and ethic of purity to be embodied within the code of practice of the temple, but also to be extended to the יחד (or community).[251] He notes that a later Pharisaic viewpoint would assert that "the purity observed in the Temple should be observed in the home and the hearth." Neusner makes the point that, during the Second Temple period, it is to be expected that the ancient biblical texts would have been well known. Therefore, he sees no reason why such a philosophy and ethic should not have been inherited from the earlier times where the centrifugal spread of purity law was not so much, temple → home and hearth → land, but rather, priestly ideology and influence → home and hearth → land. Ultimately, it was הארץ that had to be protected from impurity, as failure to do this would necessarily result in divine departure, desolation, and exile of the people. Such protection would only have been possible if the ethic and *Weltanschauung* of the priests was *mutatis mutandis* appropriately transmitted to and inculcated in the people.

Neusner's central thesis for cultic purity, is that *participation in the cult* and thereby contact with what is sacred, should be available to the pure but proscribed to the impure.

Neusner lists the causes of cultic impurity, as he sees them in the biblical, P writings as follows: [252]

---

250 See chapter 2.
251 Clines, ed., *Dictionary of Classical Hebrew*, Vol. IV, 196.
252 Adapted from: Neusner, *The Idea of Purity in Ancient Judaism*, 18–23.

	Cause	Biblical Reference
1	Forbidden foods	Lev 11:1–47, 17:15–16,
2	Childbirth	Lev 12:1–8
3	"Leprosy" = dermopathy	Lev 13:1–46, 13:59
4	"Leprosy" = moulds, mildew	Lev 13:47–59
5	Bodily discharges	Lev 15:1–33, Deut 23:10
6	Sexual misdeeds & murder	Lev 18:6–25, Num 35:32–34
7	Corpses	Lev 21:1–24, Num 31:19–20

Neusner's Idea of Metaphorical Purity/Impurity

In addition to the above notion of cultic purity and impurity, Neusner takes the view that within biblical literature can be found a usage of the terms טהור and טמא as metaphors for (im)moral behaviour. Where there is a (personal and cultic) maintenance of purity through adherence to religious prescriptions and dogma, this is indicative of an acceptance *of* God and is a reciprocal process by which the pure are within the cult and so are accepted *by* God. In contrast, impurity is the failure to follow such prescriptions and is indicative of an active rejection *of* God punishable with rejection *by* God. In Neusner's view, metaphorical purity/impurity stands in contrast with cultic purity/impurity because the former entails no consideration of the details of priestly law, whereas the latter entails specific questions about how, within a priestly worldview, to achieve, maintain and restore purity. Douglas specifically rejected Neusner's view of metaphorical impurity because she saw the entirety of the biblical purity texts as a single (priestly) symbolic system. More recently, Klawans has felt that Neusner's dichotomy is oversimplified, there is no requirement for metaphor, and that his specific association of purity and impurity with the priesthood and/or temple is unhelpful.[253]

Neusner considered a wealth of literature in arriving at his understanding of purity/impurity but, unlike Milgrom, he did not make a direct analysis of Leviticus and Numbers. His Hebrew Bible scholarship relates specifically to Ezra and Nehemiah and he also used the Apocrypha, Pseudepigrapha, Philo, and Josephus as textual sources. Pollution of the temple cult by idolatry is a major

---

253 Klawans, *Impurity and Sin in Ancient Judaism*. See below.

theme throughout much of this, and Philo²⁵⁴ and Josephus²⁵⁵ offer some thoughts—important to Neusner's argument—on צרעת and זוב which Neusner relates to the Levitical heritage.

It is difficult to see what Neusner believes to have been added by later sources to the corpus of purity/impurity law handed down in the biblical texts. Perhaps he is simply using later textual sources, not so much as a restatement of Leviticus and Numbers, but rather to reinforce his notional dichotomy of cultic and metaphorical purity/impurity. In fact, Josephus quite specifically refers to purity outside the temple among the Essenes.²⁵⁶ This allows Neusner to conclude that Josephus considered that the purity laws not only governed the temple but were more or less universally accepted *outside* the temple. However, Haber has suggested that careful study of the word μίασμα that Josephus uses for *impurity, pollution,* and *defilement,* suggests that his concept of these entities was influenced by rather different, Graeco-Roman, ideas of purity, in addition to those originating in P and transmitted abroad through the medium of the temple.²⁵⁷

Neusner's work offers a very considerable mass of interpretative information on the Jewish purity laws. However, we must be very circumspect in understanding how much of this is specifically interpretation of the biblical canon and how

---

254 Philo sticks very closely to the Hebrew Bible or, more probably, the Septuagint. Almost all occurrences are in the context of commentary upon Leviticus and offer no insight into what צרעת, and λέπρα actually meant. Miriam's affliction is mentioned, but only in commentary upon Numbers. In several instances the word λέπρα appears as a metaphor for unpleasant things, progressive nastiness and 'vice'. Philo sees "leprosy", like gonorrhoea, as the reward of the "evil man": "ἐν τῷ φαύλῳ ἡ ἀληθὴς περὶ θεοῦ δόξα ἐπεσκίασται καὶ ἀποκρύπτεται ... ὁ δὲ τοιοῦτος πεφυγάδευται θείου χοροῦ, καθάπερ ὁ λεπρὸς καὶ γονορρυής." (Philo, *Legum Allegoriarum*, III: 7). So the "leper" is one who is deprived of divine company, seemingly through his own iniquity rather than through misfortune. This was a view which was to continue for a very long time. Neusner supposes that Philo is treating the purity law first, as a second-level metaphor for moral cleanliness and secondly, by a process of allegorization, as a metaphor for self-control. In Neusner's interpretation, Philo's view of צרעת or λέπρα is not so much that of a disease but rather as symptomatic and symbolic of instability of sound judgement, moral purpose and Lebensstil.
255 Josephus, a former priest and a historian rather than a philosopher, takes a more down-to-earth approach to impurity than Philo, as is exemplified by his view of "leprosy"; offering practical advice about things for lepers to do or have done to them rather than a discourse upon divine influence. In the majority of cases he is reporting or interpreting Levitical law but from a characteristically personal viewpoint. Josephus is especially interested in whether or not Moses himself had leprosy and, if so, how this impinged on his law-making. Nevertheless, with a single exception, it is clear that to have λέπρα makes one impure and casts one amid social detritus. The word often appears in the company of γονορρυής and sufferers from either affliction are the subject of many social prohibitions: in particular the ruling that they should abide outside the city walls. Josephus takes a surprisingly compassionate and pragmatic view of "lepers": "καὶ ταῦτα παρὰ πολλοῖς ὄντων λαπρῶν ἔθνεσι καὶ τιμῆς ἀπολαυόντων, οὐ μόνον ὕβρεως καὶ φυγῆς ἀπηλλαγμένων, ἀλλὰ καὶ τὰς ἐπιστημοτάτας στρτείας στρατευομένων καὶ τὰς πολιτικὰς ἀρχὰς πιστευομένων καὶ εἰς ἱερὰ καὶ ναοὺς ἐχόντων ἐξουσίαν εἰσιέναι·" (Josephus, Jewish Antiquities, III: 266). And in stark contrast to the opacity of Leviticus (P) on this subject, makes a single, if rather unconvincing, suggestion that leprosy may be the result of excessive exposure to the sun's rays: "ἡλίου λαμπρὸν ἐξέλαμψε καὶ τῇ τοῦ βασιλέως ὄψει προσέπεσεν, ὡς τῷ μὲν εὐθέως λέπραν ἐπιδραμεῖν" (Josephus, *Jewish Antiquities*, IX: 225). It is unfortunate that Josephus, often so useful in interpreting detail, is of so little help with "leprosy". Most likely, the idea of ritual impurity engendered by the very thought of this disease was so ingrained—he had, after all, been a Jewish priest—and of such cultic significance that alternative views simply did not come to mind.
256 Josephus, *Jewish War*, II, 120–61; *Antiquities*, XVIII 18–22; Titus Flavius Josephus, Josephus, (Joseph ben Matityahu), Collected Works, trans. H. St. J. Thackeray and L. Feldman, 13 vols. (Cambridge, MA: Harvard University Press, 2004).
257 Susan Haber and Adele Reinhartz, *"They Shall Purify Themselves": Essays on Purity in Early Judaism,* EJ&L no 24 (Atlanta, GA: Society of Biblical Literature, 2008).

Milgrom: An Exhaustive Analysis

Jacob Milgrom (1923–2010), an American rabbi and scholar, wrote extensively on the Torah and in particular, on Leviticus. Between 1970 and 2004, Milgrom produced his monumental commentary on Leviticus[258] and its smaller, follow-up volume.[259] Together, these must be considered the most extensive and scholarly corpus of work on Leviticus and, by association, upon the Torah purity laws. Milgrom's analytical style and, where the purity laws are concerned, interpretation, owes much to Hoffman: both are text-based. However, Milgrom's exposition is both more thorough and more in depth. Milgrom is exhaustive in his consideration of later Jewish, Mishnaic, and Talmudic exegesis of the biblical texts.[260] Among many new ideas brought by Milgrom to the study of biblical purity is the notion that sinfulness has the power to defile the sanctuary from afar. This can occur by way of major forms of both ritual and moral impurity, but Milgrom attaches a somewhat different distinction to this dichotomy from that of Neusner and Klawans. Purification, necessary to remedy such defilement, is required, therefore, for the altar and the sanctuary more particularly than for the sinner. Milgrom arrives at this view by his exegesis of the word חטאת (√חטא = incur guilt).[261] Traditionally, this word has been translated as *sin-offering* as, for example:

ועשה אתם הכהן אחד חטאת והאחד עלה וכפר עליו הכהן לפני יהוה מזובו

> and the priest shall offer them, the one for a sin offering, and the other for a burnt offering; and the priest shall make atonement for him before the Lord for his issue. (Lev 15:15)

Milgrom argues that this translation is inappropriate because the ritual being carried out is a ritual of purification—not of the sinner but of the altar and sanctuary—rather than a ritual of atonement on the part of the sinner. The word חטאת should, therefore, be translated as *purification-offering*. Milgrom goes on to identify two sets of circumstances in which purification by חטאת is required. In both cases the personal purification of the individual must be brought about before the sacrificial offering of חטאת. A variety of means necessary to carry out this personal "pre-purification" is listed in the priestly writings. In Milgrom's first case, the impurity in the individual may have been incurred in, for example, childbirth, צרעת, or זוב. The affected individual is then required to undertake

---

258 Milgrom, *Leviticus: A New Translation*.
259 Milgrom, *Leviticus: A Continental Commentary*.
260 A similar strategy—at risk of criticism for reception history and illicit extrapolation—has been adopted in the present study in the hope that it may find justification by such an authority as Milgrom.
261 Clines, ed., *Dictionary of Classical Hebrew*, Vol. III, 198–200. *TDOT*, Vol. IV, 309–319.

personal purification by ritual ablution before bringing the חטאת to the sanctuary. Milgrom's second situation is concerned with impurity acquired inadvertently. Here, personal purification is "internal"—Milgrom describes it as "spiritually" purifying the individual—inasmuch as the individual's guilt, combined with the intrinsic inadvertency of the sinful act, serves instead of ablution. There is still, however, an eventual requirement at the sanctuary, for חטאת. In both cases, Milgrom postulates the ultimate target of חטאת to be the sanctuary, for it is there that the blood of the sacrificial beast is shed and utilized in the act of purgation.

Milgrom also identifies a hierarchy of sacrificial ritual activity at the temple after real or potential defilement of the sanctuary. This occurs on three levels[262] each of which entails a distinct category of severity counteracted by a specific process of purgation. At the lowest level of seriousness, it is the outer altar of the temple that is at risk. Established physical impurity such as childbirth, צרעת or זוב, but also the inadvertent assumption of impurity/sin, as discussed above, can both cause defilement of the altar in this way. The blood from the חטאת is used by the priest to purge this pollution. He is required to paint the horns of the altar, (Exod 27:2) and dispose of the blood at the base of the outer altar.

ולקח הכהן מדמה באצבעו ונתן על־קרנת מזבח העלה ואת־כל־דמה ישפך אל־יסוד המזבח

> And the priest shall take of the blood thereof with his finger, and put it upon the horns of the altar of burnt offering, and all the blood thereof shall he pour out at the base of the altar. (Lev 4:30)

This ritual is further described at Lev 4:25 and 9:9. Milgrom's second level of seriousness involves the same impurity/sin, both intentional and inadvertent, but now the sinner is the high priest himself or the community as a whole. The ritual of purgation also involves the blood of the חטאת in much the same way, but now involves the inner altar in front of the veil.

וטבל הכהן אצבעו מן־הדם והזה שבע פעמים לפני יהוה את פני הפרכת

> and the priest shall dip his finger in the blood, and sprinkle it seven times before the Lord, before the veil. (Lev 4:17)

In the third and most serious of Milgrom's categories, the mechanism of acquiring impurity/sin involves wanton actions which remain un-repented. Un-repented sin triggers a different and more complex set of rituals for its purgation because it causes more extensive defilement of the sanctuary. This defilement involves both the outer and inner altars, and penetrates the veil, so polluting the sacred ark and the holy of holies (קדש קדשים). There are two consequences of this form of pollution of the sanctuary that did not apply to the lesser forms of

---

262 Milgrom, *Leviticus: A New Translation*, Vol. 1, 257.

defilement. First, the wanton sinner may not now offer חטאת at the temple in expiation of his impurity, indeed, "that soul must be utterly cut off and bear his shame upon him."

כי דבר־יהוה בזה ואת־מצותו הפר הכרת תכרת הנפש ההוא עונה בה

> Because he hath despised the word of the Lord, and hath broken his commandment; that soul shall utterly be cut off; his iniquity shall be upon him. (Num 15:31).

Secondly, because both inner and outer altars have been desecrated, defilement of this gravity can only be counteracted by the purification rituals reserved for the Day of Atonement (Lev 16:16–19).

If we consider all of these situations, we can see that Milgrom is postulating a proportional relationship between the severity of the impurity/sin and the degree to which it penetrates the sanctuary thus:

> Severity of impurity $\propto$ Extent of penetration of sanctuary[263]

Milgrom also considers that the pollution of the sanctuary can be brought about remotely by sinfulness. He furthermore, makes a distinction between two types if impurity which he considers as *ritually-generated* and *morally-generated*.[264] The distinction still taxonomical, is not quite the same as that of Neusner or Klawans *(qv)*. As ever with Milgrom, the distinction is founded upon a lexical observation. Ritually-generated impurity, טמאה, he considers to be physical defilement such as congenital or acquired blemishes or צרעת or זוב. The sinner himself is not involved in the purification ritual for טמה beyond providing the חטאת. It is then up to the priest to bring about ritual purgation:

ועשה הכהן את־החטאת וכפר על־המטהר מטמאתו ואחר ישחט את־העלה

> And the priest shall offer the sin offering, and make atonement for him that is to be cleansed because of his uncleanness; and afterward he shall kill the burnt offering: (Lev 14:19)

For the inadvertent sinner, it is not merely purification but also forgiveness that is the necessary antidote. In such cases, Milgrom sees the term הטמא as describing the sin or moral impurity and the verb $\sqrt{}$סלח (in the *nifʿal* נִסְלַח = be forgiven), describing the specific process of forgiving.

ואת־כל־חלבו יקטיר המזבחה כחלב זבח השלמים וכפר עליו הכהן מחטאתו ונסלח לו

---

[263] Note: $\propto$ means "is directly proportional to".
[264] Milgrom, *Leviticus: A New Translation*, Vol. 1, 253–92.

And all the fat thereof shall he burn upon the altar, as the fat of the sacrifice of peace offerings: and the priest shall make atonement for him as concerning his sin, and he shall be forgiven. (Lev 4:26)

Where the sinfulness is wanton and un-repented, the Day of Atonement ritual must take place in order to effect adequate purgation. This involves the sacrifice of two goats, one of which (for God) provides the liquid blood necessary to purge the sanctuary and so operates as the חטאת and another is the *scapegoat* upon which the priest confesses all of the iniquities of the community. This implies that the impurity is of such a degree of seriousness that it has already polluted the people and so urgent action is necessary to prevent extension of this pollution to the land. Untreated, this would have the inevitable consequence of provoking the departure of the deity so as to leave the people in desolation and ultimately bring about their exile.[265] The sins of the people Milgrom regards as moral impurity. In the Day of Atonement ritual, the priest confesses all these iniquities (עון) of the people, and in so doing, they become heaped upon the unfortunate scapegoat who is then sent away into the wilderness: this is mass purgation. Milgrom, in his analysis, associates טמאה with the first goat and with חטאת, and he associates עונת with the second goat and with the טמאה of the people.[266]

וסמך אהרן את־שתי (ידו) [ידיו] על ראש השעיר החי והתודה עליו את־כל־עונת בני ישראל ואת־כל־פשעיהם לכל־חטאתם ונתן אתם על־ראש השעיר ושלח ביד־איש עתי המדברה

and Aaron shall lay both his hands upon the head of the live goat, and confess over him all the iniquities of the children of Israel, and all their transgressions, even all their sins; and he shall put them upon the head of the goat, and shall send him away by the hand of a man that is in readiness into the wilderness: (Lev 16:21)

It must be admitted that Milgrom's account of the Levitical purity laws, though *prima facie* seemingly exhaustive, contains a number of ambiguities that remain unclear. In particular, these relate to his distinction between ritual (i.e. physically-generated) impurity and moral impurity. For example, in Volume 2 of his commentary[267] Milgrom suggests that the distinction between ritual and moral impurity is primarily dependent upon the distinction between P and H elements of the Levitical text. P impurity he describes as "concrete, cultic-ritual impurity" whereas H impurity is "abstract, inexpungeable-moral impurity".[268] These somewhat cumbersome distinctions are not particularly helpful. The latter definition might be supposed to imply a metaphorical usage but Milgrom takes

---

265 Milgrom, *Leviticus: A New Translation*, Vol. 1, 258–9.
266 Milgrom, *Leviticus: A New Translation*, Vol. 2, 1571–84.
267 Milgrom, *Leviticus: A New Translation*, Vol. 2, 1578.
268 See also chapter 10; also Knohl, The Sanctuary of Silence and Wright, "Holiness in Leviticus and Beyond," 351–64.

pains to point out that it is as "real and potent as P's impurity". One is left feeling the need for a more concise differentiation of the two types of impurity and particularly a need for further clarification in the matter of moral impurity. Milgrom defines this latter as embodying idolatry, sexual sin, and homicide but fails to fit them together to produce a single concept and theology in the way that he so adeptly and thoroughly does in the case of ritual impurity.

Several other scholars have also taken a largely taxonomical stance in concerning themselves with Levitical impurity. These may be considered now.

Frymer-Kensky: A Classification of Impurity.

Tikva Frymer-Kensky (1943–2006), was an American Jewish theologian with a particular interest in the Ancient Near East. Her approach to impurity will always appeal to those who are tidy-minded and seek formality: it is based largely upon Milgrom but is more logical. The central feature of her analysis is that ritual pollutions that are *contagious*, and can be divided into major and minor classes principally on the basis of their duration.[269] Frymer-Kensky makes the important point, often not appreciated, that in the Israel of biblical times, the need and desire for purity was so intense that it was the essential force behind the establishment of a particular social class, the priesthood, to provide a mechanism for both controlling and educating about this phenomenon. In this respect Frymer-Kensky stands apart from the other authors considered in this chapter. She is suggesting that the intense need for purity brought about the priestly worldview rather than the converse. Frymer-Kensky retains Milgrom's and others' hierarchy of pollution's growing in seriousness from individual → sanctuary/temple → the land. In this respect Frymer-Kensky saw pollution and attitudes towards it, as having been central determinants of Israel's history. Therefore, the biblical purity laws and the related activities of the priesthood were to be seen, collectively and principally, as a national strategy for *catastrophe-avoidance*. Within this strategy could be identified curative practices, remedial for specific polluting events. Each would be based specifically upon the level of seriousness attributed to each particular infraction of the rules. Thus, if and when contact was made with a particular polluting influence, a time-period of uncleanness would begin immediately. In the case of minor pollutions this extended until the same evening or, with major pollution, for seven days. This time-period was, in either case, a period of *contagion* during which contact with other individuals and with any sacred places or objects was to be sedulously eschewed.

---

[269] Tikva Frymer-Kensky, "Pollution, Purification and Purgation in Biblical Israel: Major and Minor Pollutions," in Carol L. Meyers and Michael Patrick O'Connor, eds. *The Word of the Lord Shall go Forth: Essays in Honor of David Noel Freedman in Celebration of his Sixtieth Birthday,* Special Volume Series, American Schools of Oriental Research (Winona Lake, IN: Eisenbrauns, 1983).

Minor Impurity

For Frymer-Kensky, minor pollution consisted of the acquisition of טמאה, usually from external sources[270] and usually by direct physical contact. There was one major exception to this activity which was contact with a corpse: that instigated a major pollution. In addition, contact with someone who was already suffering a major pollution could bring about a minor pollution in any individual who made physical contact. Obviously, this process is somewhat at variance with modern ideas of contagion but, of course, any notion of an infective agent was completely absent from Levitical thinking. Frymer-Kensky supplies an extensive table of minor pollutions[271] and the remedial ritual actions to be taken in order to regain a pure state. These all involve waiting until evening of the same day; washing of the clothes in a majority of cases and bathing in about 50% of cases. The rationale for how these treatments were arrived at is unclear and perhaps somewhat illogical in the light of present day thinking. For example, if one touches a menstruating woman, this demands only waiting until evening for purification. However, if one comes into contact with her seat or her bedding, it becomes necessary in addition, to bathe and to wash one's clothes.

Major Impurity

Frymer-Kensky stresses that although major impurities are contagious, they are not dangerous: nor is any moral opprobrium attached to any of them, with the single exception of צרעת. She suggests that this single exception may stem from the view taken in certain instances in the Torah that צרעת is a form of divine punishment.[272] However, Frymer-Kensky is at pains to point out that, apart from these few instances, there is no textual evidence to suggest wrongdoing as being a feature of all cases of צרעת and there is nothing to suggest a moral deficiency in *dermopaths*. Any such idea may have originated from suspicious folklore, from prejudice or from inculcated bigotry.

Major impurities can be subdivided into those which have external causes and those with internal causes. External causes are more usually associated with minor pollutions but there are two significant exceptions: צרעת and contact with a corpse. Major internal pollutions are specifically those involved with emissions from the body: childbirth, menstruation, and genital discharges (זוב). Frymer-Kensky notes, along with Douglas, that other bodily physiological and pathological products such as blood,[273] saliva, pus, nasal mucus, sputum and all forms of excreta do not produce, on contact, ritual major or minor pollution. Although these natural *exuviae* did cross the body's boundaries, they were not associated with *life* in the sense that childbirth, menstrual blood, and semen

---

270 There was only one "internal" source of minor pollution, namely seminal discharge—chapter 6.
271 Frymer-Kensky, "Pollution, Purification and Purgation," 402.
272 E.g. Num 12:10–15; 2 Kgs 5:27; 2 Chr 26:19–21.
273 As distinct from "bloodshed".

were thought to have been. Nor were the natural *exuviae* associated with *un-life*, i.e. death as would be the case with a corpse.[274] It is interesting to compare elements of these ideas with those of Freud whose decidedly more colourful approach to taboo was centred in the developmental excursions of the individual rather than being seen as metaphors for avoidance of ills destined to fall upon society as a whole.[275]

The common factor, for all major impurities, in Levitical thought, is that they are contagious. However, according to Frymer-Kensky, although these pollutions are *contagious*, they are not *dangerous,* nor should they be expected to be. Neither is guilt attached to them in any biblical context. However, they can be transmitted to others and more importantly to sacred objects and to the land, and so a strategy for avoiding this sequence of events had to be part of Israelite society's rules. Normal life in any society would be impossible without childbirth or disposal of the dead, faeces, urine, other natural *exuviae* and the associated, unavoidable functions. It is only when *some* of these things come into contact with the sacred that danger results and it is this, above all, that must be avoided if the society is to flourish. It is a matter of some debate how much צרעת can be thought of as natural and unavoidable; however, צרעת appears to have been adopted into the category of major ritual impurity and so merits the same treatment as other impurities in this category. Medieval and later views about the nature of "leprosy" are in stark contrast to this accommodating and intelligent view of dermopathic problems. They fit the *mores* of a later civilization and presumably reflect a desire on the part of the church to wield a terrifying threat to keep the proletariat in thraldom.

Danger-beliefs and Catastrophe-deeds

Frymer-Kensky, in addition, to major and minor impurity, recognizes a further subset of impurities which she calls *danger beliefs*. The deeds that are involved have a clear implication of wrong-doing and the danger is that into which the individual places himself as perpetrator. It is, of course, the danger of divine punishment and it cannot be ameliorated by any ritual activity. Frymer-Kensky supposes that where *danger beliefs* are held, *catastrophe-deeds* may follow and divine punishment is then unavoidable. She puts this view in a Hebrew Bible context by suggesting a textual indicator for *catastrophe-deeds* which is the phrase usually translated as: "he shall bear his iniquity" (עונו ישא). The penalty for *catastrophe-deeds* is כרת, the cutting-off of the individual from his people[276] which, more particularly, means from his lineage. However, it would be wrong

---

274 Douglas, *Purity and Danger*, 150.
275 Sigmund Freud, Angela Richards, and James Strachey, *Introductory Lectures on Psychoanalysis*. Pelican Freud Library, Vol. 1 (Harmondsworth: Penguin, 1973), 187–202, 357–370. Sigmund Freud, James Strachey, and Angela Richards, On Sexuality: Three Essays on the Theory of Sexuality and Other Works, Vol. 7 (Harmondsworth: Penguin Books, 1977), 107–8, 127–8, 131–143.
276 Usually nif'al (but sometimes hif'il) as in, וְנִכְרְתוּ שְׁנֵיהֶם מִקֶּרֶב עַמָּם See Clines, ed., *Dictionary of Classical Hebrew*, Vol. IV, 465, 2b. Also, *TDOT*, Vol. VII, 339–352

to infer that the execution of the penalty of כרת is always an active process brought about by human members of society. Rather it is to be seen as an automatic penalty imposed by the will of God—it is divine extirpation.[277]

Wrong-doings that incur this penalty have been described by Frymer-Kensky as "fundamental principles of Israelite cosmology; in particular, acts that blur the most vital distinction in the Israelite classificatory system, the separation of sacred and profane".[278] Unsurprisingly, they are to be found listed in the H chapters of the Book of Leviticus and must be thought of as corresponding to the "abstract, inexpungeable-moral impurity" described by Milgrom *(qv)*. It is arguable how far they fit into the priestly worldview. The general sense of the כרת penalty goes beyond the Levitical and other purity laws, and must be seen in the generality as the proper penalty for offences against the Abrahamic covenant with God. This point is made perfectly clear in Genesis:

וערל זכר אשר לא־ימול את־בשר ערלתו ונכרתה הנפש ההוא מעמיה את־בריתי הפר

> And the uncircumcised male who is not circumcised in the flesh of his foreskin, that soul shall be cut off from his people; he hath broken my covenant. (Gen 17:14)

It is interesting to note that there is but a single case of overlap between the ritual impurity of Frymer-Kensky's *major impurities* and the violation of holiness exemplified by *catastrophe deeds* and, therefore, an overlap in P and H material. This single instance is detailed in:

ואיש אשר־ישכב את־אשה דוה וגלה את־ערותה את־מקרה הערה והיא גלתה את־מקור דמיה ונכרתו שניהם מקרב עמם

> And if a man shall lie with a woman having her sickness, and shall uncover her nakedness; he hath made naked her fountain, and she hath uncovered the fountain of her blood: and both of them shall be cut off from among their people. (Lev 20:18)

Here, in what is undoubted H material, there is a clear demand for the penalty of כרת, but apparently no requirement for the usual ritual ablution and time-serving necessary for the cleansing of a major impurity.

The punishment of כרת must be regarded as existing in order to protect those things regarded as sacred. In so doing it not only contributes to defining the boundaries between what is sacred and what is profane, but also provides a sanction against the violation of those very boundaries. We can, perhaps, see a

---

[277] Nevertheless, miscreants were often stoned to death in anticipation of divine action.
[278] Frymer-Kensky, "Pollution, Purification and Purgation," 404.

parallel between these ideas of Frymer-Kensky and those of Mary Douglas in respect of the defining and maintenance of socio-religious boundaries.

Capital Punishment in Levitical Law — כרת

Capital punishment in the Ancient Near East was widespread and differed from society to society. The subject has been extensively investigated and reported by Good.[279] Good recognizes seven law codes as having existed at different times in the Ancient Near East; that of the Hebrew Bible is number seven.[280] It is seen by Good as embodying:

- The *Code of the Covenant*—*Exod* 20:22–23:19—probably from between the twelfth and the tenth or ninth century BCE.
- The *Code of Deuteronomy*—*Deut* 12–28—possibly compiled in the seventh century BCE.
- The *Priestly Code*—P and H, see Appendix 3.

Good further classifies offences, defined in these law-codes and punishable by death, into 5 categories:

1. Offences against persons.
2. Offences involving property.
3. Defiance of authority.[281]
4. Religious offences.
5. Procedural requirements.[282]

Category 1 (and to a lesser extent category 4)[283] concerns us here with regard to the imposition of the penalty of כרת for infractions of the purity laws. There is biblical textual justification for the death penalty in murder (Exod 21:12; Lev 24:17); manslaughter (Num 35:16–18);[284] kidnapping (Deut 24:7); causing death by negligence (Exod 21:29–31); sorcery (Exod 22:17);[285] rape (Deut 22:23–27);[286] adultery[287]—both parties to be executed (Lev 20:10; Deut 22:22); harlotry, in the singular case where the offender is the daughter of a priest (Lev 21:9); incest (Lev 18:6, generally, and with one's father's wife 20:11[288]); homosexuality (Lev 20:13); and bestiality (Lev 20:15–16).

---

279 Edwin M. Good, "Capital Punishment and Its Alternatives in Ancient near Eastern Law," *Stanford Law Review* 19, no. 5 (1967): 947–77.
280 The others are the law codes of: (1) Ur-Nammu, (2) Lipit-Ishtar, (3) Eshnunna, (4) Hammurabi, (5) Middle Assyrian, and (6) Hittite.
281 Especially kings
282 Especially in relation to legal procedure but also involving trial by ordeal which often resulted in death.
283 And also category 2, inasmuch as wives and daughters were regarded as "property" in those times.
284 Although the Hebrew Bible makes the distinction between murder and manslaughter, the penalty remains the same.
285 In the Hebrew texts this is specifically referring to a sorceress (מְכַשֵּׁפָה) however the LXX has φαρμακούς which it must be supposed is the conventional use of the plural and the masculine gender to include both sexes.
286 But only if force is used and the woman is married or formally betrothed.
287 But not "fornication" which was intercourse in which at least one of the parties was not married, cf. Deut 22:13–21.
288 This is strictly and strangely an offence against one's father because it "uncovers his nakedness".

It is particularly difficult to draw generalizations from all of this. Good suggests that, whereas the Babylonians were especially severe in dealing with offences against property, the Hebrews were more concerned with offences against the person, but overwhelmingly so with those crimes that were of a sexual nature. This fits in well with their stringent application of the purity/impurity laws. Good remarks that in the Ancient Near East, "as evidenced by legislation, purity of religion was incomparably more important to the Hebrews than to any of the other people".[289] He goes on to suggest that in many cases it is possible that the death penalty was not routinely carried out but it was the formal statement of its mandatory requirement in the codified laws that led to its adoption by society as ethical dogma and thereby to a clearer and more formal definition of the moral, ethical, and behavioural boundaries with which that society proposed to invest itself.

Where it took place, the mechanism of formal execution is not clear though in some cases burning and stoning were specifically prescribed. The term כרת does not refer to the process of execution itself but rather to the cutting off of the individual from society, his family, and his lineage. The terms "extirpation", "eradication", and "uprooting" have all been widely used as a translation of כרת but "eradication" and "uprooting" seem quite inappropriate inasmuch as uprooting is quite different from cutting off. There is no suggestion that his lineage, his "stock", is in any way deleted: it is his personal attachment to it that is to be ended. "Extirpation" (Latin "*stirps*" = "stock") or "deracination" (Latin "*radix*", French "*racine*" = "root"), might be thought better words than "eradication", as they less imply uprooting than separation from one's root-stock. The sentiment of how כרת operates as a punishment is, perhaps more properly to be seen as one of excommunication than of annihilation.[290]

Wright: Permitted and Prohibited Impurities

David P. Wright[291] has contributed to the debate on the Levitical purity laws by suggesting a different classification. His work is based particularly upon that of Hoffmann, Büchler, and Frymer-Kensky but postulates a spectrum of *purity↔impurity* or, more particularly one ranging from *permitted impurities* to *prohibited impurities*.[292] The word "permitted" is perhaps better understood as "tolerated" and Wright eventually came to prefer this epithet in his writings. Wright's category of tolerated impurities corresponds, more or less, to the major impurities of Frymer-Kensky: death-related, sexual-related, disease-related, and cultic. Wright classifies these together because they are all free from any form of

---

289 Good, "Capital Punishment and Its Alternatives," 947.
290 *TDOT*, Vol. VII, 347.
291 See chapter 4.
292 D. P. Wright, "Two Types of Impurity in the Priestly Writings of the Bible," *Koroth* 9 (1988): 180–93; D. P. Wright, "The Spectrum of Priestly Impurity," in *Priesthood and Cult in Ancient Israel*, ed. G. A. Anderson and S. M. Olyan (Sheffield: JSOT Press, 1991).

what he calls "blanket prohibition" in the priestly laws. It is difficult to extract from Wright's writings exactly where each specific impurity lies along the length of the spectrum and this seems a major deficiency in his work. However, in the category of prohibited impurities he is more circumscribed. This category contains two sub-categories. The first of these embodies those impurities that arise unintentionally, often from mis-management of tolerated impurities; for example, as in the inadvertent contact with a corpse or prohibited animal.[293] Wright sees these offences as equivalent to those of other writers that involve the outer altar and require a sacrifice of חטאת in order to bring about appropriate purgation. Wright's second sub-category is the more serious case of deliberate sin. This corresponds most nearly to Frymer-Kensky's *catastrophe-deeds*. For Wright, there are two consequences of this form of misconduct. First the perpetrator must pay the penalty of כרת and, secondly because the קדש קדשים has been defiled, the purification must be that of the Day of Atonement ritual. Although Wright is rather opaque about the specific nature of each grade of impurity, at least it is clear that his spectrum has four grades, they are, in increasing order of severity:

1. Those requiring no sacrificial expiation.
2. Those requiring sacrificial expiation by the individual.
3. Those requiring sacrificial expiation by the community.
4. Those requiring the Day of Atonement sacrifice.

Wright's analysis has these four categories corresponding specifically to a progression in the *locus of pollution*; so, in the same order as above, this sequence would be:

1. The person.
2. The outer altar + the person.
3. The outer altar + the shrine (± the person).
4. The קדש קדשים ± *the person*.

There is, moreover, a corresponding inverse relationship in the degree to which the defiled individual is excluded from elements of society. Again in corresponding order:

1. Exclusion of the individual from those things and places that are sacred.
2. Exclusion from sacred places ± some forms of profane habitation.
3. Exclusion from sacred places + all forms of profane habitation.
4. Permanent exclusion from all human society + הארץ.

Wright's interpretation of the impurity laws has a clear moral basis which he believes indicates a priestly, systematic legislative scheme directed at sustaining

---

293 E.g.: Lev 4:1–5; Lev 5:2–3; Num 6:6–7; Num 15:22–29.

the priestly worldview and ideology and so the moral order of Israelite society.[294] Wright has been criticized from the entirely logical standpoint that his system is over-categorized and thereby lacks the progressive continuity necessary for a spectrum.[295]

Jenson: A Holiness Spectrum

Philip P. Jenson has been more specifically concerned with holiness *per se* than with the *purity* ↔ *impurity* tension. His spectrum of holiness has been briefly considered above. However, Jenson is the first to admit that any spectrum for holiness must concern itself with impurity. Jenson, for the most part, leans toward Douglas's viewpoint and rejects as simplistic, a purely *hygenic* or *cultic* basis for the impurity laws of Lev 11–15. As in the case of Douglas, Jenson takes an anthropological approach and considers impurity/pollution/defilement as characteristic of those things that blur the boundaries of the body. Because they are anomalous, they present a danger to ordered society. They challenge the God-given perfection of the body and so disqualify the individual from approaching God.[296] Jenson sees the dynamics of pollution as conferring a temporary blemish upon an afflicted individual. The worst case is, of course, death, where the blemish is irreversible. Jenson discusses two theories that he suggests account for the way in which impurity and holiness were seen in biblical times. The first of these he calls the *structural theory*, which he describes as idealist and focused upon the human ability to classify the world in such a way as to combine cultural, social, and theological aspects into a single structure. Holiness here *is* wholeness—Douglas's view—and wholeness means freedom from anomaly or imperfection. The converse is impurity i.e. defect and mongrelism. This theory assumes a structured system with fixed and stable parameters and processes from which deviations may be seen and measured in their degree of significance.

The second theory, Jenson calls the *death theory* and describes it as "realist" because it involves the inescapable qualities of life and death and holds the latter as an end-point for impurity. All impurities direct the individual inescapably towards death and are to be seen by the priests as a quantifiable negative exposition of life before God. Because it is concerned with irreversible events, Jenson supposes this theory to have a clearer referential content and to be less amenable to a static structural analysis than the first theory. However, he remains sitting firmly on the fence as to which theory he prefers, saying,

---

[294] Wright, "The Spectrum of Priestly Impurity," 170.
[295] Haber and Reinhartz, *"They Shall Purify Themselves,"* 27.
[296] This will be dealt with more fully in chapter 9 where "blemish" is considered.

"Anomaly is as much an offence against an ordered world as is the destructive power of death".[297]

Klawans: Ritual and Moral Impurity, Revised

Jonathan Klawans, between 1995 and the present time, has been a prolific writer on the subject of the Jewish purity laws. His work builds on, and clarifies, Frymer-Kensky but additionally is integrated with the thinking of Milgrom and Neusner and, to a lesser extent, Douglas.

Klawans's interest has been focused mainly on the exilic, Second Temple,[298] and rabbinical[299] periods, but he has, of necessity, had to consider the biblical period also.[300] There, in particular, Klawans has made three highly specific contributions to the understanding of biblical purity laws. First, being the most recent of the authors to be considered here, it is not surprising that Klawans's account is both up-to-date and comprehensive, as he has been able to draw upon and conflate previous scholarship. Secondly, in doing this, he has been able to arrive at and focus upon a personal and particular viewpoint regarding the matter of ritual and moral impurity. It is for his rationalizing of this dichotomy that he is best known and for which we must be grateful. Klawans has, furthermore, produced a study of the interaction between gentiles and the Jewish purity laws[301] and also has extensively considered the association of violence, defilement and sacrifice.[302]

Klawans's third contribution to modern scholarship in this field has been his highly convincing argument against the metaphorical nature of moral impurity *(qv)*.

Klawans's terminology for the sub-categories of impurity is not new. He recognizes *ritual impurity* and *moral impurity* in much the same was as others already have. These are summarized in Klawans's 2010 book[303] in a useful table.

---

[297] Jenson, *Graded Holiness*, 88.
[298] Jonathan Klawans, *Purity, Sacrifice, and the Temple: Symbolism and Supersessionism in the Study of Ancient Judaism* (New York; Oxford: Oxford University Press, 2010).
[299] Klawans believes that in Tannaitic times the dichotomy became somewhat simplified: ritual impurity was halakhic while moral impurity was aggadic.
[300] Klawans, *Impurity and Sin in Ancient Judaism*.
[301] Jonathan Klawans, "Notions of Gentile Impurity in Ancient Judaism," *AJS Rev* 20, no. 2 (1995): 285–312.
[302] Jonathan Klawans, "Pure Violence: Sacrifice and Defilement in Ancient Israel," *Harvard Th Rev* 94, no. 2 (2001): 133–55.
[303] Klawans, *Purity, Sacrifice, and the Temple*, 56.

Purity and Impurity in the Priestly Society of Ancient Israel 113

Impurity Type	Source	Effect	Resolution
Ritual	Natural processes and substances such as birth, death, bodily flows, certain animal carcasses, human corpses	Temporary, contagious defilement of persons and objects	Ritual purification, which can include bathing waiting and sacrifices
Moral	Sins: idolatry, sexual transgressions, bloodshed	Long-lasting defilement of sinners, land and sanctuary	Atonement or punishment and ultimately, exile.

Thus, as with Frymer-Kensky, *ritual impurities* are natural, often unavoidable, sometimes even desirable, not proscribed as sin and, although contagious, neither permanent nor dangerous. To contract any of these is not a sin[304] though the consequences, in certain cases (צרעת), and for certain people (priests—Lev 21:1–4) may be more severe than for the generality.

Klawans dismisses the idea that צרעת is a mark of sin although he recognizes that certain biblical narratives appear to imply this (Num 12; 2 Chron 26), and no less an authority than Milgrom has suggested as much.[305] Milgrom bases his argument on the dermopath's requirement to provide חטאת, but Klawans argues that this is less to address moral sin than as an expiatory precaution against the probability of the dermopath's having inadvertently defiled holy objects whilst polluted with צרעת.

However, Klawans does recognize two instances where ritual impurity leads to sin. The first of these is a refusal to purify oneself after defilement by a corpse (Num 19:13; 19:20): this defiles the sanctuary, even from afar, and in such a case the punishment is כרת. Presumably, there is an element of *moral impurity ↔ sin* here, inasmuch as a decision not to purify must surely be the product of sinful thinking. The second case, deserving of the same penalty, is defilement of the sanctuary and/or coming into contact with holy foods while knowingly in a state of ritual impurity, (Lev 7:20–21; 15:31; 22:3–7). Priests may be at especial risk of committing this misdeed.

Central to Klawans's argument about ritual impurities is that they affect the ritual status of the individual within the community. This is manifested by prohibitions and exclusions. Klawans speculates that by following the regulations for ritual purity and thereby ostracizing oneself and avoiding, for

---

304 Contrast Zoroastrianism where impurity is identified as a great evil.
305 Milgrom, *Leviticus: A New Translation*, Vol. 1, 822, 857.

example, sex, and as far as one can, death, one is voluntarily isolating oneself from those things that would make one least like God. The effect of this tidying-up of one's personal *imitatio Dei* is, in Klawans's own words, "nothing other than the theological underpinning of the entire Holiness Code: *imitatio Dei*. Only a heightened god-like state—the state of ritual purity—made one eligible to enter the sanctuary, God's holy residence on earth."

In his approach to moral impurity Klawans is more outspoken and differs more obviously in his views from those of his predecessors. In Klawans's view, moral impurity is acquired by committing *abominations* (תועבת). These are the usual trio of sexual transgression, bloodshed,[306] and idolatry[307] which bring about moral (but not ritual) defilement that involves (sequentially) the sinner, the land, and the sanctuary of Yahweh, leading ultimately to the depopulation and desolation of the land of Israel.[308] The (five) specific differences seen by Klawans as distinguishing ritual from moral impurity are summarized in the table above. Of special note is that moral impurity is not contagious and ritual impurity is never transmitted to the land.[309] Additionally, Klawans introduces a semantic dimension to distinguish between ritual and moral impurity. He observes that sources of both types of impurity are described in the Torah as טמא (unclean) but the terms תועבה (abomination) and √חנף (pollute) are reserved specifically for reference to sources of what Klawans defines as moral impurity. Klawans draws a parallel between moral impurity (as he sees it) and the Greek concept of μίασμα:[310] a form of pollution caused by blood-guilt.[311] From this he arrives at a working definition of moral impurity:

> Moral impurity is best understood as a potent force unleashed by certain sinful human actions. The force defiles the sinner, the sanctuary and the land, even though the sinner is not ritually impure and does not ritually defile ... yet the sinner is seen as morally impure.[312]

It is interesting to note that, although moral impurity defiles the sanctuary, the sinner is not excluded from the sanctuary because he is not ritually defiled. Klawans gets around this seemingly anomalous situation by suggesting that moral defilement is an all-pervading influence that can operate even from afar, but its effect is not such that it enters the sanctuary along with the sinner himself. However, neither Klawans nor the biblical texts themselves offer any

---

306 Murder was seen as a moral impurity but clearly not as a ritual impurity because murderers were admitted to the sanctuary; see: A. Buchler, *Studies in Sin and Atonement in the Rabbinic Literature of the First Century* (London: Oxford University Press, 1928), 235.
307 And, although this is not formally stated, necromancy and the somewhat esoteric sin of Molech worship.
308 Lev 18:24-25; Ezek 36:17; Lev 20:3; Ezek 5:11, Lev 18:28; Ezek 36:19.
309 See below.
310 Liddell and Scott, *Greek English Lexicon*, 1132; Muraoka, *A Greek-English Lexicon of the Septuagint*, 462; Bauer et al., *A Greek-English Lexicon of the New Testament*, 650.
311 Kittel, Friedrich, and Pitkin, *TDNT*, Vol. IV, 646. Robert Parker, *Miasma: Pollution and Purification in Early Greek Religion* (Oxford: Clarendon, 1983), 104-125.
312 Klawans, *Impurity and Sin in Ancient Judaism*, 29.

explanation as to *why* this should be so. Unfortunately, the repeated failing of the biblical authors to concern themselves with answering the questions "*how?*" and "*why?*" is a recurrent, major problem for scholars in this field.

Moral impurity, according to Klawans, degrades the status of both individual and land, and this degradation is not easily purged. There is nothing in the Holiness Code to direct how this might be done. Nor is it clear if there is a hierarchy of moral impurities and of consequences to match. It must, therefore, be supposed that, in the case of the sinner, he must retain his moral impurity and degradation throughout the remainder of his life or suffer the penalty of כרת. Likewise, the land retains its polluted state. However, the Day of Atonement ritual does effectively purge the sanctuary and its environs so that they can be used again.

Defilement of the Land — הארץ

Most modern authors agree with Klawans that whereas ritual impurity is never conveyed to, or contracted from the land, the obligatory end-point of moral impurity (sexual sins, idolatry, bloodshed, apostasy, necromancy, and Molech-worship), as far as the Levitical laws were concerned, was a long-lasting, non-contagious, defilement and pollution of the land (הארץ) and of the sanctuary of God. This idea persisted throughout the exile and into the rabbinic period.[313] However, there is a degree of unclarity about what precisely this means. Some authors consider that once the land becomes defiled by moral impurity, God departs from it and so leaves the population of Israel in metaphorical exile *in situ*. A more widely held view is that once the land has become defiled, the people are, literally, expelled from the land into exile.

ותטמא הארץ ואפקד עונה עליה ותקא הארץ את־ישביה

> And the land is defiled: therefore I do visit the iniquity thereof upon it, and the land vomiteth out her inhabitants. (Lev 18:25)

This view, of course, has served a useful purpose in that it has been used to justify the Exodus—a return from previous oppression to a land vacated by sinners as a punishment by God. The Babylonian exile itself—undoubtedly, in the eyes of the prophets—was brought about by moral impurity. The philosophy underlying the Israelites' claim of a right to possess the land of Israel, which God protects as his own, stems from the idea that it was the Israelites' god Yahweh who dispossessed the original inhabitants of this land as a punishment for their misdeeds and sinfulness:

---

313 Buchler, *Studies in Sin and Atonement*, 216–7; Klawans, *Impurity and Sin in Ancient Judaism*, 27. Frymer-Kensky, "Pollution, Purification and Purgation," 406–9.

לא בצדקתך ובישר לבבך אתה בא לרשת את־ארצם כי ברשעת הגוים האלה יהוה אלהיך מורישם מפניך ולמען הקים את־הדבר אשר נשבע יהוה לאבתיך לאברהם ליצחק וליעקב

> Not for thy righteousness, or for the uprightness of thine heart, dost thou go in to possess their land: but for the wickedness of these nations the Lord thy God doth drive them out from before thee, and that he may establish the word which the Lord sware unto thy fathers, to Abraham, to Isaac, and to Jacob. (Deut 9:5)

The Israelites' right of occupation of הארץ is, therefore, not contingent upon *their* past behaviour but results from God's punishing the misbehaviour of former occupants. The Israelites have yet to earn and justify in the eyes of God, this right of occupation, for themselves.

By the time of the prophets, Israel is seen to have become fully polluted by the actions of the people and, in particular, by the actions of their kings. Israel is down-trodden by bloody footprints (עקבה מדם—Hos 6:8); Judah is beset with violence (חמס—Ezek 8:17); Jerusalem is described by Isaiah in colourful terms (איכה היתה לזונה קריה—Isa 1:21) as being a harlot: an unhygienic, menstruous woman (טמאתה בשוליה—Lam 1:9; and היתה ירושלם לנדה ביניהם—Lam 1:17). The land and the nation as a whole have become invested by the ultimate imagery of squalor, degradation, dereliction, depravity, and defilement. It has become regarded in the way that a "leper" is seen: ostracized and despised, sitting apart and alone, wanton and unwanted, (איכה ישבה בדד העיר—Lam 1:1).

Moral Impurity as Metaphor; Ritual Impurity as Reality

A number of scholars have, over the years, come to regard the notion of moral impurity as figurative or metaphorical. Prominent among these is Neusner[314] but Milgrom[315] and Wright[316] have both entertained the possibility and discussed it at some length. Klawans, however, is sceptical. In the first place, he says that, "none of the scholars ... states clearly what is meant by the terms 'metaphorical' or 'figurative'". The problem, for Klawans, is that the use of figurative or metaphorical language must obligatorily require the transference of words or phrases that are applicable literally, onto a context where they may not be applicable literally. Klawans's definition of metaphor is therefore, language that is "a secondary, non-literal (or non-technical) usage that is informed by the prior, literal usage of the language in question." Of metaphor in the present context, he goes on to say, "What it boils down to is that when purity language is used metaphorically, then no real defilement of purification is actually taking place."

---

[314] Neusner, The Idea of Purity in Ancient Judaism.
[315] Milgrom, *Leviticus: A New Translation*, Vol. 1, 37.
[316] Wright, "The Spectrum of Priestly Impurity," 163.

Klawans is unable to see any rationale for considering moral impurity to be any less real—and therefore metaphorical—than ritual impurity. He cites the following passage (Lev 18:24) that has been widely used as a reason for postulating a metaphorical basis for moral impurity:

אל־תטמאו בכל־אלה כי בכל־אלה נטמאו הגוים אשר־אני משלח מפניכם

> Defile not ye yourselves in any of these things: for in all these the nations are defiled which I cast out from before you: (Lev 18:24)

The consequence of this was, of course, that the land was defiled (Lev 18:25). Klawans argues that it is difficult to see how this *cannot* be taken literally because self-defilement by doing sinful things is entirely plausible and if that is so, why should not defilement of nation and land likewise, be literally possible? Moreover, Klawans argues that if, by the definitions provided by the Holiness Code, the land of Israel is Yahweh's habitation, then it must be a holy place. And, if it is holy it is, *de facto,* capable of being defiled.

ולא תטמא את־הארץ אשר אתם ישבים בה אשר אני שכן בתוכה כי אני יהוה שכן בתוך בני ישראל

> And thou shalt not defile the land which ye inhabit, in the midst of which I dwell: for I the Lord dwell in the midst of the children of Israel. (Num 35:34)

Klawans considers that the entire concept of impurity in the context of sin is to be understood as standing in opposition to holiness. This was a view first suggested a century ago by D. Z. Hoffmann. If this idea is correct, there is no reason why Lev 18:24–30 cannot be interpreted literally and there is no need for metaphor—sexual misdeeds, by their intrinsic opposition to holiness, defile what is holy and that includes the land. Moreover, this cannot be ritual defilement because it is a permanent and non-contagious falling-off of status.

Although Klawans has elsewhere[317] made the point that, whereas later rabbinical authors saw ritual impurity as *halakhah* and moral impurity as *aggadah,* the latter may nevertheless be seen to also have practical legal implications. While the ritually impure person is legally obliged to eschew sacred things and places, the morally impure individual may (in extremis) face the prospect of capital punishment, or at very least (if female) significant diminution of marriage prospects. The land, in its own way, is legally affected by exile when banishment of its inhabitants is imposed in punishment for moral sin. There is really no need here for metaphor or figurative language. It is the opinion of the present author that Klawans makes this case well and although there is undoubtedly a very considerable amount of metaphorical language in the Hebrew Bible, this is not an example. Klawans, however, does not help his own argument when he re-

---

[317] Klawans, *Impurity and Sin in Ancient Judaism*, 160.

introduces the word *contagion* into the melting-pot in an altogether new context. He had previously made the categorical statement that *contagion* is a function only of ritual impurity: not of moral impurity. He now ends his argument against the metaphorical and figurative nature of moral impurity with the sentence: "Though the sources and modes of transfer of moral and ritual impurity differ, we are dealing, nonetheless, with two analogous perceptions of *contagion,* each of which brings about effects of legal and social consequence." Klawans does not make clear the precise nature of his analogy,[318] which is unhelpful[319] for it is the non-analogical social and legal consequences of moral impurity that most effectively militate against any metaphorical origin.

It is interesting to note that, in contrast to his view on impurity itself, Klawans appears to regard sacrifice—the antidote for impurity—as a metaphor. Klawans sees the process of sacrifice as a metaphor for the act of *imitatio Dei*.[320] An important example of this is to be found in the significance attached to *shepherding* in biblical narrative. The ritualistic elements of raising and caring for livestock as a prelude to the sacrificial process can be seen as a metaphorical *imitatio Dei* applicable to the notion of God's caring for the whole people of Israel. Anderson[321] has suggested six ritualistic steps in the practical side of this process:

1. Bringing the animal to the sanctuary.
2. Laying hands on the animal.
3. Slaughter and dismemberment.
4. Scattering/tossing/sprinkling the blood.
5. Burning the animal.
6. Disposal of the remains.

Other authors have variously suggested different numbers of steps though the differences are largely in minor detail. Surprisingly, all of these omit the actual process of ritual purification and say nothing of the method of selection of the specific animal. In Klawans's view, this is, once again analogical. The sacrifice and/or the priest are seen in the role of God and sacrificial animals taken from the flock are seen in the role of the people. The sacrificial ritual thereby plays-out what "ought to be" in God's society and as such qualifies as *imitatio Dei*. It has been suggested that Klawans's metaphorical interpretation of sacrifice is an oversimplification: it certainly presents something of a "chicken-and-egg" dilemma. Klawans does not make it entirely clear if he believes the process of ritual sacrifice and the *mores* attendant upon it were set up *de novo* by the Israelites in order that, by providing an *imitatio Dei* for themselves from within

---

[318] See for an informative, somewhat mathematical, account of analogies, E. L. Mascall, *Existence and Analogy* (London: Longmans, Green and Co, 1949).
[319] The matter of "contagion" will be discussed in chapter 8.
[320] Klawans, *Purity, Sacrifice, and the Temple,* 61.
[321] Anderson, *Sin: A History.*

their own society, they might, thereby, become more holy. Alternatively, is *imitatio Dei* simply a retrospectory construct of modern exegetes used, in this instance by Klawans,[322] to justify *post hoc* his notion that ritual sacrifice was symbolic?

A second viewpoint held by Klawans on the matter of ritual sacrifice as metaphor is that it functions as a symbolic means of attracting and maintaining the divine presence both within the sanctuary and, by extension, within the populace.[323] In this context, Klawans believes the daily burnt-offering sacrifice cannot be an expiatory process as has been widely held. Daily sacrifice is neither expiatory nor apotropaeic but is symbolic and there to maintain God's presence in a renewable relationship that is constantly at risk of becoming fractured by sin.

The above is a brief attempt to review the biblical concept of purity and impurity and modern opinion thereon. While the output from commentators is helpful in understanding the importance of the purity laws, it must always be remembered that these, often complex, systems of classification are all modern constructs. We cannot know if the priests operated a systematic and practical sub-classification of impurity and pollution, nor whether, if such were the case, it would have been along the lines of the sub-classifications proposed by these modern authors.

Some permutation of the Douglas/Turner anthropological idea of *wholeness* as the prerequisite for maintaining purity (and thereby holiness) offers a possible basis for priest-mediated ritual impurity but an exact priestly definition of *wholeness* remains elusive. It could be argued that the Douglas/Turner hypothesis sees *wholeness* as the absence of *category violation*—the possession of untypical (and therefore undesirable) physical attributes. The question immediately arises as to the nature and number of such categories and the process by which they have been defined. This idea does not go far enough because it does not explain why it is only certain atypicalities—צרעת, זוב the two contagious afflictions and blemishes that specifically affect the body surface and the genitals—that qualify as appropriate category violaters and precipitants of impurity through unwholeness.

Those proponents of a taxonomical approach to impurity offer a detailed and useful categorization of grades of impurity but no explanation as to a specific cause of a loss of *sacramental hygiene* such that sacred objects and places are put at risk of defilement. We are given by these authors a clear effect but no mechanism of cause. This admittedly does not rule out an infraction of wholeness by category violation as in the Douglas/Turner model, but it seems unlikely that such an important mechanism would have been tacitly assumed.

---

322 And, of course, Mary Douglas.
323 Klawans, *Purity, Sacrifice, and the Temple*, 68.

As a working hypothesis for causation in ritual impurity, the Douglas/Turner model remains the best we have.

Turning from cause to effect, it is appropriate, now to investigate specifically those categories—צרעת, זוב, blemish and contagiousness—that have been implicated in causing unwholeness/ritual impurity and thereby unholiness. However, before doing so, it is necessary to consider—from a medical point of view—the nature and origin of the textual material upon which any such analysis must, ultimately, be based.

Chapter 6

THE "LEPROSY" PROBLEM

In the King James Bible (Authorized Version or KJV), the word "leprosy"—where the present-day spelling "leprosy" had been carried over from Tyndale[324]—occurs thirty-nine times.[325] Of these thirty-nine, only four occurrences each of "leprosy" and "leper" are in the New Testament. Leprosy as we know it today—Hansen's disease (HD)—had come to England with the returning crusaders and persisted to a variable extent into the nineteenth century. Milton,[326] writing in 1667 was obviously familiar with the idea of segregating lepers into "lazar-houses" when he wrote:

> *Immediately a place*
> *Before his eyes appeared, sad, noisome, dark*
> *A lazar-house it seemed, wherein were laid*
> *Numbers of all diseased—all maladies.*

And Milton was, perhaps unwittingly, making the point that the "lepers" in the lazar-house were, most likely, suffering from a congeries of afflictions rather than any specific disease. Some of them would, undoubtedly, have had Hansen's disease, called *Elephantiasis Graecorum* (*EG*) in earlier times. By the Middle Ages[327] leprosy had become a disease that was greatly feared because of the disfigurement that followed from chronic infection and also because of its supposed contagion[328] which, in fact is not great at all. Neither of these properties figures in accounts of "leprosy" from biblical and other textual sources from the Ancient Near East (ANE): it is whiteness and scaliness that are the cardinal signs there. This difference calls into question the nature of "biblical leprosy", צרעת in Hebrew and λέπρα in Greek. It has long been held both by biblical scholars and medical writers alike that these words, (Hebrew צרעת and Greek λέπρα) though customarily translated into English as "*leprosy*" in both biblical texts and parabiblical writings do not necessarily refer to Hansen's disease (HD). Thus, the following relationship applies:

---

[324] W. Tyndale, *The New Testament*, Tyndale's 1526 Edition with Original Spelling (London: British Library, 2003). See also Coverdale (1535) and Wyclif (1395).
[325] "Leper" 17, "lepers" 6 and "leprous" 6 times.
[326] Milton, *Paradise Lost* (1667) Book xi, 477
[327] F. O. Touati, "Contagion and Leprosy: Myth, Ideas and Evolution in Medieval Minds and Societies," in *Contagion, Perspectives in Pre-modern Societies*, ed. L. I. Wujastyk and D. Conrad (Aldershot: Ashgate, 2000), 179–202.
[328] L. I. Wujastyk and D. Conrad, eds. *Contagion, Perspectives in Pre-modern Societies* (Aldershot, Hampshire: Ashgate Publishing Ltd, 2000).

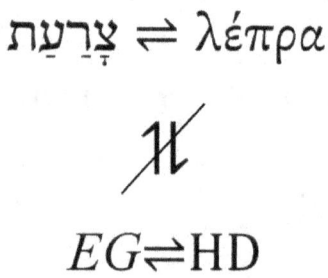

BACKGROUND

There is an extensive bibliography on the subject of *"Biblical leprosy".*[329] References from before 1873, when Hansen characterized the *Mycobacterium leprae,* are largely unhelpful, and there is confusion about what was meant by the various terms צָרַעַת, λέπρα, *Elephantiasis Graecorum* and *leprosy*. After Hansen's work, *"leprosy"* acquired a specific aetiology and symptomatology—within the medical world but not necessarily outside it—as the eponymous *"Hansen's disease".* This cast significant doubt about the nature of "biblical leprosy" since the symptoms and signs and course of the "disease" reported in texts from the Bible and Ancient Near Eastern literature, were quite different from those of Hansen's disease.

While we can be fairly certain that צָרַעַת/λέπρα was *not* Hansen's disease,[330] attempts to characterize exactly what צָרַעַת/λέπρα was have been far from fruitful.

---

[329] Johs G. Andersen, "Leprosy in Translations of the Bible," *Bible Translator (Ap, O Practical Papers)* 31, no. 2 (1980): 207–12; B. Bafverstedt, "Dermatological and Venereal Diseases Told About in the Bible," *Lakartidningen* 68, no. 34 (1971): 3793–802; R. A. Baillie and E. E. Baillie, "Biblical Leprosy as Compared to Present-day Leprosy," *South. Med. J.* 75, no. 7 (1982): 855–57; D. A. Bennahum, "Psoriasis, Leprosy and the Dead Sea Valley," *Korot* 9, no. 1–2 (1985): 86–89; R. Bennett, *Diseases of the Bible* (Oxford: Oxford University Press, 1891); G. Ceccarelli, "Leprosy in the Bible," *Minerva Med.* 85, no. 4 (1994): 197–201; R. G. Cochrane, "In Defense of the Name 'Leprosy'", *Int.J.Lepr.Other Mycobact.Dis.* 38, no. 2 (1970): 207–09; R. G. Cochrane, "Biblical Leprosy," *Bible Translator (Ap, O Practical Papers)* 12, no. 4 (1961): 202–03; Claudine Dauphin, "Leprosy, Lust and Lice: Health and Hygiene in Byzantine Palestine," *Bulletin of the Anglo-Israel Archaeological Society* 15 (1996): 55–80; M. L. Davies and T. A. Davies, "Biblical Leprosy: A Comedy of Errors," *J.R.Soc.Med.* 82, no. 10 (1989): 622–23; James Arthur Diamond, "Maimonides on Leprosy: Illness as Contemplative Metaphor," *Jewish Quarterly Review* 96, no. 1 (2006): 95–122; Barbara Doolan Heins, "From Leprosy to Shalom and Back Again: A Discourse Analysis of 2 Kings 5," *OPTAT* 2, no. 1 (1988): 20–33; A. R. Freilich, "Tzaraat—'Biblical Leprosy'," *J.Am.Acad.Dermatol.* 6, no. 1 (1982): 131–34; T. Gejrot, "Leprosy in the Bible: Incorrect Translation," *Lakartidningen* 96, no. 12 (1999): 1463; F. S. Glickman, "Lepra, Psora, Psoriasis," *J.Am.Acad.Dermatol.* 14, no. 5 Pt 1 (1986): 863–66; R. M. Heller, T. W. Heller, and J. M. Sasson, "Mold: 'tsara'at,' Leviticus, and the History of a Confusion," *Perspect.Biol.Med.* 46, no. 4 (2003): 588–91; Gilbert Lewis, "A Lesson from Leviticus: Leprosy," *Man* 22, no. 4 (1987): 593–612; K. Liddell, "Skin Disease in Antiquity," *Clin.Med.* 6, no. 1 (2006): 81–86; E. W. Massey, "Leprosy: Biblical Opprobrium?," *South.Med.J.* 71, no. 10 (1978): 1294–95; J. D. McCaughey, "The Leper," *Med.J.Aust.* 1, no. 13 (1975): 425–26; Kenneth V. Mull and Carolyn Sandquist Mull, "Biblical Leprosy: Is it Really?," *Bible Review* 8, no. 2 (1992): 32; Eugene Albert Nida, "The Translation of 'Leprosy': A Brief Contribution to the Discussion," *Bible Translator (Ap, O Practical Papers)* 11, no. 2 (1960): 80–81; M. Nuchtern, "['And the Skin Turned White as Snow...' On Skin Diseases and Leprosy in the Bible]," *Dtsch.Krankenpflegez* 42, no. 7 (1989): 425–29; John J. Pilch, "Biblical Leprosy and Body Symbolism," *Biblical Theology Bulletin* 11 (1981): 108–13; O. K. Skinsnes, "Leprosy and the New English Bible," *Int.J.Lepr.Other Mycobact.Dis.* 38, no. 3 (1970): 310–12; V. Sticht-Groh and G. Bretzel, "[Leprosy: Current Aspects of a Disease from Biblical Times]," *Immun.Infekt.* 23, no. 6 (1995): 216–21; J. L. Swellengrebel, "'Leprosy' and the Bible: The Translation of tsara'ath and lepra," *Bible Translator (Ap, O Practical Papers)* 11, no. 2 (1960): 69–80; John Todd, "Leprosy, Biblical and Mediaeval," *Modern Churchman* 34, no. 4–6 (1944): 129–37; W. W. Weed, "Biblical Leprosy," *J.Am.Acad.Dermatol.* 29, no. 6 (1993): 1058–59.

[330] There is a very small minority who dispute this—see chapters 2 and 3.

The 'Leprosy' Problem

The near non-existence or rudimentary nature, in the ANE of medical practice in the modern sense is, however only partly to blame for this. After all, biblical and other ANE texts are quite specific in their descriptions of physical signs such as whiteness and scaliness. The problem, therefore is most likely to be one of translation.

Version	צרעת in Lev 13:2
Authorized (KJV) 1611	leprosy
Revised (ERV) 1885	leprosy
Revised Standard (RSV) 1952	a leprous disease
New Revised Standard (NRSV) 1989	a leprous disease
New English Bible (NEB) 1970	a malignant skin disease
Revised English Bible (REB) 1989	a virulent skin disease
Jewish Publication Society (JPS) 1917	leprosy
American Standard Version (ASV) 1901	leprosy
Geneva Bible (GNV) 1559	leprosie
Bible in Basic English (BBE) 1949	the disease of a leper
Christian Standard Bible (CSB) 2004	a disease on the skin of his body
Douay- Rheims (DRB) 1609	leprosy
New American Bible (NAB) 1991	leprosy
New International (NIV) 1984	an infectious skin disease
New Jerusalem (NJB) 1985	a contagious skin disease
New King James (NKJ) 1982	a leprous sore
New English Translation (NET) 2004	a diseased infection

The table above shows how, taking a single verse (Lev 13:2) as an example, the Hebrew word צרעת and the Greek λέπρα have been translated into English in editions of the Bible that are in common use. It is obvious that the majority of translators have chosen to retain the word "leprosy" in one form or another and it is this choice that has caused the confusion. The meaning of the Hebrew word צרעת is uncertain primarily because there is no textual corroborative evidence as to its meaning. Nevertheless, the translators of the Septuagint (LXX) faithfully rendered צרעת as λέπρα and since there is a good etymology to associate λέπ* derivatives with scaliness, it seems likely that whatever "biblical leprosy" was, it had an element of scaliness. For this reason, Milgrom has consistently chosen to use the term "*scale-disease*" throughout his work.[331] The wisdom of this choice is undoubted in respect of the Hebrew Bible and the Septuagint. However, a problem seems to have arisen for translators into English who operated after the arrival of what was called "leprosy" and what was now undoubtedly Hansen's disease brought to England by the returning crusaders. We must ask why this new disease became so firmly identified as the צרעת/λέπρα of biblical writings. A likely possibility is that it may simply have been mistaken symptomatology at a time when medical practice was far from developed. However, for any medieval institution, committed to keeping a society in religious and social thraldom in the face of an attitude of *oderint dum metuant*, a ghastly disfiguring disease, especially if it had a supposed biblical provenance was enormously helpful in the day-to-day business of preserving a climate of fear and for dispensing damnation.

Over the years many authors have looked at the problem of "biblical leprosy", some with quasi-medical and some with doctrinal axes to grind but few, sadly, have taken a disinterested, scientific view. Before Hansen's work, of course, it would have been impossible to rule out true leprosy but it is nevertheless surprising and disappointing that no early authors seem to have noticed the differences between biblical and medieval "leprosy". After Hansen's work, HD became clearly identifiable with the *Elephantiasis Graecorum* (*EG*) of Hellenic and Roman times but not with צרעת/λέπρα, and doubts began to emerge as to the correspondence of true leprosy with the biblical affliction. We can, today, only give credence to the relatively few studies since this time[332] which have been summarized and discussed by Browne[333] in his excellent yet inconclusive study, whixh regrettably does not consider the priestly *Weltanschauung* based in ritual, and furthermore lacks the benefit of later exegetical work such as that of Milgrom.

Hansen's Disease

Leprosy, nowadays called Hansen's disease (HD), is a chronic inflammatory disease caused by the bacillus *Mycobacterium leprae*.[334] It exhibits a wide spectrum of symptoms and signs. In "tuberculoid" leprosy localized lesions containing scant numbers of bacilli are restricted to the skin and peripheral nerve in which they cause thickening. In "lepromatous" leprosy there is a

---

[331] Milgrom, *Leviticus: A Continental Commentary*; Milgrom, *Leviticus: A New Translation*.
[332] See footnote above.
[333] S. G. Browne, "Some Aspects of the History of Leprosy: The Leprosie of Yesterday," *Proc.R.Soc.Med.* 68, no. 8 (1975): 485–93; Stanley G. Browne, "'Leprosy' in the New English Bible," *Bible Translator (Ja, Jl Technical Papers)* 22, no. 1 (1971): 45–46; S. G. Browne, "Was Leprosy Common in Palestine in New Testament Times?," *Zambia Nurse J.* 4, no. 3 (1970): 10–11; S. G. Browne, *Leprosy in the Bible* (London: Christian Medical Fellowship Publications, 1970).
[334] M. F. R. Waters, "Leprosy, (Hansen's Disease)," in *Oxford Textbook of Medicine*, ed. D. J. Weatherall et al. (Oxford: Oxford University Press, 1989).

generalized bacteraemia and large numbers of bacilli are to be found in lesions in skin, peripheral nerve, upper respiratory tract, reticulo-endothelial system, eyes, bone, and testes. The kidneys, heart, lungs, and central nervous system are largely spared. It is the thickening of the peripheral nerves that causes the pachydermatous appearance and confers the cardinal sign of leprosy: anaesthesia. This may be lead to secondary mechanical and/or thermal tissue damage causing the characteristic disfigurement.

Aetiology

In 1873 G. A. Hansen in Bergen, Norway, demonstrated the existence of the bacillus *Mycobacterium leprae*[335] as a result of advances made in laboratory staining techniques. At this time the ability to culture living bacteria on agar plates was becoming established, along with histopathological techniques for staining tissues. The *haematoxylin–eosin* method of staining tissue samples and Leishmann's stain for blood smears revolutionized diagnosis. More sophisticated stains and the technique of vital staining and differential staining soon followed. The Ziehl–Neelsen "Acid-Fast" staining technique[336] was a development which led also to the characterization of a group of bacteria named *Mycobacteria* which included *Mycobacterium leprae* and *Mycobacterium tuberculosis*.

The realization that bacteria might be cultured from tissue samples, smears, blood etc. taken from infected patients was another important step forward which is seemingly obvious today.

In 2008 a variant form *Mycobacterium lepromatosis* was isolated from a fatal case of lepromatous leprosy and is now recognized as a second causative agent alongside *M leprae*.

Diagnosis

Diagnosis of leprosy is based on the presence of one or more of three cardinal signs and this method has been shown to be associated with a diagnostic success rate of >95%. The three signs are:

- Hypopigmented or reddish patches with demonstrable loss of sensation.
- Thickened peripheral nerves.

---

[335] G. H. A. Hansen, "Undersøgelser Angående Spedalskhedens Årsager [Investigations Concerning the Etiology of Leprosy]," *Norsk Mag. Laegervidenskaben* 4 (1874): 1–88; S. P. Impey, *Handbook on Leprosy* (Philadelphia: P. Blakiston, Son & Co, 1896).
[336] In contrast to most other bacteria, the high molecular weight lipid capsules of acid-fast organisms take up carbolfuchsin and resist decolorization by acids.

- Acid-fast bacilli, (*M leprae*), in skin smears or biopsy specimens.[337]

Laboratory Studies

The only known animal reservoir for leprosy is the nine-banded armadillo and consequently laboratory studies of the disease have been difficult and slow.

M leprae cannot be grown *in vitro* but the footpads of certain mice and the Guinea-pig though not natural reservoirs, allow for low-yield growth and so have been used in the studies both of the disease and its treatment. These experimental systems have helped greatly to shed light upon the natural history of mycobacterial conditions.

The Ziehl–Neelsen stain made possible the study of the two widespread and serious mycobacterial diseases, tuberculosis and leprosy, and led ultimately to cures for them both.[338]

Re-naming

Leprosy is now "officially" called "Hansen's disease" (or occasionally the ugly "Hanseniasis") by the World Health Organization (WHO). It is not entirely clear whether this was in recognition of Hansen's pioneering work or as an attempt to mitigate the persisting stigma of "biblical leprosy".[339] Whatever the case renaming has not been entirely successful and the term "leprosy" is still used widely and has proved as resistant as the disease.

Epidemiology

Incidence and prevalence

According to official reports from the WHO,[340] that monitors the HD throughout the world in 5 WHO regions incorporating 103 countries, the global registered prevalence of leprosy at the end of 2013 was 180,618 cases. In 2013, 215,656 new cases were reported globally. This compares with 232,857 new cases in in 2012 and 226,626 in 2011.

The number of new cases indicates the degree of continued transmission of infection in the community. A total of 13 countries reported zero cases in 2013; 206,107 (96%) of new cases of HD were reported from 14 countries and only these 14 countries reported more than 1000 new cases in 2013. This compares with only 4% of new cases from the rest of the world.

---

337 Usually skin: by means of Wade's 'scraped incision' technique.
338 In the sense of bactericidal treatment with antibiotics. However, the effects of these diseases, especially if allowed to become chronic before treatment begins, are still very serious and debilitating.
339 Interestingly, at a time when eponymous naming of diseases is generally discouraged.
340 WHO Factsheet No 101.

Pockets of high endemicity remain in: Angola, Bangladesh, Brazil, People's Republic of China, Democratic Republic of Congo, Ethiopia, India, Indonesia, Madagascar, Mozambique, Myanmar, Nepal, Nigeria, Philippines, South Sudan, Sri Lanka, Sudan, and the United Republic of Tanzania.

Though today the disease seldom kills, its chronicity causes serious disability. It is predominantly associated with overcrowding and a low standard of living. *M leprae* is a bacterium of extremely low infectivity and so relatively difficult to pass on. This low infectivity is in clear contradistinction to what is held to be the virulent contagion of צרעת in the Hebrew Bible.

Pathology

Nature of the Disease

The target organ for invading *M leprae* is the endoneurium of peripheral nerve[341]. This is normally an "immunologically protected site" where bacilli are rapidly engulfed by Schwann cells. The process of "delayed hypersensitivity" also seen in tuberculosis anc characteristic of mycobacterial diseases, ensues and its progress is dependent on and proportional to the antigen-load and therefore bacterial numbers. It is the delayed-hypersensitivity response that damages cells and produces the wide-ranging symptoms and signs which manifest the disease.[342] It should be emphasized, however, that the symptoms and signs of HD are very non-uniform. This has led to an attempt to classify the disease as a spectrum of conditions with the "tuberculoid" disease at one end and the "lepromatous" disease at the other:

$$TT \rightleftharpoons BT \rightleftharpoons BB \rightleftharpoons BL \rightleftharpoons LL$$

The abbreviations stand for "tuberculoid leprosy", "borderline tuberculoid leprosy", "borderline leprosy", "borderline lepromatous leprosy" and "lepromatous leprosy" respectively. The size of the lettering in the above is supposed to represent the severity which increases towards either end of the spectrum though the lepromatous forms are always more severe than the equivalent tuberculoid forms.

Physical Symptoms and Signs

Because of its heterogeneity it is extremely difficult to make the diagnosis of HD from physical signs and symptoms. This explains why the accurate diagnosis of

---

[341] T. R. Swift and T. D. Sabin, "Leprous Neuritis," in *Clinical Neurology*, ed. M. Swash and J. Oxbury (Edinburgh: Churchill Livingstone, 1991).
[342] As in the related disease tuberculosis caused by M tuberculosis. However the "caseation" typical of tuberculosis does not occur in leprosy.

leprosy could not be made with any certainty before the work of Hansen characterized the causative agent.

One of the most obvious and prominent consequences of HD is leprotic involvement of the skin so that it takes on the appearance of an erythematous pachydermatous thickening. This is the "elephantiasis" of *Elephantiasis Graecorum*. It is brought about initially by an increase in capillary permeability to produce oedema as part of the inflammatory reaction to the presence of *M leprae*. This is followed by infiltration by histiocytes and other inflammatory cells. The skin and its contained peripheral nerves become scarred, anaesthetic, and grossly hyperplastic and so may be further damaged by abrasion, heat, and sunburn. Secondary bacterial infection may supervene. Crucially, none of these reactions involves scaliness or whiteness.

Treatment

Hansen's disease, though characterized in the 19th century remained relatively unbtreatable until the 1940s with the development of the drug dapsone, which arrested the disease. Treatment had to be life-long and this presented problems, particularly in migrant populations. In the 1960s, *M. leprae* started to develop resistance to dapsone. At about this time the important notion of multidrug therapy (MDT) as a means of obverting resistance to antibiotics was formulated and this led to the use of MDT in the form of triple-therapy using dapsone, rifampicin, and clofazimine.[343]

Although the bacterial infection *per se* can be controlled and eradicated with MDT, the changes to the skin and peripheral nerves are irreversible. Surgical procedures have been devised to assist with restoration of function and offer variable success.[344] The disease remains a major cause of morbidity, disfigurement, and disability.[345]

ELEPHANTIASIS GRAECORUM

Elephantiasis Graecorum (*EG*), was the name given in the Ancient World to what is today recognized as true leprosy or Hansen's disease (HD) as it existed in the Greek and Latin-speaking World.[346] Its name distinguished it from another prevalent disease, *Elephantiasis Arabum*[347] which was unrelated except in some appearances and corresponded to the "elephantiasis" of the modern world. This, properly known as Bancroftian filariasis, is a chronic obstructive

---

[343] A parallel use of MDT for tuberculosis involved the drugs streptomycin, rifampicin, and isoniazid.
[344] M. A. Glasby, S. Evans, and C. L. H. Huang, "Nerve Regeneration Through Treated Muscle Grafts During Experimental Treatment with Antileprotic Drugs," *Neuro-Orthopedics* 8 (1989): 1–7; J. H. Pereira et al., "Nerve Repair by Denatured Muscle Autografts Promotes Sustained Sensory Recovery in Leprosy," *Journal of Bone and Joint Surgery* 90-B (2007): 220–24.
[345] Liddell, "Skin Disease in Antiquity."
[346] R. Liveing, *Elephantiasis Graecorum or True Leprosy* (London: Spottiswoode & Co, 1872).
[347] Also known as "Barbadoes [sic] Leg" (Wytton-Davies 1890)

The 'Leprosy' Problem

disease of lymphatic vessels caused by a parasitic nematode.[348] Modern usage also adopts the term "elephantiasis" to describe any gross swelling of a limb such as may follow radiotherapy. We should note, however, that the allusion to elephants derives not from the notion of oversize legs but from that of thick(ened) skin.

It is generally supposed (although there been some debate on the matter) that *Elephantiasis Graecorum* did not exist in the Ancient Near East (ANE) before the return of Alexander the Great from his Indus Valley campaign of 325/324 BCE. His biographers, Arrian and Plutarch, offer no help in this respect.[349]

Evidence for the existence of *EG*⇌HD in ancient Egypt has sometimes been inferred from the Ebers Papyrus, dating from around 1550 BCE,[350] Translations of the chapter on "Skin Diseases" mention "leprous spots"[351] but the Egyptian words ꜥJŏꜥ◯ (*wbnw* = wound) and 𓈖𓏏 (*ḥꜣyt* = disease) are very nonspecific, although the single glyph[352] ◯ may be translated as "pustule".[353] The Edwin Smith Papyrus,[354] the other major Egyptian "medical" papyrus, makes no mention of any disease of this kind. Two Egyptian glyphs relating to the generality of skin diseases have also been identified in these papyri, they are, *"uashesh"* = a skin disease 𓆑𓈖𓏏 and *"nesit"* = a kind of skin disease 𓈖𓏏𓏭.

A minority of scholars has argued thus for *EG*⇌HD being present in Ancient Egypt; papyrologists and archaeologists well know the preservative qualities of the Egyptian sands and, were it there, might expect to find evidence of *EG*⇌HD among papyri, mummies or bone specimens; but this is not the case. Leprous individuals would, most likely, have been ostracised and buried separately outside the town and not considered for mummification. However, none has been found, and the overwhelming absence particularly of osteological evidence militates strongly against this view.[355]

There is no parallel controversy about the prevalence of *EG*⇌HD in India and especially in the Indus Valley. Sanskrit texts from before 1000 BCE,[356] and from around 600 BCE,[357] contain reports which are clearly of *EG*⇌HD. Several Sanskrit words have persisted and can be shown from their incidence in cognate Indo-

---

348 Filaria bancrofti.
349 Arrian, *The Anabasis of Alexander*, LCL; C. B. R. Pelling, *Plutarch and History* (Swansea: Classical Press of Wales, 2002); Plutarch, *Lives*, 11 vols., trans. B. Perrin (Cambridge, MA; London: Harvard University Press, 1989).
350 Bryan, *The Papyrus Ebers*.
351 This is how it is customarily translated, with little or no justification.
352 Gardiner's hieroglyphic number: aa20.
353 A. Gardiner, *Egyptian Grammar* (Oxford: Griffith Institute, Asmolean Museum, 1927).
354 Breasted, The *Edwin Smith Surgical Papyrus*.
355 Nevertheless Lieber is unwilling to rule this out (see chapter 7): E. Lieber, "Old Testament 'Leprosy', Contagion and Sin," in *Contagion, Perspectives in Pre-modern Societies*, ed. L. I. Wujastyk and D. Conrad (Aldershot: Ashgate, 2000).
356 M. Bloomfield, *Hymns of the Atharva Veda* (Whitefish, MT: Kessinger, 2004).
357 K. G. Zysk, *Religious Medicine: The History and Evolution of Indian Medicine* (Edison, NJ: Transaction, 1992).

European languages to refer to $EG{\rightleftharpoons}HD$. These words are: सिध्म [sidh-má] *adj.*= leprous. श्वित्र [svit-rá] *noun(m)* = leprosy. श्वेतकाकीय [sveta-kâk-îya] *adj* = resembling a white crow, *noun* = white leprosy; a*dj* = leprous. किलास [kil&asharp;s-a] *adj* = leprous; *n.* leprosy. कुष्ठ [kú-sh*tha*] *noun (f)* = leprosy.[358]

There is very clear archaeological evidence from skulls found in and around the Indus Valley that $EG{\rightleftharpoons}HD$ was prevalent as early as 2000 BCE.[359] In the lepromatous forms of HD there is a specific tendency towards thickening of the facial skin and nasal mucosa. This eventually causes erosion of the nasal cartilages and central maxilla to produce, in life, a characteristic "saddle-nose" deformity—*gangosa*. The eroded maxillary bone when preserved in skeletons is pathognomonic of $EG{\rightleftharpoons}HD$. Indeed, it is the *only* archaeological evidence of HD and although common in India is almost non-existent in Egyptian mummies[360] and in skeletons from the ANE before the Hellenic period. This point has been widely used to support the view that leprosy arrived there with Alexander's returning armies in ~325 BCE.[361] However, this conclusion does not take account of the possibility that lepers might not have enjoyed the same burial/mummification facilities as healthy individuals.

Robbins et al[359] have reported what must now be the earliest documented osteological evidence of $EG{\rightleftharpoons}HD$ from a site at Balathal, 40 km northeast of Udaipur in the state of Rajasthan. Archaeological correlation with pottery styles and radiocarbon (C^{14}) mass spectroscopy of the bones, associated wheat grains, and cow dung have allowed these specimens to be dated to ~2000 BCE. Osteopathological evidence for $EG{\rightleftharpoons}HD$ was seen in the nasal, maxillary, and mandibular erosion which is typical "leprous" gangosa[362]

The return of Alexander appears to have been the watershed for $EG{\rightleftharpoons}HD$ in the Ancient Near East. Alexander's troops, after his death in Babylon in 323 BCE, would have taken some time to migrate westwards and one must suppose that $EG{\rightleftharpoons}HD$ went with them. As tuberculosis was also unknown before this time in the ANE there would have been no resistance to mycobacterial infection and despite the relatively low infectivity of leprosy, its introduction into a population lacking resistance would have resulted in extensive and rapid spread.

---

358 M. Monier-Williams, *A Sanskrit-English Dictionary* (Oxford: Oxford University Press, 1899).
359 G. Robbins et al., *Ancient Skeletal Evidence for Leprosy in India (2000BC)* (5) (www.plosone.org, 2009 [cited 4]); available from www.plosone.org.
360 Though Josephus citing Manetho says that leprous native Egyptians were "banished from the land": Josephus, "Contra Apionem, 1:229" in *Josephus Collected Works*, 13 vols., trans. H. St. J. Thackeray and L. Feldman; also M. Stern, ed., *Greek and Latin Authors on Jews and Judaism*, Vol. 1 (Jerusalem: Israel Academy of Sciences and Humanities, 1974), 78–84. Diodorus writing in the first century bce makes the same point: Stern, ed., *Greek and Latin Authors on Jews and Judaism*, 182.
361 See chapter 3.
362 Robbins et al., *Ancient Skeletal Evidence for Leprosy in India (2000BC)*. See also chapter 2.

By the second century BCE when the Romans had a presence in Egypt, *EG⇌HD* had arrived there.[363] One should bear in mind that a date of 132 BCE has been suggested for completion of the Septuagint (LXX) and thus there is confusion about what λέπρα might mean there.

In common with the ANE, *EG⇌HD* does not appear to have existed in the pre-Hellenic (Classical) world. Of two major works on the ANE and the Classical World, neither mentions the disease.[364] Liddell and Scott's Lexicon[365] contains no *definienda* for ἐλεφ* other than those relating to "elephants" or "ivory". Λέπρα is defined in exactly the way one might expect for צרעת and refers to scaly diseases, mould on leather and plastered walls and upon wine and vinegar. Hippocrates (*c.* 460–370 BCE) does not use the word ἐλέφαντια at all. He does, however, use λέπρα[366] a number of times and interestingly, almost every reference includes words for both scaliness and whiteness together, e.g. ἀλφοί, λέπραι ἢ τὰ τοιαῦτα. (*Epidemics 2.1:85*) or when advocating a suspension of gypsum as a "cure": Ἀλφοῦ καὶ λέπρης, τίτανος ἐν ὕδατι, ὡς μὴ ἑλκώσῃς (*Epidemics 2.6:24*).[367]

Besides using the word λέπρα alongside words for "whiteness" (λευκος), Hippocrates frequently uses the term λειχήν = tree-moss or lichen, as in: Λειχῆνες δὲ καὶ λέπραι καὶ λεῦκαι (*Prorrhetic II:43*). This has persisted into present-day dermatology where "leucoderma", "leukoplakia" and "lichen planus" are common conditions. It is interesting to speculate that "white, scaly and having the appearance of a lichen" is a near perfect description of psoriasis.

There is no clear evidence of the word ἐλέφαντια having been used before the Common Era. However, Lucretius (*c.* 99–55 BCE) refers to the "elephant disease" to be found in the Nile valley mid-Egypt and "nowhere else".[368] Although he does not list any symptoms, this has generally been assumed to be *Elephantiasis Graecorum*.[369]

> Est elephas morbus qui propter flumini Nili gignitur Aegypto in media neque praeterea usquam. (De Rerum Natura, 6:1114–5)

But it is from Celsus (*c.* 25–50 CE), writing in Latin during the reign of Tiberius, that we get the best and earliest account of what is clearly *EG⇌HD*:

> Ignotus autem paene in Italia, frequentissimus in quibusdam regionibus is morbus est, quem ἐλεφαντίασιν Graeci vocant; isque longis

---

[363] T. Dzierzykray-Rogalski, "Paleopathology of the Ptolemaic Inhabitants of the Dakhleh Oasis (Egypt)," *Journal of Human Evolution* 9 (1980): 71–74.
[364] P. Bienkowski and A. Millard, *Dictionary of the Ancient Near East* (Philadelphia, PA: University of Pennsylvania Press, 2000); M. Gagarin, *The Oxford Encyclopaedia of Ancient Greece and Rome*, 7 vols. (Oxford: Oxford University Press, 2010).
[365] Liddell and Scott, *Greek English Lexicon*.
[366] Usually in the plural, λεπραι.
[367] The word ἀλφος refers particularly to a white scaly thickening of the skin of the face.
[368] Lucretius, *De Rerum Natura* [Rouse and Smith, LCL].
[369] However there is no reason to rule out filarial elephantiasis which is always prevalent near water.

adnumeratur: quo totum corpus adficitur, ita ut ossa quoque vitiari dicantur. Summa pars corporis crebras maculas crebrosque tumores habet; rubor harum paulatim in atrum colorem convertitur. Summa cutis inaequaliter crassa, tenuis, dura mollisque, quasi squamis quibusdam exasperator; corpus emacrescit; os, surae, pedes intumescent. Ubi vetus morbus est, digiti in minibus pedibusque sub tumour conduntur; febricula oritur, quae facile tot malis obrutum hominem consumit. (De Medicina III:25)

The disease which the Greeks call elelphantiasis, whilst almost unknown in Italy, is of very frequent occurrence in certain regions; it is counted among chronic affections; and in this the whole body becomes so affected that even the bones are said to become diseased. The surface of the body presents a multiplicity of spots and of swellings, which, at first red, are gradually changed to become black in colour. The skin is thickened and thinned in an irregular way, hardened and softened, roughened in some places as if scaly; the trunk wastes, the face, calves and feet swell. When the disease is long standing; the fingers and toes are sunk into the swelling: fever supervenes and may easily destroy a patient overwhelmed by such ills.

The disease, though prevalent in the Greek-speaking part of the Empire, was still not widely known about in Italy. This is emphatically not a description of simple scaliness (? psoriasis) but of a much more severe condition. The discoloration, fever, thickening of the skin, emaciation, and generalized inanition are pathognomonic. Moreover, its progressive nature is documented along with the involvement of the extremities and digits as a result of anaesthetic injury. It would be difficult not to see a picture of modern HD, in this account and, as such, among ancient texts, this must be considered as defining *EG⇌HD*.

Galen (129–199/217 CE), uses the following description for a group of infective conditions which he calls "*dyscrasias that no one can escape*" and which he considered to be related.[370] Here Galen clearly distinguishes between ἐλελφαντιάσεις and λέπραι.

> ἐρυσιπέλατα γὰρ, καὶ φλεγμοναὶ, καὶ οἰδήματα, καὶ φύματα, καὶ φύγεθλα, καὶ χοιράδες, ἐλεφαντιάσεις τε καὶ ψῶραι, καὶ λέπραι, καὶ ἀλφοὶ, καὶ σκίρροι τούτου τοῦ γένους εἰσίν, οὐδένα λαθεῖν δυνάμεθα. (De morborum differentiis V2)

Galen identified "primary" (*per se*) and "secondary" (*per accidentem*) conditions. Among the former he includes ἐλεφαντίασις and φθίσις; the second of these is recognizable as "consumption" or tuberculosis. He was, therefore, familiar with both of the major mycobacterial diseases[23] which he rated as

---

370 I. Johnston, *Galen: On Diseases and Symptoms* (Cambridge: Cambridge University Press, 2006).

serious dyscrasias. In contrast, where Galen discusses itching (VII.197K) κνῆσις, we find this symptom associated with "lichen" and with "λέπραι" in, for example: λειχῆνας καὶ ψώρας and ψώρας καὶ λέπρας. This suggests that Galen was aware of the "scaliness" of psoriasis and that he regarded it as an altogether less serious condition than ἐλεφαντίασις.[23]

The Church Fathers of the Patristic period had higher things to think about. Lampe's Patristic Greek Lexicon,[371] provides but a single citation for the word ἡ ἐλεφαντια, defined as "elephantiasis", in the writings of John Chrysostom (c347–407 CE).

The term ἐλεφαντια/ἐλεφαντίασις appears to have been largely confined to the medical profession and so retained its specific meaning. In contrast, λέπρα/λέπραι, was widely used non-specifically in all kinds of literature.[372] Instances of λέπρα/λέπραι appearing before the return of Alexander are unlikely to refer to EG⇌HD. However, it would be unsafe to suppose that occurrences of λέπρα/λέπραι in later texts,[373] unsupported by symptomatology, can be translated in any particular way.

Between 1000 and 1200 CE, soldiers returning from the Crusades brought "true leprosy" i.e. Hansen's disease, to Europe. In Britain, the disease was prevalent from 625–1798 BCE and 326 lazar houses (*leprosaria*) were documented during this period.

By the time of the King James Version of the Bible in English (1611 CE), we must assume that the distinction between ἐλεφαντίασις and λέπρα had become blurred. While λέπρα might have been an entirely appropriate translation into Greek of the Hebrew word צרעת it was not an appropriate translation for ἐλεφαντίασις. However, by this time "leprosy" was a widespread and feared disease. Its dramatic social impetus, was far greater than that of צרעת, ἐλέφαντίασις or ψώρα.

"LEPROSY" OR צרעת IN THE HEBREW BIBLE

The Hebrew Bible is quite consistent in its use of the word צָרַעַת as a descriptor of this condition of ritual impurity or uncleanliness:[374] it is its translation that has caused disputation.[375] We know that the editors of the KJV were scrupulous in consulting both Hebrew and Greek texts and it will not, therefore, do to assume, as many have, that the use of the word "leprosy" was simply carried over from the λέπρα of the Septuagint. Given the prevalence of Hansen's disease in England at the time of Wyclif and Tyndale and for many years after, it is entirely reasonable to suppose that the editors of the KJV, in 1611, believed that λέπρα

---

371 G. W. H. Lampe, *A Patristic Greek Lexicon* (Oxford: Oxford University Press, 1961).
372 See chapters 4 and 5.
373 For example the New Testament.
374 *TDOT*; Milgrom, *Leviticus: A New Translation*; Milgrom, *Leviticus: A Continental Commentary*; Knohl, *The Sanctuary of Silence*; Poorthuis and Schwartz, *Purity and Holiness*.
375 Which is not helped by the fact that צָרַעַת is the word used in Modern Hebrew for Hansen's disease.

referred to what became Hansen's disease and what they already called "leprosy". However, one cannot make a parallel assumption about the interpretation that the translators of the LXX placed upon the Hebrew word צרעת when they chose to translate it as λέπρα. Since we know from other Greek writings that the morpheme λέπ* derives from the verb λέπω meaning "to peel, strip off bark/rind" etc, the notion of "scaliness" or "peeling" must have been central to this translation. The question, that we have to ask is, therefore, "What did they mean specifically and is λέπρα/scale-disease an accurate translation of צרעת?" Statistical analysis[376] of the Hebrew Bible looking specifically for un-pointed צרע* finds both צרעה and צרעת as nouns and also the verb צרע.

Etymology of צרעת

Understanding the etymology and meaning of the Hebrew word צרעת would be the key to biblical "leprosy" but this is probably an impossible quest.[377] Despite a very considerable body of expertise operating over many years there is no certainty: it is unlikely that we shall ever know precisely what צרעת was.

It has been said that "Any word from a Semitic Language can be completely defined in terms of root and pattern".[378] There is a wealth of Hebrew dictionaries; the best and most recent is probably the *Dictionary of Classical Hebrew* (DCH), from Sheffield.[379] The multi-volume *Theological Dictionary of the Old Testament* (TDOT), though somewhat dated, is comprehensive.[380]

Root

The obvious trilateral root for צרעת is √צרע . The well-established dictionary of Brown Driver and Briggs (BDB)[381] defines √צרע and its verb צָרַע as "to fall down, humble or prostrate oneself". BDB, along with TDOT, favours a derivation from, or common ancestor with the Arabic cognate صَرِعَة. It has been suggested that the "falling" or "prostration" is metaphorically alluding to a fall from grace as a result of sinfulness but this seems tendentious. There are no skin diseases that cause falling or prostration and many other diseases that do. Along such lines of argument, Sawyer's[382] objection to this derivation seems to be overwhelming.[383]

---

376 Bibleworks (version 8 2009); Bibleworks LLC Norfolk VA.
377 E. V. Hulse, "Nature of Biblical Leprosy and the Use of Alternative Medical Terms in Modern Translations of the Bible," *Palestine Exploration Quarterly* 107 (1975): 87–105.
378 J. Contineau, "Racines et Schèmes dans les Langues Sémitiques," *Actes du XXIe Congrès International des Orientalistes*, Paris 23–24 Juillet 1948 (1949): 93–95; A. Sáenz-Badillos, *A History of the Hebrew Language* (New York: Cambridge University Press, 1996).
379 Clines, ed., *Dictionary of Classical Hebrew*. This is a dictionary based around individual words.
380 *TDOT*
381 F. Driver, S. R. Brown, C. A. Briggs, *A Hebrew and English Lexicon of the Old Testament* (Oxford: Clarendon, 1960). This is a dictionary based around roots.
382 J. F. A. Sawyer, "A Note on the Etymology of sara'at," *VT* 26, no. 2 (1976): 241–45.
383 Vide infra.

DCH includes the √צרע root as being of the verb צָרַע meaning quite specifically "to be afflicted with a rash". It is easy to see that this is a definition derived by backward association as all of the given examples of its use are in the context of "leprosy" and there are no alternative usages for this verb.

From the verbal forms, therefore, no clear meaning can be evinced.

Pattern

צרעת is a noun of the *qaṭṭal* type. Also used as nouns are the *Qal* passive participle צָרוּעַ (הַצָּרוּעַ) and the *Pual* participle מְצֹרָע — famously and inaccurately for true leprosy in Exod 4:6 — וְהִנֵּה יָדוֹ מְצֹרַעַת כַּשָּׁלֶג

Dictionary entries are, as may be seen above, of little help in telling us about צרעת, beyond the fact that it was unpleasant, affected the skin, and possibly occurred suddenly "like a blow". We know too from Leviticus that it affected fabrics and even buildings. Its diagnosis and "treatment" were within the province of the priest and the latter involved sacrifice and the ablution of "impurity" by washing.[384] It is difficult to know if Milgrom[385] has gone too far in insisting on the term "scale-disease". This is undoubtedly a better term than "leprosy" but there is relatively little to suggest scaliness as distinct from other forms of rash or indeed a rash at all. The idea of a skin disease is based primarily on a description in Lev 13:2:

> אדם כי־יהיה בעור־בשרו שאת או־ספחת או בהרת והיה בעור־בשרו לנגע צרעת והובא אל־אהרן הכהן או אל־אחד מבניו הכהנים

> When a man shall have in the skin of his flesh a rising, or a scab, or a bright spot, and it become in the skin of his flesh the plague of leprosy, then he shall be brought unto Aaron the priest, or unto one of his sons the priests: (Lev 13:2)

which mentions neither scaliness nor a rash and whiteness is limited to the hair. In every case we are imputing to the root √צרע and to צרעת meanings that have been arrived at inductively and not deductively.

Wasps and Hornets?

An intriguing, alternative etymology for צרעת has been discussed by Milgrom and others.[386] It is doubtful that he ascribes much credibility to this view but it should, nevertheless be considered as it represents an important problem with the decipherment of Semitic languages, namely, that of pointing or vocalization.

---

384 Poorthuis and Schwartz, *Purity and Holiness*; Knohl, *The Sanctuary of Silence*.
385 Milgrom, *Leviticus: A Continental Commentary*; Milgrom, *Leviticus: A New Translation*.
386 Milgrom, *Leviticus: A New Translation*; Sawyer, "A Note on the Etymology of sara'at."

It has been noted above that there is little support for the view that צָרַעַת and צִרְעָה are the same thing. The former word with its Masoretic pointing is that which is translated as "leprosy" or "scale disease". The latter word is not found in the Hebrew Bible and the closest to be found there is צָרְעָה the town of Zorah. Nevertheless, it has been suggested that צָרַעַת may be a mis-pointing of the word צִרְעָה which means a hornet or large wasp. Both in Classical Hebrew[387] and Rabbinical Hebrew,[388] this word, besides referring to the insect, is used to describe "plague" and "terror", "dejection" and "discouragement" and any affliction of the worst sort. All of these meanings are well-attested.

Being stung by a wasp[389] combines an unpleasant and sometimes dangerous pathological process with an "assault", "strike" or "blow" and one can see how the word *might* have been used metaphorically for "leprosy". What is of particular interest here is that the angioneurotic oedema that may result from the allergic reaction to a wasp sting, presents itself, in the face particularly, as a severe pachydermatous swelling and induration very similar to that seen in lepromatous Hansen's disease—the *facies leonina*. This is probably no more than a coincidence: the pathological and linguistic aspects of this association cannot be linked by any substantive evidence and the argument for "scaliness" is undoubtedly more pressing. Nevertheless, the "wasp-sting" hypothesis returns with every new author.

Other Hebrew Words to Describe "Leprosy"

Although צרעת takes pride of place, the Old Testament (mainly Leviticus) uses several other words which we should note in passing. The significance of these words is that they all refer to what today we would call "symptoms and signs". These words—with the pointing that occurs in the Hebrew Bible—are: שְׂאֵת = *swelling, blotch*; סַפַּחַת = *eruption, scab*; בַּהֶרֶת = *a bright shiny spot*; יַלֶּפֶת = *scabby*; יַבֶּלֶת = *suppurating*; גָּרָב = *itch, scab*. They are the outward signs of צרעת rather than the condition itself and it is these that the priest has to see in order to pronounce the unfortunate individual "impure".

Cognate Languages of the Ancient Near East

Cognate Semitic Languages

It is always helpful to examine cognate[390] Semitic languages in dealing with difficult etymologies. Nuance of meaning may surface so that later usages become explained. In the present case we must look for both examples of words

---

387 Clines, ed., *Dictionary of Classical Hebrew*.
388 Jastrow, *Dictionary of the Targumim*.
389 A hornet would be much worse.
390 Non-cognate languages such as Sanskrit and Ancient Egyptian were considered in chapter 3.

The 'Leprosy' Problem

that may be true cognates of צרעת but it is also helpful to consider other words in these languages for "leprosy" even if unlikely to reveal exactly what צרעת actually was.

Akkadian

TDOT[391] suggests the Babylonian Akkadian word *ṣennītu* meaning a "skin disease"[392] to have undergone a n→r sound shift and eventually become equivalent to צרעת. Sawyer[393] has suggested the Akkadian word was *ṣerretu* 𒄑𒂍𒑊𒁇 meaning "radiance" referred to the redness of an inflammatory response. Both of these derivations seem unlikely. [394]

The Akkadian word for leprosy is *epqu(m)* which can appear in a number of forms. The Chicago Assyrian Dictionary[395] suggest the ideogram dib (𒁁) which Borger equates with KU (𒁁 Borger number 808) and sometimes E.dib (𒂍𒁁). There is too little Akkadian or Assyrian material available to be for certain what was the most common expression.

Nothing is known about its symptoms and signs but *epqu(m)* was, at least, thought serious enough for it to be recommended to male suitors that they should not entertain the idea of marrying girls suffering from *epqu(m)*.

Elinor Lieber[396] has suggested an alternative Akkadian derivation for צרעת. This word is *sa ḫar šub bū* (𒊓 𒄯 𒋗 𒁍) or *saḫar šubbū* (𒊓𒄯 𒋗𒁍) which was thought to refer to some disease that "covered the skin with white dust".[397] The question of whiteness and its place in צרעת and in true leprosy will be discussed in chapter 7.

Ugaritic

The Epic of Aqhat from Ugarit was written in Ugaritic Cuneiform in the 13th century BCE. This tells how the childless King Daniel appealed to the god El who granted him a son, Aqhat.[398] Aqhat himself has a son who gets into trouble and is killed, and Aqhat curses the loci where his son's murder may have taken place. Hillers[399] has translated one of these curses as containing the phrase, *"May you*

---

391 *TDOT*.
392 W. von Soden and B. Meissner, *Akkadisches Handwörterbuch*, 3 vols. (Wiesbaden: Otto Harrassowitz, 1965); R. Borger, *Mesopotamisches Zeichenlexikon* (Münster: Ugarit-Verlag, 2004); R. Malbran-Labat and F. Labat, *Manuel d'Épigraphie Akkadienne: Signes Syllabaire Idéogrammes,* ed. Paul Geuthner (Paris: Geuthner S.A., 1988).
393 Sawyer, "A Note on the Etymology of sara'at."
394 Kinnier-Wilson, "Diseases of Babylon," 135–40.
395 A. L. Oppenheim and E. Reiner, eds., *The Assyrian Dictionary of the Oriental Institute of the University of Chicago*, Vol. 4 (E) (Chicago, IL: Oriental Institute, 1958), 246. This attests to a number of syllabic options also: x nu sig ($ ä È), x ba ($ $), x si ($ «), x za ($ μ) and x x x NE ($ $ $ ™), where x is an unintelligible sign.
396 Lieber, "Old Testament 'Leprosy', Contagion and Sin."
397 Kinnier-Wilson, "Diseases of Babylon."
398 Bienkowski and Millard, *Dictionary of the Ancient Near East*.
399 D. R. Hillers, "A Difficult Curse in Aqht," in *Biblical and Related Studies Presented to Samuel Iwry*, ed. A. Morschauser and S. Kort (Winona Lake, IN: Eisenbrauns, 1985). El (il) presumably corresponds to the Hebrew אֵל.

be clothed with leprosy of El" though it is unclear whether the god El suffered from leprosy or dispensed it to malefactors. The words in question are *grbt il* (𐎂𐎗𐎁𐎚 𐎛𐎍). The Ugaritic root √grb is thought to refer to the acquisition of a skin disease and *grbt* (𐎂𐎗𐎁𐎚) is the corresponding noun in the construct state.[400]

This term for skin diseases may be related to the Hebrew גָּרָב as in Deut 28:27 where the Lord offers up a pathological "smiting" which seems particularly nasty:[401]

יככה יהוה בשחין מצרים (ובעפלים) [ובטחרים] ובגרב ובחרס אשר לא־תוכל להרפא:

> The Lord shall smite thee with the boil of Egypt, and with the emerods, and with the scurvy, and with the itch, whereof thou canst not be healed. (Deut 28:27)

Aramaic

The importance of Aramaic in the "leprosy controversy" is in evaluating the Targumin and especially the Talmud and other material of the Rabbinic period. These are potentially important because as exegetical and explicative discourses, they (may) offer insight into the precise meaning of the Hebrew צרעת.

If we look up √צרע in an Aramaic lexicon[402] the verb צָרַע "to strike" also "to be(come) leprous" and the noun צרעת "a plague" or "leprosy" may be found. However, in the Talmud √סגר is widely used to denote all things "leprous". This verb more commonly means "to shut out"[403] originally in the sense of "bar/bolt/lock a door" but later in the general sense of "exclude". It is thought that the verb סְגִיר "to be leprous" which is used in the Talmud, is a late stative form of סְגַר which specifically implies the "shut-out" nature of the leper.[404] The word סְגִיר (with the definite article סְגִירָא) is also used as both a noun and an adjective to mean "leper/leprous" as are the derived participial forms סְגִירוּת and סְגִירוּתָא (Hebrew ≡ הַמְּצֹרָע). A "leprous man" is usually rendered by גְּבַר סְגִיר (Hebrew ≡ אִישׁ־צָרוּעַ).

---

400 Gregorio del Olmo Lete, Joaquín Sanmartín and Wilfred G. E. Watson, *A Dictionary of the Ugaritic Language in the Alphabetic Tradition*, 2nd rev. ed. 2 vols. (Leiden; Boston: Brill, 2004), 306. It is interesting that the verb grb originally meant to 'protect' in the sense of to 'set apart from harm' and the 'setting apart' may be significant in respect of what was done to lepers.
401 So magnificently rendered in the KJV: 'The LORD will smite thee with the botch of Egypt, and with the emerods, and with the scab, and with the itch, whereof thou canst not be healed.'
402 Jastrow, *Dictionary of the Targumim*; Sokoloff, *A Dictionary of Judean Aramaic*; Sokoloff, *A Dictionary of Jewish Babylonian Aramaic*; Sokoloff, *A Dictionary of Jewish Palestinian Aramaic*; A. Tal, *A Dictionary of Samaritan Aramaic*, 2 vols. (Leiden: Brill, 2000).
403 Sokoloff, *A Dictionary of Jewish Palestinian Aramaic*; Jastrow, *Dictionary of the Targumim*; Tal, *A Dictionary of Samaritan Aramaic*.
404 This notion of 'separation' and/or 'segregation' for lepers has persisted to this day in the German and Welsh words for 'leprosy' which are *'Aussatz'* and *'gwahanglwyf'* respectively, and in the unfortunate and pejorative 'social leper'.

In Rabbinical Jewish writings, there appears to be a preference for the Aramaic forms deriving from √סגר. However, צרעת is also used, especially when referring to biblical passages where צרע occurred in the original text. This preference may indicate a desire to comment on the social status of the "leper" beyond his simple "impurity" but it is unsafe to infer too much from this finding on account of the very diverse origins of Rabbinical writings and the fact that at the time of their writing, Aramaic was the *lingua franca for* this genre. We should note, also, that √סגר does exist in Hebrew and is widely used in the sense of "shut" etc.[405] It does not, however, appear in Hebrew, to attest to "leprosy".

Arabic

In Arabic the letter ص is a velarized "s" equivalent to the Hebrew צ and Dols[406] has suggested that the Arabic root صرع meaning "throw down" in its causative form, may be equivalent to צרעת.[407]

The Arabic letters ص ر and ع are equivalent to Hebrew צ ר and ע respectively. The feminine ending (ة — taa marbutaa) would add an "-at" sound if the word was followed by a vowel or in the construct state — صَرْعَة. It is easy to see, therefore a similarity with צרעת.

However an alternative suggestion[408] has been that words such as صَرْعَة and صَرْع are more likely to mean something akin to epilepsy.[409] One can see the analogy with the Hebrew נֶגַע and נֶגֶף meaning a "stroke", "blow", "affliction", and by association a "plague"[410] but there is no evidence of this analogy in Arabic's referring to leprosy. An alternative suggestion from Sawyer,[411] has been that words such as صَرْعَة and صَرْع are more likely to mean something akin to epilepsy on account of the "falling" or "prostrating" element. However there is no clear evidence for this association. The modern Arabic word for "leprosy" is جُذَام whose root has the sense of "mutilated". This suggests a more modern aetiology for significantly, nowhere in the ancient references[412] is mention made of "disfigurement". This omission is perhaps the most telling evidence against biblical "leprosy's" having been Hansen's disease. The term جُذَام is to be found in pre-Islamic Arabic writings from the early Common Era and is widely found in medieval Arabic medical texts.[413] جُذَام clearly refers to lepromatous leprosy

---

405 Clines, ed., *Dictionary of Classical Hebrew*.
406 M. W. Dols, "Leprosy in Medieval Arabic Medicine." *Journal of the History of Medicine & Allied Sciences* 34 (1979): 314-33.
407 This is the derivation favoured by Brown, Driver and Briggs: Brown, *A Hebrew and English Lexicon of the Old Testament*.
408 Sawyer, "A Note on the Etymology of sara'at."
409 Annie Nicolette Zadoks, *Ancestral Portraiture in Rome and the Art of the Last Century of the Republic*, Allard Pierson Stichting Deel 1, Archaeologische-historische Bijdragen (Amsterdam: N. v. Noord-Hollandsche uitgeversmij., 1932). Once called "falling sickness".
410 See Exod 11:1 and 12:13 respectively.
411 Sawyer, "A Note on the Etymology of sara'at."
412 As indeed it is not in Hebrew texts.
413 Shivtiel and Niessen, eds., *Arabic and Judaeo-arabic Manuscripts*.

140

i.e. *Elephantiasis Graecorum* and descriptions make much of the disfiguring nature of the disease.

Another Arabic word بَرَص appears to be equally old[414] and is the only disease specifically mentioned in the Qur'an[415] in relation to Jesus. It is, therefore, equivalent to the New Testament λέπρα. The root from which بَرَص is derived means "white" or "shiny" but as Dols[416] suggests this is unlikely to refer to Hansen's disease because we know that whiteness and shininess are not symptoms of HD. Beyond a tenuous homophony it is, therefore, impossible to find a relationship between צרעת and صَرْعَة/صَرْع .

Non-semitic Languages

Candidates that might be considered are Sumerian and Egyptian.[417] There is nothing among available Sumerian records that is in any way helpful and therefore we cannot draw any conclusions about this civilization.

In Egyptian, four words to describe skin diseases can be found in standard lexicons and grammar books.[418] They come exclusively from the Ebers Papyrus[419] and the Edwin Smith Papyrus.[420] These words are: *"uashesh"* = a skin disease 𓂋𓏤𓈖𓏥, *"nesit"* = a kind of skin disease 𓈖𓋴𓏏𓏥𓈖𓋴𓏏𓏥, *"wbnw"* = a wound 𓂋𓏤𓈖𓏥, and *"ḥryt"* = disease 𓂋𓏤𓈖𓏥. However, they all appear to be non-specific for "dermatoses" generally and their appearance, in the two papyri, is in a purely medical context—there is no association with "impurity" and so no parallel with צרעת would be legitimate. It seems likely, therefore, that at this time, such a parallel was peculiar to Semitic or even specifically Canaanite/Israelite cultures and languages.

צרעת — SEMANTICS OR SEMIOLOGY?

The above "lexical" approach to understanding צרעת, while telling us a lot about how the terminology was used, tells us very little, if anything at all, about the physical nature of this condition. There was no "medical tradition" in the Ancient Near East; the priesthood was powerful and it suited a burgeoning monotheistic tradition to define lapses of cultic and ritual purity as punishable sins. No differentiation was made between passive afflictions—and visible deformities were considered by far the worst—and active misdeeds. In such an environment one may speculate that any visible and widespread pathological

---

414 Dols, "Leprosy in Medieval Arabic Medicine."
415 Surah 5:110.
416 Dols, "Leprosy in Medieval Arabic Medicine."
417 Sanskrit, though of not the Ancient Near East, must be considered since Elephantiasis Graecorum probably came from the Indus valley.
418 Budge, *Egyptian Hieroglyphic Dictionary*; Gardiner, *Egyptian Grammar*.
419 Bryan, *The Papyrus Ebers*.
420 Breasted, *The Edwin Smith Surgical Papyrus*.

The 'Leprosy' Problem

affection of the skin would excite great interest and be seen as a potent sign of divine indignation.

If, then, we are to distil anything from a study of the Hebrew words for "leprosy" it is probably that the idea of being "struck" a "blow" is the conceptualized consequence and punishment for a lapse of purity. One might then argue that נֶגַע and נֶגֶף are much better terms than צרעת and it is not surprising to find that in 11 out of 29 occurrences of צרעת in Leviticus, this word appears as the *nomen rectum* in construct with נֶגַע.

ARCHAEOLOGICAL EVIDENCE FROM THE FIRST CENTURY

If we accept the view that $EG{\rightleftharpoons}HD$ was introduced into the Ancient Near East and Palestine by the returning soldiers of Alexander's Indian Campaign, the disease would be expected to have become widespread by the end of the first century CE. It is surprising, therefore, that relatively little archaeological evidence for $EG{\rightleftharpoons}HD$ has turned up despite the excavation of many tombs and ossuaries. This suggests that true HD was rare unlike צרעת/λέπρα and sufferers may have been buried apart or their corpses destroyed in such a way as to leave no obvious clues.

Recently, an interesting case of undoubted Hansen's disease has been found in Jerusalem by Matheson *et al*. During the exploration of tombs at Akeldama in the Lower Hinnom Valley, a tomb—*The Tomb of The Shroud*—was discovered. Although it had been looted, it contained a number of skeletons. These included osteological remains of a single individual wrapped in a partially-degraded shroud within a plaster-sealed "*loculus*".[421] This had escaped the looting and had been protected from high and destructive levels of humidity by the unbroken seal. Radiocarbon dating of the shroud material fixed its age as 2025 ± 28 years, well within the period where $EG{\rightleftharpoons}HD$ may be expected to have been prevalent. Furthermore, genetic analysis[422] of one of the phalanges[423] revealed the presence of DNA for both *M tuberculosis* and *M leprae* although there were no obvious osteological signs of HD. It is not surprising to find co-infection of tuberculosis and leprosy. In the pre-antibiotic era complication by tuberculosis was frequently a cause of death in patients with HD. This important finding is, therefore, the earliest confirmed archaeological evidence of HD in this region.

---

421 Usually in Jewish burials at this time the body was sealed into a "loculus" until decomposition had taken place and then either transferred to an "ossilegium", a niche or shelf hewn into the rock or to an ossuary.

422 Using the polymerase chain reaction (PCR). C. J. Haas et al., "Detection of Leprosy in Ancient Human Skeletal Remains by Molecular Identification of Mycobacterium Leprae," *American Journal of Clinical Pathology* 114 (2000): 428–36; C. D. Matheson et al., "Molecular Exploration of the First Century Tomb of the Shroud in Akeldama, Jerusalem," *PLoS ONE* 4, no. 12 (2009); A. Rafi et al., "Mycobacterium Leprae DNA from Ancient Bone Detected by PCR," *Lancet* 343 (1994): 1360–61.

423 Shown by mitochondrial DNA (MtDNA) to be a male and related to other non-leprous occupants of the tomb complex.

One must assume that the stigma of צרעת/λέπρα in the Levitical sense that prevailed into the period of the Crusades when "leprosy" was brought to Europe. It is quite possible that early on in this process *Elephantiasis Graecorum* and λέπρα were used interchangeably and the two terms became confused. However, by the time medieval leper-colonies arose in England the term *Elephantiasis Graecorum* of secular "medical Latin" fell out of use. To those with doctrinal axes to grind, the idea of pestilence connoted by "leprosy"—*verbum terribilissime dictu*—as divine punishment by affliction and the lot of the sinner, must have been irresistible in the medieval, ecclesiastical ethic. Whether by policy or confusion, leprosy entered the English Bible resplendent in the full panoply of ghastliness.

Chapter 7

צרעת A MEDICAL EXEGESIS OF LEVITICUS CHAPTER 13

Chapter thirteen of the book of Leviticus contains the fullest treatment in the Hebrew Bible of צרעת. Chapter 13 may be thought to operate as what, today, is called a "checklist" to enable the identification of the symptoms and signs of צרעת and guidance for dealing with what is found. For both exegete and physician, this chapter raises questions about the nature of צרעת which are difficult to answer: perhaps unanswerable. Central to understanding the place of צרעת, both in ancient ritual and in ancient medicine, is evidence as to its nature and an important corollary is the question of why the translators of the Septuagint (LXX) chose another equivocal Greek word λέπρα to translate the Hebrew. In this chapter, the question is considered of how far we can extract from the Hebrew text of chapter 13, and its LXX equivalent in Greek, any inkling of symptoms, signs or syndrome(s) that can be identified today and how far we may equate these with צרעת/λέπρα. Much has been written and little concluded in this respect, largely because we have had no corroborating evidence as to what צרעת and λέπρα meant in everyday parlance, and especially in the esoteric worldview and language of the priesthood. The difficulty with the seemingly simple, yet elusive, meanings of these words and the condition(s) they represent, has further been complicated in English and other modern-language translations of the Bible, by their misrepresentation as leprosy—*Elephantiasis Graecorum* or Hansen's disease.

THE NATURE OF צרעת

This has been considered at length in the previous chapter. In the specific context of chapter 13 where the word occurs 17 times and is, effectively, the subject of the chapter, we must begin by asking "how is the word צרעת being used by the author(s) of Leviticus and is this usage is similar to or different from its usage elsewhere in the Hebrew Bible and beyond?" Chapter 13 presents by far the most concentrated usage of the word צרעת anywhere in ancient Hebrew literature.[424] In order to maintain a disinterested scientific approach, the Hebrew צרעת and/or the Greek λέπρα will, be used throughout this chapter without translation.

---

[424] Hulse, "Nature of Biblical Leprosy."

A Medical Exegesis of Leviticus Chapter 13

13:1 Introductory Command

In noteworthy contrast to chapter 15, the introductory command does not extend to demanding the direct passing on of the message of chapter 13 to the Children of Israel. Chapter 13 is for the ears of Moses and Aaron only. Milgrom[425] has suggested that this restriction is a measure to guard against amateur (mis-)diagnosis within the community. In contrast, it is supposed that the concealed nature of genital discharges (chapter 15) requires early recognition by the patient of the need to consult the priest. Dermatological conditions, by contrast, become and remain evident early on, especially when the head is involved. This idea, however, cannot adequately explain what triggers the consultation with the priest if the patient is unaware of the gravity of his symptoms if he has צרעת which may, not necessarily, be present on areas of the body open to public view.

13:2-17 Symptoms and Signs

This section has been described by Milgrom[426] as the *first subject* of the chapter on the basis of it's being introduced by כי which does not occur again until it introduces the *second subject* at verse eighteen. These verses mark out a list of symptoms and signs that characterize צרעת and also the appropriate actions to be taken by the Aaronic Priest (הכהן) in diagnosing the condition and thereafter. The latter most certainly cannot be considered to be treatment in the modern sense. The variability of these symptoms and signs goes a long way to suggesting that צרעת cannot be so much a disease as a group of [visible] symptoms and signs[427] that qualify for inclusion in one or another of the Levitical categories of impurity.[428] The famous *Tetrad of Celsus—tumor, rubor, calor, dolor*—is called to mind by these descriptions; it accounted for almost the whole of pathology until the nineteenth century and remains central today to any consideration of inflammation or immunity.[429] However, there is a degree of imprecision and non-correspondence with current terminology that leaves the present-day clinician unable to regard them as acknowledged identifiable syndromes. The best course, therefore, is to try to establish the semantic domains of the descriptive terms within the specific Hebrew and Greek biblical sources and then try to arrive at as near a correspondence with established pathology as is

---

425 Milgrom, *Leviticus: A New Translation*, Vol. 1, 772.
426 Milgrom, Leviticus: A New Translation, 768.
427 For a fuller discussion of the etymology of this word see: Glasby, "What was Biblical Leprosy?"
428 See chapter 5.
429 Aulus Cornelius Celsus, *De medicina,* trans. W. G. Spencer (London: William Heinemann ; Cambridge, 1935).

possible.[430] Consulting non-biblical sources, if available, may be additionally helpful.

13:2 Skin Lesions

An important anatomical term עור־בשר *the skin of (his) flesh* appears here. The Septuagint (LXX) reads δέρματι χρωτός. Both of these pairings, *prima facie,* seem to be tautologous. However, in both cases the second term is probably a refining addition as both of the first terms commonly refer to animal pelts bearing fur, hair etc.[431] The second term in each case more specifically refers to flesh and the pairing has, therefore, been taken to mean "hairless skin". This view is, perhaps, reinforced by the way in which verse 2 stands in contrast to verse 3.[432]

Three dermatological signs are introduced in this verse; these are שאת, ספחת and בהרת.[433] They are separated by the conjunction או = "or" but it is unclear whether this means that they are alternative descriptions of the same lesion or that they are different lesions each of which might be seen separately, or together, in צרעת. They have traditionally been considered as different lesions, all, may be described by *Celsus's Tetrad.*

The feminine noun שְׂאֵת in the Rabbinic literature has been customarily defined as a "swelling" (Celsus's *tumor*) with the assumed root (נשׂא). However, Milgrom,[434] points out that this would not fit in with the idea of the lesion's having penetrated deeper than the surface of the skin, as suggested in verse 3: a description that suggests active ulceration.[435] However, he notes also that the Arabic cognate شِيَاتو meaning a "mark" has a similar root. Outside Leviticus the word שְׂאֵת occurs nine times in the Hebrew Bible. In all but one of these instances it is as the *Qal* infinitive construct of √נשׂא = "to bear". The exception is Gen 49:3 where it is a noun meaning "excellence".

The noun ספחת is usually taken to mean a "scab" and there appears to be more agreement here. "Scab" implies an excoriating lesion that is healing. In verses 6, 7 and 8 the related noun מספחת appears and it is clear from the context that this represents a form of the lesion associated with a lesser degree of impurity. We can therefore classify these terms as *major scab* and *minor scab*[436] and it is

---

430 The same practice must apply in considering the various skin lesions in chapter 13 and elsewhere.
431 Clines, ed., *Dictionary of Classical Hebrew.* Jastrow, *Dictionary of the Targumim.* Sokoloff, *A Dictionary of Jewish Babylonian Aramaic*; Sokoloff, *A Dictionary of Jewish Palestinian Aramaic*; Sokoloff, *A Dictionary of Judean Aramaic.* Bauer et al., *A Greek-English Lexicon*; Lampe, *A Patristic Greek Lexicon.*
432 However that is not to say that hairy skin is spared, see v. 31 where the word נֶתֶק (LXX = θραῦσμα), implies 'scab' (KJV = "scall"), and has been assumed to refer to favus.
433 בֶּהֶרֶת is the lexical form, however Clines notes in the DCH that in the Codex Leningradensis the form בְּהֶרֶת is used: Clines, ed., *Dictionary of Classical Hebrew*, Vol. 2, 101.
434 Milgrom, *Leviticus: A New Translation*, Vol. 1, 773.
435 O.E.D. Ulcer—an erosive solution of continuity in any external or internal surface of the body, forming an open sore attended with a secretion of pus or other morbid matter.
436 It should be noted that no classification of this kind is made, or implied, in the text itself. The differentiation has been made on the basis of the consequences for the patient and the procedure that has to be followed in his purification. Haber and Reinhartz, "They Shall Purify Themselves"; Neusner, "The Idea of Purity in Ancient Judaism"; Klawans, "Notions of Gentile Impurity in Ancient Judaism."

interesting to speculate about whether they represent stages in a process that was either developing or resolving. If so, they would have supplied the priest with a rudimentary clinical history from which he might be able to predict outcome.

The third clinical sign in verse 2, בהרת is customarily translated as a "spot" or "shiny/bright mark" (Celsus's = *tumor* + *rubor* + *calor*); this implies active inflammation. This traditional view has been challenged on the authority of the Mishnah (*Neg* 1:1)[437] where it is clear that "bright" = "white".[438]

> The colours of "leprosy"-signs [that appear in the bare — non-hair-covered — skin] are two[439] which are, in fact, four [colours]: the bright spot, intensely white like snow, [and] the second [shade] to it is [as white] as the lime [used for the walls] of the Sanctuary; and the swelling, [that is as white] as the skin in an egg, [and] the second [shade] of it is [as white] as white wool, according to the view of R. Meir; but the Sages say, "The swelling is [as white] as white wool, [and] the second [shade] of it is [as white] as the skin of an egg."

Hulse[440] has made the suggestion that all of these lesions are at times shiny, i.e. inflamed, and that the *rubor* (and *tumor*) has subsided with healing so that, *red-shiny* → *white-shiny*. He justifies this by saying that in verses 6, 21, 26 and 39, the lesions are described by the adjective כהה meaning "dull", "faint" "colourless" or "faded" (LXX = ἀμαυρός), and that with this fading, the condition ceases to be fulminating צרעת but nevertheless requires a week of quarantine as a precautionary measure.

The Septuagint lumps all three lesions together as, οὐλὴ σημασίας τηλαυγὴς. Both Liddell and Scott's Lexicon (L&L)[441] and Bauer's Lexicon (BDAG)[442] define οὐλὴ quite specifically as a "wound scarred over". The noun σημασίας, L&L defines as "an indication/-tor" or "a mark" and τηλαυγὴς as "conspicuous from afar by its shining whiteness". BDAG is in agreement with these definitions. It would seem, therefore, that here, in contrast to the Hebrew text, we do not have an inflammatory lesion glowing red but an area of white scarring. This suggests an old lesion that has healed.[443] Pietersma and Wright's recent English translation of the Septuagint (NETS) sits squarely on the fence of non-commitment by translating this phrase as "a conspicuous lesion indicating disease".[444] If we turn to non-biblical Greek sources, Hippocrates reinforces the idea of scarring in an

---

[437] P. Blackman, ed., *Mishnayoth* 3rd ed., 6 vols. (New York: Judaica Press, 1965).
[438] The rabbinic view was that "whiteness" was the cardinal sign of צרעת
[439] בֶּהֶרֶת and שְׂאֵת
[440] Hulse, "Nature of Biblical Leprosy."
[441] Liddell and Scott, *Greek English Lexicon*.
[442] Bauer et al., *A Greek-English Lexicon*.
[443] The diagnostic test should be the presence of calor, but we are told nothing about it.
[444] A. Pietersma and G. Benjamin Wright, *A New English Translation of the Septuagint: and the Other Greek Translations Traditionally Included Under that Title* (New York; Oxford: Oxford University Press, 2007).

account of a child born with an omphalocoele which became ulcerated so "the navel did not form a scar":[445]

... ὁ ὀμφαλὸς οὐ μάλα οὐλὴ ἐγεγόνει, ... (Hippocrates, Epidemics IV, 171)

Verse 2 is packed with terminology and introduces, at once, the most important and most difficult term צרעת. So much has been written about the meaning of this word and so little concluded, that it would be wearisome to embark on further analysis here.

It is important, however, to note the coupling, in Lev 13:2, of צרעת with the noun נגע in construct, as נֶגַע צָרַעַת. This is usually rendered as the "plague of leprosy" or sometimes "affliction of leprosy", but of course leprosy has never behaved as a plague. Nevertheless, in ancient times any misfortune might have been seen as descending suddenly upon the unfortunate recipient as if by a blow struck by Yahweh and √נגע significantly has the meaning "touch/attack/befall/strike a blow".[446] The LXX supports this with the slightly milder ἁφὴ λέπρας, (ἁφὴ = a touch). Elsewhere in the Hebrew Bible, Yahweh is always the originator of a נגע and so the affliction of צרעת may, in all probability, be the result of Yahweh's displeasure.

We have, therefore, at the end of verse 2 three clinical signs appearing on hairless flesh that individually, or together, are suggestive of Yahweh's having brought צרעת upon an individual and this is such a potentially serious breach of purity that it *must* be reported to a priest. It, therefore, appears to be a biblical *communicable disease*.

13:3 Hair

The hair plays an important part in the priestly diagnosis of צרעת. Hair colour is defined by the ratio of *pheomelanin* (red pigment) to *eumelanin* (black/brown pigment) in the melanocytes of the hair and their presence or absence is genetically determined. The number of melanocytes in any hair follicle declines with age from about thirty years onwards but relatively few diseases cause greying or whitening of the hair. In pathological states, hair whitening and loss of hair are likely to be due to poor nutrition of the hair follicles by unsatisfactory circulatory or metabolic conditions. Hypothyroidism and malnutrition may cause whitening and thinning of the hair but Hansen's disease does not. Among the candidates for צרעת, only *bejel, favus,* and *vitiligo* are associated with whitening and loss of hair.[447]

---

445 Hippocrates et al., *Hippocrates*, Vol. VII, 128. An omphalocoele is a herniation of the gut at the umbilicus resulting from incomplete closure of the latter by scarring, during foetal development. Omphalocoeles become secondarily infected and show an inflammatory response.
446 And by extension the terms "affection" or "lesion" have been used by various commentators.
447 Glasby, "What was Biblical Leprosy?" See table on page 74.

There appears to be an immediate problem with verse 3. If, as Milgrom suggests, the expression עור־בשר (δέρματι χρωτός), means "hairless skin", why is this expression used here in a verse specifically referring to hair? This raises the question of whether it is referring to abnormal hair growth within the lesion but this is known to be so rare as to be highly unlikely. It seems, therefore, that two situations are being considered, and at the same time confused in this verse. One is that which pertains to hairy skin, the head and beard area; the other is a description of ulceration taking place in hairless skin such as was considered in the previous verse. The word מראה, however, introduces a further element of confusion. This word usually means "seeing" or "appearance" and thus begs the question about whether ulceration is really present or only appears to be present. Milgrom[448] suggests the rabbinic view was that white lesions *appeared* to be deeper than the skin surface and this idea has been used by others to justify the relatively benign conditions of *psoriasis* and *favus* as being צרעת. However, it is very difficult to suppose that a white scar or skin flake could be confused with an ulcer even by the untrained eye. What can be said with certainty here is that if either of these affections was found to be present, this would be—to the priest—pathognomonic of צרעת and so, call for him to declare the *dermopath* unclean/impure/טמא.[449] At this point no mention is made of precisely what such a declaration entails.

13:4 Diagnostic Pointers

The next five verses are about what is, today, called *differential diagnosis* i.e. those observations, made over time, that allow the examiner to arrive at a clear diagnosis by the inclusion and exclusion of evidence. Whiteness of the skin without ulceration or any change in hair colour is not enough to declare the patient טמא, but it does arouse suspicion and so demands further investigation. How the condition progresses, is the information that would be required to confirm the diagnosis. Therefore, so as not to risk spreading the disease by contagion, it becomes necessary for the priest to quarantine the patient. In the LXX, ἀφορίζω = "separate" fits the idea of quarantining in the modern sense but the Hebrew uses הִסְגִּיר the *hiph'il* of √סגר = "cause to be shut up" and so it is unclear whether some enforced form of separation/isolation was intended. The quarantine period of seven days appears to be arbitrary and probably a reflection of the ritualistic/mystical association with the number seven in the P-writings— a reflection in the cosmic element of the priestly worldview in which creation took seven days.

There is no indication as to where the quarantine was to take place. Two possible explanations have been put forward from biblical examples. Either, like Miriam (Num 12:14-15), the unfortunate *dermopath* is to be sent outside the camp or,

---

448 Milgrom, *Leviticus: A New Translation*, Vol. 1, 778.
449 The LXX uses the verb μαίνω = "be defiled".

צרעת A Medical Exegesis of Leviticus Chapter 13

like Uzziah (2 Chr 26:21), he is removed to isolation in special quarters. Whether his social status may have been significant in making this differentiation is unknown.

13:5 והנה

In this verse we encounter, for the first time, the Hebrew expression והנה ("behold"); a much-used word in the Hebrew Bible that occurs 20 times in Lev 13, where there is some dispute as to its significance. Milgrom[450] citing Joüon[451] suggests that the "... ו ... ו ..." sequence (exemplified here by והנה ...→... והסגירו), represents the *protasis* and *apodosis* of a conditional clause and this arrangement is to be found in P text, used in a particular way, after the verb ראה. These clauses are, therefore, often translated with an "*if ... then*" formulation which would fit in well with the diagnostic process. However, an alternative viewpoint has been put forward[452] that the recurrent והנה is a marker for meta-re-presentation.[453] This is then considered to be a higher-order presentation with a lower-order representation[454] embedded within it—the whole thing is then re-presented in entirety as the *meta-re-presentation*. The term והנה is functioning as a *parametric operator* telling the *reader* to process the ensuing string as a *re-presentation* of a perception, thought or comment from an earlier time. In the present verse this is quite clearly the exposition to the reader of an earlier clinical observation—again after the verb ראה. In all probability these two approaches add up to the same thing with the practical manifestation that, as the condition has persisted, a further period of seven days' quarantine has become necessary. However, an important additional factor is the notion that the lesion may have *spread*, פשה.

13:6 Reassessment of the Patient

The patient is reassessed at a third meeting with the priest on the fourteenth day after his initial presentation. This verse sets out the criteria for confirming the condition as being a *minor impurity*. For this to be the case, the lesion must have faded and must not have spread in the skin, כהה הנגע ולא־פשה; the "official diagnosis" is, therefore, מספחת (LXX = σημασία) i.e. a scab; and the priest may, as a result, declare him clean/cleansed/pure/purified. The verb that is used is the *pi'el* of √טהר, i.e. טִהַר which is considered to be a *declarative pi'el*.[455] The Septuagint says καθαριεῖ αὐτὸν ὁ ἱερεύς using the simple future indicative active

---

[450] Milgrom, *Leviticus: A New Translation*.
[451] P. Joüon and T. Muraoka, *A Grammar of Biblical Hebrew*, Vol. 2 (Rome: Editrice Pontificio Instituto Biblico, 2005), 651 §177i.
[452] T. Muraoka, M. F. J. Baasten, and W. Th van Peursen, *Hamlet on a Hill: Semitic and Greek Studies Presented to Professor T. Muraoka on the Occasion of his Sixty-fifth Birthday* (Leuven; Dudley, MA: Peeters, 2003).
[453] Note the second hyphen—re-presentation has the sense of "present again".
[454] Note the lack of hyphen—representation as in an image etc.
[455] Wilhelm Gesenius, A. E. Cowley, E. Kautzsch, Julius Euting, and Mark Lidzbarski. *Genesius' Hebrew Grammar: With a Facsimile of the Siloam Inscription by J. Euting and a Table of Alphabets by M. Lidzbarski*, 2nd English ed. (Oxford: Clarendon, 1910), 141, §52g.

of καθαρίζω = cleanse, presumably also in a declarative sense, though this is not attested in L&S. Importantly now, we are told the ritual procedure that *must* follow the diagnosis of a *minor impurity* in order to obtain full purification. This involves bathing and laundering of one's clothes. From this we may infer that the degree of impurity here is equivalent to that seen after, for example, eating or transporting forbidden foodstuffs.[456] However, whereas the process of recognition and ritual purification of these other peccadillos is completed within a single day, there is, with מספחת, the additional burden of a week's quarantine.

By this point in the chapter, we have been introduced to three "clinical scenarios".

1. Suspected but unproven/unconfirmed impurity → 1 week of quarantine → if no further development → patient declared טהור.
2. Minor impurity מספחת → טמא → 2 weeks of quarantine + bathing and laundering.
3. Major impurity, צרעת, →טמא → the treatment of this is ritualistic not medical and is described, at some length, in Lev 14.

13:7–46 Further Symptoms and Signs

This group of verses deals with reappearing signs and more specific features seen in the differential diagnosis of צרעת. There is a substantial amount of repetition in the text, but also pointers to additional diagnostic features and presentations in specific anatomical situations.

13:7–9 Spread

Spreading of a מספחת after the above declaration of purity has taken place demands a further visit to the priest who, if he finds clear evidence that the lesion has spread, must declare the patient unclean טמא—again by means of a *declarative pi'el*—but now with the certainty that this is נגע צרעת. In verse 7 the use of the passive, *niph'al* נִרְאָה implies that the patient "be seen" by the priest perhaps even unwillingly.

13:10–12 Whiteness

Whiteness is emphasized here; a white swelling in the skin that has turned (הפך) the hair white. There is no obvious physiological or pathological reason why this should have happened. Moreover, the association made here with raw flesh seems unlikely. Whiteness is usually associated with old scarring, scarred, or avascular flesh. Raw or ulcerating flesh, in contrast, exposes granulation tissue which usually has a good blood supply and a velvety-red appearance. Very

---

456 This is in contrast to the much more elaborate procedure that must be undertaken in dealing with a major impurity and which is described in Lev 14.

frequently it becomes secondarily infected by bacterial invasion and the presence of pus may mislead one into believing it to be turning white.

However, in verse 11 the whiteness, but not the ulceration, is perhaps justified in referring to it as a chronic condition צרעת נושנת or λέπρα παλαιουμένη. But even the word "chronic" seems unlikely given the context of this verse. More likely would be the translation "established", meaning that the lesion has had time to develop. Either way, an important point is made here: the patient has overt צרעת, there is therefore no need to quarantine this patient for diagnostic purposes, as his uncleanness is clearly evident for all to see and the Hebrew word טמא implies that major form of impurity that is beyond the ability of man to undo.

The question of spread is again considered in verse 12. In both the Hebrew and the Greek, the analogy with a budding/sprouting/blossoming flourishing plant is made: פרח and ἐξανθέω. No indication is given as to whether the spread is a manifestation of the chronicity of the condition or a fulminating acute phase. Extent appears to matter more, yet only inasmuch as it is immediately visible to the priest, presumably without the patient's having to undress and with no concern being given to a history from the patient himself. While the spread of the dermatological signs may—or even perhaps must—be from head to foot,[457] it may be considered only where the priest can see it without unduly compromising the patient's modesty.[458] This extraordinarily un-clinical approach was later justified by the rabbis[459] who indicated twenty four anatomical sites where טמא *should not/could not* be diagnosed on the basis of raw flesh.[460] Moreover, raw flesh not extending more than the diameter of a lentil, was not to be diagnosed as צרעת and therefore did not imply that the patient was טמא.

13:13 Extensive Spread and Whiteness

Verse 13 is, at first, very confusing. The inclusion of והנה suggests a conditional clause with the protasis referring back to the symptoms and signs seen by the priest in the patient of verse 12—"if the צרעת /λέπρα has spread so as to cover all his flesh". In the apodosis, however, he is declared טהור on the grounds that it has all turned white. The Hebrew is confusing at first because the והנה appears to refer to the צרעת "covering all the flesh",[461] rather than to the *whiteness* covering the whole body but it makes sense to suppose that the declaration of recovered purity is due to the צרעת having turned white. There is no such confusion in the Septuagint which makes the point quite clearly that the priest

---

457 מֵרֹאשׁוֹ וְעַד־רַגְלָיו/ἀπὸ κεφαλῆς ἕως ποδῶν
458 לְכָל־מַרְאֵה עֵינֵי הַכֹּהֵן/καθ' ὅλην τὴν ὅρασιν τοῦ ἱερέως
459 Blackman, ed., *Mishnayoth*, Negaim 6:7, Vol. 6, 345.
460 It is interesting to note that several of these are precisely those anatomical points where Hansen's disease reveals itself most prominently.
461 כִּסְּתָה הַצָּרַעַת אֶת־כָּל־בְּשָׂרוֹ

is required to declare the patient clean because everything has turned white—ὅτι πᾶν μετέβαλεν λευκόν καθαρόν ἐστιν. We can only speculate as to what this whiteness was in pathological terms. It is rather a strong argument against צרעת being psoriasis, as has been suggested, because the white scaly appearance would be indicative of active disease and the description here seems to imply a late, healing phase. Milgrom[462] suggests healing has occurred by desquamation of now-dead skin cells; but for this to be the case, we still need a diagnosis to identify the desquamatory disease that has healed. Moreover, for this to have involved almost the entire body seems very unlikely. For this reason, Hulse's suggestion of *exfoliative dermatitis* seems equally improbable.[463] The viewpoint shared by Milgrom and Hulse and indeed a majority of scholars writing on צרעת/λέπρα, is that somehow *whiteness = scales.* The analogy is, perhaps, made with fish scales which, seen in appropriate light, may appear white. But fish scales also commonly show iridescence and no mention of this phenomenon is made anywhere. An alternative view, suggested by Wevers,[464] is that *whiteness = normal skin colour* and so, as the scabs have healed, the appearance of the skin has returned to its normal [white] colour and the patient must, therefore, be clean. This view is supported in the text of the LXX by the πᾶν of πᾶν μετέβαλεν λευκόν καθαρόν ἐστιν being in agreement with τὸ δέρμα τοῦ χρωτός which is neuter and *not* in agreement with either λέπρα or ἁφή, both of which are feminine. This ingenious suggestion perhaps makes greater medical sense than the more conventional view, but it has not been widely accepted. This is almost certainly because of the poorly thought-out but entrenched view that צרעת was invariably associated with *whiteness*: any alternative view would conflict with important textual references such as Exod 4:6, Num 12:10 and 2 Kgs 5:27. However, it might be argued that the comparison with snow, made on these occasions, reflects its flakiness and not its whiteness. We must ask about the evidence that צרעת really was associated with scaliness too. It seems entirely likely that this idea owes its existence simply to the translation, by the authors of the Septuagint, of צרעת by λέπρα. The origins of the λεπ- morpheme in Greek are unclear. A group of related words containing this morpheme are all associated with the idea of a "rind", "husk" or "skin" and those containing the λεπτ- morpheme by extension a thin "film".[465] The notion of scales or scaliness is, therefore but one of many possible ideas that λεπ-words convey. It is even possible that the word simply means "skin" and that צרעת in the eyes of the LXX translators was intended to convey no more than *dermatosis* conveys in modern medicine.

---

462 Milgrom, *Leviticus: A New Translation*, Vol. 1, 785.
463 Hulse, "Nature of Biblical Leprosy."
464 John William Wevers, *Notes on the Greek Text of Leviticus*, ed. by Bernard A. Taylor, Society of Biblical Literature Septuagint and Cognate Studies Series 44 (Atlanta: Scholars' Press, 1997), 176. This viewpoint, of course, rests on Wevers's assumption that the natural skin colour of those who wrote Leviticus was "white".
465 Cf., for example, "leptomeninges", leptospirosis', where the lep- morpheme implies, "filminess" rather than "scaliness".

13:14 – 17 Ulceration

These verses are a consideration of what should happen if the disease breaks out again in the form of ulcerating flesh. By ביום is meant "whenever" with "if ever" implicit and in the form found in the text, וביום, the ו signifies a continuation of the previous string and is usually translated as "but". New ulceration, therefore appears to result in the patient's being declared טמא but whiteness triggers a declaration of טהור.

13:18–28 Boils and Burns

In the second half of the chapter, which Milgrom describes as his *second subject*, we are introduced to a further case of צרעת resulting from a pre-existing "boil" שחין. Today, the expression *boil* is taken to mean an acute infective lesion usually due to an infecting bacterial agent such as *Staphylococcus aureus* and producing a localized inflammatory swelling showing at least all of Celsus's original signs (*tumor + rubor + calor + dolor ± functio laesa*).[466] The lesion progressively becomes distended with pus and resolves to a scar once the swelling has ruptured or has been incised and the pus has drained. Boils are associated with poor skin hygiene and there is nothing to suggest their specific association with any of the traditional contenders for צרעת. In the Hebrew Bible, boils are viewed as a dreaded condition imposed upon an individual who has ignited the wrath of Yahweh. This idea is to be found especially in violation of the covenant, (Exod 9:9–11; 2 Kgs 20:7; Isa 38:21; Job 2:7 and most emphatically, Deut 28:27, 35). It is very easy, in an age where antibiotics are taken for granted, to dismiss the seriousness of such a condition. One should note that in the LXX the word that corresponds to שחין is ἕλκος which is usually translated as "ulcer"—but an *ulcer* is quite a different thing from a *boil*.[467] It is unclear, therefore, whether in this verse, we are dealing with a different presenting lesion or whether this is simply repetition. The latter seems more likely given the fact that the author has already dwelt at some length upon the presentation of צרעת as שאת ספחת.

13:19 Spots

The two Hebrew words שחין and בהרת remain to be further elucidated. The former, as we have just seen, is probably a white purulent spot or *boil*. בהרת is usually translated as a "shiny spot", by which it may be supposed we mean a reddish inflamed swelling: Celsus's *tumor + rubor ± calor ± dolor*. It may be no more than the early manifestation of this same condition, before the invasion by inflammatory cells and the formation of pus. We are re-entering the field of confusion brought about by the term "white". In the likely pathology, there are

---

466 Functio laesa, loss of function, may occur as a direct result of the disease process; i.e. by destruction of tissue or as a side effect of the tumor or dolor. A swollen hot, painful joint, for example, cannot function normally.
467 For the definition of an ulcer, see above. A boil is a lay term indicating a hot red swelling on the skin that may or may not contain pus. It is a simple manifestation of the inflammatory process and is usually the result of bacterial infection by agents such as Staphylococcus aureus.

two very distinct processes that are associated with whitening of the flesh. One of these is healing, whereby the tissues are rendered avascular by the fibrosis of scarring and so become white. The other process is the development of pus as a result of the invasion of the lesion by inflammatory leucocytes, monocytes, and macrophages. All of these cells, in the business of engulfing bacterial invaders and the products of local necrosis, themselves die and their remains form the pus characteristic of advanced inflammation. The colour of pus varies from whitish to a yellowish green or, in the case of infection with *Pseudomonas aeruginosa*, even a fluorescent green. The difference in the presentation of these two processes would be that in healing by scar-formation the lesion is white and dry while purulent tissue would be white and wet. It seems likely here that we are dealing with the latter—true boils—whereas in earlier verses we were dealing with a healing/scarring process. This makes sense as a further reason for a consultation with the priest. However, it does not fit in with a diagnosis of an autoimmune condition for צרעת such as psoriasis; if we accept this presentation, we must think of an acute inflammatory condition.

13:20–23 Persistent Spots

The sequence of events, consequent upon the presentation of בהרת/שחין symptoms to the priest, is similar to those observed with a מספחת/ספחת/שאת presentation. White hair in the lesion indicates clear צרעת but its absence, fading of the redness and lack of ulceration, calls for a further seven days' quarantine. As before, overt spread requires a declaration of טמא whereas a single, healing lesion does not.

13:24–28 Pre-existing Burns

These verses deal with the somewhat unlikely situation in which צרעת may develop in a pre-existing burn מכות־אש. It might be supposed that minor burns were a not uncommon consequence of routine domestic activities in the Israelites' daily life and secondary infection of burnt skin would be a frequent and potentially serious complication. The priest is here looking for the same signs as hitherto. White hair and ulceration breaking out in the burnt area are pathognomonic of צרעת; their absence and fading of the lesion necessitate a further seven days' quarantine and if spread has occurred after that time, the condition is confirmed as צרעת. Failure to spread and fading indicate, by contrast, that this is simply the resolving burn and the patient must be טהור.

13:29–32 Lesions on the Head and Beard Area

Lesions affecting hair-bearing skin, notably the head and beard, are considered next. A new masculine noun, נתק is introduced here. It is translated in the ERV and KJV as "scall"[468] but in the RSV and NRSV simply as an "itch" though in all these cases it is qualified as *leprosy of the head and beard*, צרעת הראש או הזקן. The introduction of נתק has led a number of authors to suggest that a different disease is under consideration here. *Psoriasis*, *scabies*, and *favus* have been particular favourites though the first two of these seem unlikely. Favus, named because of its "honeycomb" presentation, is a fungal disease caused by *Tricophyton schoenleinii*. It is a recurrent, persistent infection of the scalp and beard area that causes highly disfiguring encrustations (*scutula*) which periodically drop off to reveal shiny red and white areas. These *scutula* have frequently been confused with the pachydermatous thickening—e.g. the *facies leonina*—seen in Hansen's disease. Today, treatment is relatively straightforward with anti-fungal drugs.

In such cases, the procedure that priest and patient must follow is the same as that laid out previously with the exception that fine yellow hair, שער צהב דק (LXX: θρὶξ ξανθίζουσα λεπτή), is now held to be pathognomonic of צרעת and black hair along with failure of the lesions to spread delivers the "all-clear". The yellow hair, it has been suggested, might indicate *favus* on the grounds that, in this condition, the hair turns a yellowish colour and then drops out; however, this is open to dispute.

13:33–37 Scall

Unsurprisingly, shaving is advocated along with seven days' quarantine. The *hithpaʿel* הִתְגַּלָּח implies that the patient must shave himself but how extensive this shaving must be we are not told. It is emphasized that the scall itself must be sedulously avoided and never be included in the shaving, ואת־הנתק לא יגלח . Thereafter follows a further seven days' quarantine after which a further examination is carried out as before, to look for spread and ulceration.

If these observations are negative, the patient is declared clean but must still launder his clothes; oddly, no mention is made of his having to wash himself. If spread or ulceration is shown to recur after this cleansing, he is undoubtedly טמא and there is no need to continue the examination in search of yellow hair. But if the spread of lesions appears static and only black hair is to be found in the remains of the scall, he may be declared טהור.

13:38–39 Tetters

These verses introduce the term *tetter*[469] (בהק) in the ERV and RSV. This is translated as "freckled spot" in the KJV and "rash" in the NRSV. Here is our first

---

468 Which the O.E.D., perhaps unhelpfully, describes as a "scabby disease of the skin, especially the scalp" and indicates two forms, a "dry scall" = psoriasis and "humid or moist scall" = eczema. However, ringworm is also mentioned but not favus which must surely be the best contender.
469 The OED defines tetter as: "A general term for any pustular herpetiform eruption of the skin, as eczema, herpes, impetigo, ringworm, etc."

clear instance of differential diagnosis. The *tetter*, (בהק) is not צרעת because it is dull white and not shiny white. This suggests it is not an inflammatory spot: *tumor without calor, rubor* or *dolor*. The important point here is that the white spot is dull-white (LXX = ἀλφός) which Hulse[470] has suggested means *leukoderma* or *vitiligo*: both benign, though not particularly common, conditions. Both the Hebrew Bible and the Septuagint make the point that this condition—*tetters*—does not confer impurity.

13:40–44 Baldness

Again, the head is a special case. Baldness, as a result of hair falling out (*niph'al* ימרט; μαδάσκομαι) is not *per se* indicative of any disease process and there is no impurity. This is apparently also the case if the baldness occurs on the forehead.[471] In Hebrew and in Greek there is a clear distinction between קרח (φαλακρός) which is baldness on the crown of the head and גבח (ἀναφάλαντός) which is baldness of the forehead. Neither of these implies צרעת unless either appears to be accompanied by נגע לבן אדמדם (ἀφὴ λευκὴ ἢ πυρρίζουσα). This, a clear sign of צרעת, is variously described as "*a reddish white mark*" or "*a reddening white infection*". Milgrom[472] suggests that it is the *brightness* of the lesion, regardless of whether *bright white* or *bright red*, that is pathognomonic of צרעת of the head.

13: 45–46 צרעת

The next two verses make generalizations about צרעת and about the behaviour of anyone diagnosed as having the condition (הצרוע). We see in the Septuagint that ὁ ἄνθρωπος λεπρός has now become ὁ λεπρός. He is not looked-upon kindly by society nor by his compatriots. His clothing, perhaps seen as a source of contagion, must be destroyed. He must dishevel his hair ראשו יהיה פרוע or perhaps as the Septuagint says, his head should be uncovered (ἡ κεφαλὴ αὐτοῦ ἀκατακάλυπτος). But his mouth must be covered[473] על־שפם יעטה presumably as a guard against infection. Most humiliatingly of all, he must announce his presence to the world by crying out "*unclean, unclean!*" — וטמא טמא יקרא (ἀκάθαρτος κεκλήσεται).[474]

On a more practical point, the "leper" must also, for the duration of his period of enforced impurity, dwell alone and outside the camp, בדד ישב מחוץ למחנה מושבו.

---

470 Hulse, "Nature of Biblical Leprosy."
471 And, according to the rabbis, the temples.
472 Milgrom, *Leviticus: A New Translation,* Vol. 1, 801.
473 Technically שָׂפָם is a moustache. It is sometimes translated as "upper lip" but "mouth" is the translation that makes the most sense here.
474 A rare use of the Classical future-perfect tense in late Greek.

13:47–58 צרעת upon Fabrics

The text now turns to the medically unlikely, if not absurd, state of צרעת affecting fabrics such as cloth and leather, clothing, furnishings, and sails. It is this notion, along with that of צרעת's affecting buildings (Lev 14:34–53) that is, perhaps the strongest argument for the case that צרעת cannot be a disease in the modern sense, but refers to any visible and unsightly affection of a surface in both animal and mineral material—*platydysmorphism*. As such it would encompass diseases, especially those with dermatological involvement, moulds growing upon fabrics and foodstuffs, and fungal or lichenaceous growths upon the walls of damp buildings.[475] While the aetiologies of these may be widely-differing, the common factor, to the Israelite mind would be that of [visible] disfigurement and the likely explanation for this would be that offence had been caused to the deity.

Whereas the modern exegete might incline towards translating צרעת/λέπρα in these latter verses as "mould/mouldiness, mouldy" etc. the Hebrew Bible and LXX continue to use צרעת and λέπρα and the KJV and ERV are unwavering in rendering these as "leprosy". Even the RSV and NRSV, somewhat half-heartedly, say "leprous disease". Milgrom,[476] at this point, exchanges *scale-disease* for *mould-disease* noting that in semi-tropical latitudes any dampness will often facilitate the growth of fungal mycelia upon fabrics of animal or plant origin. One must suppose that the appearance of the fungal hyphae and fruiting bodies must somehow have resembled that of צרעת/λέπρα in human subjects. Today, this is a difficult assumption to make; our familiarity with, and discernment of, these things is based on a greater awareness of the world about us than might be expected of an ancient Israelite. Milgrom suggests that the symptoms of צרעת affecting both humans and fabrics can easily be confused because the surface appearances are similar [Milgrom's mildew?] but this seems unlikely and tendentious. Fungal mycelia and fruiting bodies give a furry appearance to the surfaces upon which they live and this is totally different from scaliness or the peeling or scarring of skin. It seems very unlikely that anyone could confuse the two. However, we should note that both may be white in colour although, in verse 49, Leviticus notes that upon fabric צרעת/λέπρα may present as red or green[477] ירקרק או אדמדם (χλωρίζουσα ἢ πυρρίζουσα) both of which colours occur in fungal infestations such as *dry-rot* and species of the *Penicillium* mould. Much is made in these verses of the involvement of both the warp and the weft/woof of the cloth. This may be no more than poetic licence but it has led Milgrom to suggest it indicates that it may be the yarns—wool and linen were almost exclusively used in these times—rather than the woven cloth that becomes

---

475 Typically "mildew" for which the OED gives: "A morbid destructive growth upon plants, consisting of minute fungi, and having usually the appearance of a thin whitish coating. Also, a similar growth on paper, leather, wood, etc., when exposed to damp."
476 Milgrom, *Leviticus: A New Translation,* Vol. 1, 809.
477 It has been suggested that no distinction was made between yellow and green in ANE cultures.

affected by the צרעת. His reasoning for this is that, in the woven cloth, there would be cross-infection of warp by weft or *vice versa*, and it would be impossible to identify which component part(s) of the finished cloth was the causative agent.

13:50–9

As with the human patient, the mouldy fabric must be examined by the priest who, seemingly whatever the appearance, must shut-up the affected thing for seven days at which point he must re-examine it, looking for spread.

13:51–52

If the affection has spread, the remedy is the simple one of burning[478] the garment (or whatever it was) for the spreading of צרעת characterizes the condition immediately as צרעת ממארת הנגע. The KJV and ERV translate ממארת by the somewhat archaic term *fretting*,[479] the RSV says, "malignant" and the NRSV as ever sits on the fence of dubiety with "spreading". The DCH[480] defines √מאר "be painful" or in the *hiph'il* as here "cause pain". It is difficult to know what this means with reference to a fabric but one must suppose that it is something akin to "serious" or "severe" though for whom—the fabric itself, its owner or the world in general—remains unclear. In contrast, the LXX says λέπρα ἔμμονός ἐστιν which implies chronicity rather than severity. The word ἔμμονός (= continual, persistent) occurs only four times in the LXX and on three of these occasions it is with λέπρα: there appears to be no apparent reason for choosing it to translate ממארת about whose meaning there is no uncertainty.

13:53–58

If no spread has occurred, the article must be washed and quarantined for a further seven days after which time it is inspected again. If, either no change in colour is seen and/or spread has occurred, the item must nevertheless still be burnt as it is irretrievably damaged with impurity.

However, if the affection has faded,[481] the priest can cut out or tear out the affected part from the whole with no concern as to whether this renders it useless. It must now be washed once again before it can be declared טהור. However, if, after this treatment, the mildew appears again, the entire item must be burnt immediately.

With regard to the tearing out of the affected area, both the HB and the LXX say that it can be torn quite specifically out of the garment or skin or selectively out

---

478 This can occur within the camp as burning brings about total destruction and there is no risk of further contagion.
479 OED = "A slow gnawing or eating away; erosion, corrosion; also, the process of decaying or wasting."
480 Clines, ed., *Dictionary of Classical Hebrew*.
481 Was this simply due to the washing?

of the warp *or* out of the weft, מִן־הַבֶּגֶד אוֹ מִן־הָעוֹר אוֹ מִֽן־הַשְּׁתִי אוֹ מִן־הָעֵרֶב (ἀπὸ τοῦ ἱματίου ἢ ἀπὸ τοῦ δέρματος ἢ ἀπὸ τοῦ στήμονος ἢ ἀπὸ τῆς κρόκης): this last feat is clearly impossible and reinforces the suggestion that this, in fact, refers to the individual yarns before they reach the loom.

13:59 A Summary Verse

The final verse is a statement that this chapter summarizes the law and procedures for צרעת/λέπρα.

What then, can we conclude from chapter 13 about the nature of צרעת/λέπρα? The array of symptoms and signs is so diverse that it is impossible to assemble them into any known modern syndrome or disease. The contenders have been summarized by Glasby[482] according to their symptoms and signs but the point is made that nothing fits exactly and that צרעת almost certainly did not refer to a specific disease but to a range of conditions that the untrained and uncritical Israelite mind perceived as being similar to one another. It remains unclear whether these conditions were characterized by scaliness or by whiteness. The present author believes that Milgrom's term *scale disease*, cannot be justified by the symptomatology. Moreover, the switch from *scale-disease* to *mould-disease* simply because of the change of subject is unacceptable as either a logical or a pathological possibility. The only justification we have for "scaliness" is that the translators of the LXX chose λέπρα to translate צרעת. But the λέπ* morpheme, besides alluding to *scales*, can also refer to *rind, coating, surface, skin, peel,* etc. We have no clear idea which of these meanings the authors of the Septuagint had in mind when using λέπρα to translate צרעת. The only thing they all have in common is that they refer to the external surface of a plant or animal. In this respect they may do no more than equate the *dermato-* prefix of modern pathology. The same may be said of *leproidosis* which, though a less specific term than *scale-disease*, nevertheless is entrammelled in the same dubious etymology. Another neologism, suggested by the present author is (*dermopathic*) *platydysmorphism* which means nothing more precise than disruption, misshapenness or disfigurement of a (skin) surface. Though cumbersome it has a certain attractiveness because it is appropriately and accurately descriptive and at the same time wholly non-specific.

Particularly controversial is the reference to *whiteness* in the various descriptions of צרעת. Whiteness is the single epithet most consistently applied to צרעת/λέπρα in the HB and LXX. It has been dismissed by commentators, perhaps too readily, because of the lack of any association of whiteness with modern Hansen's disease. Moreover, the appearance of whiteness may be due both to the scarring process and/or the flakiness of desquamating skin. These two appearances are to be seen in many of the contenders for צרעת and so may have led to the

---

482 Glasby, "What was Biblical Leprosy?", 74.

dismissal of this important sign as being confusing on account of its non-specific nature. There can be little doubt that even those of the most modest intellect in the ANE knew what "white" meant. It is, hard to dismiss whiteness as being relevant to צרעת because it is the adjective that recurs in this context in *all* of the relevant texts from Exodus to the Mishnah and Talmud.

Lieber has proposed a highly specific *scenario* for biblical "leprosy". She bases her argument on the observation that the Levitical rules for dealing with צרעת suggest a more serious affliction than one might expect from a perusal of the various biblical case-histories relating to the condition.[483] Lieber suggests that there may have been at least two categories of צרעת one being a more serious condition than the other. She postulates that during the Exodus and the period of wanderings in the desert, צרעת was probably the highly contagious disease *bejel*[484] (one of the non-venereal *treponematoses*), that is a common *sequela* of poorly-hygienic living in hot dry environments. It was, and is today, rarely seen in towns. Once the Israelites had settled in Canaan, Lieber suggests that *bejel* ceased to be prevalent but chronic *psoriasis* became prevalent and the two conditions became confused. This theory is attractive but has no direct evidence to support it, particularly regarding the Exodus and the wanderings. Nevertheless, Lieber has pointed out that in Lev 13, the diagnostic assessment of צרעת practised by the priests was based, principally, upon visible skin signs and these allowed for a differentiation into what Lieber has called "unclean" and "clean" cases inasmuch as they do, or do not, require the full treatment with isolation etc. She supposes that the "unclean" cases may have been bejel whilst those designated "clean" were probably chronic psoriasis or something related. Lieber suggests that, by deliberately collecting these conditions together as צרעת, they were all subjected to a process of triage which reduced the possibility of both false negatives and false positives.[485] If this is correct, it suggests that the priests were operating a public-sacramental-health policy designed to protect their sanctuary at least if not the community as a whole.

THE LEVITICUS RABBAH AND צרעת

While one must be cautious of extrapolation from one period and one worldview to another, the Leviticus Rabbah (LR) offers an irresistible opportunity to enlarge the lamentably meagre understanding of the word צרעת. This step may be partially justified by the fact that Leviticus Rabbah is quite specifically a rabbinic attempt to explain biblical Levitical material. Admittedly the attraction of the LR material is that it fits in somewhat with the Hellenic → Medieval "medical" *theory of humours*. Of course it is therefore open to the criticism of

---

[483] See also chapter 11.
[484] And much more contagious than Hansen's disease with similar signs, such as: depigmentation, ulceration, scaliness, deformity of the face and nose—gangosa—but not facies leonina. Also unlike leprosy this disease exhibits periods of latency and has a remitting course.
[485] Lieber, "Old Testament 'Leprosy', Contagion and Sin," 132–133.

invoking *hyperdiagnosis* and *anachronism* and at best we are allowed to conclude that LR is nothing more than a late interpretation brought about by progress. This is probably so, but it nevertheless highlights an interesting point. In chapter 11 under the heading *Context Logometrics* I shall propose that statistical analysis of the biblical usage of the word צרעת suggests that even if its meaning is completely lost to us, the writer(s) of Leviticus had a clear and specific understanding of its meaning. By rabbinic times it is possible that Hellenic and other influences had affected the interpretation given to this pathophysiological situation so that its original meaning had become enlarged or altered. In either case the possibility of retrojecting this meaning must not be overlooked.

The way in which *Leviticus Rabbah* deals with צרעת has been extensively discussed by Ostrer[486] in a paper that shows great insight and imagination. We are, however, dealing twice with a "sample of one" as both LR and Ostrer's paper stand alone and unchallenged. Uniquely, chapters 15 and 16 of LR offer some insight into what may be called, very loosely, "diagnosis" though hardly in the modern sense.[487] For the modern leprologist, this is perhaps the most interesting passage to be found in Hebrew/Aramaic literature. Chapter 15 of the Leviticus Rabbah deals extensively with skin diseases: the first two verses read:

1. When a man shall have in the skin of his flesh a rising, or a scab, or a bright spot, and it become in the skin of his flesh the plague of leprosy.
2. This is [alluded to in] what is written, "He appointeth a weight for the wind, and meteth out the waters by measure".

(Leviticus Rabbah 15:1–2)

The quotation is from the Book of Job:

לעשות לרוח משקל ומים תכן במדה

To make a weight for the wind; yea, he meteth out the waters by measure. (Job 28:25)

The Rabbinical view of disease-processes in general appears to have been akin to that of the Hippocratic School of Medicine and was based upon the notion of a maintained but dynamic equilibrium between certain bodily components.[488] Two such quantities-in-equilibrium were wind רוח and water מים, which were natural phenomena "measured out", i.e. dispensed, for humans by Yahweh. In the body it is necessary to postulate the materialization of the רוח (wind/spirit) into a physical form. Water (מים) was supposed to constitute 50% of the body's

---

486 B. S. Ostrer, "Leprosy: Medical Views of Leviticus Rabba," *ES&M* 7, no. 2 (2002): 138–54.
487 Hulse, "Nature of Biblical Leprosy."
488 A view that persisted generally for a very long time and which, in certain instances still holds today.

total make up, with the remaining 50% apparently made up of blood (דם).[489] It is interesting to speculate how the ancients reconciled this duality of liquids with what they could have observed in *post mortem* examination of bodies.[490] It was essential that this 50:50 equilibrium was maintained for the good health of both body and soul and the means by which the equilibrium was maintained intact was meritorious behaviour and the avoidance of sin. When the equilibrium was upset in the direction of an excess of water, dropsy[491] occurred and when there was an excess of blood, צרעת was the result. This is quite explicitly stated in the final *derashah* of 15:2:

אדם היה משוקל חציו מים וחציו דם בשעה שהוא זוכה לא המים רבין על הדם ולא הדם רבין על המים ובזמן שחוטא פעמים שהמים רבין על הדם ונעשה אדריפיקוס ופעמים שהדם רבין על המים ונעשה מצורע הה״ד אדם או דם

> Man is evenly balanced, half of him is water, and the other half is blood. When he is deserving, the water does not exceed the blood, nor does the blood exceed the water; but when he sins, it sometimes happens that the water gains over the blood and he then becomes a sufferer from dropsy; at other times the blood gains over the water and he then becomes leprous. This is [indicated by] what is written, ADAM [i.e. A MAN.] read as if O dam.[492] Or [if it be] blood [that exceeds].

Menstruation,[493] though apparently not a pathological genital discharge, was viewed similarly, as an upset of the water/blood equilibrium, and the conception[494] of a child by a mother whilst in such a ritually impure state was supposed to result in the [still]birth of a child afflicted with צרעת. As stillborn children were thought to have a scaly appearance, this provided a convenient pathological explanation and a means of apportioning blame. As Job contemplates his dermatological afflictions he asks why he was not stillborn[495].

או כנפל טמון לא אהיה כעללים לא־ראו אור

> Or as an hidden untimely birth I had not been; as infants which never saw light. (Job 3:16)

The idea of a water/blood dis-equilibrium presented for the rabbis a means of explaining the spots, scabs, scales, blisters, and the whitening of the hair all described (but not explained), in Lev 13, as symptomatic of צרעת. An excess of blood over water in the body (*plethora*) occurs as a result of some aspect of sin or impure living. The plethora causes such a degree of engorgement that the

---

489 Ostrer points out that we have to accept that the terms "blood", "heat", and "spirit" are synonymous. Ostrer, "Leprosy: Medical Views of Leviticus Rabba," 153.
490 It is possible that levitical laws relating to corpses meant that such examinations were rare or even non-existent.
491 ὑδρωπικος in Hippocratic medicine. Hippocrates et al., *Hippocrates*.
492 Not the vocative! In Hebrew או means "or".
493 See also chapter 8.
494 Unlikely, though not impossible.
495 Cf. μὴ φῦναι τὸν ἅπαντα νικᾷ λογον. (Sophocles: *Oedipus at Colonus*, 1224–5).

boundaries of the body become fractured and large quantities of blood pour forth.[496] The result is a generalized *anaemia* that causes the hair to turn white and all of the the various dermatological lesions to develop.[497] While this sequence of events makes no pathological sense today, one can see how such an explanation might have satisfied curiosity at the time, and indeed such an explanation would have been quite acceptable later, in Greek medicine.

Ostrer,[498] in his study of the Leviticus Rabbah—which he describes as an *allegorical commentary*—has tried to bring a sense of *Gleichschaltung* to the idea of biblical "leprosy" by drawing particularly upon material from Douglas, Milgrom, and Neusner. Ostrer draws also upon Hippocratic medicine to postulate that the Levitical priests were operating a rudimentary system of health awareness parallel to, but less sophisticated than, the Greek educational principle of παιδεία. By "health", of course, in the Jewish view was still meant principally, the avoidance of impurity. For the Greek, there was a much wider purview. There was, in the Greek mentality, a notion of unity between microcosm and macrocosm: individual and universe. The Greek doctor, through παιδεία, was supposed to make the individual aware of the universe. Ostrer believes that, with a different concept of universe, and (*mutatis mutandis*) this was also the duty of the Levitical priest. To the Israelite, this notion stretched no further than the society to which he belonged. Douglas[499] has suggested that there was a clear correspondence in the mind of individuals between the social macrocosm and the individual microcosm and that any situation in which their boundaries were transgressed, either legitimately or otherwise, represented a potential or real violation of the purity of both individual and society (ארץ). Therefore, the rules that govern what enters or leaves the body, become a reflection of the rules for society as a whole.[500] Violation of one set of boundaries *ipso facto* entails a violation of the other set. One can see that, since the number of individuals and the variation among them is very large compared with only a single limited society, the probability of violation beginning with the individual and diffusing to society as a whole is significantly greater than the reverse.

However fanciful all this might appear today, we must be grateful to the rabbis for this insight into their thought-processes. They may have been uncomfortable with צרעת in purely Levitical terms and so were attempting to find a [quasi]-rational explanation for what was overwhelmingly seen as an act of God. Alternatively, they were conscious of a need to upgrade their thoughts in the light of Greek medicine and its *theory of humours*. They probably were not

---

496 However, there seem to be no accounts of serious haemorrhage associated with צרעת and we have to suppose a process perhaps akin to evaporation. These "boundaries" do not appear to be defined in any anatomical sense.
497 Anoxic necrosis?
498 Ostrer, "Leprosy: Medical Views of Leviticus Rabba."
499 Douglas, *Purity and Danger*; T. M. Lemos, "The Universal and the Particular: Mary Douglas and the Politics of Impurity," *J.Rel* 89, no. 2 (2009): 236–51.
500 Cf. رمضان (Ramaḍān), in Islam.

wholly unaware of the fact that there might be some organic basis for צרעת and, in a different worldview from the Levitical priests, saw no reason not to develop this idea. Nevertheless, disease as divine punishment remained the order of the day.

צרעת IN THE DEAD SEA SCROLLS

For purposes of comparison this important later source is also helpful. Feder has reviewed the case for צרעת on the basis of a study of 4QMMT.[501] His thesis is that in the late Tannaitic and early Amoraitic periods there was, among the rabbis, a change of attitude regarding צרעת. Feder's wider aim which uses צרעת as a paradigm, is to understand how the process of *halakah*—by which he means the conversion of legalistic text into practice—was brought to bear in the matter of purity/impurity in a non-priestly milieu. Feder suggests that by the time of 4QMMT, rabbinical attitudes towards צרעת had softened considerably from the Levitical position and the treatment by the priesthood of the individual afflicted with this condition had changed from that demanded in Lev 13:46 and 14:8. In particular, the rules had changed regarding his dwelling outside his tent. Two seminal texts from the Hebrew Bible are:

כל־ימי אשר הנגע בו יטמא טמא הוא בדד ישב מחוץ למחנה מושבו

> All the days wherein the plague is in him he shall be unclean; he is unclean: he shall dwell alone; without the camp shall his dwelling be. (Lev 13:46)

וכבס המטהר את־בגדיו וגלח את־כל־שערו ורחץ במים וטהר ואחר יבוא אל־המחנה וישב מחוץ לאהלו שבעת ימים

> And he that is to be cleansed shall wash his clothes, and shave off all his hair, and bathe himself in water, and he shall be clean: and after that he shall come into the camp, but shall dwell outside his tent seven days. (Lev 14:8)

The new stricture, imposed by the rabbis, was that the *dermopath*,[502] although he could return to his tent, should abstain from sexual intercourse during the period of his purification.

---

[501] Y. Feder, "The Polemic Regarding Skin Diseases in 4QMMT," *DSD* 19 (2012): 55–70. 4QMMT is sometimes called the "Halachic Letter" and is supposed by some to have been directed to the priests in Jerusalem. Another view is that it was a letter written by Qumran's 'Teacher of Righteousness' and/or his followers, to his rival, the "Wicked Priest".

[502] It is almost impossible to find an appropriate word in English. To use leper or even "leper" (cf. Feder) would seem counterintuitive to the spirit of this study. The word צרעת in participial form is too general as it would include inanimate objects besides humans. The rather unattractive word dermopath at least is correctly derived and implies a human sufferer from a skin disease and fits in with other modern neologisms such as arteriopath and sociopath.

This exegesis, Feder suggests, is the result of interpreting a passage from the *Sifra* covering similar topics;[503] Feder bases his idea upon Deut 5:30,

לך אמר להם שובו לכם לאהליכם

Go say to them, Return ye to your tents. (Deut 5:30)

And he extends this by means of a text from the Sifra[504]

. יהא כמנודה ויהא אסור בתשמיש המיטה.וישב מחוץ לאהלו ישב מחוץ לאוהלו

.אהלו אין אהלו אלא אשתו שנ' שובו לכם לאהליכם

"And he shall dwell outside his tent"—he shall dwell outside his tent, (meaning) he shall be like an ostracized person and be forbidden in sexual relations. "his tent"—there is no other tent besides his wife, as it is said: "Go back to your tents".

Feder's contention is that the rabbis saw "tent" (or "house") as a metaphor for "wife" and so by extension for sexual intercourse. There is some small literary precedent for this, for example, we find in relation to Noah's drunken episode (Gen 9:21):

וישת מן־היין וישכר ויתגל בתוך אהלה

and he drank of the wine, and was drunken; and he was uncovered within his tent. (Gen 9:21)

Although it may not be obvious in the text of the Hebrew Bible, in the Genesis Rabbah 36:4,[505] the following explanation is proffered:

בתוך אהלו אהלה כתיב בתוך אהלה של אשתו

within his tent (ahaloh): this is written ahalah, (her tent), viz. his wife's tent

The author of the *Genesis Rabbah* is suggesting that Noah, through his drunkenness and in contradistinction to the canonical tale, failed in his sexual advances towards his wife.

The word "house" is also found as a metaphor for "wife" in the *Talmud,* although not necessarily in a sexual context. For example, in relation to the rules for *Yom Kippur, (Mas Yoma 2a:1)* we find the phrase:

שנאמר וכפר בעדו ובעד ביתו ביתו זו אשתו

---

503 The Sifra, (Aramaic: ספרא), is an halakic midrash devoted specifically to Leviticus. It was traditionally studied after the Mishnah. Its original authorship is uncertain but its redaction into the version studied by rabbis along with the Mishnah and widely quoted in the Talmud, is attributed to Rabbi Hiyya (c. 180–230 BCE).
504 MSS Vatican 66.
505 Soncino, *The Soncino Classics Collection.*

it is written, "and he shall make atonement for himself and for his house." "His house" that means "his wife".[506]

Words such as "house" or "tent" are, therefore attested as being used metaphorically for "wife" in both a sexual and a domestic context. If one accepts this idea, the *dermopath* did not, literally, have to dwell outside his tent but merely refrain from coition. However, it seems particularly curious that there is no parallel passage relating to those afflicted with any of the genital effluxions mentioned in Leviticus chapter 15. These individuals, and especially those with venereal associations, would be expected today to be at the top of any list of coital prohibitions. Of course the canonical *Sifra* and the *Mishnah* and *Talmud* were written after the Qumran community ended in 68 CE. Nevertheless, we may suppose that halakic principles therein might well have been handed down to the rabbis, perhaps from their pharisaic forebears in Jerusalem who were extant during the period of the Qumran community. Feder makes an assumption along these lines and supposes that the passage in 4QMMT (below) was a specific polemic from the Qumran community, challenging this "plunge into leniency" on the part of the Jerusalem Pharisees, who were later to become rabbis. The passage he cites is: "

> 4. ...And also concerning lepers: we
>
> 5. s[ay that] they should [not] enter (a place) with hol[y] purity, but in isolation
>
> 6. [they shall stay outside a house. And] also it is written that [from] the moment he shaves and washes he should stay outside
>
> 7. [his tent for seven d]ays. But now, even when they are still unclean
>
> 8. [lepers approach (a place) wi]th holy purity, to the house. And you know
>
> 9. [ ] and it is taken away from him, must bring it
>
> 10. [a sin-offering. And concerning him who acts offensively it is wri]tten that he is a slanderer and a blasp[he]mer.
>
> 11. [And also: when they have the uncleanness of leprosy] they should not eat any of the ho[l]y things
>
> (4Q396 (4QMMT-c) III:4—11)

This instruction, Feder argues, is unequivocal in its adherence to the message of Lev 13:46 and 14:8 (above), which it reaffirms as the view which should be that

---

506 Ibid, there is nothing in the ensuing Gemara to explain this usage, so we may suppose it was a common metaphor.

of those belonging to the Qumran community. The rabbis, with their mollifying approach are, therefore, taking inappropriate and unjustified liberties with biblical exegesis. Feder's argument is strengthened by the observation that elsewhere, there can be found no evidence of a requirement placed upon any sort of ostracized individual (מנודה) to abandon his home. More likely, he might be expected to take refuge there and remain therein in either isolation/quarantine or banishment. In the absence of such an instruction, the equation of "tent" or "house" with "wife" seems both feasible and likely. The undoubted notion of the Hebrew Bible where, in Levitical priestly dogma, a dermopath, at any time, could cause *defilement by habitation* appears to have been revised by rabbinical times where it became limited to the pre-purificatory period (מוחלט), before the cleansing protocol formulated in Lev 14:8. Some uncertainty has, however, been mooted about this idea on the basis of a passage from the *Mishnah*. After the shaving and washing, Lev 14:8 demands that "he shall come into the camp, but shall dwell outside his tent seven days." In contrast the *Mishnah* (*Mas Nega'im 14:2*), has the following to say:

מנודה מביתו נכנס לפנים מן החומה והרי הוא מטמא כשרץ טהור מלטמא בביאה ואסור בתשמיש המטה שבעת ימים

> he is then clean so far as not to convey uncleanness by entering in, but he still conveys uncleanness like a creeping thing. He may enter within the wall, but must keep away from his *house* for seven days, and he is forbidden marital intercourse

It is irritatingly unclear whether two different sets of instructions are combined in operation here or whether "house" is again a metaphor for "wife" and the words that follow are explicative and/or emphatic. Whatever the case may have been, there is clear evidence that the strictures imposed upon the dermopath by Levitical law, in particular those relating to defilement by habitation, were attenuated by time and the midrashic processing of the rabbis. Moreover, in addition, the rabbis decreed that there was a hierarchy of "camps" inasmuch as walled cities were considered to be more holy (and therefore more defilable) than less permanent encampments or settlements.

עירות המוקפות חומה מקודשות ממנה. שמשלחין מתוכן את המצורעים. ומסבבין לתוכן מת עד שירצו. יצא. אין מחזירין אותו

> cities that are walled are holier, for lepers must be sent out of them and a corpse, though it may be carried about within them as long as it is desired, may not be brought back once it has been taken out. (Mishnah, Kelim 1:7)

This rather goes against Feder's argument for the metaphorical usage of "camp/tent/house" to mean wife. By Second Temple times, it must be supposed that, because Yahweh occupied the temple and the priests and Levites occupied the Temple Mount that was walled, this, they felt, created for themselves a precinct that demanded a higher standard of attention where prevention of contagion was concerned.

From a medical point of view, all of this is very interesting because it appears to show a greater concern, on the part of written *halakah*, for the risk of contagion for the community than for the individual. The act of sexual intercourse today would be seen as undoubtedly putting the individual more at risk of acquiring a contagious disease—venereal or non-venereal and not merely a skin disease—than would the sharing of commodities and commonalities of existence under the same roof. Were the rabbis then, themselves having no modern idea of infection or contagion, simply more concerned for the health of the community than for that of the individual? This seems likely if we accept a hierarchy—inherited from the priestly worldview—in the purity laws from individual to community to land.[507]

This is well summed-up in two verses from Num 5:2–3 which bear the fullest quoting here:

צו את־בני ישראל וישלחו מן־המחנה כל־צרוע וכל־זב וכל טמא לנפש

> Command the children of Israel, that they put out of the camp every leper, and every one that hath an issue, and whosoever is unclean by the dead:

מזכר עד־נקבה תשלחו אל־מחוץ למחנה תשלחום ולא יטמאו את־מחניהם אשר אני שכן בתוכם

> both male and female shall ye put out, without the camp shall ye put them; that they defile not their camp, in the midst whereof I dwell.

Two important points are made here. First, there is a triad of states that demands the ostracizing of the individual from the camp. These are, in what appears to be a descending order of seriousness, skin disease צרעת, a genital discharge זוב, or defilement by touching a dead body. The second point is that Yahweh dwells in the land, within the (walled) camp even, and so any defilement puts this arrangement at risk. The loss of Yahweh's presence was, in the eyes of the ancient Israelites and especially their priests, the ultimate catastrophe for a land bereft of Yahweh would be bereft of his covenant and the inhabitants would lose their status as a chosen people.

One of the most disappointing and indeed irritating problems associated with any attempt to understand צרעת is the complete absence in the Hebrew Bible of any evidence to suggest incidence or prevalence. Admittedly a great deal of text-space was given to צרעת both in the Hebrew Bible and especially in later

---

507 See chapter 3.

Jewish literature but never is there an indication of how often any given priest might encounter a case. In considering any form of pathology the first things one wants to know are who is at risk, what is the geographical extent of the disease and how many cases might one expect to see? We have no idea how often the priests were called upon to use their diagnostic skills and so we cannot know whether צרעת was something they encountered daily or only infrequently, in isolated cases or in "clumps".

In addition, it is impossible from the textual evidence to decide if the priests used their skills in a truly differential way to arrive at a specific diagnosis or whether they were content simply to accept the presence of platydysmorphism as pathognomonic of defilement without needing to know anything about its specific nature. It appears that only establishment of the presence of צרעת was necessary for them to institute appropriate ritual measures.

What can we conclude from this medical exegesis of Leviticus 13? The evidence available in this chapter, although highly descriptive, allows us no more than to arrive at the proposition that צרעת is a *portmanteaulogism*[508] used to describe a congeries of conditions that, collectively, exhibits (roughly) those symptoms exemplified by another portmanteau word, *platydysmorphism*. By its very nature, this is usefully, non-specific, widely inclusive, and appropriate to what [little] we know of צרעת under the ancient priestly worldview: but it cannot be translocated to a modern, medical environment.

What then are we entitled to say about צרעת/λέπρα?

1. It is a visible disfigurement of a surface upon which it may spread—platydysmorphism.
2. It exhibits a range of symptoms which are not consistent with any modern, recognizable disease.
3. Whiteness may be a feature in human cases.

This strongly suggests that the Israelite perception of צרעת was of a very non-specific thing that, serving as a general determinant of טמא, was more important to Hebrew priestly thoughts and deeds directed at the establishment and preservation of sacramental ritual than was any consideration of its medical/pathological nature. We must energetically no longer try to think of צרעת as a disease, rather it should be seen as a spectrum—perhaps of *affections* rather than *afflictions*—all of which contribute to the ritual impurity of the individual. We may profitably employ the terms *dermopath*[509] and

---

508 Applied attributively to a general description or category, or to a word or expression which has a general or generalized meaning. Originally applied by 'Lewis Carroll' to a factitious word made up of the blended sounds of two distinct words and combining the meanings of both."
509 But only where human skin is involved.

platydysmorphism[510] to describe the condition in a highly appropriate but entirely non-specific way.

The word itself will be discussed yet further in chapter 11 and its theological implications in chapter 12.

Chapter 14 of Leviticus deals at length with the sacrificial duties of both priest and מצרע. It has nothing significant to add to the present investigation. Chapter 15, however deals with a detailed consideration of another "medical" condition that came within the province of the priesthood. This is זוב, a term used to describe a number of physiological and pathological genital effluxions whose presence conferred varying degrees of impurity upon the sufferer. It is proposed to discuss this in the following chapter.

---

510 Wherever any sort of surface is involved.

Chapter 8

זוב GENITAL EFFLUXIONS: A MEDICAL EXEGESIS OF LEVITICUS CHAPTER 15

Chapter 15 of the Book of Leviticus is concerned with the second supposedly medical reason for טמא/ἀκάθαρτός, namely, genital discharges. It is part of the P material in Leviticus and, if we susbscribe to the views of Milgrom, Knohl *et al*,[511] this dates it before the H material of chapters 17–26.[512] The above authors cite the absence of any mention of the *sojourner* or *resident alien* (גר) as being indicative of an origin earlier than H. Because of this, it is reasonable to suppose that the chapter was written for, and concerns only Israelites and that non-Israelites were either thought not to be susceptible to the impurity conferred by these discharges, or were not worthy of and/or appropriate for consideration. It is not strictly accurate to refer to these conditions, as some authors have, collectively as pathological because effluxes such as menstruation and involuntary seminal emissions are known today to be physiological. Clearly, this fact was not appreciated in the ANE. Modern commentaries, such as those of Milgrom,[513] are sedulous in differentiating *pathological* from *physiological* or "abnormal" from "normal" discharges. However, neither the Hebrew Bible (HB), nor the Septuagint (LXX), makes any such distinction which, therefore, rests entirely upon modern medical knowledge. The essential point about genital discharges collectively is that they all were seen to confer impurity (טמא) and that this impurity was *contagious* and transferable to other individuals both venereally and by non-venereal practices, such as spitting.

It is important to note also that it is only a *genital* discharge (זוב/ῥύσις) that qualifies for טמא/ἀκάθαρτός in the Hebrew Bible and later Jewish religious writings and for the scrupulous attention of the priesthood. This puts it alongside that other pathological cause of impurity, צרעת/λέπρα. Surprisingly, other bodily discharges that today would undoubtedly be regarded as unpleasant, if not defiling, are not considered. One might imagine a variety of unpleasant effluxions or suppurations, both visible and invisible, such as perianal abscess, Bartholin's cyst, haemorrhoidal bleeding, abnormal salivation, dental infections, urinary and faecal incontinence, to be considered as leading to impurity; but they are not. The physiological processes of micturition and defaecation and their products are nowhere mentioned in either the Hebrew Bible or the Septuagint as being connected with impurity.[514] It appears to be the

---

511 Milgrom, *Leviticus: A New Translation*; Milgrom, *Leviticus: A Continental Commentary*; Knohl, *The Sanctuary of Silence*.
512 See chapter 2.
513 Milgrom, *Leviticus: A New Translation*.
514 It was not to say, however, that these were not considered unattractive. For example cf Ezek 4:12; and 2 Kgs 18:27.

association of the discharge specifically with the *genitalia*—when and where these are seen as behaving specifically as *organs of generation* but not when operating in their excretory/defaecatory capacities—that defines these discharges as causing impurity. So (despite this medical illogicality, at least in present-day terms), this moves them from the sphere of medicine into the priestly worldview of ritual purity and impurity.

In searching for a reason as to why this very specific association should obtain, there appear to be two possibilities. It seems likely that the ancients were fearful that any progeny conceived when either parent was in a state of זוב/ῥύσις (and therefore טמא/ἀκάθαρτός), would in some way be irretrievably damaged, perhaps even permanently damned, by an irreversible form of both spiritual and physical defilement. In the priestly worldview, such an individual would challenge the maintenance of the cosmic order. In support of this idea, Milgrom[515] has noted that the very clear bipartite structure of Lev 15 has, at its centre, a single verse (18) prohibiting sexual intercourse—or more precisely, intercourse in which internal ejaculation takes place—in the presence of any of the specified forms of זוב/ῥύσις. He believes this declaration of *caveat* to be pivotal for this chapter and the *raison d'être* for the participant's becoming טמא/ἀκάθαρτός in this way. Surprisingly however, the consequences of this activity—considered more fully below—are only those expected of *minor impurities*,[516] namely bathing and remaining unclean until sunset.

ואשה אשר ישכב איש אתה שכבת־זרע ורחצו במים וטמאו עד־הערב

> The woman also with whom a man shall lie with seed of copulation, they shall both bathe themselves in water, and be unclean until the even. (Lev 15:18)

An alternative, though not mutually exclusive, view that contrasts significantly with modern ideas about genital discharges, requires the observer to consider them as *something lost* rather than *something gained*. Today, we talk of getting/picking-up, for example, a "dose" of gonorrhoea, and so see the condition as something we have gained by incautiousness, poor hygiene or even sinfulness. Such an approach could not possibly apply to the physiological discharges and it is important to note that the Levitical viewpoint never suggests this. The only way in which Levitical impurity can be reconciled with both physiological and pathological discharges as described in Lev 15 is if we consider *all* of these forms of genital discharge to represent *something lost*. The "something" is, of course, the *seed of generation* i.e. semen, which is seen as the potential *life force*. In support of this idea we have already noted that no watery discharges nor urine itself ever bring about impurity. It is always the loss of this

---

515 Milgrom, *Leviticus: A New Translation*, 905.
516 See chapter 5.

easily identifiable life-giving body-fluid that results in impurity.⁵¹⁷ There is a further implication that, not only are life-giving body-fluid(s) lost from the body when genital discharges occur, but they are also destroyed in the course of the effluxion/ejaculation. Whether the emission is intentional or not, the destruction appears to be an ineluctable consequence, and in every case it is defiling. In the story of Onan and Tamar (Gen 38:9), most English translations (and also the LXX), speak of Onan's merely "spilling his seed" upon the ground, (ἐξέχεεν ἐπὶ τὴν γῆν). The Hebrew Bible uses the *pi'el* form of the verb שחת that quite specifically means "spoil" or "ruin" and it has been suggested that this is to emphasize that the life-giving potential of his seed has been ruined utterly. However, the root שחת has no recorded *Qal* form and is normally found in the *niph'al* (נִשְׁחַת) with the sense of "be destroyed".⁵¹⁸ The *pi'el* (שִׁחֵת) may, therefore, simply operate as the normal active voice. Nevertheless, as Joüon and Muraoka have pointed out, the meaning of the *pi'el* is still something of a mystery and almost certainly has a more complex role to play than being merely emphatic.⁵¹⁹ Perhaps in this case it is being used in a *factive* sense where one might more usually expect the *hiph'il*. The implication is, nevertheless, considerably more than Onan's simply missing the target; it is the intentional destruction of his semen not only as a contraceptive measure, as we may assume—from the Masoretic vocalization—that לְבִלְתִּי נְתָן־זֶרַע לְאָחִיו implies, but also to avoid the totality of the responsibilities that would be conferred by an unwanted levirate marriage. It thus amounted to a crime for which the punishment of death would be fitting, or at least not unreasonable, in the climate of legalistic thought entailed by the priestly worldview and Levitical ideology.

STRUCTURE OF LEVITICUS CHAPTER 15

The structure of Lev 13 is as follows:

- Pathological male (♂) discharges, (vv. 2–15).
- Physiological male (♂) discharges, (vv. 16–17).
- Sexual intercourse (v. 18).
- Physiological female (♀) discharges, (vv. 19–24).
- Pathological female (♀) discharges, (vv. 25–30).

There is a clear symmetry around verse 18 which perhaps supports Milgrom's view of its pivotal place. Given the relatively large portion of Leviticus, and of the Torah in general, that is concerned with צרעת/λέπρα and with זוב/ῥύσις, one might think, *prima facie*, these matters shared a wide prevalence and considerable importance in the ANE. However, nowhere is there any indication as to the incidence or prevalence of these conditions and we are left to make rather ill-informed guesses as to the magnitude of these variables. This does not

---

517 A parallel idea but in a different context, would be loss of blood.
518 Clines, ed., *Dictionary of Classical Hebrew*.
519 Joüon and Muraoka, *A Grammar of Biblical Hebrew*, §52 a & d.

go unnoticed either in the many highly speculative accounts of what these conditions might have been, or in critical responses to such accounts.[520] We cannot legitimately conclude that the large amount of space given over to them in the Torah was in any way a reflection of their being commonplace—they may have been rare—but nevertheless because of their inherent nastiness and their potential for contagion, they were considered important and fearsome enough to warrant a substantial degree of consideration in the ritual prescriptions and proscriptions issuant from the priesthood. Likewise, although *what* they were is perfectly clear, we are not told anything about the incidence of physiological seminal emissions and little distinction is made as to whether these were voluntary (masturbation, *coitus interruptus*), or involuntary.[521] Neither should we use present day *mores* or criteria to presume that menstruation was thought of as it is today; and, even more importantly, nor should we imagine it to have been as common as it is today.[522] The Israelite wife spent a much greater proportion of her reproductive life than is common today in either pregnancy or lactation (Hos 1:8). Normal menstruation, which is suppressed by these conditions, would not, therefore, have been seen as the regular monthly event expected by most women today.[523]

It is the question of genital *infections* that causes the greatest controversy. What these may have been is a matter of considerable dispute. Whilst we can draw some conclusions about the various forms of genital effluxion that are the subject of this chapter, we are nevertheless left with some uncertainties that will be considered below in relation to their occurrence in specific verses.

For the moment we may suppose:

- Pathological (♂) discharges: infections—see discussion below.
- Physiological (♂) discharges: voluntary or involuntary emissions of semen.
- Physiological (♀) discharges: menstruation (post partum lochia).
- Pathological (♀) discharges: infections + menorrhagia /metrorrhagia.[524]

It has been suggested by Milgrom that, with the exception of the final three somewhat homiletical verses, Lev 15 was written by a single author.[525] He bases

---

520 See the preceeding chapter for similar thoughts about צרעת
521 It would probably be just as difficult today to obtain meaningful statistics about the incidence of these conditions and the practices relating to them.
522 The Islamic view of menstruation was also that it conferred impurity. Hayim ben Yosef Tawil, *An Akkadian Lexical Companion for Biblical Hebrew* (Jersey City, NJ: KTAV Publishing House, 2009). Abdullah Yusuf Ali, *The Holy Qur'an* (text and translation) (Birmingham: IPCI: Islamic Vision, 1999), 2:222.
523 It is highly unlikely that the ancients had any idea of the physiological significance of menstruation. They almost certainly saw it at least as semi-pathological. Moreover, puberty would have been later and overall life-expectancy shorter then. Goodman has suggested that the Israelites eschewed any form of contraception and also the practices of abortion and infanticide that were common at the time among other Mediterranean communities. Geller, *Ancient Babylonian Medicine*, 61.
524 Menorrhagia = prolonged or excessive menstruation; metrorrhagia = abnormal uterine bleeding. The distinction is one of time as well as pathology: the former being a cyclical phenomenon and the latter being random.
525 Milgrom, *Leviticus: A New Translation*, Vol. 1, 905.

this conclusion on observations of style, syntax, and vocabulary—and particularly upon the way in which the second half of the chapter is wholly dependent on the first half and that both pivot around the all-important verse 18. If this is correct, we at least can assume that we have a unified view about the nature of the various types of discharge as well as their place in early Israelite society. This is a great bonus and in contrast to what we know about צרעת.

On the larger scale of the book of Leviticus, Milgrom sees an interesting structure in the block of chapters 12 to 15. They appear to specify a descending order for the times taken for purification after the acquisition of טמא/ἀκάθαρτός.

- Chapter 12—Post-parturient: ♂ child 40 days; ♀ child 80 days.
- Chapter 13 & 14—צרעת/λέπρα ♂ or ♀ 8 days + 4 sacrifices + anointing.
- Chapter 15—Genital discharges.
  - Pathological discharge ♂ or ♀ 8 days + 2 sacrifices.
  - Menstruation—7 days.
  - Seminal emission—1 day.

The individual verses of chaper 15 may now be considered using the same format—medical exegesis—as in the preceeding chapter.

A MEDICAL EXEGESIS OF LEVITICUS 15

15:1–2 Pathological Discharge in Males—Nature of the Condition

The involvement of Aaron is in response to the need for sacrifices to be made. Because these conditions, in contrast one supposes to צרעת, are not exposed and obvious for all to see, there is a clear and vital need for the patients themselves to recognize the problem and to initiate its treatment. As mentioned above, this chapter is quite specifically aimed at Israelites. Later, and as a supposed deterrent to sodomy, the rabbis decreed that all non-Israelite males above the age of nine years should also be included.

Several important facts about the nature of the discharges can be gleaned from the grammar employed in these verses. The use of the imperfect tense of the verb "to be" plus a participle, forms a compound tense indicating the continuing nature of the discharge (יִהְיֶה זָב). We are, therefore, dealing here with *chronic* conditions that may be expected to persist into the future. We are introduced here also to the term describing male and female sufferers, זב /זבה literally "one discharging" from the Hebrew root[526] זוב and the Akkadian cognate *zâbu* (𒀭𒁺𒁉), meaning "ooze".[527]

---

[526] Clines, ed., *Dictionary of Classical Hebrew*. Note also Exod 3:17, זָבַת חָלָב וּדְבָשׁ
[527] Tawil, *An Akkadian Lexical Companion for Biblical Hebrew*, 90; Borger, *Mesopotamisches Zeichenlexikon*, 390 #641; Soden and Meissner, *Akkadisches Handwörterbuch*, Vol. 3, 1501; H. F. Lutz, "A Contribution to the Knowledge of Assyro-Babylonian Medicine," *AmJSLL* 36, no. 1 (1919): 67–83.

In verse 2 we are asked to accept the usage of בשר, normally translated as skin/flesh/meat/body, as being here a euphemism for genitals. The KJV and ERV nevertheless persist in translating this word as "flesh" and the RSV as "body"; only the NRSV says "member". The evidence that has been cited for translating this word as "genitals/penis" is very tenuous indeed: Gen 17:11; Exod 28:42; Ezek 23:20; and it is not supported by the LXX which uses the word σῶμα. Despite this lack of hard evidence, Wevers[528] is, nevertheless, firmly of the view that "member/penis" is what was intended and we must perhaps put away modern clinical thoughts about suppurating flesh and try to see this problem as it would have appeared in the Ancient World. Milgrom[529] is helpful here in pointing us in the direction of the rabbis who—agreeing for once—in elucidating the nature of the male discharges, make it quite clear whence they originate. The physiological and pathological male discharges are demarcated by the fact that the words זרע and זב, although they may occur in the same verse (Lev 22:4), are clearly referring to different things. Moreover, in the Talmud (*Nidah 35b*), we find the following observation:

> Rabbi Huna stated: The discharge of a zab resembles the dough-water of barley. The discharge of the zab issues from dead flesh while semen issues from live flesh. The former is watery and resembles the white of a crushed egg while the latter is viscous and resembles the white of a sound egg.

We must suppose, since *post mortem* events are not under consideration, that "dead flesh", is a somewhat over-dramatic euphemism for *membro flaccido* and "live flesh", in contrast, refers to a state of being *membro erecto*. This would cohere with the analogies chosen for the discharges. What we are dealing with therefore, seems perfectly clear; although there is nothing to identify the pathological discharge specifically except to say that it has a less viscid consistency than semen.[530]

The most immediately obvious contender for the pathological discharge is the condition that we know today as *gonorrhoea*. Older exegetes left the reader in no doubt that זוב *was* gonorrhoea. Later work, both theological and medical, has thrown doubt upon this conclusion and making the connection (or not) of gonorrhoea with the pathological discharge(s) of Lev 15 has become central to an understanding of this chapter.

---

528 Wevers, *Notes on the Greek Text of Leviticus*, 224
529 Milgrom, *Leviticus: A New Translation*, 907. Milgrom's helpfulness is not, however, unlimited. The sheer mass of rabbinic material on this matter and its wide variability is overwhelming.
530 It has been said earlier that watery discharges in the sense of urine, serum, plasma, etc. are not relevant to what is being considered here. By "watery", in the levitical context, we must suppose is meant something with a lower coefficient of viscosity than semen which, like all proteinaceous body fluids (and egg-white!), itself becomes less viscous with time and exposure to air.

The present-day definition of gonorrhoea is that it is a sexually-transmitted infectious disease of the lining mucosa of the genito-urinary tract. It is caused by the gonococcus *Neisseria gonorrhoeae*, which was identified by Albert Neisser in 1879.[531] Non-venereal transmission is sometimes seen, most usually during parturition, and apart from the genito-urinary tract, the rectum, oropharynx, eyes, epididymis, Fallopian tubes and perihepatic tissues may become infected. Dissemination, to produce lesions in joints, skin, meninges, and endocardium, has also been reported. The Gram-negative diplococcus *N. gonorrhoeae*, has been described as a *fastidious bacterium* because it does not survive for long outside the body. Traditionally, it has always been sensitive to the tetracycline class of antibiotics though resistant strains are beginning to appear as a result of antibiotic over/mis-use and the incidence of the disease is once again rising. The disease is most common today in heterosexual men, though both sexes can be affected and, although less common in females, the disease there is often more severe because it is harder to recognize and diagnose, especially early-on. It may consequently persist and lead to pelvic inflammatory disease and to sterility. In the uncomplicated case, the presenting symptoms, after a short incubation period (range: 1–12 days), are dysuria and a purulent urethral discharge that may first be noticed as cloudy urine.[532]

Milgrom[533] is over-generalizing, perhaps too emphatic, and certainly misleading, in his statement that "Scientific opinion is nearly unanimous that the only illness we know of that can be referred to here is gonorrhoea." He goes on to say that the identification of זוב as gonorrhoea "has been already made by the LXX and Josephus (Ant 3:261; Wars 5:273 and 6:426)." If not wholly wrong, this is very confusing because of the considerable historical unclarity that surrounded this condition before Neisser's identification of the gonococcus in 1879. The situation is somewhat parallel to that for צרעת/λέπρα and "leprosy".[534]

Milgrom does not help by going on to say that biblical gonorrhoea is not gonorrhoea as it is known today and also by using terminology which has been out-of-date since the early nineteenth century. To understand his position—unsurprisingly more that of an etymologist than a venereologist—we must bear in mind that the word *gonorrhoea* ultimately has its origins in γόνος, meaning "that which is begotten" and by extension "seed" as in the "seed of generation". Thus, the basic etymology of gonorrhoea implies a flowing of seed and it is to this etymology, rather than to modern venereology, that Milgrom appears to be looking for an explanation of pathological זוב/ῥύσις.

---

531 G. W. Csonka, "Gonorrhoea," in *Oxford Textbook of Medicine*, ed. D. J. Weatherall, J. G. G. Ledingham, D. A. Warrell (Oxford: Oxford University Press, 1989). V. Bevan, "Gonorrhoea: An Unlikely Love Affair," *Microbiologist December* (2004): 30–31.
532 5–10% of cases may be entirely asymptomatic and so the individual may spread the disease unwittingly. As the disease progresses the fresh discharge becomes more purulent and viscid—not watery!
533 Milgrom, *Leviticus: A New Translation*, 907.
534 Glasby, "What was Biblical Leprosy?"

Milgrom[535] compounds the problem by the use of undefinable archaisms. He asserts that זוב was "*not Gonorrhoea virulenta*"[536] by which he intends us to understand that he means not neisserial gonorrhoea, but something else. Milgrom makes the point that *Gonorrhoea virulenta* was unknown before the fifteenth century, though this is open to question. The appellation, *Gonorrhoea virulenta* was, indeed in the past, used for severe but otherwise un-specified venereal disease, but it was abandoned in the first half of the nineteenth century, even before Neisser's discovery of the gonococcus. Its virtue was, possibly, to contrast recognizable and relatively virulent venereal infection(s) with other conditions that were more benign. However, we must remember that in "pre-antibiotic" days, what are today considered as innocuous infections all had the potential, if left untreated, to become serious and even life-threatening.[537] It seems unfortunate that Milgrom should feel it necessary to resurrect out-of-date terminology to explain that זוב was probably not gonorrhoea. This could have been achieved more elegantly and with proper respect for modern bacteriological scientific-rigour by more careful attention to medical terminology that was in everyday use at the time of Milgrom's writing. Milgrom's choice of obsolete, nineteenth-century medical terms for benign venereal diseases seems entirely out of character for an author who is usually so fastidious. Nevertheless, so significant is Milgrom's exegetical work that these terms have become entrenched and the reader needs to be disabused of them.

Chief amongst these relatively benign conditions were so-called *Gonorrhoea benigna* and *Blenorrhoea urethrae*.[538] It is all very well for Milgrom to implicate these conditions as "possibles" for זוב but in fact today, neither of them can be identified as a specific disease. In nineteenth century European medicine, especially in Victorian Britain, there was a somewhat sanctimonious element among doctors who held that the "solitary and unholy" practice of *onania*—self abuse, or masturbation—was harmful and resulted in disease, even blindness.[539] The premonitory symptoms and signs of an overindulgent practice of *onania* were apparently genital discharges of a muco-serous nature.[540] In British medical practice this early sign of *onania* became [over]frequently diagnosed and known as *spermatorrhoea*;[541] a word that has also been used to describe involuntary

---

535 *Leviticus: A New Translation*, 907.
536 His words. Gonorrhoea virulenta is unknown in modern medicine but probably the term was used in the past for neisserial gonorrhoea, but also for a range of venereal diseases. It is, therefore, unsafe to use this term as a means of identifying זוב.
537 It was quite possible too, that common treatments for these ailments usually involving mercury and arsenic could cause as much, if not more, morbidity and mortality than the infections themselves.
538 These conditions were almost certainly what was commonly diagnosed as gleet up until the end of the nineteenth century, though it was quite likely that neisserial gonorrhoea was included in this term also. With no systematic, established, bacteriology, mis-diagnosis would have been common.
539 There was no thought of infection here.
540 Michael Stolberg, "Self-Pollution, Moral Reform, and the Venereal Trade: Notes on the Sources and Historical Context of Onania (1716)," *JHS* 9, no. 1/2 (2000): 37–61.
541 Efforts to remove this word from the medical vocabulary and literature have encountered a resistance out of all proportion to the ease with which the condition itself may be eradicated.

nocturnal emissions of semen and which, thereby has added to the confusion.[542] The term *blennorhoea* is even more obfuscating as it has been employed very loosely indeed with different meanings at different times. The Greek word βλέννος means "slime" and by extension "mucus". Today blennorrhoea is a generic term meaning an excessive discharge of mucus from any source. It is most frequently used as the term *ophthalmic blennorrhoea* to describe the conjunctivitis that may be seen in cases of congenital (true) gonorrhoea, (*Ophthalmia neonatorum*). However, the term *Blennorrhoea urethrae* was used loosely in nineteenth century medicine initially to describe *any* (muco-purulent) genital discharge and, after 1879, any such discharge that was *not* neisserial gonorrhoea. We cannot, therefore, in the quest for זוב, safely use any of the terms: *Gonorrhoea, Gonorrhoea virulenta, Spermatorrhoea, Gonorrhoea benigna* or *Blennorrhoea urethrae*, in the knowledge that we are describing a particular disease, past or present. The common denominator of all these is quite simply that of a mucous or muco-purulent urethral discharge and there are many causes of this. For once, we cannot rely on Milgrom because he does not cite any convincing or particular evidence for his assertion that true gonorrhoea, which he calls *Gonorrhoea virulenta*, was unknown before the fifteenth century and there is a considerable body of evidence to suggest that this may not be so.[543]

Some evidence may be evinced from records of treatment for genital discharges. Nothing exists from biblical times but if we consult the Talmud, a "cure" for זוב is described. Of course, we have no idea of whether this remedy existed in Levitical times. This "cure" does, however, show quite an advanced knowledge of herbal pharmacology and since it was applied by the rabbis to what we may assume was the same זוב as that described in Levitical texts, we must conclude that it was viewed and treated with a rationale much the same as that applied to infectious diseases today.

> R. Johanan: A potion of roots: the weight of a zuz of Alexandrian gum is brought, a zuz weight of liquid alum and a zuz weight of garden crocus, and they are powdered together. For a zab, two thirds thereof [mixed] with beer [is drunk], and he [the sufferer] then becomes impotent. For a zabah, a third thereof [mixed] with wine [is efficacious] that she shall not become barren. (Talmud Shabbat 110)

The rabbis, presumably by chance, hit upon what seems to be an appropriate treatment for an infectious bacterial disease. Alum (potassium aluminium sulphate), is well known to be a mild antiseptic. In ancient times it would have been used primarily in the tanning of leather: its effect, in high doses or long-term, upon the urethral mucosa would have been similar to its effect in the

---

542 G. G. Gascoyen, "On Spermatorrhoea and its Treatment," 1(577), *BMJ* no. 1 January 20th (1871): 67–69.
543 R. H. Boyd, "Origin of Gonorrhoea and Non-specific Urethritis," *British Journal of Venereal Diseases* 31 (1955): 246–48.

tannery! The use of the garden crocus indicates a relatively advanced knowledge of what herbs can do. The garden (or autumn) crocus, *Colchicum autumnale* is different from the saffron crocus not least in its being very poisonous.[544] This is because it contains the compound *colchicine* which is a powerful anti-mitotic agent. It is widely used today in chemotherapeutic treatment of malignant disease because of its power to inhibit cell division. In very low concentrations, it would have a similar effect on bacteria and so be effective in controlling the proliferation of bacterial colonies. Together with an antiseptic such as alum, this, in theory at least, would be a most effective (pre-antibiotic) treatment for bacterial diseases such as gonorrhoea. The rabbis clearly recognized the potency of this mixture and that large doses in females might result in sterility. It would be fascinating to know how effective this treatment was; it is entirely probable that, side-effects apart, it would have had some beneficial effect.

We must then, look for contenders for זוב besides true gonorrhoea which, despite Milgrom, we cannot entirely discount. There are two principal contenders and the evidence for both is compelling. These are *non-specific urethritis* (NSU), or as it is more often called these days, *non-gonococcal urethritis* (NGU),[545] and *schistosomiasis* (or *bilharzia*). Although he does not make the point specifically, it is possible that Milgrom's *Gonorrhoea benigna* or *Blennorrhoea urethrae* might have been NGU if indeed it was a venereally transmitted disease—but we cannot be certain of this. Non-gonococcal infectious urethritis is, as its name suggests, an inflammation of the urethral mucosa caused by an (originally unspecified) organism other than *N. gonorrhoeae*.[546] It was originally strictly defined as a group of conditions and a number of bacterial, viral, and parasitic agents was identified as causing the eponymous symptomatology. However, by far the most commonly seen causative agent is *Chlamydia trachomatis* and today NGU/NSU and *chlamydial urethritis* are considered to be synonymous in all but the most exceptional circumstances. This condition is widespread and becoming more prevalent in Western society. Chlamydial urethritis is symptomatically similar to gonorrhoea though much less fulminant. It is readily treatable with antibiotics and often resolves spontaneously. Complications seen in men are proctitis, prostatitis, and epididymitis. In women, proctitis, cervicitis, pelvic inflammatory disease with subsequent sterility and secondary risk of ectopic pregnancy, are encountered. Dysuria and acute or chronic pelvic pain are frequently seen. *C. trachomatis* is also an important neonatal pathogen, where it can lead to lung infections. The infecting organism may spread to the eye and

---

544 It is vital not to confuse them. The saffron (spring) crocus, Crocus sativus (Hebrew כַּרְכֹּם—see Song 4:13–14) is harmless and widely used in cookery. Zohary, *Plants of the Bible*.
545 Probably this was the condition classified as "gleet" up until the mid-twentieth century. It had no aetiological connection with the Peccatum Onanum.
546 J. Allen McCutchan, "Epidemiology of Venereal Urethritis: Comparison of Gonorrhea and Nongonococcal Urethritis," *Reviews of Infectious Diseases* 6, no. 5 (1984): 669–88.

cause *trachoma*: it is the single most important infectious agent associated, worldwide, with blindness, of which it is the commonest cause.[547]

There is no residual evidence for the incidence or prevalence of either gonorrhoea or NGU in the Ancient Near East as neither disease leaves any archaeological trace. Nor is it possible from paleo-anthropological studies to gain any insight into the frequency of practices that might result in sexually-transmitted infections among peoples of the Ancient Near East.

On the grounds that its symptomatology *can* include the excessive secretion of mucus from the urethra, Milgrom[548] has suggested *bilharzia* as another possible cause of זוב. He appears to attribute this view to no less an authority than Kinnier-Wilson.[549] It is unclear, however, whether Milgrom is implying that bilharzia is what Kinnier-Wilson means by *Gonorrhoea benigna/Blenorrhoea urethrae* (which he surely does not!) or that he is suggesting bilharzia *per se* as an alternative, non-venereal, cause of זוב. Milgrom refers to the condition as "urinary bilharzia"; the correct generic term for the disease today is *schistosomiasis*. This condition was originally known as "snail fever" and the infecting agent was first characterized by Theodor Bilharz in 1851. The complicated life cycle of the infecting and host organisms was described by Pirajá da Silva in 1908. Schistosomiasis is a parasitic disease caused by platyhelminth trematode worms of the genus *Schistosoma*. It involves two hosts, the fresh-water snail and the human.

Outside the human body the trematodes infect and develop in fresh-water snails. Having completed this stage of their life-cycle in the snail, they are released into the surrounding water where, as larval forms, *miricidia,* they may infect humans who use the water. The *miricidia* secrete enzymes that allow them to penetrate human skin and so infection is a very simple process with an incidence proportional both to the vast number of organisms in the water and the frequency of human usage of that water. It is, therefore, very difficult to remain free of this disease if one utilizes water populated by snails. The Nile delta[550] is infamous as a source of bilharzia and the disease was certainly known in ancient Egyptian times. Archaeological evidence has been found both in the form of snail shells which have been carbon-dated and more importantly, calcified schistosome ova have been found in the urinary tracts of mummies.

Once the human is infected, the schistosome parasites congregate in small veins, especially the pelvic veins around the bladder and in the bladder wall itself. Here

---

[547] Affecting 41 million worldwide today. The C. trachomatis initially affects the eyelid mucosa just as it does the urethral mucosa in NGU, causing chronic granulomatous change. It is friction from this that causes corneal erosion and blindness.
[548] Milgrom, *Leviticus: A New Translation*, 907.
[549] Kinnier-Wilson, "Medicine in the Land and Times of the Old Testament."
[550] But also Upper Egypt. It seems likely that the disease originated in central Africa and spread north along the Nile.

they lay eggs which are excreted as *cercariae* in the faeces or urine. If these reach water, they hatch and re-infect the snails, so beginning the cycle again.

Schistosomiasis is a chronic disease and in endemic areas re-infection follows recovery with relentless certainty. There are several species of schistosome and the symptoms and signs each produces are characteristic. *S. mansoni* and *S. haematobium* are the commonest species to infect man.[551] The former of these shows a predilection for the lower digestive tract and the latter for the genito-urinary tract. So, if זוב were schistosomiasis, it would most likely have been caused by *S. haematobium*. There is, however, cause for some uncertainty here. The presence of large numbers of schistosomes in the urinary bladder is known to stimulate the deposition of calcium salts so that bladder stones are formed. This is not necessarily so in all cases, but it is relatively common. Bladder stones, consequently, have been frequently observed in those mummies from Egypt that also contained *S. haematobium* ova. The effect of stones in the bladder is that they cause chronic abrasion and bleeding. Thus the cardinal sign of *S. haematobium* bilharzia is haematuria. There is no mention at all in the Levitical texts of the זוב being bloodstained and, given the fascination with blood shown by all ancient peoples and the Israelites and the later rabbis in particular, it seems almost impossible that they would fail to mention this important sign. It is, therefore, very difficult to agree with Milgrom that זוב was schistosomiasis: nevertheless, we should keep an open mind. Adamson[552] has reviewed the subject with great thoroughness and provided convincing evidence to support the view that schistosomiasis, besides being widely endemic in Egypt, almost certainly spread through Syria-Palestine to Mesopotamia. However, he points out that there is only circumstantial evidence for this. Hulse,[553] on the other hand, has suggested schistosomiasis as being endemic in Jericho at the time of Joshua and that the plague of the Philistines (1 Sam 6:4) was due to *S. mansoni*.[554]

To summarize therefore, in trying to identify the pathology of זוב when it is the result of an infection, we must consider two possibilities. If the discharges had a venereal origin, then the two principle contenders are *Neisserial gonorrhoea* (despite Milgrom) and *non-gonococcal urethritis*. We know nothing about the incidence and prevalence of these diseases in the Ancient Near East, but the symptoms and signs do appear to fit the descriptions in the texts and in the extensive Talmudic discourses.

---

551 And other primates and some monkeys. Monkeys have undoubtedly been involved with the spread of the disease and monkeys kept as pets have been implicated in the spread of the disease to distant parts.
552 P. B. Adamson, "Schistosomiasis in Antiquity," *Med Hist* 20, no. 2 (1976): 176–88.
553 E. V. Hulse, "Joshua's Curse and the Abandonment of Ancient Jericho: Schistosomiasis as a Possible Medical Explanation," *Medical History* 15, no. 4 (1971): 376–86.
554 The more usual explanation has been a Yersinia pestis infection such as bubonic or pneumonic plague.

If the disease was not sexually transmitted, endemic infection by *Schistosoma haematobium* remains a possibility. However, in contrast to the two venereal infections, while we have a good provenance for the disease's incidence and prevalence in the Ancient Near East at the appropriate time, the absence of any mention of bladder stones, or particularly of haematuria, militates very strongly against a disease of which these are the cardinal signs.

Whatever the condition, the view taken by the rabbis was that it was entirely absent among the Hebrews when they arrived at Mount Sinai:

> Rabbi Simeon ben Yohai taught: When Israel stood at Mount Sinai, and said, "All that the Lord hath spoken will we do, and obey" (Exod 24:7). There was none among them with an issue, or leprous, or lame, or blind, or dumb, or deaf, or imbecile. (Midrash Rabbah, Lev 18:4)

15:3 זוב *Properties of the Flow*

This verse is difficult to interpret. English translations imply that uncleanness occurs with genital discharges regardless of whether they are flowing or have flowed and dried up. If we understand בשרו ("from his flesh") to be euphemism for "from his penis", we must ask what "stopped" means. Clearly, it is used in apposition to "flowing" and the implication is "dried up". Nevertheless, effluxions such as occur in venereal diseases are not necessarily continuous and would be expected to show a sporadic occurrence at the exterior. However, when we consult the Masoretic Text (MT), we see that the verb הֶחְתִּים is used.[555] This is the *hiph'il* perfect of √חתם meaning "to seal" with a causative sense. This would seem to imply more than a simple drying up of the discharge; however, blockage of the urethra is not a feature of any of these diseases,[556] the effect of which on the urinary system, if prolonged, would lead to renal failure. The LXX[557] uses the verb συνιστημι here and this verb is usually taken to mean "stand together". It may be being used here in the sense of "cohere" or "dry up". The modern term for the cessation of flow in a viscus, whether physiological or pathological is of course, *stasis*. As with any secretory process the rate of discharge is inconsistent and among other things depends on the over-all state of hydration of the subject. It may be unwise, despite the MT therefore, to speak of "blockage" and to read anything more into this verse beyond that the discharge is intermittent and its volume is variable. The important point is that the state of impurity is maintained throughout the time of these fluctuations.

---

[555] This is also the case in the Samaritan Pentateuch and in 11QLev.
[556] Very occasionally blockage of the urethra by cercariae has been reported in schistosomiasis, but this is exceptionally rare.
[557] In the LXX, Samarian Pentateuch and 11QLev this verse is almost twice the length of the MT but this is largely due to repetition and no additional information is added.

15:4–10 Spread of Infection

The next eight verses are concerned with potential transmission of the infection. We should note, however, that nowhere is it specifically asserted that a venereal cause is to be assumed for זוב. By Rabbinic times, even over-indulgence in food had been implicated though it is not clear whether this was the primary cause or the trigger of an acute attack:

> Our rabbis taught: To one afflicted with gonorrhoea one assigns food or too many kinds of food as the cause of an attack of gonorrhoea. (Talmud Yoma 18a)

The prescription for the individual who has acquired secondary impurity in any of these ways is that he must bathe, launder his clothes, and remain unclean until the evening. Anything the זב/זבה may have touched,[558] slept on, or sat upon, becomes unclean and anyone who touches them or touches the flesh of the זב/זבה becomes similarly tainted. The same prescriptions apply to anyone unfortunate enough to have been spat upon by a זב/זבה or with whom a saddle has been shared.

In verse 4 the LXX introduces the word ὁ γονορρυής which Wevers[559] describes as, "a neologism to designate one suffering form γονόρροια, 'spermatorrhoea' not to be confused with 'gonorrhoea' an infectious sexual disease." This exegesis is unhelpful for the reasons discussed, at length, above. There is an interesting syntactical point to be made from the MT. The phrase כל־המשכב is open to two alternative translations. There is a strong syntactical case to be made for כל plus the definite article's being translated as "any" or "every" (bed)[560] and an alternative case for the simpler translation as "all the", "the entire" (bed). The safe translation here might seem to be the latter: infection first spreads locally and it would seem unnecessarily pedantic to specify the general case. However, the former translation, "every bed" is that preferred by the ERV, KJV, RSV and NRSV.

Milgrom[561] derives an interesting conclusion from the use, throughout the chapter, of the imperfect tense in phrases such as, וכל־הכלי אשר־ישב עליו יטמא. He believes that this choice of tense indicates that the זב/זבה in contrast to the sufferer from צרעת remains at home and is not isolated from the community. This Levitical leniency is in contrast to Num 5:2–4 where both "leper" and זב are banished.[562] If this speculation is correct, it seems that זוב, was, therefore, considered to be less of a risk as a communicable disease then צרעת. Nevertheless, in chapter 15, זוב is afforded a more logical chain of impurity in its

---

[558] Milgrom, assumes, with good reason, that the זָב is likely to have touched his genitals during micturition. Milgrom, *Leviticus: A New Translation*, 911.
[559] Wevers, *Notes on the Greek Text of Leviticus*, 226.
[560] Gesenius et al., *Gesenius' Hebrew Grammar*. This is the preferred translation in ERV, KJV, RSV and NRSV.
[561] Milgrom, *Leviticus: A New Translation*, Vol. 1, 909.
[562] Deut 23:10–12, goes even further and banishes those having nocturnal emissions of semen.

passage to subsequent generations by whatever means of contagion. In surprising contrast, there is no mention made of whether or not impurity is passed on if, for example, a man enters a house infested with the fungous variety of צרעת: we are not told if he remains contagious when he goes elsewhere. In addition, the use of יִטְמָא, the imperfect tense, is likewise supposed by Milgrom, to indicate the temporary nature of the impurity (compare with טמא הוא in verse 2).[563]

15:11-13 Hygienic Measures

These three verses deal with the actions the זב/זבה must take after having touched something without first having washed his hands. If he has touched another person, that person takes on the same impurity and must perform the same ritual ablution of himself and his clothing. He too shall remain unclean until the evening.

There is an interesting linguistic point to be made concerning the various verbs used in Hebrew and in Greek for "wash". Three senses of "washing" appear in this verse. First, there is washing of hands, then the washing of clothes and finally the bathing of the whole body. Both Hebrew and Greek have three quite specific verbs: שטף/νίπτω = to wash one's hands; כבס/πλύνω = to wash one's clothes; רחץ/λούω = to wash/bathe oneself; and these are all used precisely in these contexts in verse 11. This degree of attention to detail underlines the importance of these processes in the acquisition and treatment of טמא/ἀκάθαρτός.

In verse 12 we find, in surprising contradistinction to what we might imagine today, that ceramic vessels touched by a זב/זבה must be destroyed whereas wooden vessels can simply be washed. Modern considerations of hygiene would lead one to expect quite the opposite on account of the wooden vessel's being more porous and one must suppose that the rules here were a reflection of the respective cost of manufacture and availability of these utensils.

There is some uncertainty as to the water that is to be used for cleansing. The LXX is content to use the word ὕδατι (dative case of ὕδωρ) whereas the MT is more specific with מים חיים literally = "living water". This has variously been interpreted "fresh water", "running water", and "spring water".[564] It is unclear whether the water needs to be "fresh" in order to effect purification or "running" in order to remove potentially infectious material. It is used, similarly, on the first day of purification for sufferers of צרעת and for houses, or with fungal צרעת (Lev 14:5-6) and also in the purifications of those contaminated by handling

---

563 Milgrom makes the interesting point that in Islamic law, transference of impurity by objects does not exist whereas in ancient Arabia it did. Milgrom, *Leviticus: A New Translation*, 910. However, with reference to the rabbis, he goes on to say (p. 919), that this passage provides "a golden opportunity for fanciful exegesis."
564 See classically John 4:10-11; but also Jer 2:13 and Lev 14:52.

human or animal corpses (Num 19:17). Milgrom is inconsistent here: having stated his preference for "spring water" as a translation for מים חיים, he rather has his cake and eats it by suggesting that the term "living water" emphasizes the contrasting symbolism of a "living" or "life-giving" force with impurity which, in all forms, symbolizes death.[565] As justification for this idea, he notes that in the Mishnah, the rabbis classified water to be used in ritual cleansing baths into six grades of which מים חיים was the sixth and most efficacious.[566] It seems likely that the choice of whatever this water was, arose not out of modern principles of hygiene, but rather for its symbolizing purity.

15:14–15 Rituals to Follow Quarantine

As with צרעת, the hygienic treatment of זוב must be followed by ritual purification and this is outlined in verses 14–15. Verse 14, once again deals specifically with the זוב sufferer. After the washing, seven days must elapse: a quarantine period identical to that required for the individual with צרעת. The formula is very much like that dealt with in great detail in Lev 14 (and elsewhere by the rabbis) and presumably reflects time-period of creation according to the cosmic ritual requirement of the priestly worldview. On the eighth day, two turtle-doves or young pigeons are required to be "brought before the Lord" (לפני יהוה/ἔναντι κυρίου). By this is meant that they are to be presented to the priest at the entrance to the sanctuary or tent of meeting. The priest subsequently, "makes atonement for the issue before the Lord" by sacrificing the two birds, the one of them as a sin offering (חטאת/περὶ ἁμαρτίας), and the other as a burnt offering (עלה/ὁλοκαύτωμα).

15:16–17 Physiological Discharges in Males

The text turns briefly now to physiological male discharges. In fact, only one is considered, namely that of semen. It is clear that the discharge of semen during conventional sexual intercourse is not being considered in these verses; that is reserved for verse 18. Nor is it immediately obvious whether the discharge of semen leading to impurity is voluntary (*manu*)[567] or involuntary, as in a nocturnal emission (קרה־לילה, *cf.* Deut 23:11). However, examination of the grammar suggests that both are being considered. Verse 16 says:

ואיש כי־תצא ממנו שכבת־זרע ורחץ במים את־כל־בשרו וטמא עד־הערב

> And if any man's seed of copulation go out from him, then he shall bathe all his flesh in water, and be unclean until the even. (Lev 15:16)

---

[565] Milgrom, *Leviticus: A New Translation*, 923–4. Milgrom, prefers "spring water" from an artesian well and believes that the important point is that the water is not "stored" water drawn from collected, static water, in a cistern.
[566] Mikva'oth 1:1–8. See H. Danby, *The Mishnah*. Oxford: Oxford University Press, 1933.
[567] The notion of masturbation in order to produce a gratuitous orgasm is nowhere considered. No explanation is ever offered as to why involuntary seminal emissions seemingly, always took place at night.

The verb תֵּצֵא is *Qal* imperfect, third person feminine singular and must, therefore be intransitive and have זרע as its subject, *not* איש. If the voluntary process alone were being considered, one would expect the verb to be *hiph'il* (יוֹצִיא) agreeing with איש as its subject.

There is a clear technical term for this seminal emission in Hebrew though not in Greek, where the authors of the LXX resorted to using the phrase κοίτη σπέρματος as a calque for the Hebrew שכבת־זרע.[568] The feminine noun שכבה properly means "a coating" or "that which is laid down" (in a layer), often in the sense of "the morning dew".[569] However, the parent verb (√שכב) simply means "to lie" and it is also frequently used in the sense of "to copulate". Thus, it is unclear whether the incorporation of the noun into שכבת־זרע that is clearly a technical term, occurs by virtue of its allusion to the sexual act or to the "deposited seed". Most authors and exegetes conflate the two ideas. The KJV and ERV translate it as "seed of copulation" and the RSV and NRSV as "emission of semen". We cannot tell for sure, therefore, if ritual impurity was conferred by both voluntary acts: the one, the *Peccatum Onanum,* in its exact, biblical sense as a means of contraception, or the other, simple masturbation, the *Peccatum Onanum* that Victorian moralists vilified as "solitary and unholy". Whatever the case, the remedial treatment is a relatively minor one, being simply the subject's bathing himself—his clothes are not mentioned as he presumably slept naked—and remaining unclean until the evening. The same goes (verse 17) for any article contaminated by the spilt semen.

15:18 Sexual Intercourse

It might be thought that the transmission of semen in normal, sexual intercourse would be entirely desirable and would/should *not* result in impurity. However, verse 18 very clearly suggests otherwise.

ואשה אשר ישכב איש אתה שכבת־זרע ורחצו במים וטמאו עד־הערב

> The woman also with whom a man shall lie with seed of copulation, they shall both bathe themselves in water, and be unclean until the even. (Lev 15:18)

This verse contains nothing to suggest infection with זוב nor does it seem to imply *Peccatum Onanum/coitus interruptus*. The difference—that the one process begets life whilst the others waste life—has already been discussed. However, if we consider other ancient, and some modern civilizations, it is apparent that in many cultures the act of (normal) copulation was/is always profaning and requiring to be followed by some form of ablution and/or other forms of (ritual) purification. In particular, sexual activity should not take place

---

568 Clines, ed., *Dictionary of Classical Hebrew.*
569 See Exod 16:13, הַטַּל סָבִיב לַמַּחֲנֶה.

in or near sacred places and, in some cultures, before sacred events. Herodotus noted with characteristic snobbishness that apart from the Egyptians and Greeks, many of what he considered to be more primitive peoples copulated in sacred places and did not wash afterwards.[570] However, as was not unusual, Herodotus was wrong and there is evidence, besides that from Leviticus, to indicate that other civilizations in the Ancient Near East were as, if not more, scrupulous in engaging in post-coital purification.[571] This has persisted not only in Judaism but into the Hindu religion and into Islam where the process is known as "ghusl" (غسل). Milgrom states that "the entire ancient world is unanimous in its concern for cultic purity ... in all cultures sexual intercourse disqualifies a person from participating in the cult ... and the same rite, bathing, is prescribed for purification from sexual impurity."[572] This does not, however, explain the seemingly paradoxical situation of why "normal" sexual intercourse—with the implicit intention of procreation—should be so widely regarded as defiling: for procreation is, after all, a supposedly desirable process—it is Yahweh's will, to be encouraged enthusiastically, within the legal and religious framework of marriage and society in virtually every religion. The mechanism of its achievement logically would be expected not to cause defilement. Milgrom[573] turns to Maimonides[574] for an explanation and this, which although of a much later date, appears to be based in Exod 21:10:

אם־אחרת יקח־לו שארה כסותה וענתה לא יגרע

> If he take him another wife; her food, her raiment, and her duty of marriage, shall he not diminish. (Exod 21:10)

The critical word is ענה (ὁμιλία) defined as "cohabitation" and, by extension, "conjugal rights". It is a husband's legal and moral obligation, upon marriage, to supply this and other commodities.[575] Such an obligation persists, even if the wife is too young to bear children, barren, pregnant or post-menopausal. And, according to Maimonides, (*Mishneh Torah, Issurei Biyah 21: Halacha 9*) and at considerable variance with present-day attitudes to the rights of individuals:

> A man's wife is permitted to him. Therefore a man may do whatever he desires with his wife. He may engage in relations whenever he desires, kiss any organ he desires, engage in vaginal or anal intercourse or

---

570 Herodotus, *The Persian Wars*, trans. A. D. Godley, Vol. 2:64, 351.
571 Such rules were clearly operative in ancient Sabean culture in Southern Arabia. See: J. B. Pritchard, ed., *Ancient Near Eastern Texts Relating to the Old Testament*, 3rd ed. (Princeton, NJ: Princeton University Press, 1969), 665.
572 Milgrom, *Leviticus: A New Translation*, 933. Milgrom reaches this conclusion after citing numerous examples of post-coital impurity/purification from Greek, Egyptian, Arab, Persian and Hittite civilizations and all social classes amongst them.
573 Milgrom, *Leviticus: A New Translation*, 934.
574 F. Rosner, *Encyclopaedia of Medicine in the Bible and the Talmud* (Northvale, NJ: Jason Aronson, 2000).
575 Ten such obligations are specified in Jewish Law.

engage in physical intimacy without relations, *provided he does not release seed in vain.*

"In vain" quite clearly means that measures must not be taken against the opportunity and potential for the act to result in conception. There is, therefore, a conflict of obligation between these two passages because some of these activities, whether undertaken by choice and to fulfil the husband's conjugal duties, will involve the emission of semen at times or in situations where conception cannot take place nor procreation ensue. Moreover, copulation is never a process guaranteed to be 100% successful in conception and the provision of offspring: there is always an element of probability. It might therefore, reasonably be argued that as it is impossible to know which acts of copulation will result in conception, and also that those that do not are, *de facto*, "wasting seed in vain" and therefore defiling; the logical course of action is to treat *every* act as potentially defiling.[576]

Wenham has taken a different approach to the exegesis of this verse.[577] For the "wasting of seed" idea he coins the phrase "loss of life liquids" (LLL) and relates this to Douglas's thinking that the Levitical laws were expressions of the notion of physical wholeness and perfection in the created order.[578] LLLs, therefore, become associated with movement, on the part of the organism, away from life towards death, and defilement is due to the fact that the organism, in so doing, acquires an "aura of death". A body, free from any sort of discharge would, according to Wenham, preserve its "fullness of life intact" but the impending defilement caused by the "aura of death"—which is itself caused by the LLL—would be such as to necessitate legislation in order to vouchsafe the perfect holiness that is to be the nation's character. This is not an easy argument to understand or to accept. Wenham pitches the LLL argument almost entirely in respect of blood-loss, claiming that, ultimately, this would lead to death and so constitute an aura of such. One cannot argue with the pathophysiology of *that* statement. However, it does not seem to hold for the loss of semen, about which he is somewhat opaque and fails to project his argument onto hypothetical unborn children. How something that is only *in posse* and not yet *in esse* might have an aura of death about it is difficult to understand.

Whitekettle,[579] in contrast to Wenham, suggests that because the sexual union of husband and wife is designated "one flesh", there can be no loss of seed during marital intercourse because the entire process takes place within this one "composite body". He postulates that in such circumstances there can be no LLL

---

576 There is perhaps a parallel in this logic with today's use of the "morning after pill".
577 G. Wenham, "Why Does Sexual Intercourse Defile? (Lev 15:18)," *ZAW* 95 (1983): 432-34.
578 Douglas, *Purity and Danger*; Douglas, *Leviticus as Literature*.
579 Richard Whitekettle, "Leviticus 15:18 Reconsidered: Chiasm, Spatial Structure and the Body," *JSOT*, no. 49 (1991): 31-45.

because the semen moves only from an "environment of origin to an environment of growth". Defilement cannot, therefore, occur in the way Wenham suggests because no "body boundaries" have been crossed. This conveniently destroys part of Wenham's argument but even so, is scarcely helpful as it leaves us no further forward in explaining verse 18. Whitekettle's counter-argument that follows his critique of Wenham's proposition is, to this author, interesting but equally unconvincing. It entails a lengthy and perhaps tendentious, discourse on the perceived chiastic structure of chapter 15 as a whole. Whitekettle eventually arrives at the conclusion that the chapter is concerned—in a highly structured, almost diagrammatic way—with the "physiological functioning of the reproductive system". In answer to the question "Is the reproductive system functioning so as to bring about reproduction?", Whitekettle sees a divergence away from the perfection of the procreative copulation of verse 18 in both directions, schematically:

1←18→33

The degree of malfunction apparently increases with distance from verse 18. Whitekettle sees this continuum as a homology with the way the sanctity of the tabernacle wanes linearly with distance through the encampment and onward, away into the wilderness:

Increasing Purity ⎯⎯⎯⎯⎯⎯⎯⎯⎯⎯⎯⎯⎯⎯⎯⎯⎯⎯⎯⎯→

                Wilderness ↔ Encampment ↔ Tabernacle

Decreasing Purity ←⎯⎯⎯⎯⎯⎯⎯⎯⎯⎯⎯⎯⎯⎯⎯⎯⎯⎯⎯⎯

However, it is hard to see where this gets us in explaining verse 18. In a somewhat tangential way, Whitekettle now invokes the duplex function of the penis to explain the polluting effect of marital coition. In his scheme the wilderness is equated to "non-life" or "waste" and the tabernacle to ideal sexual function, i.e. the production of new life. Douglas has suggested that holiness demands the separation of distinct categories of creation[580] and this entails both anatomical structures and physiological processes. The penis fulfils both a reproductive and a micturatory *physiological* role; but while these can be seen as functionally distinct and separate, there is no way they can be separated *anatomically*. The unfortunate penis is damned by its embryological heritage *and* by its structural efficiency! This is notwithstanding the fact that nowhere in the Levitical code is it suggested that urine[581] is a pollutant or a cause of defilement and impurity.[582] Whitekettle sidesteps this argument by means of an opaque statement suggesting that urine is "of the periphery": it is akin to the wilderness in the above scheme. It is, therefore, the role of the penis, with its

---

[580] Douglas, *Purity and Danger*, 51–71.
[581] Or faeces for that matter.
[582] Frymer-Kensky, "Pollution, Purification and Purgation."

ambiguous structure and ambivalent function, that defiles marital sexual conjugation and this is what Whitekettle believes to be the message of verse 18. One is apt to wonder if Whitekettle has, perhaps, read a little too much into some of Freud's more colourful ideas.

One final point about this verse is the contrast, and therefore a possible difference in meaning, between the Masoretic Text and the Samaritan Pentateuch (SP).[583] The former reads:

וְאִשָּׁה אֲשֶׁר יִשְׁכַּב אִישׁ אֹתָהּ שִׁכְבַת־זֶרַע וְרָחֲצוּ בַמַּיִם וְטָמְאוּ עַד־הָעָרֶב

And the SP reads:

ואשה אשר ישכב אישה אתה שכבת זרע ורחצו במים וטמאו עד הערב

While the underlined word clearly means "a woman" and is the referent of אשר as in "A woman who"; the subject of the sentence (underlined) and of the verb ישכב ("to lie") is different in the two cases. The traditional translation, shown by the ERV and the KJV[584] begins with the relative clause:

> The woman also with whom a man shall lie with seed of copulation, they shall both bathe themselves in water, and be unclean until the even. (Lev 15:18)

This is a perfectly proper usage of אֲשֶׁר and the syntax of beginning the sentence in this way is relatively common in Hebrew.[585] In the unvocalized text of the Samaritan Pentateuch, the unpointed אישה must, from the context, be אִישָׁהּ "her man" = "her husband"[586] and this has a legal and moral implication. It is generally supposed that Levitical law was not concerned with legal formulations in the sense of halachic law. While Mosaic, halachic, law technically did not prohibit polygamy, Samaritan law did.[587]

15:19–24 Menstruation

The remainder of chapter 15 is concerned with physiological and pathological discharges affecting females. The first of these categories deals solely with menstruation. Uterine haemorrhage that was irregular and/or excessive was always considered to be abnormal and so considered together with genital infections. It is not difficult, however, given the contrasting knowledge about

---

583 Mark Shoulson, *The Torah: Jewish and Samaritan Versions Compared*, Leac an Anfa, (Co. Mhaigh Eo: Evertype, 2008). A. Sperber, ed., *The Bible in Aramaic Based on Old Manuscripts and Printed Texts*, 5 vols. (Leiden: Brill, 1973).
584 The RSV and NRSV, make the man the subject of the whole sentence and remove the relative clause this: "If a man lies with a woman and has an emission of semen, both of them shall bathe themselves in water, and be unclean until the evening."
585 Gesenius et al., *Gesenius' Hebrew Grammar*, 112 (§155), 485; Joüon and Muraoka, *A Grammar of Biblical Hebrew*, 118 (§38), 591 (§158).
586 Not, of course, to be confused with אִשָּׁה "a woman".
587 A. Cowley, "Some Remarks on Samaritan Literature and Religion," *JQR* 8, no. 4 (1896): 562–75; Kerr B. Tupper, "The Samaritan Pentateuch," *Heb Stud* 1, no. 2 (1882): 7–8.

menstruation, then and now, to understand how and why these distinctions came about.

Verses 19 to 23 outline the typical prohibitions that might be expected for the menstruant. Verse 19 reads:

ואשה כי־תהיה זבה דם יהיה זבה בבשרה שבעת ימים תהיה בנדתה וכל־הנגע בה יטמא עד־הערב

> And if a woman have an issue, and her issue in her flesh be blood, she shall be in her impurity seven days: and whosoever toucheth her shall be unclean until the even. (Lev 15:19)

Milgrom[588] draws our attention to the word בבשרה, literally "in her flesh/body" and the use therein of the inseparable pronoun ־ב "in" rather than מִנ־ "from". He suggests that this implies that, even if the woman senses her incipient menstruation before there is any visible evidence, her impurity is upon her from that time. This argument seems somewhat tendentious; the ־ב perhaps rather more simply indicates that the flow begins within her body; although of course, that could be said for all discharges. It is true, nevertheless, that while the menstruant is referred to as זבה the term זב in males was restricted to those with pathological discharges and was not applied to those having seminal emissions.[589]

A feminist approach to both parturition[590] and menstruation in Leviticus has been posited by a number of authors, notably Brenner.[591] However this work has been challenged by Trible as being overly tendentious.[592] Although it is possible that a particular feminist view of menstruation may have obtained or equally that the prevalent male attitude to women in biblical times either over- or understated the case, it seems likely for the reasons stated above that menstruation as זוב would not have been specifically differentiated in terms of its effects, from those other forms of זב categorized in Lev 15. Notwithstanding this, in the second half of verse 19 we note that although the menstruant woman is called a זבה, the *condition* is not referred to as זוב but rather as נדה.

Verses 20 to 23 follow what has now become an expected formula. Verse 20 implicates anything upon which the זבה lies or sits and verses 21, 22 and 23, anyone who has touched any such *fomites*. In all of these cases the contaminated individual must wash his/her clothes and him/herself and remain unclean until the evening. There is, however, no indication that the *fomites* themselves have

---

588 Milgrom, *Leviticus: A New Translation*, 934.
589 Milgrom suggests that the distinction may have been made according to the velocity of flow!
590 Cf. Lev 12.
591 Athalya Brenner, *The Israelite Woman: Social Role and Literary Type in Biblical Narrative*, 2nd ed. (New York: Bloomsbury T&T Clark, 2015).
592 Phyllis Trible, "The Israelite Woman: Social Role and Literary Type in Biblical Narrative by Athalya Brenner Review," *JBL* 106, no. 4 (1987): 700–01.

to be decontaminated—this would have been an extraordinarily difficult business to carry out especially at monthly intervals. The same might be said for sacrifices of which no mention is made with respect to נדה. No mention is made of the menstruant's having to perform specific acts of ablution or laundering, though we are told that her impurity will last for seven days (v19). A similar period of seven days' impurity is imposed upon any man who "lies with her" and upon the bed upon which this act takes place. Thus, contamination by menstrual blood during intercourse confers impurity for seven days in contrast to that of a single day conferred by the shedding of semen during copulation (v18).[593]

This completes the instructions for the זבה in her נדה. Over the years there has been much dispute about what "seven days" means. Some count from the first sighting of the discharge, others begin counting from a notional time twenty-four hours before this, supposing a recognizable "internal flow" prior to its manifestation. Later some, Rabbinic[594] authors suppose that the "seven days" refers to a separate period of "clean-days" after the flow has abated and there is no visible evidence remaining. The implications of this variation are significant and their understanding is not entirely helped by the extensive debate on the subject to be found in the Talmud. It seems likely that in Levitical times at least, the seven-day period began at the first sighting externally of the menstrual flow and to add a further seven "clean-days" would have aligned the menstruant with the pathological זבה — see verse 28 below. It would seem that this alignment by the addition of the further seven "clean-days" came about later in Amoraim times,[595] possibly as a means of differentiating between normal menstruation and menorrhagia/metrorrhagia. In any case, the observance of seven additional "clean-days" has persisted into modern times for Orthodox and Conservative Jews.[596]

15:25–30 Pathological Discharges in Females

This group of verses deals with abnormal/pathological discharges in women and in contrast to those verses dealing with נדה, we see here that sacrifices are included in the treatment. This is almost certainly a reflection of the more sporadic nature of זוב compared with נדה. In the first place, a menstruating woman would not be permitted to enter the temple,[597] and even if the sacrifice were delayed until after menstruation had ceased, the imposition of such a duty every month would be excessive. The distinction between נדה and זוב appears to

---

593 See Ezek 18:6.
594 The Niddah section of the Talmud is extensive.
595 Talmud Mas. Niddah 2a, 31a, 57b, 68a–69a.
596 In the Ashkenazic tradition the niddah state lasts at least twelve days calculated as 5 days for the flow + 7 "clean days" after menstruation has been shown to have ceased. The Sephardic tradition favours a minimum of 11 days.
597 This rule persists in many religions today. The Man Mo temple in Hong Kong has a large and explicit notice outside to enforce this.

have been made more in respect of the timing and length of the bloody discharge rather than upon either its amount or its quality. In verse 15:25,

> ואשה כי־יזוב זוב דמה ימים רבים בלא עת־נדתה או כי־תזוב על־נדתה כל־ימי זוב טמאתה כימי נדתה תהיה טמאה הוא

The conventional translation given in the ERV is:

> And if a woman have an issue of her blood many days not in the time of her impurity, or if she have an issue beyond the time of her impurity; all the days of the issue of her uncleanness she shall be as in the days of her impurity: she is unclean. (Lev 15:25 ERV)

The LXX gives:

> καὶ γυνὴ ἐὰν ῥέῃ ῥύσει αἵματος ἡμέρας πλείους οὐκ ἐν καιρῷ τῆς ἀφέδρου αὐτῆς ἐὰν καὶ ῥέῃ μετὰ τὴν ἄφεδρον αὐτῆς πᾶσαι αἱ ἡμέραι ῥύσεως ἀκαθαρσίας αὐτῆς καθάπερ αἱ ἡμέραι τῆς <u>ἀφέδρου</u> ἀκάθαρτος ἔσται

And the NETS translation is:

> And a woman, if she flows with a flow of blood for rather many days, not at the time of her period, even if she flows after her period, all the days of the flow of her impurity are like the days of her period; she shall be unclean. (Lev 15:25 NETS)

The key-words are בלא "not in" and על־ "beyond". The differential diagnosis of זוב and נדה depends upon the former's being either at a different time from the expected menstrual period or an abnormal prolongation of it. In the LXX there is a specific word ἡ ἄφεδρος for "menstruation",[598] with *time how long* being expressed by the accusative case and *time when* by the genitive case.

This verse encompasses both of the modern diagnoses of menorrhagia and metrorrhagia[524] but it is interesting that no attention was paid to the nature of the flow itself, which, today, would be of the utmost importance in reaching any diagnosis. This is undoubtedly illustrative of the somewhat fixated priestly worldview that it was *that* these things occurred that mattered rather than *why* or *how* they came about. Unsurprisingly, the text (v26), goes on to say that anything upon which the זבה lies, sits or by implication rides upon becomes contaminated and (v27), that anyone who comes into contact with these things must bathe, launder his/her clothes, and remain unclean until the evening. We may note the increased severity in response to having touched a זבה that incurs the need to launder one's clothes. This was not obligatory (vv. 21–23), after contact with a נדה.

---

598 Liddell and Scott, *Greek English Lexicon*.

In the case of a זבה it is made quite clear (v28) that the seven-day clean period can only begin after the discharge has abated and she is not טהורה until this time has passed. Furthermore, on the eighth day, she must make a sacrifice by presenting to the priest at the tabernacle/tent of meeting (אהל מועד), two turtle doves or young pigeons. One of the pair is to be a sin-offering (חטאת), and the other a burnt-offering (עלה). This is the formula we have already encountered in the expiation of the more serious instances of טמאה.

Some support for this formula, with minor variations, can be acquired from other sources. In the Qumran Community the זב/זבה went through a similar cleansing process but was required to wait for eight rather than seven days before entering the temple for the atonement sacrifice.[599] The passage, 4Q274 f1i:0–4Q274 f2ii:1, in particular deals extensively with much of the subject matter in Leviticus Chapter 15 and the approach is very much the same. The fate of the זב/זבה is spelt out in no uncertain terms:

[-- אל]

יחל להפיל את תחנונו. משכב יג[ו]ן ישכ[ב ו]מושב אנחה ישב. בדד לכול הטמאים ישב ורחוק מן

הטהרה שתים עשרה באמה בדברו אליו. ומערב צפון לכול בית מושב ישב רחוק כמדה הזות.

[Let him not] begin to present his suppli[cati]on. He shall lie down on a bed of sorrow, and in a seat of sighing he shall sit. He shall sit apart from all those who are unclean and at a distance

of twelve cubits from the purity when he speaks to them. He shall dwell to the northwest of any habitation at a distance of the same measurement. (4Q274 f1i:0–f1i:2)

Josephus says that both the זב/זבה and the נדה (and the parturient), were banished from the city for seven days.[600] This is in contradistinction to Leviticus who demands this quarantine only from those with צרעת.

15:31 An Interpolation from H?

There is some debate in the literature as to whether this verse was interpolated either by the author of H or by some later redactor. Milgrom[601] adds the *caveat* that the verse is specifically about the purity of the sanctuary—typically a priestly concern—and not about the purity of the land, which would be more in keeping with H. Verses 15:32 and 15:33 provide a summary of what has been said already

---

599 4Q266 (4QDa 6i, 4), 4Q397 (4QMMT-d II 10), 11Q19 (11QT 45:7–17). See also: Devorah Dimant and Lawrence H. Schiffman, Time to Prepare the Way in the Wilderness: Papers on the Qumran Scrolls, Vol. 16 (Leiden: Brill, 1995).
600 Josephus, *Josephus Collected Works*, 13 vols., trans Thackeray and Feldman.
601 Milgrom, *Leviticus: A New Translation*, 945–947.

but they lack force as a concluding statement. The question regarding verse 31 is perhaps less to do with what it is about (defilement of the sanctuary), than to whom it is directed:

> והזרתם את־בני־ישראל מטמאתם ולא ימתו בטמאתם בטמאם את־משכני אשר בתוכם

> Thus shall ye separate the children of Israel from their uncleanness; that they die not in their uncleanness, when they defile my tabernacle that is in the midst of them. (Lev 15:31)

This verse is the chapter's summarizing motive statement and clearly a paraenetic for the sons of Israel. Its style is characteristic and therefore, highly suggestive of H material.[602] In particular it contains two important, potential, stylistic identifiers of H. The first of these is the use of the first person singular. This is referring to Yahweh who is saying "my sanctuary" (משכני), when he addresses to Moses and Aaron and through them the priesthood as a whole. There is a parallel to the undoubted H material of Lev 26:11:

> ונתתי משכני בתוככם ולא־תגעל נפשי אתכם

> And I will set my tabernacle among you: and my soul shall not abhor you. (Lev 26:11)

While P concerns itself with the priesthood and their activities, it is generally thought that H is for transmission either directly or, more usually, through the priests to the population as a whole. Yahweh, therefore speaks in the first person to his priestly audience and thus speaks of "my sanctuary". There is no corresponding usage of the first person in the Levitical P material.

The second stylistic feature of 15:31 suggesting H material, is the particular use of the verb √נזר. It is in verse 15:31 in the *hiph'il* which, (also with the *niph'al*) followed by מִן, implies separation and withdrawal.[603] The causative *hiph'il* "make separate", suggests a command to someone other than the sons of Israel and we must suppose this to be Moses, Aaron, and the priesthood. Yahweh is instructing them to clean up the Israelites' shoddy practices in order to prevent them from defiling his sanctuary. Moreover, he is warning them that not to do so risks the punishment of death by divine agency.

The translators of the Septuagint clearly had some difficulty with: καὶ εὐλαβεῖς ποιήσετε τοὺς υἱοὺς Ισραηλ ἀπὸ τῶν ἀκαθαρσιῶν αὐτῶν but arrived at the same endpoint because they realized that the second person plural ποιήσετε was a command from Yahweh to Moses and Aaron (*cf.* 15:2), and thereby to priests in general to act in a way that was εὐλαβεῖς = "cautious" or "discreet" in their

---

602 See chapter 2.
603 Clines, ed., *Dictionary of Classical Hebrew*; TDOT.

dealings with the Israelites whose uncleanness was at risk of defiling the sanctuary.[604]

The verb √נזר appears in a similar context in Lev 22:2, which is undoubted H material. Both verses are hortatory and from the mouth of Yahweh. In verse 31, we must surely translate ולא in the sense of "lest", warning of impending death ימתו for those who persist in their uncleanness. It might be argued today, that a penalty of death is rather severe for the misdeed of acquiring a genital issue. However, this would be to miss the point and verse 31 makes the point quite clearly—the acquisition of the זוב under the circumstances outlined in the preceding verses of this chapter, results in the defilement of the sanctuary and it is *that* which is punishable by death. Verse 31, therefore becomes a summary of the *direction* of the whole chapter and it may be surmised that the later H redactor felt that such a rounding-up was necessary to focus the mind of the reader.

15:32–33

These two verses make for a rather anticlimactic ending after verse 31. They do nothing more than rather weakly summarize (זאת תורת הזב) the foregoing verses. In all probability, they were the summarizing conclusion of the original P text before the interpolation of H in the form of verse 31. It remains to be seen why they were retained as stylistically, they offer no improvement. It is possible that their removal would have been seen as defacing a sacred text so that only addition was possible: there is a strong precedent for this view.

THE LEVITICUS RABBAH & GENITAL DISCHARGES

The *zab** morpheme does not appear in the Leviticus Rabbah but the word *issue* used in the appropriate context occurs 25 times. Unfortunately, none of these occurrences offers any insight beyond what is to be found in biblical Leviticus. As a *midrash* on scriptural Leviticus, the *Leviticus Rabbah* operates along strictly Talmudic lines, going to great lengths to expound upon and interpret the biblical text but contributing little or nothing new to the understanding of the pathophysiology of these conditions.

For the modern medical mind, the idea of זוב is much easier to grasp than that of צרעת. All of the instances of זוב that have been discussed above are explicable in terms of modern medical symptomatology whether physiological or pathological. The specific incidence of venereal disease in ancient Israel is quite unknown but it is quite likely that conditions such as non-specific urethritis were relatively common.

---

604 Cf. Lev 10:10–11 and Ezek 44:23 for a similar instruction.

All of this makes it easier to see a relationship between conditions of this sort, the potential compromise of reproductive capacity that they bring about, and the notion of uncleanness and impurity. It is unlikely that the early Israelite mind made any distinction between these physiological and pathological symptoms and signs in any consideration of contagious transmission (see chapter 10).

As in the case of צרעת, the Hebrew Bible offers no clue to the incidence or prevalence of זוב, especially when of a solitary or venereal nature. In contrast to צרעת, it is much easier to make a provisional differential diagnosis as there is a much closer correspondence with present-day diseases. The physiological seminal and menstrual discharges are obvious and there is strong evidence to suggest that pathological discharges were likely to have been either non-gonococcal urethritis or schistosomiasis.

There is also clear evidence that other seemingly unpleasant discharges from the nether regions (urine and faeces) did not result in ritual impurity. This is a clear pointer to the underlying principle rearding זוב as compromise of either reproductive function *per se* or the more complex notion that the discharge is evidence of some sort of "anti-life" or "life-wasting" process. That the Israelites may have considered anything issuing from the genitalia as concerned with the generation of new life is not especially difficult to understand.

Because of the strictures on sexual intercourse during זוב it is suggested that it was compromise of quality rather than quantity of reproductive capacity that was feared. Clearly it was held that it was still possible to conceive in a state of זוב but the result should be expected to be abortion, stillbirth, and disfigurement.

Chapter 9

BLEMISH, DEFORMITY & DISABILITY

Blemish occupies a significant but equivocal place in the Hebrew Bible and Septuagint and the purpose of the present chapter is to investigate whether this reflects a parallel ambiguity in the priestly ideology. The definition of blemish to be found in the Levitical writings is somewhat different from that of modern usage where it has, in any case, largely fallen from favour as a descriptive term.[605] Like צרעת and זוב, *blemish* (מום/μῶμος), was viewed in a very negative light. Today most examples of blemish reported in the Scriptures would be seen unequivocally in a medical context. In biblical times however, מום—or at least certain specified cases of מום—appears to have occupied the province of priests. It is necessary to ask why and how מום fitted into the priestly worldview and the ritual practice of sacramental hygiene and why מומים necessitated a different priestly response from צרעת and זוב.

TERMINOLOGY AND LOGOMETRICS

The *Oxford English Dictionary* gives the following definitions for the noun "blemish":

1   Physical defect or disfigurement; a stain.
2   (transferable) A defect, imperfection, flaw, in any object, matter, condition, or work.
3   (figurative) A moral defect or stain; a flaw, fault, blot, slur.

From a medical point of view, blemishes can be both congenital and acquired. Congenital blemishes have traditionally been called "deformities" though today both words are increasingly avoided and seen as indelicate.[606] Acquired blemishes have traditionally been referred to as "disabilities" especially when they are the result of injury. This word persists in usage today but has become stretched to include congenital deformities.

The ancients did not mince their words: the Hebrew Bible uses the word מום for "blemish" almost exclusively. The Greek equivalent to be found in the LXX is μῶμος. However, it should be noted and seen as significant,[607] that the phrase "without blemish" is used at least as often. In this case the word תמים (ἄμωμος) is found. It is interesting to search out the number of instances of these terms in the Bible as a whole and this becomes a simple task if one uses electronic

---
605 Butterfield, *Fowler's Dictionary of Modern English Usage*, 219.
606 Today, the words "blemish" and "deformity" have lost favour and are often seen as derogatory. With the current, modish predilection for clichés and word-mincing, a plethora of euphemisms has evolved to replace it, not always effectively; see, Butterfield, *Fowler's Dictionary of Modern English Usage*, 219.
607 See below for attitudes to beauty and ugliness.

concordances.[608] The following graph shows the results of searching the entire Hebrew Bible for instances of the Hebrew word, מום:

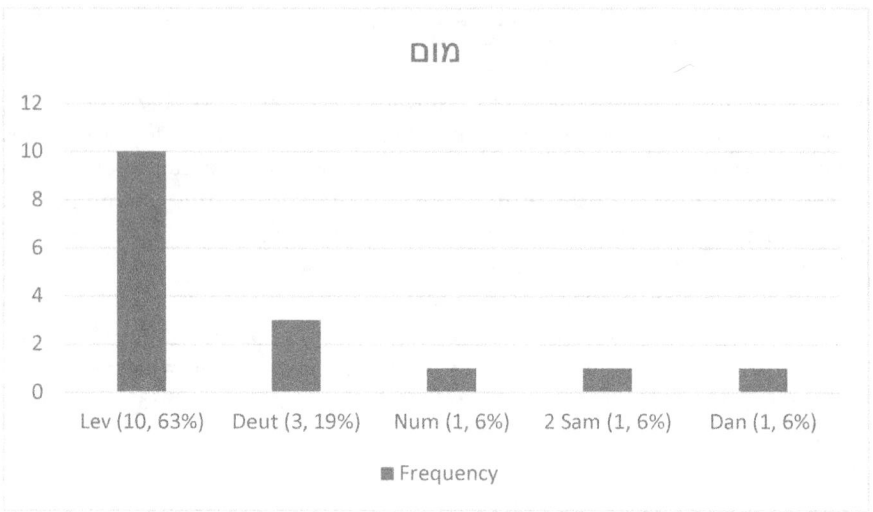

We can search the Septuagint and the New Testament if we use the lexeme μῶμ* which allows for cases, numbers and genders in the Greek declension of μῶμος. This produces the following distribution:

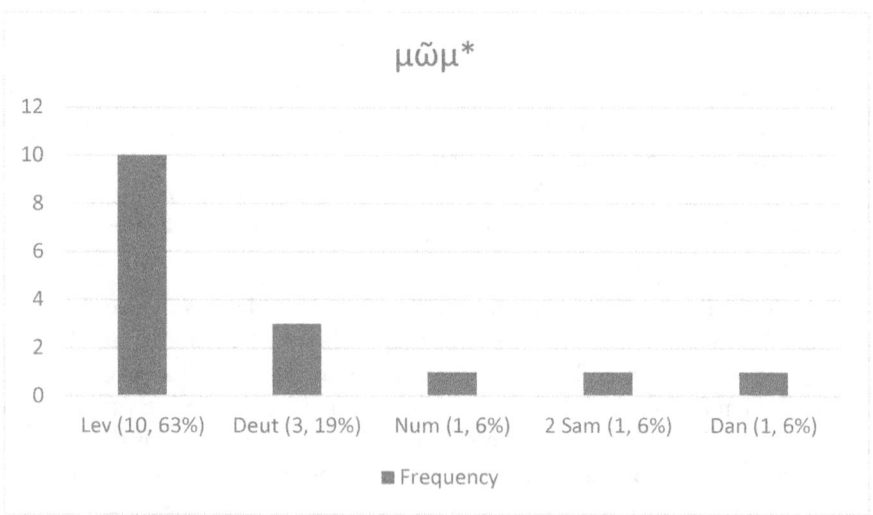

---

608 Bibleworks, "Software for Biblical Exegesis and Research." Accordance, "Bible Software."

Searching for "without blemish" תמים/ἄμωμ* we get:

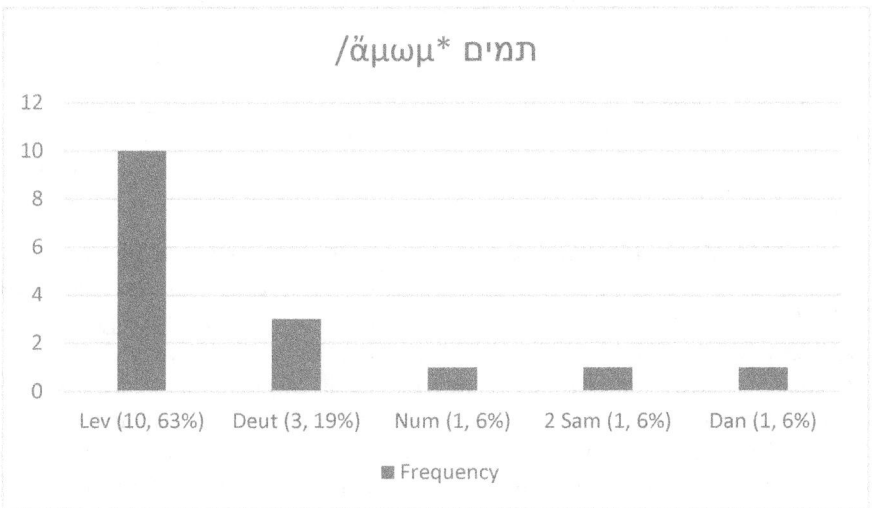

In a very small number of instances (e.g. Exod 12:5), the LXX uses τέλειος instead of ἄμωμος but this is very rare; the use of מום/μῶμος and its antithet תמים/ἄμωμος is remarkably consistent.

NEGATIVE IMAGERY AND DISABILITY

The negative imagery of disability and deformity is a key feature of the Hebrew Bible and indeed, of a great deal of other literature from the Ancient World. This attitude stretched into the Middle Ages and well beyond. Sullivan, has drawn attention to the fact that whereas the negative stereotype of the disabled person or cripple has generally been considered to have its origins in the cultural ethos of Greek civilization, an association of disability with ritualistic and religious practices can be found in more ancient cultural groups, notably in Egypt.[609]

However, in Egyptian culture, disability appears never to have been viewed in a negative way and was sometimes seen even as a positive feature. For example, dwarves were esteemed and allowed to hold high positions; they featured particularly in the worship of Seneb. Deformed individuals were often mentioned in a positive way in Egyptian religious and magical texts. Their deformity made them unusual and thereby objects of curiosity, respect, and even veneration. They were never stigmatized or ostracized except where the mutilation had been brought about by their own society as a sanctioned act of retribution, vengeance or punishment. Sullivan's conclusion is that it was in Greek culture, where there developed a necessary and desirable philosophical relationship between form and actuality and consequently an ideology of

---

[609] R. Sullivan, "Deformity: A Modern Western Prejudice with Ancient Origins," *Proc RCPE* 31 (2001): 262–66.

perfection, that deformity/disability/blemish eventually became a full-blown stigma. In the context of the Greek world, physical perfection was seen as all-important. Sullivan's review is scholarly and interesting, and makes a good case for the persistence of the Greek view of disability into later art and thinking, and perhaps even further as a basis for modern attitudes. Unfortunately, Sullivan misses out the Ancient Near East completely and so makes no comment on the very obviously and easily-observed negative attitudes to disability that are found in the Hebrew Bible.

It is curious to speculate upon why Sullivan allowed this lacuna in his survey. It leaves open the very important question of whether Israelite culture's negative attitude arose *de novo,* or whether it may have been influenced by neighbouring cultures. An appropriate substrate for investigation might have been priestly ideology, at least in the case of the Levitical material. The priestly *Weltanschauung* held no particular place for an ideology of perfection such as that of Greek culture, but it was intensely concerned with the preservation through ritual, of the cosmic order. Whatever the case, Olyan[610] has suggested that ideas about blemishes and deformities might have been equated with the observation of the [necessary] motor and sensory dysfunctionality of idols. Olyan turns to the Psalms for textual evidence in support of his suggestion.

פה־להם ולא ידברו עינים להם ולא יראו

אזנים להם ולא ישמעו אף להם ולא יריחון

ידיהם ולא ימישון רגליהם ולא יהלכו לא־יהגו בגרונם

כמוהם יהיו עשיהם כל אשר־בטח בהם

> They have mouths, but they speak not; eyes have they, but they see not;
>
> They have ears, but they hear not; noses have they, but they smell not;
>
> They have hands, but they handle not; feet have they, but they walk not; neither speak they through their throat.
>
> They that make them shall be like unto them; yea, every one that trusteth in them. (Ps HB & ERV 115:5–8; LXX 113:13–16)

These disabilities leave the idols helpless and unable to do those things that Yahweh, who possesses these faculties, *can* do:

ואלהינו בשמים כל אשר־חפץ עשה

---

610 Saul M. Olyan, *Disability in the Hebrew Bible: Interpreting Mental and Physical Differences* (Cambridge: Cambridge University Press, 2008), 8; S. M. Olyan, "The Ascription of Physical Disability as a Stigmatizing Strategy in Biblical iconic Polemics," in *Disability Studies and Biblical Literature,* ed. Candida R. Moss and Jeremy Schipper (New York: Palgrave Macmillan, 2011).

> But our God is in the heavens: he hath done whatsoever he pleased. (Ps HB & ERV 115:3; LXX 113:11)

It is possible that Sullivan was drawing over-generous conclusions from his small number of examples from Egyptian culture. Olyan, who has studied extensively the specific case of disability both in the Hebrew Bible and in the wider world in which it was written, concludes,[611] "the representations of disability in the non-Israelite West Asian texts that I have compared with biblical materials resemble biblical representations more than they differ from them".

If this is correct, we may suppose that those with disabilities were seen in Israelite society as a specific group wherein they appear to have been the recipients of prejudice and to have found themselves significantly disadvantaged in both religious and social environments.

Margolis and Shapiro[612] have studied the negative imagery of disability and deformity in literature, especially that of the Classical World. They stress the association of disability with induced fear, shame, and debasement. This is in stark contrast with the supposedly civilized present-day attitudes of Western societies, where toleration of disabilities is encouraged and the principal negative association, if any, is more likely to be that of embarrassment.

Margolis and Shapiro categorize those fruits of society that have been historically and traditionally denied or withheld from the disabled: *right to life, freedom, education, shelter, and employment*. They believe that the stereotypical negative imagery of disablement operates subliminally and is implanted at an early age: children have been found to accept negative subliminal attitudes easily, learning to despise early in life from parents, peer-groups, literature, and the mass media.

Lemos[613] has considered an important practical application of stigmatization by disfigurement which operated in the Ancient Near East and is to be seen widely in Israelite culture and in the Hebrew Bible. This is the practice of mutilating one's enemies, usually carried out by victors in battle but seen also on a domestic level. This practice was widespread in Mesopotamia and in Egypt. Lemos supposes that the mutilation of enemies was more than simple brutality and revenge and that it discharged a very specific symbolic function by signalling the establishment of a new power-dynamic between agressor and vanquished. We are perhaps familiar with the following two verses from Lev 24:19–20 in the context of retaliation applied to murder but in fact, it is in the context of blemish that the *lex talionis* is first encountered.

ואיש כי־יתן מום בעמיתו כאשר עשה כן יעשה לו

---

611 Olyan, *Disability in the Hebrew Bible*, 120.
612 Howard Margolis and Arthur Shapiro, "Countering Negative Images of Disability in Classical Literature," *Eng J* 76, no. 3 (1987): 18–22.
613 T. M. Lemos, "Shame and Mutilation of Enemies in the Hebrew Bible," *JBL* 125, no. 2 (2006): 225–41.

And if a man cause a blemish in his neighbour; as he hath done, so shall it be done to him;

שבר תחת שבר עין תחת עין שן תחת שן כאשר יתן מום באדם כן ינתן בו

breach for breach, eye for eye, tooth for tooth: as he hath caused a blemish in a man, so shall it be rendered unto him. (Lev 24:19–20)

Mutilation brought shame not merely upon the victim, but also on his family and his community. The act of mutilation[614] left the defeated individual with the *appearance* of one with a *natural* deformity or blemish and so indicated his having fallen into a lower status-group such as would be occupied by cripples. Thus, mutilation becomes a blemish[615] and is subject to the full compass of stigmata attached thereto. The key ingredient of this stigmatization is *shame* which Lemos defines in three ways:[616]

(1) The (internal) experience of disgrace together with fear that others will see how we have dishonoured ourselves.
(2) The feeling that others are looking on with contempt and scorn at everything we do and don't do.
(3) A preventative attitude (hiding or disappearing in order not to be disgraced).

Lemos's arguments about shame and mutilation can, at times, seem tendentious but we can discern, nevertheless, a theme familiar in the Hebrew Bible concerning negative imagery. Importantly, mutilation and natural blemishes along with the Levitical disease-stigmata (צרעת and זוב), all have one or the other of *only two* features in common. The affliction must either be *visible* and so on public display or, if not visible, *it must involve the genitals*. In the former category we also have most of the biblical examples of מום (and צרעת) and in the second category we have זוב and, as an example of מום, "He that is wounded in the stones or with his privy member cut off", (פצוע־דכא וכרות שפכה)—Deut 23:2 HB and LXX 23:1 in English translations).

BEAUTY AND UGLINESS IN THE HEBREW BIBLE

Whereas Greek thinking on this subject has been widely written about, there is significantly little textual material on the subject in the Hebrew Bible and nothing substantive to explain the meaning of the words *beauty* and *ugliness*. In the ERV translation of the Hebrew Bible the word "beauty" (תפארת) occurs 47 times and "beautiful" (יפה), 23 times. In contrast, words for "ugliness" and "ugly" do not occur at all in English translations. The nearest Hebrew adjective appears

---

614 Which Lemos defines, rather prolixly, as "a negatively constructed somatic alteration".
615 Though, of course, not all blemishes are mutilations.
616 Lemos gives examples from the Hebrew Bible which include: 1 Sam 10:27–11:11; 2 Sam 5:8; 2 Sam 10; Judith 13–14; Judg 1-1–7; Jere 34:18–20.

to be רע which is generally translated as "bad". Olyan[617] has compiled a list of those positive physical attributes that, in the Hebrew Bible, are associated with human beauty. They are: plumpness, thick hair on the head, ruddy clear skin, dark eyes, symmetrical teeth and breasts, significant height, agility of movement and physical strength. The idea of being "well fleshed-out" appears to have been particularly important:[618]

ומקצת ימים עשרה נראה מראיהם טוב ובריאי בשר מן־כל־הילדים האכלים את פתבג המלך

And at the end of ten days their countenances appeared fairer, and they were fatter in flesh, than all the youths which did eat of the king's meat. (Dan 1:15)

Within the Hebrew Bible the Song of Songs offers perhaps the most useful source material. A later specific case is that mentioned in the Genesis Apocryphon, written in Qumranic Aramaic.[619] Although from a time and milieu different from that of the Levitical priests it is helpful because, as Fitzmyer[620] in his commentary on the Genesis Apocryphon from Qumran suggests, it introduces a descriptive style that makes much of "*the beautiful fair-skinned female*".[621] It is thought to be an extension of a literary genre that may have migrated from ancient Arabic literature.[622]

---

617 Olyan, *Disability in the Hebrew Bible*, 18.
618 A catalogue of the prerequisites of beauty can be found in a later text (4Q186) from Qumran. This passage, (4Q186 f1i:4–f2i:9), in several ways is at variance with Olyan's account.
> Anyone, the ha[ir of whose head] shall be [... and whose head and forehead] are broad and curved [...] intermediate, but the rest of [his] head is not [...] [...] unclean [... his stone is] granite. [And] anyone [whose] eyes are [... and lo]ng, but th[e]y are fix[e]d, whose thighs are long and slender, whose toes are slender and long, and who was born during the second phase of the moon: he possesses a spirit with six parts light, but three parts in the house of Darkness. This is the birth sign under which such a person shall be born: the haunch of Taurus. He will be poor. This is his animal: the bull. and whose head [...,] [whose] ey[es] inspire fear [and are ...,] whose teeth protrude (?), whose fingers are thick, whose thighs are thick and extremely hairy, and whose toes are thick and short: he possesses a spirit with [ei]ght parts in the House of [Darkness] and one from the House of Light regula[r,] whose [e]yes are neither dark n[or] light (?), whose beard is sp[arse] and medium curly, whose voice resonates, whose teeth are fine and regular, who is neither tall nor short but is well built, whose fingers are thin and long, whose thighs are hairless, the soles of whose feet [and whose to]es are as they should be: he possesses a spirit [...] eight parts [from the House of Light] and o[ne] [in the House of Darkness. This is the birth sign under which] such a person shall be born....

Translation from: Michael Owen Wise, Martin G. Abegg, and Edward M. Cook, *The Dead Sea Scrolls: A New Translation* (London: HarperCollins, 1996).
619 T. Muraoka, *A Grammar of Qumran Aramaic*, Ancient Near Eastern Studies, Supplement 38 (Leuven; Walpole, MA: Peeters, 2011).
620 Joseph A. Fitzmyer, *The Genesis Apocryphon of Qumran Cave I*, B&O 18a (Rome: Biblical Institute, 1971), 119.
621 Fair skin was particularly admired by the dark-skinned Mediterranean and Near Eastern races. This point is made repeatedly in Homer and by the Greek Tragic Dramatists.
622 The subject of this eulogy is Sarai/Sarah, the wife of Abraham whose beauty is being recounted to Pharaoh by his courtiers.

2	[]כמה ושפיר לה צלם אנפיהא וכמא[]
3	[נ]עים וכמא רקיק לה שער ראישה כמא יאין להון לה עיניהא ומא רגג הוא לה אנפהא וכול נץ
4	אנפיהא כמא יאא לה חדיה וכמא שפיר לה כול לבנהא דרעיהא מא שפירן וידיהא כמא
5	כליל וחמיד כול מחזה יד[י]הא כמא יאין כפיהא ומא אריכן וקטינן כול אצבעת ידיהא רגליהא
6	כמא שפירן וכמא שלמא להן לה שקיהא וכל בתולן וכלאן די יעלן לגנון לא ישפרן מנהא ועל כול
7	נשין שופר שפרה ועליא שפרהא לעלא מן כולהן ועם כול שפרא דן חכמא שגיא עמהא ודליהא
8	יאא

A similar proposition comes from Greenfield[623] and both of these accounts appear to have been based on the earlier work of Goshen-Gottstein.[624] These authors suggest that this passage describing Sarai's beauty belongs to a genre of Arabic literature known as وصف (*waṣf*) which, in literal translation, means "description" but in the present context is a technical term for passages that highlight the personal charms of a beloved one. Goshen-Gottstein believes this to be the only such usage in Jewish writings outside the Song of Songs; its purpose being to encomionize Sarai before Pharoah. There is no reason to suppose that the epithets used had not evolved over time and were still thought appropriate. It is noteworthy, in the light of any consideration of blemishes such as deafness (see below), that all of these positive attributes of beauty are mediated through the visual system.

All of this stands in opposition to biblical images of emaciation, where such dysphemisms as "weak" (דל) and "thin" (דק), are to be found. Shaving the head was also a form of self-debasement that was a common, expected, and tolerated sign of mourning in Israelite culture. Natural baldness, in contrast, probably because of its association with this debasement, appears to have been considered as unattractive.

Ugliness *per se* is seldom described in biblical texts; where it does occur it is largely confined to descriptions of animals and the adjective רע is the most common rendering. Olyan[625] has considered the relationship of beauty and ugliness in Israelite society as depicted in the Hebrew Bible. He believes that although it would be reasonable to conclude, from analysis of the texts, that the most generally and widely-applied criterion for beauty was simply the absence of visible physical defects (מומים), he nevertheless, considers it an over-simplification to believe that physical, somatic beauty was seen by the Israelites *always and only* as a lack of such physical flaws. Despite this, Olyan finds two verses in the Hebrew Bible that may be thought to justify this proposition:

כלך יפה רעיתי ומום אין בך

Thou art all fair, my love; and there is no spot in thee. (Song 4:7)

---

2. "[ ]how and beautiful is the aspect of her face, and how[ ]
3. [pl]easant and how supple is the hair of her head. How lovely are her eyes; how pleasant her nose and all the radiance of
4. her face . How shapely is her breast, how gorgeous all her fairness! Her arms, how comely! Her hands,
5. how perfect—How [lovely] is every aspect of her hands! How exquisite are her palms, how long and delicate all her fingers! Her feet,
6. how attractive! How perfect are her thighs! Neither virgins nor brides entering the bridal chamber exceed her charms. Over all
7. women is her beauty supreme, her loveliness far above them all. Yet with all this comeliness, she possesses great wisdom, and all that she has
8. is beautiful." (1Q20 (1QapGenar) XX:2–8) See: Martinez and Tigchelaar, *The Dead Sea Scrolls*. Study Edition.
623 J. C. Greenfield, "Early Aramaic Poetry" *JANES* 11 (Bravmann Memorial Volume) (1979): 45–51.
624 M. Goshen-Gottstein, "Philologische Miszellen zu den Qumrantexten," *RQ* 2 (1959-60): 43–51.
625 Olyan, *Disability in the Hebrew Bible*, 21–25.

וכאבשלום לא־היה איש־יפה בכל־ישראל להלל מאד מכף רגלו ועד קדקדו לא־היה
בו מום

> Now in all Israel there was none to be so much praised as Absalom for his beauty: from the sole of his foot even to the crown of his head there was no blemish in him (2 Sam 14:25)

The relationship, according to Olyan, must have been more complex than the above idea which, he believes, does not go far enough. A more logical case would, almost certainly, be that while "it is possible to lack 'defects' and still be deficient with respect to beauty, ... those who are described as beautiful must be without 'defects'."[626]

A Neuro-Biological Approach to Blemish

Recently, evidence has accrued from studies using functional magnetic resonance imaging (*fMRI*) of the existence within the human brain of "hard wiring" relating to those things we all perceive as beautiful and ugly. If this is so and given the rate of human evolution, it is entirely probable that there has always been an organic element of the appreciation of beauty operating alongside that engendered by culture and society. In other words, our reactions to beauty and ugliness are most probably *conditioned reflexes*.

This neuro-biological, evolutionary approach to blemish and disability appears to have developed along the lines of the oft-quoted, but never attributed, adage that while "Fear evolved to keep us away from large animals that want to eat us from the outside, disgust evolved to keep us away from smaller animals that kill us from the inside." It is easy from this clever but rather generalized viewpoint to understand disgust as a protective mechanism if we consider, for example, the stimulation of nausea and the vomiting reflex by noxious smells, unpleasant sights, and ingested bacteria and their toxins. However, in the human, we must go beyond the simple reflex and consider this response to have evolved into a Pavlovian *conditioned reflex* where the conditioning is the result of our evolution into gregarious and social animals. The most extreme forms of stimuli that trigger such reflexes will never be overcome by training or social *mores*. However, further back in the evolutionary spectrum of triggering events, it is quite possible to imagine sights and other sensory experiences that have become active triggers as a result of fear, social habituation or even fashion. This semi-physiological distaste for what Mary Douglas has called the "out of place"[627] has traditionally been seen as the reason behind the aversion shown by ancient societies to physical deformity and disfigurement resulting from disease or injury. Today, we take a mildly smug pride in believing that we can be much more selective in choosing our conditioning factors to fit in with perceived

---

626 Olyan, *Disability in the Hebrew Bible*, 21.
627 See chapter 5; also, Douglas, *Purity and Danger*, 36–50.

morality, social customs, *Zeitgeist*, and even fashion. To this end, the overused, convenient but frequently meaningless word-duality *appropriate/inappropriate* is endlessly defined and re-defined to suit the particular pleadings of any *special interest group*.

Disability studies, nowadays widely seen as an academic discipline, is fast becoming a modish and popular subject for study, both in its present-day and historical contexts. The idea that the human response to disability is the product of a very highly conditioned reflex is a particularly favoured viewpoint because it can be seen in both of these time-contexts. *Disability Studies* as a discipline has, however, been criticized on the grounds that the philosophical and sociological standpoint has often been established *before* the evidence is examined. Recently, this approach has been questioned on the logical and concrete grounds that, not only is it over-simplified and overly convenient to followers of present-day fashions and attitudes but, more significantly, there may, in reality, be a permanent element of *hard-wiring* within the brain that, at least to an extent, defines *ab initio*, our aversive and pleasurable reactions to particular sensory inputs. While such an element may be considered to be *hard-wired* inasmuch as its neural connections are defined initially by anatomical development, it will always be susceptible to modification by learning in a manner analogous to the learning of e.g. motor skills. This will involve input-convergence into sensory, memory, and effector pathways in which spatial and temporal summation of new inputs with data stored in existing circuitry takes place. This process is known to stimulate dendritic and synaptic proliferation which, along with positive and negative feed-back and feed-forward systems, is the anatomical basis of both *data-storage* and *functional integrative activity* in the brain.[628]

A diffuse interconnected network of grey-matter nuclei and white-matter tracts within the brain and known as the *limbic system* is the most likely candidate for this role. The anatomy and wiring of the limbic system was worked out from dissection, ablation studies and examination of neurological dysfunction long ago.[629] Its association with emotional status and memory was established later,[630] but it is only since the advent of *functional nuclear-magnetic resonance* imaging studies (*fMRI*)[631] that it has been possible to demonstrate, in conscious individuals, a direct association between electrical activity in the limbic system and specific sensory inputs of an unpleasant or unaesthetic nature. While no researcher, perhaps understandably, appears to have gone so far as to define ugly

---

628 See, M. A. Glasby, "The Control of Posture and Movement" in *Applied Physiology for Surgery and Critical Care*, ed. M. A. Glasby and C. L-H. Huang (Oxford: Butterworth-Heinemann, 1995).
629 Stephen Walter Ranson and Sam Lillard Clark, *The Anatomy of the Nervous System*. Revised by Sam Lillard Clark (Philadelphia; London: W. B. Saunders Co., 1959).
630 A. Brodal, *Neurological Anatomy: In Relation to Clinical Medicine* (Oxford: University Press, 1972).
631 Henry Gray and Susan Standring, *Gray's Anatomy: The Anatomical Basis of Clinical Practice* (Edinburgh: Churchill Livingstone, 2008).

faces and employ their unfortunate owners in his experiments, there has been a considerable degree of study of facial recognition using both normal individuals and those who, through congenital or acquired neurological causes, have lost the ability to recognize and/or memorize faces—*prosopagnosia*. From these studies has emerged the idea that facial recognition is dependent upon two neural sub-processes: *recognition* and *memory*. Intuitively, one might suppose the former to be associated with the visual processing system[632] and the latter with those parts of the brain that serve memory. In particular the *hippocampal-limbic* connections in the temporal lobe have been implicated both in the processing of short-term memories into long-term memories and in the association and integration of memory with emotion. Eimer,[633] using electroencephalographic techniques to investigate brain activity, after facial recognition in normal and prosopagnostic subjects, found that the activation of stored visual representations of familiar faces was not sufficient for conscious, explicit, facial recognition and that prosopagnosia was, therefore, a disconnection between visual and memory sites for faces. It followed that multiple brain sites were necessary to recognize faces. Observations carried out on patients with identifiable, specific neural lesions and on animals with neural ablations, implicated the *amygdaloid nucleus*[634] as being vital for this memory element of facial recognition.

Fox[635] and others have located an area close to the *parahippocampal gyrus* (Brodmann area 37)[636] on the ventral surface of the temporal lobe and on the lateral side of the *fusiform gyrus* which they have shown by *fMRI* to be specific for the visual part of facial recognition and which is malfunctional in prosopagnostic patients. This has been called the *fusiform face area* (FFA) and has been shown to be preferentially activated when faces are seen before the eyes of an observer. It has been suggested, as a result of these and similar studies, that the FFA operates as a *neural centre for identity* by encoding multiple types of visual information, such as expression, gaze-direction, age, and sex, among others.

It is the limbic system and, in particular, the *amygdala,* that integrates this identifying information with appropriately related memories and thereby with neural and hormonal effector systems. Adolphs[637] extended this idea to involve unpleasant stimuli: specifically fear and anger, but he again fell short of including ugliness, deformity or blemish in his catalogue of stimuli for

---

632 Not the parts of the brain that enable us to see images but rather those parts that allow us to interpret them.
633 M. Eimer, A. Gosling, and B. Duchaine, "Electrophysiological Markers of Covert Face Recognition in Developmental Prosopagnosia," *Brain* 135 (2012): 542–54.
634 Named thus because it is shaped like an almond — ἀμύγδαλος, ἡ = almond tree.
635 C. J. Fox, H. M. Hanif, G. Iaria, B. Duchaine, J. J. S. Barton, "Perceptual and Anatomic Patterns of Selective Deficits in Facial Identity and Expression Processing," *NPA* 49, no. 12 (2011): 3188–200.
636 Brodal, *Neurological Anatomy*.
637 Ralph Adolphs, James A. Russell, and Daniel Tranel, "A Role for the Human Amygdala in Recognizing Emotional Arousal from Unpleasant Stimuli," *Psy Sci*, no. 2 (1999): 167–71.

amygdalar activation. Nevertheless, Adolphs widened the field significantly by showing that the amygdala was specifically involved with the arousal of at least some negative emotions.

Anderson and Phelps[638] added to the observation that the amygdala may be a critical neural substrate for visual/emotional processing, by demonstrating that damage to the human amygdala impairs the normal appraisal of social signals of emotion. He postulated that effective social communication depends on both the ability to receive (emotional appraisal) and the ability to send (emotional expression) signals of emotional states. Patients with bilateral amygdalar lesions, despite a severe deficit in *interpreting* facial expressions of emotion including fear, exhibited an intact ability to *express* this and other basic emotions. This dissociation suggested that a single neural integrating module did not support all aspects of the social communication of emotional status. One well-established function of the amygdala is its contribution to emotional learning and memory and so it may be important for the acquisition of understanding and formulation of response to the significance of facial expressions of whatever form.

Kawabata[639] continuing to avoid the "hot potato" of living human ugliness, chose to examine its antithesis (beauty), using *art* as a stimulus for brain activity to be assessed by *fMRI*. This study set out to address the question of whether there are brain areas that became specifically engaged when subjects viewed paintings of male and female faces that were considered to be beautiful or ugly, presumably in the opinion of experts. Within this framework, it was found that the perception of different categories of paintings was associated with distinct and specialized visual areas of the brain, and specifically that the *orbito-frontal cortex* was differentially engaged during the perception of "beautiful" and "ugly" stimuli. An important finding in this study was that, although there was a differential response in the *fMRI* to the presentation of various examples of artwork for visual delectation, the results showed that there was no separate structure specifically engaged when stimuli were perceived as ugly.

From all of this we cannot draw any definite conclusions about the brain's response to unpleasant images such as might be presented by the sight of ugliness, deformity, disfigurement or blemish. However, we *can* conclude that the brain does have specific areas dedicated to the recognition of new sights, particularly faces, and to their association with data acquired in the past—memory—and also to the motor or effector responses to these processed and updated memories. It remains, therefore, a matter for debate whether we are fully pre-programmed to show aversive activity when confronted by unpleasant

---

638 Adam K. Anderson and Elizabeth A. Phelps, "Expression without Recognition: Contributions of the Human Amygdala to Emotional Communication," *Psy Sci*, no. 2 (2000): 106–11.
639 Hideaki Kawabata and Semir Zeki, "Neural Correlates of Beauty," *J Neurophys* 91, no. 4 (2004): 1699–705.

sights. However, it seems likely that we have at least evolved the neural hardware and software to do so.

Mortal Flesh as a Symbol of Defilement

Trevaskis[640] has argued that צרעת, זוב and מום, whatever they may actually represent in modern medical terms, were all used by the P authors in the way suggested by Douglas, namely as *antitypes of wholeness*. The afflicted person then becomes an *antitype of holiness*. If we make a small allowance for זוב, Trevaskis suggests that צרעת, זוב and all the subsets of מום might have been selected—perhaps arbitrarily—by the P authors as [specifically visual] symbols of a more over-reaching anti-typical tension between flesh and defilement.

טמא ↔ בשר

However, it is important that we understand the usage of the idea of *flesh* in the Hebrew Bible. The word for flesh (בשר) appears in Hebrew two hundred and sixty-seven times in the singular, and once in the plural, in the Hebrew Bible. Sixty-one of these occurrences are in Leviticus. It also appears three times in Aramaic. A great deal has been written on the meaning of this word[641] and, at the very least, it is necessary to consider it in both secular and theological-cultic usage. In the simplest form of its secular guise, בשר is used for "meat"—flesh as food—but this usage extends beyond food to the meat used for sacrifice in cultic practices. Commonly, בשר is used both to mean "the body", often in conjunction with עצם (bone), and variously also to mean "body parts" such as skin. Lev 13:2 uses the expression, בעור־בשרו, literally, "in the skin of his flesh", to describe symptoms of צרעת. Other secular usages of בשר are "man" and as a euphemism for genitals.[642] The theological-cultic usage of בשר, apart from referring to sacrificial meat and to circumcision, is restricted to the idea of, "man" and "man's body". In particular, the form כל־בשר, "humanity", "everyone", "any man" is used as an idiom to represent those things which all humans share in their essence but which distinguishes their essence from the essence of Yahweh.[643]

---

640 Leigh M. Trevaskis, *Holiness, Ethics and Ritual in Leviticus* (Sheffield: Sheffield Press 2010).
641 See: Clines, ed., *Dictionary of Classical Hebrew*, Vol. II, 277–280. *TDOT*, Vol. II, 317–332. Jastrow, *Dictionary of the Targumim*, 199.
642 Much has been written about this last usage and even more assumed. The question remains unclear though less unclear than the supposed usage of "feet" to euphemize the same antomical structures.
643 *TDOT*, Vol. II, 327.

If we ponder Douglas's analogy of dirt with *matter out of place*,[644] so we may think of צרעת, זוב and מום as representations of *flesh out of place*. This displacement occurs in such a way as to convert the relationship between בשר and טהור to one between בשר and טמא. A diagrammatic scheme might be:

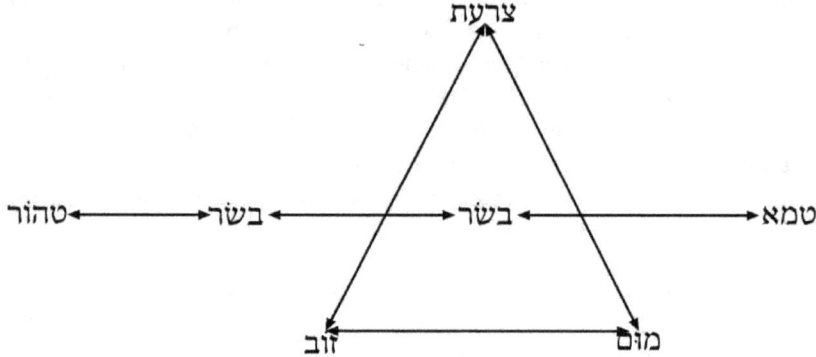

Where: the equilateral triangle represents a *zone of impurity* affecting flesh, caused by interaction of the stigmatizing factors at its apices, and operating upon the linear relationship, טמא ↔ בש ↔ טהור as a whole.

If this idea is reasonable, צרעת, זוב and מום were perhaps being used by the P authors as *exemplars* of בשר in its טמא state. The choice of example may have been made purely on the dramatic and visible appearance of these conditions or, in the case of זוב, its association with other people's sexual activity, always a favourite topic of interest and discussion.

When the perfection of flesh becomes deranged by whatever mechanism, so as to result in טמא, this uncleanliness visited upon the individual becomes symbolic of his exclusion from Yahweh's immediate presence.[645] Trevaskis proposes that although צרעת, זוב and מום may have been considered by the P authors as the consequence of divine judgement upon flesh, this does not mean that they considered these afflictions to be specific punishments imposed from on high for specific sins. Trevaskis sees them rather as an educational contrivance, *pour encourager les autres*. Deranged flesh, therefore, becomes a metaphor for sinful humanity standing under Yahweh's judgement.[646]

BLEMISHES IN THE HEBREW BIBLE

It is important to investigate those physical blemishes that impinge upon the priestly concepts of *ritual impurity*,[647] and equally to question those that do not.

---

644 Douglas, *Purity and Danger*, 43–50.
645 See also chapter 5.
646 Trevaskis, *Holiness, Ethics and Ritual in Leviticus*, 170.
647 See chapter 5.

It would seem reasonable to begin by examining blemishes in search of qualities in parallel with צרעת and זוב; i.e. having the qualities of *platydysmorphism* and/or *reproductive compromise* involving the genitalia. In present-day thought, blemish/disfigurement/disability or whatever we choose to call it can, as noted above, be either congenital or acquired. The Hebrew Bible makes no such distinction regarding the stigma(ta) that blemish imparts. However, certain very clear distinctions are made in the text regarding specific forms of blemish/disability.

Classification of Blemishes in the Hebrew Bible

Leviticus, followed by Deuteronomy, contains the most extensive textual material dealing with specific blemishes and the important biblical texts outlining these blemishes have become called, in the jargon, *mum-lists*.[648]

The Mum-lists

The most significant mum-list appears at Lev 21:17–23 and is, therefore, part of the Holiness Code (H).[649] Here and elsewhere it is important to distinguish animal and human lists of מומים but also to note their similarities. While the human lists are presented with little real anatomical and physiological detail, considerably more scribal attention was given to the regulations and prohibitions concerning animals, in Exodus, Leviticus, Numbers and Deuteronomy. The majority of these regulations and prohibitions concerning blemish in animals relates to their fitness for sacrifice. The principal mum-list regarding animal sacrifice appears at Lev 22:22–24; this is H material:

עורת או שבור או־חרוץ או־יבלת או גרב או ילפת לא־תקריבו אלה ליהוה ואשה
לא־תתנו מהם על־המזבח ליהוה

> Blind, or broken, or maimed, or having a wen, or scurvy, or scabbed, ye shall not offer these unto the Lord, nor make an offering by fire of them upon the altar unto the Lord.

ושור ושה שרוע וקלוט נדבה תעשה אתו ולנדר לא ירצה

> Either a bullock or a lamb that hath any thing superfluous or lacking in his parts, that mayest thou offer for a freewill offering; but for a vow it shall not be accepted.

ומעוך וכתות ונתוק וכרות לא תקריבו ליהוה ובארצכם לא תעשו

---

648 The Talmud expands the 12 blemishes listed in Leviticus to a total of 90 conditions, (Bekoroth 43–46). These include conditions which might reasonably be expected such as epilepsy, and more exotic conditions such as the absence of eyebrows.
649. While H is not P, the influence of P upon H is debateable. See chapter 2.

That which hath its stones bruised, or crushed, or broken, or cut, ye shall not offer unto the Lord; neither shall ye do thus in your land. (Lev 22:22–24)

This is partially restated in Deut 15:21,

וכי־יהיה בו מום פסח או עור כל מום רע לא תזבחנו ליהוה אלהיך

And if it have any blemish, as if it be lame or blind, any ill blemish whatsoever, thou shalt not sacrifice it unto the Lord thy God. (Deut 15:21)

and the terrible consequences of offering a blemished animal for sacrifice are recorded in Mal 1:14:

וארור נוכל ויש בעדרו זכר ונדר וזבח משחת לאדני כי מלך גדול אני אמר יהוה צבאות ושמי נורא בגוים

But cursed be the deceiver, which hath in his flock a male, and voweth, and sacrificeth unto the Lord a blemished thing: for I am a great king, saith the Lord of hosts, and my name is terrible among the Gentiles. (Mal 1:14)

We should compare the blemishes here with the very similar list for humans to be found in H, at Lev 21:17–20:

דבר אל־אהרן לאמר איש מזרעך לדרתם אשר יהיה בו מום לא יקרב להקריב לחם אלהיו

Speak unto Aaron, saying, Whosoever he be of thy seed throughout their generations that hath a blemish, let him not approach to offer the bread of his God.

כי כל־איש אשר־בו מום לא יקרב איש עור או פסח או חרם או שרוע

For whatsoever man he be that hath a blemish, he shall not approach: a blind man, or a lame, or he that hath a flat nose, or any thing superfluous,

או איש אשר־יהיה בו שבר רגל או שבר יד

or a man that is brokenfooted, or brokenhanded,

או־גבן או־דק או תבלל בעינו או גרב או ילפת או מרוח אשך

or crookbacked, or a dwarf, or that hath a blemish in his eye, or is scurvy, or scabbed, or hath his stones broken; (Lev 21:17–20)

The possession of a blemish by a human prevents that individual from making sacrificial offerings although he may partake of the propitiatory bread as long as he does not enter the sanctuary, penetrate the veil or approach the altar. Lev 21:21–23 is seen as the best summary of the legal position regarding sacrifice and blemish though it should be noted that this portion of the Holiness Code deals specifically with priests—the seed of Aaron.

כל־איש אשר־בו מום מזרע אהרן הכהן לא יגש להקריב את־אשי יהוה מום בו את לחם אלהיו לא יגש להקריב

> No man of the seed of Aaron the priest, that hath a blemish, shall come nigh to offer the offerings of the Lord made by fire: he hath a blemish; he shall not come nigh to offer the bread of his God.

לחם אלהיו מקדשי הקדשים ומן־הקדשים יאכל

> He shall eat the bread of his God, both of the most holy, and of the holy.

אך אל־הפרכת לא יבא ואל־המזבח לא יגש כי־מום בו ולא יחלל את־מקדשי כי אני יהוה מקדשם

> Only he shall not go in unto the veil, nor come nigh unto the altar, because he hath a blemish; that he profane not my sanctuaries: for I am the Lord which sanctify them. (Lev 21:21–23)

From a study largely of the mum-lists, Olyan has written extensively on the types of blemish to be found in the Hebrew Bible.[650] The term מום/μῶμος he considers to be a native category of classification largely, but not exclusively, occurring in legal texts concerned with the cult. His preferred translation "defect" he defines as "a technical term in biblical usage, referring to a specific set of negatively constructed physical characteristics inconsistent with biblical notions of beauty." Olyan's interest in blemish is more specifically concerned with the Israelite concept of beauty than with the purity/impurity tension. However, it rapidly becomes clear that certain of his "defects" impinge less upon the aesthetic and more upon the socio-cultic milieu in a manner strikingly akin to that of צרעת and זוב. In such cases, the "defect", as with צרעת and זוב, becomes the object of stigmatization but, in the case of מומים, it is more closely and specifically associated with the business of sacrifice and the entry of the individual into the sanctuary of the Lord's assembly (קהל). This prohibition is formally stated in Deut 23:2:

לא־יבא פצוע־דכא וכרות שפכה בקהל יהוה

> He that is wounded in the stones, or hath his privy member cut off, shall not enter into the assembly of the Lord. (Deut 23:2)

---

650 Saul M. Olyan, "Honor, Shame, and Covenant Relations in Ancient Israel and Its Environment," *JBL* 115, no. 2 (1996): 201–18; Saul M. Olyan, "What Do Shaving Rites Accomplish and What Do They Signal in Biblical Ritual Contexts?" *JBL* 117, no. 4 (1998): 611–22; Saul M. Olyan, "The Exegetical Dimensions of Restrictions on the Blind and the Lame in Texts from Qumran," *DSD* 8, no. 1 (2001): 38–50; Olyan, *Disability in the Hebrew Bible*.

For the modern reader, it is surprising and interesting to note that any notion of personal misfortune in the acquisition of disability appears to have been a totally alien concept.

Somatic Defects — מומים

Olyan supposes that, for the Israelites, the cardinal sign of a "defect" was a "lack of symmetry". This is interesting since symmetry has, particularly in Western civilization and art, so often been held up as a sign of beauty. However, we may equate a lack of symmetry with what Olyan calls a "blurring of physical boundaries" and it has already been noted that a similar set of criteria operated for Mary Douglas in her understanding of taboo and impurity. From the mum-lists, Olyan identifies the following conditions: blindness, lameness, loss of body parts (eye, tooth, etc.), deformity (e.g. flat nose), superfluous parts, fractured limbs, kypho-scoliosis, dwarfism, *coloboma iridis*, dermatitis (but see צרעת chapter 6) and, of course, injury or abnormality of the genitalia.

It is important to understand that neither צרעת nor זוב were seen as *blemishes* or *defects* although they share the same two defining criteria either of being a visible sign of (usually dermopathic) *platydysmorphism* or of involvement of the genitals. Moreover, there is no textual evidence to suggest that any distinction was made as to the extent of these physical defects either in time or space, nor to whether they were congenital or acquired. The only possible distinction appears to have been between naturally-occurring blemishes and those inflicted judicially under the *lex talionis* or upon those vanquished in battle. This lack of distinction was, of course, shared by צרעת and זוב. Nor was asymmetry obligatorily a prerequisite of stigmatization by a defect.[651]

In the Hebrew Bible, therefore, a defect appears to have been definable no more precisely than by saying it was a congenital or acquired blurring of somatic physical boundaries, not necessarily visible (if we include genital afflictions), and not necessarily with any clear asymmetry, time-course, degree of severity or associated dysfunction. One cannot help but marvel at this imprecision which must have offered great scope and convenience for stigmatizing others.

Priests with defects were destined for a miserable lot: a high priest fared even worse. Since the acquisition of congenital defects is a function of parental genetics and the presence of acquired defects an entirely fortuitous consequence of life-style and its misfortunes, it was inevitable that some priests would necessarily exhibit defects. The stigma of this was undoubtedly made worse by the closed shop restricting the priesthood to the seed of Aaron. This

---

[651] This has, in the past, been seen as having been the case by reference to Num 12:12: "Let her not, I pray, be as one dead, of whom the flesh is half consumed when he cometh out of his mother's womb" אל־נא תהי כמת אשר בצאתו מרחם אמו ויאכל חצי בשרו.

arrangement had the advantage of providing guaranteed employment and status for Levi family members but also the disadvantages of inbreeding. An afflicted priest was not, however, totally barred from practising. As long as he did not offer sacrifices or approach the veil of the tabernacle, his condition did not imperil the sanctuary and its offerings, and we can assume he could find other more menial sacerdotal tasks to occupy his time. His stigmatization, in the eyes of his fellows, was that he had much greater potential than they to pollute the sanctuary and his marginalization and/or relegation to a lower status was, for them, prophylactic sacramental hygiene, justifiable as an apotropaic measure in the interest of society as a whole. This is not to suggest that the defective priest's lot was a happy one, for banishment from the sanctuary distanced him from the deity. This was, in cultic terms, a significant social and religious disadvantage for any individual, not least a professional hierophant.

The above treatment combines as מומים, visible anatomical blemishes and genital affections. Olyan is less willing to make this conflation and although he broadly subscribes to the above ideas, he is quite specific that the individual with any sort of genital affliction was stigmatized for an entirely different reason. He also asserts that the prohibition that those with blemishes may not enter the assembly of Yahweh (קהל יהוה) implied a greater geographical involvement than the sanctuary. The principal misfortune of the genitally disabled, according to Olyan, is that they cannot reproduce and this capacity was an essential condition for the eugenic management and maintenance of the cult of the Israelite community. Whatever the mechanism by which they acquired their genital mutilation, they were no longer thought of as being part of the same group as the other priests. Whatever the pathology of מומים involving the genitalia, the result was to put the sufferer exactly on a par with the זב/זבה of Lev 15.

Circumcision: An Exception

Olyan points out the interesting exception of circumcision.[652] This procedure undoubtedly shares, with some defects, the fact that it is an imposed physical alteration of the body and involves the genitals to boot.[653] Circumcision was viewed as a barbarous mutilation by Greek and Roman cultures yet in other cultures it was the foreskin (ערלה/ἀκροβυστία)[654] that was viewed as abhorrent and consequently it became an object of stigmatization associated with disgrace (חרפה—Gen 34:14). Circumcision was seen by the Israelites as an *enabling rite*: the definitive sign, at the level of the individual, of the covenant made for them between God and Abraham, ברית מילה:

---

[652] Olyan, "Honor, Shame, and Covenant Relations." Olyan, *Disability in the Hebrew Bible*, 36–38.
[653] However we should note that tattoos were not seen as "defects". This is mildly ironical since στίγμα was any injury caused by a sharp pointed instrument and particularly a tattoo.
[654] ἀκροποσθία in Classical Greek, and it is this form that has been used in medical terms such as posthitis.

המול ימול יליד ביתך ומקנת כספך והיתה בריתי בבשרכם לברית עולם

περιτομῇ περιτμηθήσεται ὁ οἰκογενὴς τῆς οἰκίας σου καὶ ὁ ἀργυρώνητος καὶ ἔσται ἡ διαθήκη μου ἐπὶ τῆς σαρκὸς ὑμῶν εἰς διαθήκην αἰώνιον[655]

> He that is born in thy house, and he that is bought with thy money, must needs be circumcised: and my covenant shall be in your flesh for an everlasting covenant. (Gen 17:13)

The state of remaining uncircumcised within the Israelite community was, therefore, a misdeed deserving of ostracism and even the punishment of כרת—termination of one's lineage. This applied not only to natives but to their imported slaves and retainers.

וערל זכר אשר לא־ימול את־בשר ערלתו ונכרתה הנפש ההוא מעמיה את־בריתי הפר

> And the uncircumcised male who is not circumcised in the flesh of his foreskin, that soul shall be cut off from his people; he hath broken my covenant. (Gen 17:14)

Such prohibition obviously extended to the metaphorical usage of uncircumcision (in heart) as we can see in this verse from Ezekiel:

כה־אמר אדני יהוה כל־בן־נכר ערל לב וערל בשר לא יבוא אל־מקדשי לכל־בן־נכר אשר בתוך בני ישראל

> Thus saith the Lord God, No alien, uncircumcised in heart and uncircumcised in flesh, shall enter into my sanctuary, of any alien that is among the children of Israel. (Ezek 44:9)

And we are left in no doubt as to the consequences of failing to apply this extension from anatomical circumcision to its metaphorical counterpart in Jer 4:4,

המלו ליהוה והסרו ערלות לבבכם איש יהודה וישבי ירושלם פן־תצא כאש חמתי ובערה ואין מכבה מפני רע מעלליכם

> Circumcise yourselves to the Lord, and take away the foreskins of your heart, ye men of Judah and inhabitants of Jerusalem: lest my fury go forth like fire, and burn that none can quench it, because of the evil of your doings. (Jer 4:4)

Unsurprisingly then, the state of being circumcised would have been viewed as normal in Israelite society and as such it would not have been seen as a blemish in the way that another form of somatic re-arrangement might have been seen.

---

655 It is interesting to note that Greek distaste for circumcision appears to have had no influence on the authors of the Septuagint.

The contrasting Graeco–Roman view of circumcision has been extensively and fascinatingly reviewed by Hodges.[656] The Hellenistic world was so vehemently against the mutilation of circumcision that, among others, Celsus devised an operation[657] to reverse the condition and this and related procedures later became referred to as *epispasm* by association with the notion of "drawing-out". Celsus's operation has been variously improved upon and compared, by a number of surgical authors, with modern techniques of preputial reconstruction, (*acrobustioplasty*).[658]

Non-defects

It is important now to consider those conditions which, intuitively, might be thought to have been seen and treated as מומים but which were not. Most notable for their absence from the mum-lists are deafness, mutism, and all forms of mental disability. Nowhere in the Hebrew Bible or Septuagint are any of these specifically defined and stigmatized as מומים yet deafness and mutism are nevertheless stigmatized in a lesser way. In the Hebrew Bible, deaf (חרש) and mute/dumb (אלם) individuals were not restricted by any cited law, in any way, from access to any cultic place or sacred activity. This is the case both for priests and for members of the general population. Despite this lack of restriction, as Olyan points out, deaf and dumb individuals frequently find themselves, in the biblical texts, associated with those suffering from other מומים; especially the blind and lame. This happens often and is surely not a random process. Olyan surmises that although deaf and dumb individuals were not seen as *somatically defective* in the way that, for example, the blind and lame and those with other listed מומים undoubtedly were, at the time there may have existed a wider generic classification that stretched so as to encompass both of these sub-categories. If there was any such sub-classification, it has not survived. There is no clear evidence to substantiate this idea; Olyan bases his assumptions on the fact that in Exod 4:11, Yahweh takes responsibility for the creation of the disabled along with the able-bodied,

ויאמר יהוה אליו מי שם פה לאדם או מי־ישום אלם או חרש או פקח או עור הלא אנכי יהוה

> And the Lord said unto him, Who hath made man's mouth? or who maketh a man dumb, or deaf, or seeing, or blind? is it not I the Lord? (Exod 4:11)

---

656 F. M. Hodges, "The Ideal Prepuce in Ancient Greece and Rome: Male Genital Aesthetics and Their Relation to Lipodermos, Circumcision, Foreskin Restoration, and the Kynodesme," *Bull Hist Med* 75 (2001): 375-405.
657 Celsus, *De Medicina*, trans. W. G. Spencer, Vol. III, Book VII: 25, 420-425.
658 S. B. Brandes and J. W. McAninch, "Surgical Methods of Restoring the Prepuce: A Critical Review," *BJU* 83, no. Suppl 1 (1999): 109-13. D. M. Greer, P. C. Mohl, and K. A. Sheley, "A Technique for Foreskin Reconstruction and Some Preliminary Results," *J Sex Res* 18, no. 4 (1982): 324-30. J. P. Rubin, "Celsus' Decircumcision Operation. Medical and Historical Implications," *Urol* 16, no. 1 (1980): 121-24.

This statement by Yahweh is a specific paraenetic aimed at Moses who is dithering at the prospect of confronting Pharaoh and his henchmen, and it is difficult to see a more specific intention. Nevertheless, the deity's role as creator of all things is a central pillar of Yahwistic theology. Lev 19:14 showers further confusion upon the question by appearing to associate blindness, which is clearly a מום, with deafness which clearly is not. However, although he counsels not to trip-up the blind on purpose, his remarks are not in any way of a legalistic nature nor do they, in any way, imply stigmatization.

לא־תקלל חרש ולפני עור לא תתן מכשל ויראת מאלהיך אני יהוה

> Thou shalt not curse the deaf, nor put a stumblingblock before the blind, but thou shalt fear thy God: I am the Lord. (Lev 19:14)

It seems possible that the priests, in formulating the Levitical laws, may have treated *sensory* dysfunction with a more lenient viewpoint than *motor* defects. Perhaps they saw an association of these sensory deficits with weakness, dependence, and vulnerability in a way that aroused their sympathy. The consequence of this sympathy[659] might have been the real or tacit operation of a sub-category of deficiencies combining established מומים with inherent sensorimotor elements with non-defects having similar properties. In contrast, we also find in the Hebrew Bible, instances of a less generous appreciation of these defects and non-defects where they are used figuratively so that deafness and blindness become metaphors for incomprehension and ignorance. This metaphorical association of sensorimotor deficiency with intellectual dysfunction was widespread throughout the Ancient Near East and, as seen earlier (Ps 115), it proved a useful argument against idolatry.

Unfortunately, we are left with no explanation that fully encompasses the observed textual instances that combine Olyan's *defects* and *non-defects*. It is possible that this sub-classification was overly pedantic and that the mum-lists could better be seen as having encompassed all of the physical and sensorimotor dysfunctions that are mentioned in the texts. If so, we have to postulate that there was a spectral gradation of the seriousness of all of these and, likewise, of the degree of stigmatization they engendered. This is an attractive theory but unfortunately there is no hard evidence to support it.

The Barren Female

Olyan avoids this special case but it has been considered in some detail by Ackerman.[660] There is no question but that the זב or any male with a specific מום involving his genitalia, would be stigmatized on account of the real or perceived compromise of his reproductive capability. If we may paraphrase Isa 56:3, the

---

[659] Not a quality to be found in abundance in the Torah and entirely untypical of the priesthood.
[660] S Ackerman, "The Blind, the Lame and the Barren Shall Not Come into the House," in *Disability Studies and Biblical Literature*, ed. Candida R. Moss and Jeremy Schipper (New York: Palgrave Macmillan, 2011), 29-45.

male sufferer from any such reproductive dysfunction becomes, like the eunuch, a "dried-up tree" (עץ יבש). In the female, we know that זוב, menstruation, and parturition are all associated with a relatively low-level of stigmatization and impurity that precludes the woman in question from entering the sanctuary. This proscription for women is, therefore, precisely equivalent to that imposed upon both זב and זבה, having those מומים involving genital mutilation and, by implication, reproductive incapacitation.

In the case of barrenness, the most obvious case of reproductive incapacitation in the female, the situation becomes complicated by the time-course of the condition. Barrenness is an oft-recurring subject in the Hebrew Bible and the centrepiece of a number of important narratives.[661] Ackerman has, from the viewpoint of the Documentary Hypothesis, examined all of the *barren woman stories* in the Hebrew Bible.[662] Her conclusion, based on these texts, is that the specific prohibitions of Deut 23:2 are, in principle, equally applicable to barren women in that access to the sanctuary becomes forbidden to them. However, this prohibition differs in that it is not immediate but requires the passage of a certain time without the production of children before the woman can be formally declared to be barren (1 Sam 1:7). Olyan[663] too, agrees that barrenness, alone among what might be categorized as female genital blemishes, results in prohibitions and stigmatization commensurate with זוב and the genital מומים seen in men, but, again, *only* after an appropriate period has elapsed in order to prove the chronicity and/or irreversibility of the barrenness. Ackermann summarizes this viewpoint by concluding that "The cult, even when providing some leeway, still marginalized barren women as a particular subgroup on account of their reproductive inability."[664]

The Emphasis on Sexual Function and Dysfunction

It is impossible not to notice the very considerable emphasis given to sexual function and dysfunction among the מומים and also in the broader field of the purity/impurity laws. Sexual disability, for the most part, is treated in a negative way throughout the Hebrew Bible and sexual activity in one form or another is a frequently recurring theme therein.[665]

---

661 J. S. Baden, "The Nature of Barrenness in the Hebrew Bible," in *Disability Studies and Biblical Literature*, ed. Candida R. Moss and Jeremy Schipper (New York: Palgrave Macmillan, 2011). For an exhaustive account of the Greek view on this subject, see περι αφορων, in: Hippocrates et al., *Hippocrates*, Vol. X, 327–395.
662 Ackerman, "The Blind, the Lame and the Barren Shall Not Come into the House."
663 Saul M. Olyan, *Rites and Rank: Hierarchy in Biblical Representations of Cult* (Princeton, NJ: Princeton University Press, 2000).
664 Ackerman, "The Blind, the Lame and the Barren Shall Not Come into the House," 43.
665 There is however, in the Hebrew Bible in general, a refreshing lack of the polar opposites of vulgarity and prurience served up in equal measure with hypocritical sanctimony and hyper-genteelness, such as we may find elsewhere in relation to the over-worked subject of sexuality and sexual peccadillos. Ullendorf, in a scholarly yet highly amusing paper, has investigated the Bawdy Bible from a lexical and linguistic point of view. He concludes, "there is in the Hebrew Bible, in prose and in poetry, in religious admonition and in secular love songs, a healthy and unabashed outspokenness which, in a sense, constitutes one of the great glories of the Old Testament. It can

Stewart has raised the question of why a whole and sexually perfect body should be regarded as ritually pure in the first place.[666] In attempting to answer this question he rehearses the mum-lists in some detail and in relation to textual examples from the Hebrew Bible. He sees an initial contradiction between the effusive praise given to the blemish-free (female) body that is תמה:

כלך יפה רעיתי ומום אין בך

Thou art all fair, my love; and there is no spot in thee. (Song 4:7)

and the more matter-of-fact Levitical usage of תמים to denote those persons, or items, which by virtue of the absence of disqualifying מומים are acceptable for sacrificial rituals and as sacrificial animals but apparently fail to reach the empyrean of beauty. However, if we consider the notion of *wholeness* as having the meaning of *perfect somatic integrity and outward appearance* and thus paving the way to *perfect holiness*, we can see the special case for sexual disorders of all forms representing a real or perceived category-violation of the *wholeness* necessary for proper reproductive function. As Douglas has pointed out, there appears to have been "a clear relationship between wholeness and holiness",[667] such that where:

Absence of all מומים → somatic wholeness → purity → holiness

we may draw the parallel:

Absence of genital מומים → wholeness of reproductive potential → purity → holiness

Today, we are universally concerned[668] with sexual performance and it is deficiencies in this capacity that are, today, seen as stigmatizing. In the Hebrew Bible, by contrast, it was the endpoint of sexual function, reproductive success, that was central to the achieving of *wholeness* and, thereby, *holiness*.

Of course, we know today, that some of the Levitical מומים would not necessarily result in reproductive failure but it is easy to see how the ancients might have thought otherwise.

---

and does touch upon subjects and issues, candidly and ingenuously and with unvarnished vigour, and will give offence only to the squeamish and the lecherous." Edward Ullendorff, "The Bawdy Bible," *Bull* SOAS 42, no. 3 (1979): 425–56.
666 D. T. Stewart, "Sexual Disabilities in the Hebrew Bible," in *Disability Studies and Biblical Literature*, ed. Candida R. Moss and Jeremy Schipper (New York: Palgrave Macmillan, 2011), 67.
667 Douglas, *Purity and Danger*, 64–71. See also, Poorthuis and Schwartz, *Purity and Holiness*.
668 Indeed, obsessively fascinated, especially in the popular media.

We can be reasonably certain also, that זוב did not carry the stigma that later generations applied to venereal diseases:[669] it would have been seen entirely as a manifestation of a failure of reproductive capacity.[670]

The menstrual taboo has been largely dealt with in chapter 8. Phipps believes it to be a significant and continuing reason why women in Judaism and Islam—and even Christianity which has no impurity axe to grind, are to this day, excluded from positions of authority.[671]

A passing mention must be made of "female circumcision" since Cohen has raised the question of why Jewish females are *not* circumcised.[672] There is no evidence, from any source, that procedures of this kind have ever been performed for ritualistic reasons among Jews. However, Cohen questions whether, if circumcision is the cardinal symbol of the Abrahamic covenant with God, the absence of any equivalent anatomical sign in females means that they are excluded from the covenant *or* that they are partakers in it but to a lesser degree. This observation may imply one or more of three things: (1) men have a privileged position within the covenant; (2) circumcision has become theologically over-rated; (3) women already possess some quality that is conferred upon men by circumcision. Cohen's analysis of this situation relies most heavily on material from rabbinic texts but it is his consideration of the Torah that matters here. He notes a decline over time in the symbolic nature of the foreskin and its replacement, in symbolic importance, by the *blood of circumcision*.[673] The later rabbis considered the shedding of menstrual blood to be the female equivalent of this necessary blood-loss of circumcision and argued for a symbolic equivalence. However, there is no evidence of such sophistry in biblical times and the inescapable conclusion is that circumcision, as the prime indicator of Israelitishness/Jewishness, lay exclusively with the male and relegated the female to a lower status. The briefest consideration of many cultures, before and after the Ancient Near East, and even today, does not make this a difficult proposition to accept.

---

669 It was only with the advent of the AIDS pandemic in the 1980s that VD Clinics emerged from deepest obscurity, usually in dark corners of hospital grounds and were re-named Departments of Sexually Transmitted Diseases. The abbreviation STD thereby took something of a downturn from its former, Sacrae Theologiae Doctor.
670 See chapter 8 for a more detailed consideration.
671 William E. Phipps, "The Menstrual Taboo in the Judeo-Christian Tradition," *J R&H* 19, no. 4 (1980): 298–303.
672 Shaye J. D. Cohen, *Why aren't Jewish Women Circumcised? Gender and Covenant in Judaism* (Berkeley; London: University of California Press, 2005). Female genital mutilation (FGM) is a particularly topical, indeed one might almost say fashionable, subject in 2015 and the World Health Organization today recognizes four categories of this mutilation. Type I is partial clitoridectomy i.e. excision of the clitoral prepuce and it is this procedure that is, presumably, being considered by Cohen because it would be anatomically the near-equivalent of conventional circumcision in the male. Type II is the removal of the clitoris and labia minora; Type III (infibulation), is partial external vulvectomy with midline closure to leave a small orifice for urine and menses. Type IV encompasses a range of symbolic piercing of the clitoris, and cutting into the vagina to widen it. World Health Organization, *Eliminating Female Genital Mutilation: An Interagency Statement* (WHO, 2008).
673 In ritual Jewish circumcision—בְּרִית מִילָה—the mohel is obliged to supply visual evidence of blood-shedding. In the more Orthodox communities, this precludes the use of a crushing clamp which might be applied, in conventional surgical practice, to reduce blood-loss on excision of the prepuce.

Mental Disability

Mental disability in the Hebrew Bible does not figure in the mum-lists but it was undoubtedly a stigmatized condition which usually led to the ostracism or at least marginalization of the affected individual. The mentally disabled individual was described, as a rule, as either a *fool* or a *madman* and was always the subject of contempt. There is a precedent for this in the Ancient Near East, in Babylonian wisdom literature, where it is made clear that it was the fate of the mentally disabled to be marginalized and consigned to lowly rank. The underlying reason for this rejection and/or contempt in Israelite society was, presumably, that the mentally disabled were rejected by Yahweh as inferior and/or imperfect beings. The classic example of this is Saul's madness in 1 Sam 16:14

> ורוח יהוה סרה מעם שאול ובעתתו רוח־רעה מאת יהוה

> Now the spirit of the Lord had departed from Saul, and an evil spirit from the Lord troubled him. (1 Sam 16:14)

Madness appears along with a number of other מומים in the extended covenantal curse to be found in Deut 28:28–34.

> יככה יהוה בשגעון ובעורון ובתמהון לבב

> The Lord shall smite thee with madness, and with blindness, and with astonishment of heart: (Deut 28:28)

The priestly authors appear to have been somewhat eclectic in their interpretation of the nature of mental disability and, on some occasions, they cast it in the form of florid psychosis while at other times they imply mild neurosis, feeble-mindedness or modesty of intellect.[674] The latter interpretation is also favoured by the author(s) of Proverbs where fools figure prominently and where *fool* implies one who fails to apply common sense, understanding and sometimes, one unwilling to toe the line of orthodoxy.

In the Wisdom Literature of Proverbs and Qoheleth, the preferred words for *fool* are אויל, כסיל and סכל. These frequently stand in opposition to *wisdom* (חכמה). Similarly, a word to be found in Psalms and Proverbs specifically meaning "simple-minded" is פתי. Outside the wisdom literature, the idea of a fool is more often established using a verb such as סכל or נבל. The more serious state of *madness* is also rendered verbally (√הלל or √שגע), usually in the form of a *puʿal* participle (*poʿal* מְהוֹלָל or *puʿal* מְשֻׁגָּע). However, these choices cannot be categorized with any certainty and the language of mental disability in the

---

[674] Until quite recently the terms moron, imbecile, and idiot were used in psychiatry as technical terms to classify increasing levels of metal deficiency and to distinguish them from psychoses, neuroses, and personality disorders. These categories have, today, acquired wholly pejorative meanings and so are considered indelicate and have fallen into desuetude.

Hebrew Bible must be considered both complex and ambiguous.⁶⁷⁵ Nevertheless, we can deduce that all of the words used throughout the Hebrew Bible to describe the various facets of mental disability have some common denominators. They all imply a loss of self-control in one form or another and to a greater or lesser degree. Words such as, anger, shock, anguish drunkenness, insanity, hot-headedness, carelessness, risk-taking, and intellectual retardation may all qualify as appropriate to describe the מהולל or the משגע at one place and time or another.

Biblical narratives containing accounts of mental disability are much less common than those involving somatic מומים. It is interesting to speculate how far the notion of מומים requiring a visual component may or may not be relevant. Mental disability is, traditionally, associated with devaluing qualities such as weakness, vulnerability, over-dependency. This is true throughout the Hebrew Bible and in much literature from other quarters up until modern times. In literature generally, we encounter two reactions⁶⁷⁶ to the mentally disabled and in either case, it is to these same qualities that each reaction takes place. Both are *ex grege* in the sense of the sufferer's failing to achieve Douglas's wholeness. Mentally disabled individuals were either seen as a threat or as a menace to the individual, community or land; or as an object requiring care and attention. In some cases of the latter, which on the whole belongs to more recent times, we even see the simpleton surrounded by an aura of mystique and becoming an object of religious veneration.

The Moron as a Menace

The Hebrew Bible certainly does not see anything good in the mental defective. However, there appears to be two different reactions to mental deficiency. In the P texts and worldview, it has been seen that mental disability was not a מום but was stigmatizing to a lesser degree. Perhaps it was sub-classified in a wider scheme of categories that has been lost to us. The best we can do, since neither "fool" nor "mad" nor "madness" appear anywhere in Leviticus, is to suppose that the level of stigmatization afforded by priests to the mentally disabled was quite low. Most likely, neurosis went unnoticed except perhaps by the immediate family; psychosis was almost certainly perceived (visually) as "raving madness" and incurable.

From the story of Saul (1 Sam 16:14–23), we know that mental disability was seen as a specific sign of divine rejection. It was clearly something to be noticed but equally clearly, not a matter for the priests and their rituals.

More difficult to understand is the inclusion of *madness* in the malediction of Deut 28:28–34. To be included in a curse would surely be highly stigmatizing

---

675 Olyan, *Disability in the Hebrew Bible*, 64. Clines, ed., *Dictionary of Classical Hebrew; TDOT*.
676 Never equal and opposite!

and, therefore, important. Admittedly, this is D material from a later date when it may have been seen fit, for political reasons, to stiffen-up the consequences of misbehaviour. It is interesting, nevertheless, to see the close association in verse 28 (above) of madness, not a מום, and blindness, one of the true מומים. The association of madness and vision continues into verse 34:

והיית משגע ממראה עיניך אשר תראה

> so that thou shalt be mad for the sight of thine eyes which thou shalt see. (Deut 28:34)

This literally means that what the cursed one "*sees in his blindness*" will drive him mad: this is surely describing an unpleasant hallucination, possibly schizophrenia. We have to go back to verse 15 to find out for what crime this was condign punishment. It turns out, unsurprisingly, to be a failure to observe all of the Lord's commandments and statutes. Here then, we see, not punishment *for* madness, but punishment *by* madness. Either way it is madness that stigmatizes and threatens individuals, society and, ultimately, הארץ.

The Innocent Simpleton

The *pure fool* or *holy fool* is a well-known literary and artistic device. We are all familiar with the simple-minded but innocent, kindly and generous *Quasimodo* of Victor Hugo;[677] or *Parsifal*[678]—the *Pure Fool*—totally innocent until enlightened by compassion ("*Durch Mitleid wissend, der reine Tor*") in Wagner's eponymous *Gesamtkunstwerk;* or the *Holy Fool* (юродивый) in Mussorgsky's opera, *Boris Godonov*. The last of these characters is a well known feature of the ascetic wing of the Eastern (especially Russian) Orthodox Church and has been considered in detail by Ivanov.[679] The "official" view of the Eastern Orthodox Church is that holy fools feign insanity in order to conceal their perfection from the world. They thus avoid praise which would be unacceptable to their austere and abstinent ethic. A more likely explanation, according to Ivanov, is that the юродивый, in order to achieve his aim, behaves as an innocent and feeble-minded simpleton to stimulate, among his gullible audience, a misplaced perception and empathy, towards his (supposed) sobriety, morality, and piety, unsullied by the detritus of run-of-the-mill humanity.

This idea of the innocent yet ingenuous and benign simpleton is wholly absent from the Hebrew Bible. It is a construct of later thought processes requiring a more abstract philosophical mental temperament.

---

[677] Victor Hugo, *The Hunchback of Notre-Dame* (1831).
[678] The innocent and ill-fated "Sir Percival" of Arthurian legend.
[679] S. A. Ivanov, *Holy Fools in Byzantium and Beyond* (English; Oxford: Oxford University Press, 2006).

Blemished Individuals in Israelite Society

Blemished individuals, though consigned to a lower social degree were, nevertheless, widely tolerated and not necessarily ill-treated. Olyan has suggested that they were seen as sub-human[680] only inasmuch as they were restricted in their fulfilling *all* of the functions one should expect of whole human beings.[681] This is Douglas's viewpoint also, but Olyan goes a step further and suggests the paradigm for this departure from wholeness was derived from a consideration of the negative features of idols. This association has been mentioned above (Ps 115:5–8) in relation to sensorimotor dysfunction. The blemished and idols may be seen as *sui generis*: innocuous and not objects of fear, as we are told in Jer 10:5,

כתמר מקשה המה ולא ידברו נשוא ינשוא כי לא יצעדו אל־תיראו מהם כי־לא ירעו וגם־היטיב אין אותם

> They are like a palm tree, of turned work, and speak not: they must needs be borne, because they cannot go. Be not afraid of them; for they cannot do evil, neither is it in them to do good. (Jer 10:5)

Olyan, therefore, supposes that the holders of מומים and those with related disabilities are analogous to idols by virtue of their inertia. Society is, nevertheless, saddled with them and, although they may be non-contributors within the community, they are harmless and, most importantly, their defects are not contagious.

An important conclusion based on the above is that we cannot view מומים in relation to the טהור/טמא tension in the way we have come to view צרעת and זוב. In general, cases of physical and mental disability, while undoubtedly lowering the social standing of the afflicted individual, were treated by a policy of *laissé faire*.

In summary we find that mutilation, natural blemishes and the Levitical disease-stigmata (צרעת and זוב) all have in common one or the other of *only two* features. They must either be *visible* and so on public display or, if not visible, they *must involve the genitals*.

In the Hebrew Bible, the possession of both physical and mental disabilities clearly resulted, to a variable degree, in the marginalization and stigmatization of affected individuals. We can distinguish a hierarchical spectrum of defilement to simple disfigurement ranging from those conditions, צרעת and זוב, that unequivocally caused overt ritual impurity, to those that merited a lesser and often rather opaque form of marginalization and stigmatization. At the more serious end of the spectrum were the two overarching categories: (1) visible

---

680 There is an unattractive odour of "Untermenschen" here.
681 Olyan, *Disability in the Hebrew Bible*, 127.

major disfigurement of the body's surface *dermopathic platydysmorphism* (צרעת) and (2) involvement of the genitalia so as to compromise reproductive capacity (זוב). The texts suggest that blemish, although stigmatizing, occupied a lower order within the hierarchy and so appears to have interested the priests only when it affected one of their own number and in such cases, restrictions were imposed exclusively over entering the sanctuary.

The deaf are seen nowhere in the Hebrew Bible as ritually impure, but were undoubtedly viewed as socially inferior to the whole-bodied. This distinction is more often implied than specified and it is never formally quantified in the texts. Among the ordinary people, such a response was, perhaps, simply a fear of ugliness, weakness, incapacity, ignorance, immobility, and those things that Douglas has classified as *antitypes* of an ingrained, mentally-programmed *wholeness paradigm*. Blemish, tells us therefore, that not every category violation of wholeness went on to cause ritual impurity. These lesser category-violations were still antitypes of wholeness and so consigned the sufferer to a lower social stratum. However, as far as we can tell from the available evidence, they did not transgress the strict purity requirements of the priestly *Weltanschauung*. This may be because blemish is never associated with contagion which is the cardinal feature of those major causes of ritual impurity צרעת and זוב. Contagion, therefore, must be the subject of the next chapter.

Chapter 10

CONTAGION

Contagion today, for us, is a feature of certain disease processes; for the Israelites, it appears to have been an important function of ritual impurity. The Oxford English Dictionary[682] defines contagion as "The communication of disease from body to body by contact direct or mediate", and this is, perhaps, the most widely understood definition. However, one should also be mindful of the noun "contagions" in the sense of, "a contagious disease or sickness; a plague or pestilence"; for this is a usage that was more common in former times than it is today.

> *And of thy light my soule in prison lighte*
> *That troubled is by the contagioun*
> *Of my body, and also by the wighte*
> *Of earthly luste and fals affeccioun;*[683]

The question to be addressed in this chapter is whether, for the Israelites, contagion was seen as intrinsic to the essence of ritual impurity (i.e the concept of impurity *per se*), or whether it was regarded primarily as part of the pathology of the specific impurifying (disease) process (צרעת, זוב etc.), thereby becoming entailed secondarily as a feature of ritual impurity. In either case it was a sign of major rather than minor impurity. This dilemma calls into question the role of the priest as mediator of both theological and public health matters, since it was he who identified the presence and risks of contagion and dictated the course of action to be taken.

In previous chapters, consideration has been given to healthcare in ancient Israel, the Levitical purity laws and their textual representations, and to the spectrum of Levitical stigmata (צרעת, זוב and מום). The first two of these, if we apply the modern definition that has been given above, quite clearly share the common features either of *contagion* itself or of the *fear of contagion*. The priestly ideology appears to have understood a spectrum of contagion running in the direction of decreasing severity thus: צרעת → זוב (→ מום). This relationship needs further investigation, beginning with words used to imply transmission and how their semantic usage differed among Ancient Near Eastern civilizations and from usage in modern times. Such a process must logically begin along comparative lines and account for how modern

---

682 J. A. Simpson and E. S. C. Weiner, *The Oxford English Dictionary*, 20 vols. (Oxford: Clarendon, 1989).
683 Chaucer, *Prologue to The Second Nun's Tale* c.1386

terminology regarding *contagion* evolved within the nosologies of the Ancient Near East and its daughter civilizations.

Nosologies of the Ancient Near East

Each of the Ancient Near Eastern civilizations[684] had its own approach to, and understanding of, illness and disease and it is reasonable to suppose that the notion of contagion would have figured, to some degree, in all of these.

In seeking a common origin for the concept of contagion and the transmissibility of disease, we should look first to the largely pastoral nature of ancient societies. This would have entailed the care of animals in addition to crops. It may be hard today to imagine the social importance of the herd in ancient society, but this cannot be overstressed. Healthy animals were essential for the livelihood and even survival of the individual and the community. The seasonal transfer of grazing animals to fresh pastures, often over substantial distances (known as the *transhumance*) must have been associated with a considerable risk of injury and disease among the flocks. It is not difficult to imagine that a need for at least a rudimentary system of animal healthcare must have evolved and how the notion of contagion might have arisen from observation of the behaviour of healthy and unhealthy domestic animals and the need to nourish and protect them.

A Comparative Approach

It is debateable how far, even if the regular caveats are applied, *a posteriori* arguments can contribute significantly to studies of this kind. The risk of criticism for reception history and revisionism is always present. A potential virtue is the opportunity a comparative approach gives us to identify ethnological and ecological *parallels* which, while not necessarily identical across civilizations, may nevertheless point to common features. For example, we have a great deal of nosological information from the Mesopotamian civilizations (see below) which can be followed-through sequentially into pre-Islamic Arab civilization, the *Golden Age of Islam,* and then into modern Islamic culture. This is invaluable in any study of the evolution of medical practice especially, since it offers the bonus of a near-continuum from a highly polytheistic civilization to a firmly monotheistic one. In contrast, we know very little regarding the parallel nosology of early Canaanite/Israelite civilization. Second Temple texts and those from the rabbis tend to be interpretative rather than innovative and so offer only half the picture.[685] A brief review of contagion in other ANE cultures and what they became is an appropriate starting point for comparison.

---

684 See also chapter 3.
685 Conrad and Wujastyk, *Contagion, Perspectives in Pre-modern Societies*, xiii.

Egypt

There is no textual evidence that the concept of contagion figures in Egyptian medicine. The word 𓇋𓐍𓏏𓅪 (iȝdt)[686] is often seen to mean "pestilence", "disease", "scourge" or "plague" and this is the nearest that one comes at least to the alternative, modern meaning of contagion. The famous Egyptian *Medical Papyri* make no mention of the specific idea of the transmission of disease by contagion.[687]

Mesopotamia

Mesopotamia is quite another matter. There is a wealth of cuneiform material, much of it still untranslated and some of what has been translated, is concerned with medical matters. What has been described as the "earliest written account [so far recorded] of a case of contagious disease"[688] is to be found on one of the tablets from Mari in present-day Syria.[689] The Mari tablets, most of which are to be found in the Aleppo National Museum,[690] date from the 18th century BCE.

It has been claimed by Neufeld that the Mari Tablet *ARM* X, 129 contains examples of the following, all of which were recorded in Akkadian cuneiform, here for the first time:

i.   The association of contagion with disease.
ii. Recognition of direct and indirect transmission of diseases.
iii. The idea of isolation for the protection of uninfected individuals.
iv. Infection by fomites.[691]
v.   The neologistic usage of the Akkadian word "muštaḫḫiz" (𒈲𒋫𒄭𒄑𒍣) = "catching" applied to disease in the sense of its being transmissible.

The importance of the Mari tablets and their primacy in the establishment of the above concepts and principles for future medical practice, cannot be overstressed.

Tablet *A2099* was unearthed in Room 108 of the palace at Mari and is a letter from the king of Mari, Zimrilim (a contemporary of Hammurabi), to one of his wives Queen Šibtu. It is worth recording the whole text[692] here and noting its

---

686 Budge, *Egyptian Hieroglyphic Dictionary*. E. A. Wallis. *Egyptian Language: Easy Lessons in Egyptian Hieroglyphics with Sign List* (London: Routledge and Kegan Paul, 1910). Gardiner, *Egyptian Grammar*.
687 Bryan, *The Papyrus Ebers*. Breasted, *The Edwin Smith Surgical Papyrus*.
688 Edward Neufeld, "The Earliest Document of a Case of Contagious Disease in Mesopotamia, (Mari Tablet ARM X, 129)," *JANES* 18 (1986): 53–66.
689 W. Heimpel, *Letters to the King of Mari* (Winona Lake, IN: Eisenbrauns, 2003).
690 Assuming it is still standing. At the time of writing, a civil war is raging in Syria and the town of Aleppo has sustained some of the worst fighting and artillery-damage.
691 OED → "Latin fōmes, fōmitis touchwood, tinder: The morbific matter (of a disease). More commonly, in medicine today, a technical term for any porous substance capable of absorbing and retaining contagious effluvia."
692 Which should be compared with the hygiene regulations in Lev 13, 14 and 15.

complete lack of either moral tone or sympathy for the unfortunate Nanname. The translation here is by W. L. Moran (1980).

Line	Akkadian Transliteration	Translation
1	[a-na^m] Ši-ib-tu	[To] Šibtu (my wife)
2	[qi-b]i-ma	[s]ay:
3	[um-m]a be-el-ki-i-ma	your lord (husband) says:
4	eš-me-e-ma^mi Na-an-na-me	I have heard that Nanname
5	si-im-ma-am mar-ṣa-at	is suffering from a skin lesion
6	u it-ti ekallim^lim	yet she frequents
7	ma-ga-al wa-aš-ba-at-ma	the palace
8	sinnišatim^meš ma-da-tim it-ti-ša-ma	it will infect many
9	i-sa-ab-bi-ik	women with her (ailment).
10	i-na-an-na dan-na-tim lu-uk-ni-ma	Now, then give strict orders
11	i-na ka-as i-ša-at-tu-ú	that no one drink
12	ma-am-ma-an la i-ša-at-ti	from the cup she uses
13	i-na ^giškussem la úš-ša-bu	and no one sit
14	ma-am-ma-an la úš-ša-ab	on the seat on which she sits
15	ú i-na ^gišeršim ša it-ti-il-lu	and no one lie
16	ma-am-ma-an la it-te-e-el-ma	on the bed on which she lies
17	sinnišatim^mes ma-da-tim	so it should not infect
18	it-ti-ša-ma	many women
19	[f]a i-sa-ab-bi-ik	with her (ailment)
20	[si-im-m]u-um šu-ú mu-uš-ta-aḫ-ḫi-iz	that [skin les]ion is catching.

Zimrilim appears to have been away from Mari at the time of writing so it is unclear how he knew of the illness of one of the women there. Neufeld has suggested that the rather matter-of-fact tone of this document could mean that it was concerned with procedures and activities that were well known and

---

693 W. L. Moran, "Review of ARMTX," *JAOS* 100 (1980): 186–89.

understood in the society of Mari and that, while communicable diseases were seen as a serious problem, they were something which was entirely customary in Mesopotamian society. Neufeld goes on to observe that the document is lacking in four seemingly important points about which it would have been interesting to know more. These are:

i. Any indication as to the duration of the proposed period of isolation.
ii. The proposed location of any quarantine.
iii. How one should deal with any fomites.
iv. Any indication of the time/season which might help in identifying the disease.

These questions are, of course, raised and answered, to some degree, in Leviticus. The language of Tablet *ARM* X 129 is classical Akkadian, with the single exception of the proper name of the sufferer *Nanname*, which appears nowhere else in Akkadian or any other Semitic language. Moran translates the word *simmu(m)* (*si-im-mu*/GIG = 𒋛 𒅎 𒈬/𒄈) specifically as "skin lesion" and in line twenty he associates it with another Akkadian word *muštaḫḫiz*, (𒈬 𒌑 𒉺 𒄴 𒄭 = *catching*), so that we are left in no doubt as to the contagious nature of this condition. However, other authorities give a more general translation of *simmu(m)* as "wound" or "disease".[694] Neufeld suggests that this may, therefore, signify a wound that has become infected. However, he appears to regard *simmu* as a relatively mild disease on the grounds of the existence, in Akkadian, of another word *epqu(m)*, 𒂊 𒄣, which is widely thought to be equivalent to the Hebrew צרעת. In the Chicago Assyrian Dictionary,[695] the word *epqu(m)* 𒂊 is translated simply (and unhelpfully) as "leprosy". It appears to be a specific case of the generic *epqennu/epeqennu* (*ep-qé-en-nu* = *ga na* = 𒂊 𒆠/GAN=𒃶) meaning "skin disease" which itself is noted as a synonym for *simmu(m)* (*si-im-mu*/GIG = 𒋛 𒅎 𒈬/𒄈). In Von Soden's Akkadian Dictionary,[696] *epqu(m)* is translated simply as "*Aussatz*". Its precise meaning, however, appears to be as obscure as צרעת, and several alternatives, from Old Babylonian, are attested, for example, ^{lú}*saḫar-šub-ba*, (𒇽 𒊓 𒄯 𒋗). The phrase, *ša e-ep[ib]-qa-am ma-lu-ú*, (𒐼 𒅁 𒅗 𒄠 𒈠 𒇻 𒌑), which means "*become covered with epqu*", is also attested in several tablets. The question is whether there is, indeed, an "equation", צרעת = *epqu(m)* = *simmu*, but if so, it remains unsolved and probably unsolvable. Neufeld is almost certainly correct in his rejection of the suggestion by several authors that צרעת/*epqu(m)* was the lepromatous form of Hansen's disease (true leprosy), while *simmu* was the milder tuberculoid form. This reasoning would seem both unjustifiably tendentious and highly improbable, given numerous arguments *passim*, in this

---

694 Soden and Meissner, *Akkadisches Handwörterbuch*, Vol. 2, 1045. Borger, *Mesopotamisches Zeichenlexikon*, 586, #705.
695 Oppenheim and Reiner, eds., *The Assyrian Dictionary*, 246.
696 Soden and Meissner, *Akkadisches Handwörterbuch*, Vol. 1, 230.

book and elsewhere, about the nosology of *Elephantiasis Graecorum* and Hansen's disease. Huehnergard, in the vocabulary provided with his Akkadian Grammar Book,[697] defines *epqu* as "leprosy" [*sic*], and *simmu* as "skin disease".

It is, however, the presumed neologism *muštaḫḫiz* (𒈲𒋫𒄴𒄭𒄑) that is of particular interest in Tablet *ARM* X 129 because it is used (in line 20) in conjunction with *simmu*. This combination of a disease and the notion of transmissibility clearly implies contagion and/or infection. Although the word in line 20 of the tablet is *muštaḫḫiz* (*mu-uš-ta-aḫ-ḫi-iz* = 𒈲𒋫𒄴𒄭𒄑), Neufeld suggests that this may be a variant, or scribal error for the similar word *muštanḫiz* (*mu-uš-ta-an-ḫi-iz* = 𒈲𒋫𒀭𒄭𒄑). His rationale for making this assertion, is that the latter can be linked semantically to the *Štn* verbal stem, which is the iterative stem, of *Š* verbs in Akkadian.[698] Huehnergard, notes that the use of the *Štn* stem is especially common in Old Babylonian and, therefore, highly characteristic of the Mari letters.[699] The parent verb, according to Neufeld, is *aḫazu* (𒄴𒄭) when the word is spelt syllabically. However it may alternatively be represented by a single ideogram (dab₅/ku, 𒁀).[700] This word *aḫazu* is a cognate of the Hebrew verb √אחז [701] and means, in both languages, to "hold", "seize" or "grasp".[702] Neufeld argues that if we add the additional meaning of the iterative *Štn* stem and use the participial (i.e. adjectival) form, *muštanḫiz*, we can arrive at meanings something like "always infectious" or "continually communicable", "ever catching" and therefore, by extension, "contagious". However, since this word is effectively a *hapax legomenon*[703] in Akkadian, we are obliged to take regard of the speculative nature of Neufeld's argument. Nevertheless, Zimrilim, in ordering the isolation of the unfortunate Nanname, quite clearly perceived her affliction as *muštaḫḫiz*, ("catching") and this undoubtedly caused him alarm and raised concern and a need for the institution of some urgent community health measures.

Even though the evidence under discussion comes from a single text, it may still go a long way towards, convincing us that the notion of contagion, isolation/quarantine and the idea of fomites was extant and active as early as Mesopotamian tradition.

---

697 Huehnergard, *A Grammar of Akkadian*.
698 Huehnergard, *A Grammar of Akkadian*, 436 (§36.2).
699 Huehnergard, *A Grammar of Akkadian*, 326 (§29.4).
700 Neufeld, "The Earliest Document of a Case of Contagious Disease in Mesopotamia." Borger, *Mesopotamisches Zeichenlexikon*.
701 Clines, ed., *Dictionary of Classical Hebrew*.
702 Also "learn and "begin". For the various stems for this verb, see: L. W. King, *First Steps in Assyrian* (London: Kegan Paul, Trench, Trübner & Co, Ltd, 1898), 319. Soden and Meissner, *Akkadisches Handwörterbuch*.
703 The only other known occurrence is on Tablet ARM X 130.

Arabia

The medical traditions of both pre-Islamic and Islamic Arabia are important because they represent the end-point of what began in Mesopotamia. The interest in the present context is to compare the history of *contagion* in this progression with the parallel progression from Israelite to later Jewish medicine. Arabian and early Islamic medicine—once, in the "Golden Age", the most well-developed and forward-looking—declined over time into the Dark Ages.

In pre-Islamic society, Arab tribal tradition considered epidemics and diseases to have been caused by demons and other forms of evil spirit. Modern Islam, except in the most extremely fundamentalist instances, fully embraces modern medicine and must, of course, concern itself with the modern pathological concepts of contagion and infection. The Arabic word for contagion, which has remained unchanged from the time of the Prophet and is used today in both religious and medical circles, is عَدْوَى ('*adwā*) from √عدو (= run, course). It undoubtedly has, over time, enjoyed a much wider usage than the "contagion" of modern English. In particular, the √عدو is associated with ephemeral actions and transitiveness and especially in the passage of something from one locus to another.

لَيْسَ عَلَى الْأَعْمَى حَرَجٌ وَلَا عَلَى الْأَعْرَجِ حَرَجٌ وَلَا عَلَى الْمَرِيضِ حَرَجٌ وَلَا عَلَى

> It is no fault in the blind, nor in the lame, nor in one afflicted with illness (Qur'an, Surat 24, al-Nur v 61)[704]

On account of this absence of fault, the Prophet Muḥammad is said to have proclaimed "No contagion" ('*la'adwā* لاعَدْوَى), and as a result, the more fundamentalist among Islamic religious scholars have felt unable to accept the idea of contagion's being a *purely* medical concept and so deny any notion of the transmissibility of disease from afflicted to healthy human individuals. Such a stance has been seen as reinforcing a much more fundamental and important doctrine of Islam, namely, the denial of any possibility that events occurring in the world are independent of the will of God/Allah. The situation is further compounded by the doctrine of the immutability of the words of the Prophet.[705] We have no direct evidence to make us suppose that a parallel approach was taken under the Levitical priestly worldview. However, this must remain as a possibility.

---

704 Ali, *The Holy Qur'an* (text and translation).
705 A. Hourani, *A History of the Arab Peoples* (London: Folio Society, 2009); L. I. Conrad, "A Ninth-Century Muslim Scholar's Discussion of Contagion," in *Contagion, Perspectives in Pre-modern Societies*, ed. L. I. Wujastyk and D. Conrad (Aldershot: Ashgate, 2000), 137–177.

Greece and Rome

There is no obvious word in Greek for *contagion*; a number of authors have suggested the noun ἐπᾰφή = "touch", "touching", "handling" and the verb ἐπᾰφάω = "touch on the surface", "stroke"; or the noun, (συν-) ἀναχρωσις = "discolouring", "taint", "infection", possibly from the verb ἀναχρώννῡμι = "colour anew", "discolour".[706] There is scant evidence to attest to this usage in either Hippocrates or Galen. However, the word عَدْوى (*'adwā*, see above) does appear in translations of Galen into Arabic and appears to imply transmission by contagion as understood in modern medicine. The Latin *contagio*, unsurprisingly, appears in Roman medical writings but is nowhere specifically defined. It has been suggested that, as far as the Greeks concerned themselves with contagion, as we see it today, they embodied it in metaphors of sharing and pollution. With the translation of Greek medical writings into Latin and Arabic, these metaphors became substantivized into the more concrete ideas of touching and transferring.[707]

It is important to remember that both Greek and Roman nosologies, subscribed to the humoral theory of disease which saw disease as the result of emanations or miasmata (Greek: μίασμα "pollution", and μιαίνειν "to pollute"). Such a system of transmission might be loosely compatible with the modern notion of airborne infection but it does not fit in with the modern idea of contagion. It has been suggested that the establishment and development of the doctrine of *miasma* was sufficient, for the Greeks, as an explanation of the dissemination of disease and there was, therefore, no need for the idea of contagion.[708]

All of this suggests that Greek and Roman medicine embodied a completely separate and distinctly different etymological and nosological concept of contagion from those of Egypt, Mesopotamia or Syria-Palestine which was, therefore, in all probability not the result of its having been handed down from any of these sources. We must suppose that by the time of Hellenic influence in Israel, an opportunity for the mingling of these contrasting views had arisen. How far this may have influenced the redactors of priestly writings is a matter for speculation and further investigation.

By the time of Pliny the Elder (23–79 CE), the modern understanding of contagion had become firmly established in both Greek and Roman thought. Pliny gives an account of a skin disease called *mentagra*,[709] which he says was transmitted by kissing and exhibited a most unlikely social prevalence.

---

706 Liddell and Scott, *Greek English Lexicon*.
707 V. Nutton, "Did the Greeks Have a Word for It? Contagion and Contagion Theory in Classical Antiquity," in *Contagion, Perspectives in Pre-modern Societies*, ed. L. I. Wujastyk and D. Conrad (Aldershot: Ashgate, 2000), 137–62.
708 Parker, *Miasma*.
709 OED, sycosis: an eruption about the chin, caused by inflammation of the hair follicles of the beard; also known as chin gout. Mentagra was probably a fungal disease, possibly lichen, λείχην, "the despair of the medical

> *Non fuerat haec lues apud maiores patresque nostros... ...nec sensere id malum* feminae aut servitia plebesque humilis aut media, sed proceres veloci transitu osculi maxime.
>
> This plague was unknown to our fathers and forefathers.... Women were not liable to the disease, or slaves and the lower and middle classes, but the nobles were very much infected through the momentary contact of a kiss. (Plinii, Naturalis Historiae, Liber XXVI, iii)

It is easy to see that women (lacking beards) would be spared, but why slaves and the *plebes* should likewise be immune is unclear. The upper classes may have indulged themselves in an excess of kissing—perhaps as in the fashionable and ostentatiously modish greeting that is gaining popularity in present-day society—and by so doing put themselves at greater risk of contagious diseases.

ANCIENT SYRIA-PALESTINE

It is necessary now to grasp the nettle of the understanding of contagion in Israelite society. Lieber, makes the point that the inference of contagion, in the modern sense, can only be made "unequivocally"[710] from a single reference in the Hebrew Bible. This comprises two verses from Lev 14:46–47, and even then, it somewhat stretches the imagination to believe contagion as a (unlikely) mode of transmission for צרעת between a house and its occupant.

> והבא אל־הבית כל־ימי הסגיר אתו יטמא עד־הערב
>
> והשכב בבית יכבס את־בגדיו והאכל בבית יכבס את־בגדיו
>
> Moreover he that goeth into the house all the while that it is shut up shall be unclean until the even.
>
> And he that lieth in the house shall wash his clothes; and he that eateth in the house shall wash his clothes. (Lev 14:46–47)

Snaith,[711] in contrast, dismisses any notion of "medical contagion" in respect of צרעת as irrelevant and says: "Whether they are medically contagious is not the point at issue; what matters here is that they are ritually contagious. The resultant contagion is ritual, not medical." Snaith believes that any implication of contagion made from the Hebrew Bible necessarily refers *only* to the transmission of ritual impurity and that any inferences about hygiene or community health are spurious and have no cause-and-effect relationship with ritual impurity.

---

historian"—indeed one of many! See, Glasby, "What was Biblical Leprosy?" Also passim in, Pliny the Elder, *Naturalis Historia*, trans. H. Rackham.
710 Lieber, "Old Testament 'Leprosy', Contagion and Sin," 100.
711 N. H. Snaith, *Leviticus and Numbers* (London: Nelson, 1967).

Lieber's View of Contagion

Lieber, taking an opposite viewpoint, remains a firm protagonist for a medical interpretation of contagion in the Hebrew Bible especially in relation to צרעת. While Lieber sedulously tries to avoid any taint of a hyperdiagnostic approach, she inclines, nevertheless, towards what must be a medical/hygienic explanation and justifies this, against the opposing view of Snaith *et al*, by proposing a difference between the Levitical text of the P authors, that she believes was intentionally paraenetic, and those non-P texts that involve צרעת found elsewhere in the Hebrew Bible.[712] These latter she describes as "narrative case histories"[713] standing in contrast to Lev 13 (and, presumably, chapter 15), which is an index of differential diagnosis for priests. Its purpose was to answer legalistic (that is, ritualistic) questions pertaining to the relationship טמא/טהור, but, for Lieber, this in no way denies, or makes less important, the underlying medical and hygienic principles it embodies. In this way it served a real, if rudimentary and perhaps secondary, public health function, by identifying any risk of spread within the community. The futility of any attempt to classify צרעת as a single disease or syndrome was entirely irrelevant because it was the *contagion* of *any* condition that mattered. For Lieber, in contrast to Snaith's view, a cause-and-effect relationship between pathology and impurity *was* identifiable, and the only, albeit crucial, question for the priest to answer was whether, in any given case, the sufferer was טמא (unclean/impure) or טהור (clean/pure).[714] The priest, therefore, became responsible not merely for diagnosing incipient contagion, but also for determining whether each diagnosed instance of צרעת would be susceptible to containment by simple hygienic measures such as washing and quarantine, or whether more stringent measures—usually sacrificial and, paradoxically, not at all medical—would be necessary. Such a view makes it virtually impossible—in Lieber's opinion—to suppose that this activity on the part of the priests could have come about with no thought as to what the symptoms and signs of צרעת conferred. *Even* if the affliction were seen to be the result of divine wrath, this ritual impurity showed itself in symptoms and signs that were manifestly pathological. Lieber further justifies her stance by suggesting that an examination of Leviticus (chapter 13 in particular), reveals diagnostic tests intended for use by the priests. These were typically arranged in a binary *protasis→ apodosis* configuration and so required simple "*yes*" or "*no*" answers. Similar binary tests often beginning with the phrase "*If a man ...*", are to be seen elsewhere in the Hebrew Bible and in texts from the Ancient Near East, especially in the *omen texts* from Mesopotamia.

---

712 E.g. Exod 4:6, Num 12:10, 2 Chron 26:19.
713 For a fuller discussion of this idea see chapter 11.
714 Poorthuis and Schwartz, *Purity and Holiness*.

Lieber's argument is, therefore, that *fear of contagion* in a clearly medical sense was absolutely central to the priestly concept of צרעת (and probably זוב), and because of this doubt must be cast upon any notion that the priestly view of צרעת was nothing more than ritualistic.

In comparing Lieber's viewpoint with that of Snaith, the crucial but unanswerable question is, "What was going on in the minds of the priests?" It is quite possible to believe that, although the priests may have been operating valuable public health measures, they were completely unaware of their practical potential and significance as they were wholly absorbed by the necessity to diagnose and treat ritual impurity. It is possible, therefore, to suggest, three scenarios that might have been operating.

1. The priests identified צרעת and זוב specifically as afflictions/diseases, albeit with a divine aetiology, and were operating a policy of preventative medicine within their society.
2. The priests had no conception of public health/hygiene and were solely concerned with protecting the individual, the sanctuary, and the land from the effects of ritual impurity.
3. The priests saw צרעת and זוב as the physical manifestation, in the form of illness, of ritual impurity. They were concerned primarily with the diagnosis and treatment of ritual impurity and had no particular interest in medical matters. However, the quarantining and cleansing measures they instituted proved, incidentally, to be advantageous in the field of public health.

From what has been discussed in earlier chapters, option (1) seems unlikely, but it is so far impossible to arrive at any clear conclusion as to distinction between (2) and (3). Perhaps we should not repine at this difficulty but rather note that the idea that *controlling contagion* is the highly desirable common denominator in all three of these scenarios.

Contagion as Symbolism and Metaphor

In view of Mary Douglas's interpretation of the purity laws as a system of social symbolism, it is pertinent to inquire into the symbolic nature of the notion of contagion in the society of ancient Israel. In a more wide-reaching study of evil in general, Ricœur has stated the view that, since (he believes) religious experience is mediated through symbolism, an analysis of the symbols from past civilizations will reveal useful historical information.[715] Ricœur says, "defilement was never literally a stain; impurity was never literally filthiness, dirtiness ... [impurity] never attains the abstract level of unworthiness, otherwise the magic of contact and contagion would have disappeared. The representation of

---

715 Ricœur, *The Symbolism of Evil*, 33–40.

defilement dwells in the half-light of a quasi-physical infection that points toward a quasi-moral unworthiness. This ambiguity is not expressed conceptually but is experienced intentionally in the very quality of the half-physical, half-ethical fear that clings to the representation of the impure." If this is so, defilement, as the object of ritual suppression and a symbol of evil, becomes a symbolic stain which, according to Ricœur, enters the human sphere through speech and the word so that the resultant development of a related vocabulary educates the individual into a feeling of guilt.

The particular difficulty with Ricœur's theory of *symbolic stain* is that he argues it with examples entirely from early Greek culture. Tantalizingly he admits, "The Hebrew example is still more striking ... it might be alleged that the Greeks never attained the feeling of sin in its peculiar quality and with the intensity of which only the people of Israel supply an example, and that is why the Greeks had no recourse than to "transpose philosophically" the schema of defilement." This can be no more than rather bold speculation given that Ricœur thereafter leaves the matter alone and supplies no evidential material, textual or otherwise, from Israelite civilization, nor indeed from any civilization previous to that of the Greeks. In failing to take account of the very real differences between these early civilizations and that of the Greeks, Ricœur leaves his suppositions dangerously exposed.

Feder, working more recently, has taken up the germ of Ricœur's premises to apply them in an investigation of the situation in ancient Israel. Feder suggests that the linguistic symbolism found in biblical texts relating to impurity and contagion is evidence of its all having been grounded in bodily experience. His hypothesis is, therefore, that the biblical representation of the concept of pollution (טמאה) is an example of what he calls "embodied rationality".[716] This idea entails the belief that several types of ritual pollution began their existence in the bodily experience of infectious diseases. Noting the absence of any Israelite secular medical literature, he seeks a parallel elsewhere and finds it in evidence supplied by the Mari tablets. The justification for this extrapolation may raise questions, if not eyebrows; but Feder is careful to protect his position by pointing-out the ever-present risk of ambiguity. This, he affirms, is especially the case in the heterogeneous[717] usage in Semitic languages of cognate words; for example, two highly pertinent words צרעת and טמאה which appear in the relevant Hebrew texts. This heterogeneity, emanating from a "lexicographic predisposition towards the abstract", he further indicts as "blurring the domains of hygiene and morality" and so resisting systematic analysis—this comes as no surprise to anyone investigating this phenomenon!

---

716 Feder, "The Polemic."
717 For a fuller discussion of heterogeneity in Hebrew word-usage, see chapter 11.

Mary Douglas's symbolic view of the purity/impurity tension demands that, before one can identify a specific instance of defilement, one must first identify the specific system of categorization that is being violated. For example, those animal foodstuffs that confer impurity do so because they all have in common some anomalous characteristic (scales, a creeping gait, absence of fins etc.), that leaves them outside the socially accepted paradigms. In a biblical context, Douglas argues, these *ex grege* anomalies threatened the equation of *wholeness* with *holiness*.[718] Douglas's approach is akin to the classical view of categorization expressed by Aristotle,[719] but such a theory necessarily demands that all categories are clearly defined, mutually exclusive and collectively exhaustive. This notion is inherently weakened by the demonstration of *any* exceptional case and this problem appears often, to have been open to convenient circumvention by the serial addition, of further categories and sub-categories, as situation arose. Feder remarks that one cannot help but be impressed by the (futile) efforts expended in attempting to preserve established abstract categories by deriving more and more concrete rules relating to bodily conditions as when, for example, the explicative dichotomies life/death, control/loss of control etc., simply fail to fit the observed data. As a result, further distinctions are invoked *ad hoc* in order to preserve the categorization but, in reality, the situation is obfuscated rather than clarified.[720] It is because of the absolutely necessary requirement of *category violation* that Douglas's view of symbolic impurity might be seen to fail. An alternative, emotional and/or intuitive viewpoint stemming largely from inductive reasoning has been suggested by a number of other authors, for example, Meigs.[721] For Meigs, an anthropologist studying present-day Papuan civilization, defilement is perceived as *embodied cognition* where the cognitive element has been triggered by an innate visceral distaste for such things as death, decay, and waste matter. However, if this were the case, the argument would seem to fail, just as Douglas's argument fails, because it is too selective and does not include things like rotting food, vomit, urine, faeces, phlegm, mucus, and pus. Its illogicality is illustrated by Feder in a colourful example: the dog-walker who "hygienically" picks up his pet's faeces, with an inverted (and assumed to be clean) plastic bag, but then nevertheless feels an obligation to wash his hands. This is illogical, since no direct contamination of the hand can have taken place, and yet it is probable that more people will wash than will not. Feder's conclusion is that contagion operates in the cognitive sphere as an *emotional bias* according to ontological assumptions embodied in the subject's cultural make-up and which the

---

718 Douglas, *Purity and Danger*. Douglas, "The Forbidden Animals in Leviticus."; Douglas, *Leviticus as Literature*.
719 Aristotle, *The Complete Works of Aristotle*, ed. J Barnes, Vol. 1 (Princeton, NJ: Princeton University Press, 1984), 3–24.
720 Y. Feder, "Contagion and Cognition: Bodily Experience and the Conceptualization of Pollution (ṭumah) in the Hebrew Bible." *Journal of Near Eastern Studies* 72, no. 2 (2013): 151–67 [155].
721 A. S. Meigs, "A Papuan Perspective on Pollution," *Man* 13 (1978): 304–18.

individual does not, necessarily, feel the need to accept as consistent with logic and the application of scientific rigour.

There is no doubt that it has become fashionable among modern biblical commentators to reject the idea of an ontological relationship between hygiene and purity. Typical arguments for example, used to support this view are, (1) that the Israelites could not possibly have known about, let alone taken prophylactic measures against *Taenia solium* infestation, by not eating pork; and (2) the lack of any evidence to suggest that Jews, on account of their dietary habits, were healthier than Gentiles.[722]

From early times until relatively recently,[723] notions of infectious diseases relied almost totally on metaphor and some of these persist in modern quasi-medical usage. Wootton has written recently, "Our language is littered with the flotsam and jetsam of a vast historical castrophe, the collapse of ancient medicine, which has left us with half-understood turns of phrase that we continue to use because metaphorical habits have an extraordinary capacity for endurance."[724]

Because of this, the risk to the biblical scholar is that of imposing modern, and therefore anachronistic, category-distinctions on the [sparsely] available evidence. For example, Smith comments that, "Distancing yourself from poisons, dust and dirt is one thing; but distancing yourself from invisibly 'unclean' people and objects is quite an achievement of the imagination.... Religious purity has a distinct role in the history of personal hygiene ... not functional, not rational ... but a key component that determined the lives and cleansing behaviour of very large numbers of people."[725] This view contrasts noticeably with that of Parker, who believes that all of these effects may be ascribed to no more than an aspect of popular perception, which he terms the "contagiousness of misfortune."[726]

The contagiousness of bad luck appears often as a theme in Greek drama—undesirable qualities are able to be wiped-off the hands and thereby can contaminate others. Pentheus, in *The Bacchae,* addressing Cadmus and fearing the contamination of contagion cries:

οὐ μὴ προσοίσεις χεῖρα,

Keep your hands to yourself! (Euripides, Bacchae,344)[727]

---

722 If health was not behind the dietary laws it is hard to imagine what was!
723 In some cases as recently as the mid-nineteenth century.
724 David Wootton, *Bad Medicine: Doctors Doing Harm since Hippocrates* (Oxford: Oxford University Press, 2006), 13. Such metaphors might be: "cold-blooded", "hysterical", "melancholic".
725 Virginia Smith, *Clean: A History of Personal Hygiene and Purity* (Oxford: Oxford University Press, 2007), 29–30.
726 Albeit in a study of miasma in Greek culture: Robert Parker, *Miasma: Pollution and Purification in Early Greek Religion*, 218–220.
727 Euripides, *Bacchae,* trans. D. Kovacs (Cambridge, MA: Harvard University Press, 2002).

Such a viewpoint requires the making of the metaphysical assumption that the contagiousness of misfortune is ontologically real and culture-specific and can be transmitted in either a tangible or a miasmatic form. Whereas Greek culture might be appropriate for taking such a philosophical step, it is doubtful if one could discover any justification for such an explanation in the worldview of the priests and the culture of ancient Israel.

Reaching once again for a parallel, we might consider the *contagion of curses* that figured significantly in Mesopotamian culture. It seems both possible and likely that the ideas of a curse and of an illness often became conflated. In the Mari tablets (and elsewhere in cuneiform literature) the term *māmītu* (𒈠 𒄩 𒌅),[728] was used to mean both an *oath-curse* and an illness and, significantly, the two of them appear to have been indistinguishable from one another. Transmission (of either or both) was supposedly effected by contact with the accursed/infected person. This argument is reinforced by the finding that the Akkadian verb *la-pā-tu(m)* (𒆷𒉺𒌈), usually translated as "touch" (*anfassen*),[729] is a cognate of the Hebrew verb נָגַע (√נגע) or the Aramaic verb, נגע which are widely used in the sense of "strike down" with a curse *or* with an illness, throughout the Hebrew Bible. The Hebrew noun (נֶגַע) is also widely used to mean "plague" as well as "blow" and indeed is one of the several biblical words used as an alternative for צרעת and, therefore, (mis-)translated into English as "leprosy". It seems likely that in both Mesopotamian culture and in that of ancient Israel, it was divine punishment that produced the pathological manifestations of טמאה (or of *māmītu,* 𒈠 𒄩 𒌅), *and* was contagious.

Feder has suggested that, in Israel, defilement (טמאה) operated in society as a *judgment heuristic*. In practical terms, this means that external events, and an intuitive, cognitive certainty about טמאה, trigger appropriate behavioural responses. In the text of the Hebrew Bible, Feder believes it is possible to identify three basic forms of טמאה that may all be classified as *embodied rationality;* that is, in the minds of the ancient Israelites, as models or images, of bodily experiences causing טמאה along with the emotional responses engendered by those experiences. Feder asks us to consider three specific models of טמאה in increasing order of seriousness. The first of these models is the simple *cleanliness model* in which the object or person requires only to be kept at a distance from God and the sacred realm. What is at risk of being transgressed here is the need to be pure when approaching God. An exact parallel is to be found in a number of other cultures both ancient and modern and it figured significantly in the culture of Mesopotamia. The second model, the *infection model* is associated with more stringent purificatory requirements and importantly, it embodies the central notion of contagion. The third model,

---

728 Soden and Meissner, *Akkadisches Handwörterbuch*, Vol. 2, 599.
729 Soden and Meissner, *Akkadisches Handwörterbuch*, Vol. 1, 535–537.

termed by Feder the *stain of transgression model*, is the most serious. It is a derivative of both the cleanliness model and the infection model and pertains to such violations of cultural standards as sexual misconduct and murder. As such it encompasses the ideas of both ritual impurity *and* moral impurity. This model cannot be mitigated by ritual cleansing; it ultimately defiles the land and demands the penalty כרת, the extirpation of lineage. The priests' employment of the binary *protasis→ apodosis* diagnostic tools mentioned above, would have been important in distinguishing between these models. There will be a familiarity about these models if the reader has assimilated chapter 5. They are little more than variants and compilations of the classes if impurity described, *passim*, by Milgrom, Frymer-Kensky, and Klawans *et al.* Feder's contribution has been to consider them as the single entity of *"embodied rationality"*. The overwhelming problem with Feder's idea, however, is that to some extent, we are once again, confronted with the notion of *category violation* with all its attendant baggage. Nevertheless, Feder's approach is helpful because it implies that, if the purity laws were based on specific models of contagion themselves derived from bodily experiences, then the much sought-after and elusive idea of an underlying abstract logic becomes unnecessary. To a degree at least, the identification of parallel models in coeval civilizations, reinforces this understanding of טמאה and its role within the genesis of contagion.

Chapter 11

צרעת AND UN-WHOLENESS

In the present chapter and that which follows, particular attention will be given to צרעת because of the pride of place that it occupies as the most serious and the most contagious cause of ritual impurity under the *Weltanschauung* of the Levitical priesthood. As the most virulent causative factor of impurity it therefore must be supposed to have had a commensurate effect in generating un-wholeness and unholiness. In the present chapter the place of צרעת in un-wholeness will be considered from an etymological and literary standpoint and in the following chapter, the effects of צרעת on unholiness will be investigated from a theological viewpoint.

The problem of ascribing a precise date, either to the *Vorlage* (source material) or the redaction(s) of the Levitical text, is considered in detail in chapter 2. Without at least an idea of this date, it is impossible to analyse textual material in its proper historical context. In the present case, the *working hypothesis* attributes to the book of Leviticus some material of considerable antiquity but also a long evolutionary process of textual accretion and redaction that came to an end when the text reached its present form in the post-exilic, *Persian period* (538–332 BCE).[730]

Lewis has remarked, "The lamentable history of social attitudes to leprosy [*sic*] is a lesson on the consequences of paying great attention to words but small attention to facts."[731] Unfortunately, when one collects together the available material, there is a significant excess of words (both primary and secondary) to weigh against a depressing dearth of facts. Nevertheless, words must be the starting point.

For the present study, two approaches will be adopted in an attempt to frame, within a literary context, the textual, medical, and historical evidence that has been presented in the above chapters. Coincidentally, an effort will be made to refer this to the priestly worldview. First, the particularities of the language pertinent to the question will be examined to assess certain words that may be relevant to the question and to quantify their relative theological and medical import. Once these words have been categorized, we may consider how other, more recent, authors have chosen to interpret their biblical standing.

---

730 See this author's attempt to present this in diagrammatic form in chapter 2.
731 Lewis, "A Lesson from Leviticus," 593–612.

Evidence From the Language of the Texts

The approach used here is that of *context logometrics* (see below), where the usage of a word in a particular context is examined and expressed as a fraction (or percentage) of its overall usage in a given text. Where a word has been used in a particular context, it may have been employed to identify something specific or a generality. Context logometrics is aimed at examining and differentiating key words in this way, to elucidate their precise meanings within specific textual contexts.

Language and Thought in the Hebrew Bible

Although his work may now have been superseded (or is otherwise seen as unfashionable) in the field of advanced linguistics, there is wisdom in the writings of James Barr on matters of language.[732] Barr has commented, "Language and thought [or language and culture—for our present purposes either term will suffice] are connected; but the connection is logically haphazard.... One does not dispute the possibility that cultures may be found in which the common language was accompanied by a uniform way of thinking; but ancient Israelite society was not such a culture."[733] Barr is implying an inherent ambiguity in the use of words in biblical Hebrew and this may be difficult to understand for someone used to modern English. Three factors must be in operation. Firstly, there is the significantly different structural, grammatical, and syntactical nature of Semitic languages when compared with those of Indo-European origin; secondly, there is the effect of changes brought about by the elapse of time; and thirdly, there is the difference between Western and ancient Hebrew thinking *per se*.

James Barr has written at length on the subject of Hebrew thought and its relationship to language.[734] He writes of Greek "analytical thought" and Semitic "totality-thought" and especially of the Hebrews' penchant for "revelation through history". Not that Barr subscribed slavishly to this distinction: he found it an oversimplification that, "Greatly and for the worse has affected the examination of linguistic evidence from the Old Testament." He acknowledges certain differing features common to the cognitive process in each of these cultures, but cautions against over-valuing their place in scholarship. Elsewhere too, the Greek mind has been considered supposedly "static", "conceptualizing", and "preferring abstractions" where, in contrast, the Semitic mind has been supposed to be "dynamic", "actualizing", and "preferring concrete facts". For the

---

[732] The Ancients were not altogether blameless when it came to "Humpty Dumpty hermeneutics".
[733] James Barr, John Barton, and Ernest W. Nicholson, *Bible and Interpretation: the Collected Essays of James Barr*, Vol. 1 (Oxford: Oxford University Press, 2013), 227–228. See also "Barr's Rhombus" in chapter 5.
[734] James Barr, *Semantics and Biblical Theology, a Contribution to the Discussion; J Barr, History and Ideology in the Old Testament* (Oxford: Oxford University Press, 2000); Barr, Barton, and Nicholson, *Bible and Interpretation*, Vol. 1, 236; Vol. 2, 16, 125; Vol. 3, 269–376.

Greek, *man* was a duality of body and soul; for the Hebrew, *soul* and *flesh* were inseparable in both space and time. This noetic dichotomy has sometimes been extrapolated to suppose that, since language is the vehicle of thought, Hebrew favours the verb and Greek the noun. Barr warns that this is simplistic: in studying the Hebrew Bible we should not be making negative comparisons with Greek but should rather be "attempting to establish a correlation between a dynamic way of thought and a grammatical phenomenon." In order to find the precise meanings of words in Hebrew texts, therefore, one must surely consider each word in its highly specific space-time (worldview) context; at the same time being aware that any given word may have several context-driven meanings and that these may be no more than very loosely related to one another. Feder[735] has approached the same problem from a more modern linguistic standpoint and avows: "One can distinguish between a 'top-down' model of semantics, whereby the lexicon of a given language is governed by rules dictated by the rational mind and a 'bottom-up' model whereby the linguistic system is the result of countless localized instances of semantic development." He goes on to opine, "only the latter model is appropriate for a natural language."[736] However, he is somewhat unclear as to precisely what he means by a "natural language".

Top-down logic (deductive reasoning) and bottom-up logic (inductive reasoning) are polar opposites but can complement one another in problems of the present kind. In deductive reasoning, a conclusion is reached reductively by applying general rules that are valid over the entirety of a closed domain of discourse. This process narrows the range under consideration until only the conclusion is left—it is the only permissible way of reasoning for the experimental scientist once an experiment has been devised. In inductive reasoning, the conclusion is reached by generalizing or extrapolating from initial information: the conclusion is, therefore, not necessarily tested but, as can be seen from Bacon's important contribution to scientific thought, it is usually as a result of inductive reasoning that the hypothesis and experiment are devised in the first place. Bacon was wise enough to add the caveat, "*Quod enim mavult homo verum esse, id potius credit*,"[737]—testing any hypothesis ultimately requires an experiment and analysis of its results by a deductive approach. All of this must be borne in mind, alongside the priestly worldview, when attempting to see ancient textual material from the standpoint of the modern thinker or present-day physician.

---

735 Feder, "Contagion and Cognition."
736 Which Feder, perhaps conveniently, does not define.
737 "For what a man would like to be true, that he more readily believes," Francis Bacon, *Novum Organon*.

Context Logometrics

Context-logometrics is an attempt to extract and quantify, from a corpus of literature, those instances in which a given word is used in a specific way.[738] In the present study, we are particularly interested in, the Hebrew words זוב and צרעת and *en route* to these, words such as "doctor/physician" or "apothecary" (רוקח, רופא). As an example of the technique we may look at "holiness" (קדוש), as used particularly in the H portion of Leviticus. The process is much simplified by the use of the *search-engines* included in proprietary biblical software.[739] One must first specify an example of the word used, in the context that one wishes to investigate. A search is then made throughout the text(s) for all instances of the word in all of its contexts. There follows the (necessarily laborious) detailed examination of every one of these instances, both in the original language and in translation,[740] and their sorting into specific *context-bins*. The result may be displayed in a table or graphically as a bar-chart or pie-chart and/or the frequency of any particular context may be expressed as a fraction or percentage of all the contexts in the whole sample.

A potential major source of error in dealing with Hebrew words is, of course, their vocalization and the presence of proclitics and pronominal suffixes etc. In such cases exhaustive scrutinization becomes even more time-consuming as every permutation must be tested. It may not be a simple matter in Hebrew to use a *wild-card* search term as it is in English or Greek (e.g. lep*, or λέπ*) to include different parts of speech and case-endings.

In the example of the unvocalized Hebrew word קדש the context in which it is used to mean "holy" or "abstract holiness" is chosen as the starting point.

The choice of search-material largely depends upon what is available though both of the common biblical search-engines[741] offer an extremely wide range of options—see table(s) below. It makes sense, however, to restrict one's search to relevant material especially avoiding examples from widely differing eras and where possible agreement across sources should be supportive

The paradigmatic example given in the table below is taken from the H material of Leviticus (e.g. 19:24). The choice of sources here is particularly wide as an illustration of the scope of the technique.

---

[738] The search may be extended by the inclusion of Boolean operators.
[739] Accordance, "Bible Software." Bibleworks, "Software for Biblical Exegesis and Research." Since I began this research, a 9th volume of Cline's *Dictionary of Classical Hebrew* has emerged. This contains a list of English words used in the Hebrew Bible and their Hebrew equivalents in all of the contexts used in the Hebrew Bible. As a starting point for context logometrics this is an invaluable aid.
[740] In the present study the ERV, KJV, RSV and NRSV.
[741] Accordance and Bibleworks were used in this study and were cross-referenced with one another.

Word = קדש — Context = "Abstract Holiness"				
Source	Total	Context	Other	% Context
Qumran	714	97	617	13.6
Targums	678	73	605	10.8
Hebrew Bible (BHS)	583	40	543	6.9
Mishna	362	8	354	2.2
DSSB	345	8	337	2.3
Jesus Ben Sira	19	2	17	10.5
Judean Desert Manuscripts	8	0	8	0
North West Semitic Iscriptions	3	0	3	0
Aramaic Inscriptions Egypt	1	0	1	0

In this example it can be seen that this context is not one in frequent use; the Hebrew Bible has only 7% of nearly 600 "hits" and there is a similar low percentage of correlation in both of the sources from Qumran.[742]

One should not impute too great an importance to study of this sort nor draw too specific a conclusion. *Context-logometrics* is but a semi-scientific, inexact tool at best: it is a means of arriving at a quasi-semantic domain in a more simplified and less formal way than that employed by professional linguists. What it does usefully is to identify the variability[743] of meaning that may be attached to a given word and the frequency of usage of a particular word in a particular context, text, time and place. Where it will be most helpful, of course, is where it illustrates large, undisputable differences. As it turns out, this is the case with צרעת.

Doctors and Physicians

The evidence presented in chapter 3 leads inevitably to the conclusion that, whatever non-priestly *healthcare* existed in ancient Israel, it was unlikely to have been much more than *ad hoc* first aid. If sorcerers and magicians, like the *āšipu* of Mesopotamia, were involved they were afforded little space by the writers of the Hebrew Bible. This view is supported by context-logometrics.

---

[742] The term "Qumran" is used to refer to non-biblical material from Qumran; the term DSSB refers to biblical material of similar origin.
[743] % specificity or % ambiguity.

There are 66 "possibles" returned by a search for permutations of what reduces algebraically to *±א*פ*ר±* in the Hebrew Bible. Nine (13.6%), are found on examination to be context-related to the idea of "healing", "healer" or "healthcare" but most of these are verbal forms of the √רפא. When a parallel English search of the ERV is performed to focus specifically upon the noun "physician", the result reduces to only a single "hit" in this exact context (Jer 8:22).[744]

Word = רפא — Context = "Physician/Surgeon"				
Source	Total	Context	Other	% Context
Hebrew Bible (BHS)	66	9	57	13.6
DSSB	38	1	37	2.6
Qumran	25	0	25	0
Mishna	16	6	10	37.5
Jesus Ben Sira	11	6	5	54.5
Hebrew Inscriptions	6	0	6	0
Aramaic Inscriptions Egypt	1	0	1	0
Targums	1	1	0	100

In contrast, a search of the Hebrew text of Jesus Ben Sira reveals a correlation of 55% using the same search parameters. Moreover, a new word *apothecary*[745] appears twice with a correlation of 100%. Elsewhere, this word רקח is quite widely used in the sense of *perfumer*. The word is derived from the late Latin *apothecarius* meaning "One who kept a store or shop of non-perishable commodities, spices, drugs, comfits, preserves, etc." An apothecary is not strictly the same thing as a pharmacist, the former diagnoses the condition then

---

[744] And only 5 in the New Testament.
[745] OED → One who prepared and sold drugs for medicinal purposes—the business now (since about 1800) conducted by a druggist or pharmaceutical chemist. From about 1700 apothecaries gradually took a place as general medical practitioners, and the modern apothecary holds this status legally, by examination and licence of the Apothecaries' Company; but in popular usage the term is archaic.

prescribes *and* dispenses drugs whereas the later only dispenses remedies. However, it seems unlikely that this distinction operated in ancient times. Before 1617 when the Apothecaries' Company of London was founded, apothecaries in London had belonged to the Grocers' Company. It was at the time of the *Enlightenment* that apothecaries took on a specific medical and pharmacological role.

Word = רקח — Context = "Apothecary"				
Source	Total	Context	Other	% Context
Hebrew Bible (BHS)	14	0	14	0
DSSB	7	0	7	0
Jesus Ben Sira	2	2	0	100
North West Semitic Inscriptions	1	0	1	0
Qumran	1	0	1	0
Aramaic Inscriptions Egypt	1	0	1	0

While these observations hardly add up to scientific precision, they add weight to the suggestion that the medical practitioner may have been a late-comer in the Israelite world. Much has been made (*passim*) of the appearance of the physician in the writings of Jesus Ben Sira and Ben Sira *nepos*. By Jesus Ben Sira's time, Hippocrates's writings might have been available in Palestine. They would certainly have been available to Ben Sira *nepos* in Alexandria. The Greek notion of the physician was, almost certainly, eventually known to the Israelites although we do not know how well it had become established in Israelite culture either in Judah or with the exiled Jews in Babylon. Furthermore, we must remember that the Ben Sira text was to a large extent a panegyric upon important people and their important job-descriptions:[746]

[אהללה נא [אנ]שי] חסד [[ ]] את אב[ותינו בדורותם]:

Let us now praise famous men, and our fathers that begat us. (Jesus Ben Sira, 44:1)

If, as seems likely, the pre-exilic *Vorlage(n)* for Leviticus did not specifically mention physicians, we must ask why, if they existed at all, they were not considered important enough to appear in the so-called "hygiene" passages of the book. The priestly worldview would not have contemplated them as *eiusdem generis* and even if, during the exile, contact with Mesopotamian medicine had been influential upon the population at large, the priestly exilic redactors of

---

746 Or for Ben Sira nepos: αἰνέσωμεν δὴ ἄνδρας ἐνδόξους καὶ τοὺς πατέρας ἡμῶν τῇ γενέσει.

Leviticus may have seen no reason to incorporate such inclusions in their writings and rituals.

The two "disease words" of Leviticus, זוב and צרעת, may now be considered in this way.

זוב

One may begin with the word זוב because it is easier to understand how the Israelites used it (as opposed to צרעת). For the modern mind, problems and even stigmata relating to the compromise of reproductive capacity persist especially in some less well-developed communities. As the priests were exponents of the virtue of expanding the Israelite population, the degree of space afforded to זוב in Leviticus (and other biblical books) makes sense. Failure of reproductive capacity both in the individual and in society as a whole was wholly undesirable and was seen as failure both in the context of the individual and—by extension—of the community. There is a wealth of literature that has accrued over the ages which involves reasoning of this kind with, and without, elements of poetic licence. Today, prejudices still abound in this sphere of thought so that even in self-proclaiming "civilized" societies such as our own Western society, eyebrows may be raised, noses looked down, and tongues wagged at those who fail to reproduce, or choose not to.

It is obvious that the terms זב/זבה/זוב are used much more precisely than רפא. Where they are used in another (non-medical) context, this is generally related to everyday things that "flow" in some way or another. In the Hebrew Bible, in about half (53%) of the instances in which the terms are used, the context is that of discharge (of a man or woman with discharge). There is even a relatively high degree of correlation in the Talmud where the words appear many times in the lengthy and exhaustive disquisitions aimed at interpreting the Levitical text. These are secondary and derivative and hence of no particular relevance to the problem in question here. It is, nevertheless, interesting to speculate that the rabbis clearly attached such great significance to these terms that they expended a great deal of effort in explaining them: the same, of course, holds true for צרעת. It is interesting to note that זוב does not appear in Jesus Ben Sira, or Ben Sira *nepos* at all in the context of any sort of pathological or physiological discharge. We must assume that it was omitted from these texts simply because it was not relevant to the subject matter.

When *context-logometrics* is applied to זוב and its English equivalent "genital discharge" it yields the following relationships.

צרעת *and Un-Wholeness*

Word = זוב/זבה/זב — Context = "[Genital] discharge"				
Source	Total	Context	Other	% Context
Talmud	578[747]	180[748]	398	31.1
Mishna	68	5	63	7.4
DSSB	58	14	44	24.1
Hebrew Bible (BHS)	51	27	24	52.9
Targums	26	25	1	96.2
Qumran	32	0	32	0
Jesus Ben Sira	2	0	2	0

It seems probable that these words, where they appear in Leviticus, are used specifically to describe a *discharge, emission, effluxion* or *effluvium, menstruum* or *lochia* all of which have a clearly apparent common factor in that they may be considered as issuant from the genitalia. Because there was no common understanding of the pathophysiology of such discharges, what *was* considered to be a hallmark of all instances of זוב, was that it always, in one way or another, compromised reproductive capacity in a way that was unacceptable because it put at risk the future of Israelite society. This stance, which combined fear and disapproval, was maintained even more rigorously in the case of צרעת.

צרעת

In earlier chapters, the point has been made repeatedly that this word is virtually untranslatable: moreover, its root √צרע is equally unyielding to explication. This is principally because we do not have adequate collateral textual data from which to extrapolate and so make it possible to arrive at a definition by an indirect route. The word is relatively rare in the Hebrew Bible. The frequency distribution for the noun צרעת in its pure lexical form and vocalized as in Lev 13:2 throughout the books of the Hebrew Bible is as follows:

If we search for the various inflected forms for √צרע expressed as hits × 10^{-3} words and as percentages, we get the following:

---

[747] Seminal discharge = 261; Emission = 177; Menstrual = 140.
[748] Menstruation = 99; Discharge/emission of semen = 81.

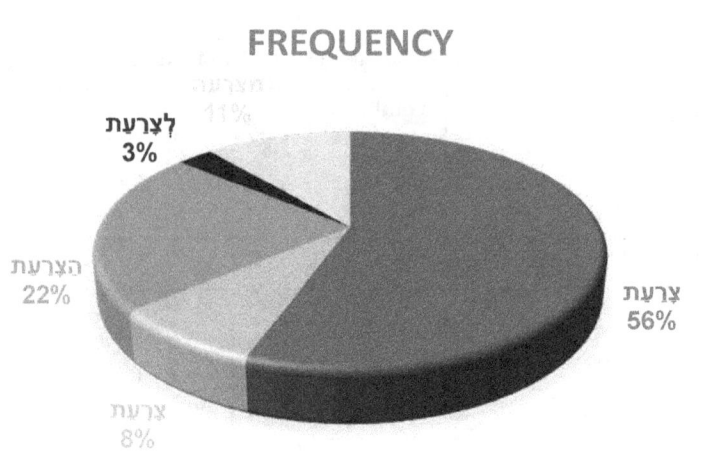

If asked, "What do we suppose to be special about צָרַעַת?", we might reply, "Almost everything and yet nothing; it is a very general term for a very important defiling thing." An examination of its backward-cognates (Akkadian, Ugaritic, Egyptian) or its forward-cognates, (Arabic, Aramaic, Syriac and Coptic) is of no help either: there is no clear evidence about where the Hebrew word came from or that it turned into anything recognizable in any of these languages.[749] Various attempts have been made by linguists, lexicographers, and exegetes to fill this etymological gap and arrive at both meaning and derivation: none is convincing.[750] What is striking, however, is that given all this uncertainty about meaning and etymology for צרעת, an exceptionally high correlation is obtained when צרעת and its participial form מצרע are subjected to scrutiny by context-logometrics.

Word[751] = צרעת/מצרע Context = [Dermopathic] platydysmorphism				
Source	Total	Context	Other	% Context
Hebrew Bible (BHS)	70	68	2	97.1
Mishna	53	40	13	75.5
DSSB	26	20	6	76.9
Qumran	23	14	9	60.9

---

749 See chapters 6 and 7.
750 For example in Clines, ed., *Dictionary of Classical Hebrew*. Also extensively in TDOT, 468–475.
751 The Talmud is not included as both Hebrew and Aramaic terms are used there. Neusner's English edition has 668 instances of "leper" and 392 instances of "leprosy".

Prima facie, this might seem paradoxical: צרעת is a word that appears to be untranslatable, and yet analysis of its usage in the Hebrew Bible indicates an exceptionally high degree of correlation (97%) in every instance to be found there. This means that even if we cannot arrive at an appropriate definition of the word, it is clear that the ancient Israelites could; so we must accept that they—or at least the priestly authors of the biblical texts—knew exactly what they meant. The strong correlation, found by context-logometrics, appears to be relatively well-maintained throughout the DSSB, non-biblical texts from Qumran, and important midrashic texts such as the Mishnah. One may surmise, therefore, that the word underwent little or no change of meaning during the elapse of time for the evolution of those texts.[752] What is more, the later commentators, because they nowhere offer a definition or explanation of this word, must be supposed to have known its meaning beyond equivocation.

It is clear, for reasons discussed elsewhere, that צרעת in the Hebrew Bible is not referring to Hansen's disease/*Elephantiasis Graecorum* and its appearance upon inanimate objects such as masonry and fabrics makes its definition as any known *dermatosis* impossible. In the present work, it has been suggested that the (admittedly cumbersome) term *platydysmorphism* might be useful because all it signifies is a disruption or corruption of a previously smooth surface. It is probably fair to say that this is the only common factor in all ascriptions of the word. When all textual accretions have been chipped away from biblical examples of צרעת including the lengthy discourses in Lev 13, this is, in fact, all that is left. The problem with Lev 13 is that the symptoms and signs simply do not add up to anything known to pathology. Therefore, we are, forced into seeking a consistent lowest common factor among the symptoms and signs, to describe something that affects animate *and* non-animate objects and is free from the wide equivocations and confusing repetitions within Leviticus. The only contender, when as far as possible all dubiety and conflict are removed, must, inductively, be something along the lines of *platydysmorphism*. Where human cases are involved, we may logically and reasonably allow ourselves to add an epithet to localize the condition to skin (i.e. body surface), and so arrive at *dermopathic platydysmorphism*. Anatomists and physiologists know, from studying the phenomenon of referred pain, that the human brain is unable to perceive or formulate sensory images of the body's interior and so refers sensations generated by, for example, internal pathology to the body's surface.[753] As the body's surface is essentially skin, it is easy to speculate that the scientifically untutored mind might somewhat reverse the process and perceive those things affecting the body's surface as projecting deeper goings-on to a mentally constructed whole-body-image or map and so to an understanding of

---

752 This is true also of the Talmud where an English search for "lepr*" scores 576 hits.
753 A classic example is the pain of appendicitis which begins in the middle of the abdomen and localizes to the right iliac fossa.

body-wholeness. In its turn, perception of disturbed body-image impinges psychologically upon the psyche to engender abstract feelings such as low self-esteem, depression, inadequacy, and doubts about one's place among one's family, tribe, or in society as a whole. The defilement of a surface, צרעת, when identified within a set of socially unacceptable conditions, may be the only symptomatology necessary to trigger this chain of events.

It is now important to examine specific examples of how these words may have been used in an Israel largely influenced by the rituals of a priestly ideology.

צרעת—*Evidence from the Hebrew Bible*

Examples of the word צרעת are to be found in other biblical books besides Leviticus. There seems to be little doubt from context-logometrics that the same primary meaning is intended. However, several authors have suggested nuances of meaning that may be revealing. If a search is made by book for occurrences of the word צרעת, the following frequencies are obtained:

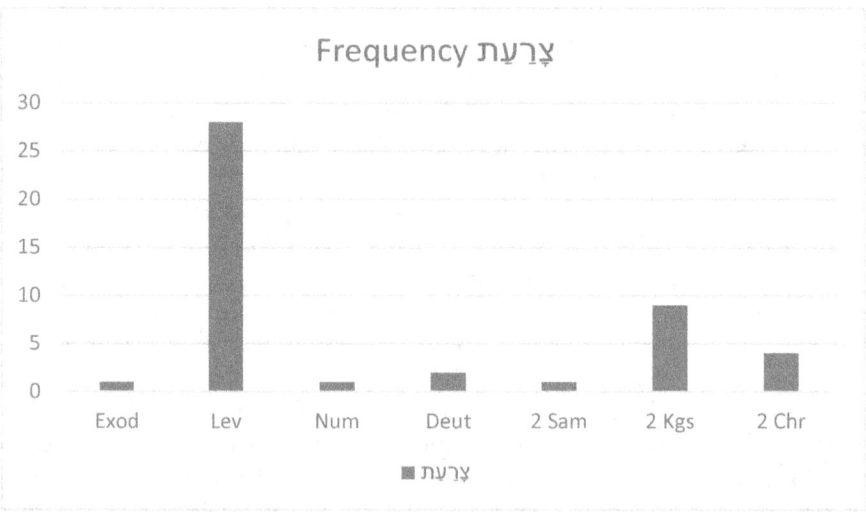

These frequencies tally perfectly with those obtained from a search of the Septuagint using λέπρ*. A search of the ERV, KJV, RSV and NRSV using *lep**, also corresponds exactly.[754] If we accept the notion that exceptions prove the rule—or at least shed light upon it—it is important further to explore the extra-Levitical cases (even though the logometrics imply similarity) in search of helpful nuances.

---

754 Glasby, "What was Biblical Leprosy?"

If we consider how the word צרעת (and/or the idea it represented) was used in a wider context—and in particular its interrelationship with religious and social events taking place in ancient Israelite society—the most obvious differentiating factor might be supposed to be the use of the word צרעת in a priestly and non-priestly context. This approach has been a central factor in the two major studies to be considered below. A secondary aim would be to see if any sort of notion of *healthcare* was actively involved in these interrelationships. The distinction, priestly/non-priestly material has, in the eyes of some authors, been interpreted as strictly Levitical (P) *versus* non-Levitical material within which most authors have included H. There have emerged several important lines of thought and two of these which are specific about Levitical and non-Levitical usage of צרעת, offer important interpretative information.

The first of these is from Lieber and approaches the subject from a largely medical point of view. As ever, with such an approach, it potentially incurs, but takes great pains to avoid, criticism for *hyperdiagnosis*. The second, from Baden and Moss,[755] takes a theological stance with *sin* as the discriminator. It too may be criticized as being somewhat eclectic about the inclusion of sin in ritual impurity. Nevertheless, both studies make important substrates for further discussion. For comparison we should also note Feder's opinion that, nowithstanding context logometrics, the meaning of צרעת changed significantly over time because its role was not to define a disease but rather a process, *contagion*. Contagion Feder supposes to be the defiling principle as it operates as an *emotional bias* and is therefore not a concrete entity but a property of cognition.[756]

What צָרַעַת Might Have Been if it Were a Disease

The risk of hyperdiagnosis has already been addressed where any attempt to extract, from textual sources, a modern explanation for the biblical condition צרעת or λέπρα is contemplated. This is especially the case where authors persist in attempting to relate צרעת/λέπρα to leprosy. This approach, in the past, has yielded information about what "leprosy" *was not,* but it has not been of help in firmly identifying whether צרעת/λέπρα was a specific disease.

Nevertheless, putting aside the difficult problem of צרעת/λέπρα infecting non animate things, we can identify a number of conditions worthy of consideration as possible contenders for צרעת at least in the human.

---

755 See chapter 12.
756 See chapter 10.

Elephantiasis Graecorum

This has been largely ruled out—see chapter 6—on the grounds of there being no archaeological evidence and the likelihood of its emergence from the Indus valley only with Alexander's return. This is the most widely held view but we must note a dissenting voice from a few authors[757] who, though thinking it unlikely, are not prepared to dismiss completely the possibility that $EG \rightleftharpoons HD$ existed in ancient Egypt and the ANE.[758] Although in Hansen's disease the lesions are never "white as snow", they may be pale. In HD, the hair never turns white and the skin is not really scaly but is pachydermatous. A major pathognomic pointer for $EG \rightleftharpoons HD$ that is missing from the Bible is the cutaneous anaesthesia of HD which is surely one of its most dramatic and consistent signs.

Vitiligo—Leucoderma

This relatively common condition is characterized by whitening of the skin[759] probably because of melanocyte depopulation. There are no scaly lesions although the hair does turn white. It is cosmetic, non-progressive, and entirely benign. The cause is unknown; in any given population the present-day incidence is <1%.

Scabies

This is a highly contagious condition associated with poor personal hygiene. The agent is the mite *Sarcoptes scabei* and the predominant symptom is itching. There may be a rash and excoriation. This condition would undoubtedly have been found in the ANE in biblical times but seems an unlikely contender for צרעת as the symptomatology does not fit. However, a secondarily infected, serious case of scabies could cause a more frightening array of signs that might possibly be interpreted as צרעת. It is known that repeated bathing can cure scabies and it may be because of this that scabies has been implicated as a possible contender for צרעת.

Favus

Favus (Latin = honeycomb) is unique among the contenders for צרעת in being a fungal disease. It is caused by the fungus *Trichophyton schoenleinii* and it is restricted to the scalp where it may grow, persist, and remit over many years. As its name suggests it manifests itself by its honeycomb-like appearance which

---

[757] Notably Lieber Lieber, "Old Testament 'Leprosy', Contagion and Sin."; Lieber, "'Cleansing' the 'Leper' in the Old and New Testaments."; Lieber, "Asaf's 'Book of Medicines.'"; E. Lieber, "Leprosy in the Lands of the Bible, and the Demons Bes and Pazuzu. Part I: Ancient Egypt and the Bes-image." *Korot.* 10 (1993): 25–43.
[758] Prioreschi, *A History of Medicine.*
[759] This condition in the late Michael Jackson—an entertainer—aroused interest in the popular press.

first forms large highly disfiguring encrustations (*scutula*) which periodically fall away to reveal shiny pale hairless areas. Although limited to the scalp area, in Western countries it has frequently, in the past, been confused with Hansen's disease presumably because of a resmblance to the *facies leonina*. It was undoubtedly present in biblical times in the ANE.

Pellagra

Glickman[760] has suggested pellagra as צרעת. This is caused by a deficiency in vitamin B3 (niacin) and has the pathognomonic tetrad, "*diarrhoea, dermatitis, dementia and death*". The second of these presents as a rough thickening with induration of the skin though there is no whiteness or change in the hair. Niacin is present in cereal crops and is unlikely to have been in short supply in the ANE except in times of famine. Pellagra is, therefore, an "outside" contender for צרעת.

Leishmaniasis

Leishmaniasis[761] is a complex of related diseases caused by members of the protozoon genus *Leishmania*. Its cutaneous form (usually due to *Leishmania donovani*), was known to have been prevalent in Mesopotamia at the time of the Babylonian exile.[762] It is highly infectious and its vector is the common sandfly. The lesions themselves are not contagious and take the form of shiny furuncles that leave permanent scars that may be grossly disfiguring. There is also a diffuse cutaneous form that resembles psoriasis and leaves behind a pachydermatous scarring of the face. The cutaneous nerves are often involved and it is not surprising therefore that this condition has often been confused with Hansen's disease. However, it does not entirely fit the symptomatology of צרעת inasmuch as there is no whitening or change in the hair.

Chronic Psoriasis

Chronic psoriasis is an autoimmune condition, probably with a genetic component, affecting 1% of the worldwide population. Among those who accept that צרעת was not *EG*⇌HD, it has proved over the years to be the most popular and enduring contender for צרעת although the symptomatology is not a perfect fit. The pathology is essentially an uncontrolled overgrowth of skin cells which form whitish scaly plaques over the whole body in serious cases but, in milder forms, show a preference for extensor surfaces. The plaques outrun their nutritional supply-lines and are desquamated to leave behind a salmon-pink shiny surface. Psoriasis is, thus, a good contender for "scale disease", especially

---

760 Glickman, "Lepra, Psora, Psoriasis."
761 Few diseases are able to boast a more evocative series of names: "Baghdad Boils", "Aleppo boils", "Bay sores", "Biskra buttons", "Chiclero ulcers", "Delhi boils", "Kandahar sores", "Lahore sores", "Oriental sores".
762 Prioreschi, *A History of Medicine*.

since the plaques are white. However, the hair does not change in colour and subdermal invasion does not take place; though if the plaques are scraped off there may be bleeding from the skin—Auspitz's sign. Chronic psoriasis can be exceptionally disfiguring and since the face and limbs are often involved, it would have been apparent in those wearing the dress of biblical times. The disease is not life-threatening and periods of remission are common. Chronic psoriasis is not at all contagious, however secondary bacterial and fungal infection of psoriatic plaques can occur. The condition undoubtedly has a psychological element also but this is poorly understood.

Köbner Phenomenon

The onset of episodes of psoriasis is thought to be triggered by quite minor injury to the skin. This is mediated by a protein *köbnerisin* whose production is up-regulated in psoriasis. However, there is at present some uncertainty as to whether this is cause or effect.

Acute Generalized Pustular Psoriasis (AGPP)

In a small number of cases, chronic psoriasis may progress to a fulminating acute form, AGPP. There is generalized excoriation and secondary infection is highly likely so that a truly contagious state ensues. This may be life-threatening.

The Treponematoses

These bacterial diseases caused by the spirochaete genus *Treponema* are widespread geographically, of variable infectivity and associated with a wide range of symptoms and signs.

Syphilis

Many attempts have been made over the years to implicate syphilis in biblical leprosy but none has been convincing.[763] Syphilis appears to have not existed in Europe before the time around which the Americas were discovered. Whether it was imported from the New World or was a result of a mutation in the Old World remains a matter for continuing and heated debate. The disease is caused by the subspecies of spirochaete *Treponema pallidum pallidum* and the symptoms and signs are so specific—and unlike צרעת—as to make it a most unlikely contender.

---

[763] Rosner, *Encyclopaedia of Medicine in the Bible*.

Non-venereal Treponematoses

There are several less serious treponematoses that are transmitted by contagion but not venereally.[764] Two of these are:

Yaws

This is a highly infectious skin disease caused by the spirochaete *Treponema pallidum pertenue*. It is endemic in tropical climates but not in the Middle East. The "mother yaw" and "daughter yaws" are so specific in their appearance that it is likely they would have been mentioned in texts if this were צרעת.

Bejel

This disease is endemic to the Middle East, known in Arabic as بَجَل/البَجَل and is caused by the spirochaete *Treponema pallidum endemicum*. It must, along with chronic psoriasis and AGPP, be considered a major contender for human צרעת. Bejel is a highly contagious disease associated with poor hygiene and today largely restricted to nomadic peoples: it is uncommon in town dwellers. It is characterized by pityroid scales, depigmentation of skin and hair with deep ulceration and scarring. It especially affects the face (but there is no *facies leonina*) and limbs and, as in HD, there may be destructive erosion of the maxilla (*gangosa*). Although as disfiguring and potentially as serious as Hansen's disease and syphilis, bejel can spontaneously remit to become latent or disappear altogether.

Lieber's Medical View of צרעת

Lieber has suggested that a distinction should be made between Levitical and non-Levitical צרעת on the grounds that the former is integral to the priestly concept of ritual impurity whereas *all* instances of the latter may be considered simply as case-histories. Lieber believes non-Levitical צרעת most probably and commonly to have been psoriasis, although she excepts from this the story of King Uzziah (2 Chron 26:19), because the circumstances of Uzziah's death are suggestive (to her) of Hansen's disease.[765] This seems highly unlikely to the present author given what is known of the origins, aetiology, incidence, and prevalence of Hansen's disease. Possibly, if Uzziah's affliction were manifestly more serious than everyday צרעת, it could have been the exacerbation of chronic psoriasis to produce *acute generalized pustular psoriasis (AGPP)*. Equally possible is *bejel* (بَجَل/البَجَل), which is discussed above. It is endemic to the Middle East, highly contagious and associated, then and today, with poor

---

[764] Even a "Scotch Pox" known as "Sibbens"—R. S. Morton, "The Sibbens of Scotland," *Medical History* 11, no. 4 (1967): 374–80.
[765] Lieber, "Leprosy in the Lands of the Bible"; "Cleansing the Leper in the Old and New Testaments"; "Old Testament 'Leprosy', Contagion and Sin."

hygiene.⁷⁶⁶ Bejel can be as disfiguring as Hansen's disease, for both may exhibit *gangosa*. In bejel, but not in Hansen's disease, the hair may turn white. Bejel *per se* is not usually fatal and may remit spontaneously. However, super-added bacterial infection is possible and likely in bejel and may result in a fatal outcome.⁷⁶⁷

It is fair to say that Lieber favours HD and never suggests that Uzziah had bejel. While *prima facie* Lieber offers a good argument for psoriasis as the צרעת of the non-Levitical case histories, she immediately breaks her own rule by postulating a different aetiology for Uzziah. Lieber suggests that Levitical צרעת was bejel and that it was during the Exodus and the Israelites' sojourn in the desert—reported in Exodus and Numbers—that they became exposed to this highly contagious, endemic disease. This idea depends, therefore, on historical veracity of the Exodus. Lieber's logic is based upon the idea that the various tests and rituals of Lev 13 are directed specifically at making a differential diagnosis so that those cases that are contagious (bejel) may be treated differently from those that are not (psoriasis). Lieber is not altogether logical in justifying her textual dichotomy, as she presents no textual evidence to suggest that two (or more) different considtions are being considered by the priests in Lev 13. Equally, there is nothing to suggest that the *protasis↔apodosis* algorithm was being applied in the extra-Levitical cases. *That* Levitical and non-Levitical צרעת were different may be a valid conclusion, but there is nothing to suggest that the priests were making any such distinction through differential diagnosis. Rather, they seem to have been carrying out what today is called "*staging*" of a single affliction to establish its progress and its potential for contagion.

Lieber⁷⁶⁸ has produced a table of characteristics of symptoms and signs that appear in Lev 13 and might account for צרעת—see below. In column 6 she suggests modern diseases that *might* account for the symptomatology. The danger of this approach has been pointed out above (*passim*). This table has been modified and extended by the present author. While columns 1 to 6 are useful in summarizing Lev 13, it is column 7 of the table that is indicative of the end point of any priestly diagnostic testing as to whether each situation results in major (טמא) or minor impurity (טהור). In column 8 is recorded the equally important contagiousness or otherwise of the condition. If we omit column 6, this table becomes a diagnostic tool for the priests to use in deciding who did or did not imperil their ritual purity. As such it would be operating with no truly medical function whatsoever. This is not what Lieber's intends, but it is important to note that her ideas, stripped of all "medicality" are not in any way incompatible with priestly ideology and function as recorded in Leviticus.

---

766 Occurring almost exclusively in the countryside but rarely found in towns. The reason for this is unknown.
767 Glasby, "What was Biblical Leprosy?", chapter 7.
768 Lieber, "Old Testament 'Leprosy'."

צרעת and Un-Wholeness

Lev 13	Scales	Depigmented skin lesions	Whitening of Hair?	Subdermal invasion?	Modern Disease	טמא or טהור	Contagious?
9–11	Yes	Yes	Yes	Yes	Bejel	טמא	Yes
18–20	Yes	Yes	Yes	Yes	Bejel	טמא	Yes
24–25	Yes	Yes	Yes	Yes	Bejel	טמא	Yes
43–46	Yes	Pale	Uncertain	Yes	Bejel	טמא	Yes, very
ditto	No	Never white as snow	Never in HD	Yes	?? Hansen's disease	טמא	Yes mildly
29–37	No	Pale scalp encrustations (scutula)	Yellowish colour then hair loss	Scutula fall off to leave shiny skin	Favus	טהור ? טמא	No Yes if 2° infection
6	No	Yes (pure white)	Yes	No	Vitiligo	טהור	No
12–13	Yes	White scales upon salmon pink skin	No	No but NB (Auspitz's sign)	Chronic psoriasis	טהור	No
17	Yes	White scales upon salmon pink skin	No	No but NB (Auspitz's sign)	Chronic psoriasis	טהור	No
14–16	Yes	Old scales may persist	No	Yes extensive	Acute generalized pustular psoriasis	טמא	Uncertain
4–6	No	No	No	Yes shiny furuncles and diffuse scarring	Diffuse cutaneous Leishmaniasis (Baghdad boils)	טָמֵא	"Yes" i.e. infectious by sandfly vector

The important points to note are that:

- There is no single symptom/sign (or constellation of these) that fits all cases.
- This suggests that צרעת cannot be a single disease.
- The symptomatology is consistent with צרעת's being sundry observable symptoms and signs all of which involve the disruption, corruption and disfigurement of all or part the body's surface—platydysmorphism.
- The priests regarded these symptoms and signs as permitting a differential diagnosis of major impurity (טמא) or minor impurity (טהור).

- All of those symptoms seen as producing major impurity (טמא) share the property of contagion.

In summary, therefore, word analysis tells us nothing medical about צרעת but the use of context logometrics strongly suggests that that the priests knew exactly what they meant by צרעת. Moreover, the later rabbis presumably also understood what was meant because they attempted first to interpret צרעת and latterly to extend its meaning. Within the Hebrew Bible we are justified in assuming a clear and consistent intended meaning for the word. This evidence does not, however, support the conclusion that every case of צרעת seen by every priest was necessarily the same. It seems likely that צרעת "represented" a spectrum of conditions all platydysmorphic in symptomatology but not necessarily of similar aetiology. Priestly differential diagnosis allowed for decision-making about what ritual anti-צרעת procedure should be instituted.

The compact neatness of Lieber's analysis *prima facie* raises suspicions of hyperdiagnosis. Hers is, nevertheless, a highly attractive theory *if* we do *not* try to believe that צרעת was a single condition or that the priests had any particular interest in medical matters. Lieber's work is important because it sets out a framework based upon *protasis↔apodosis* questioning, for the priests to operate a system of differential diagnosis for טהור/טמא and *contagious/not contagious*. Lieber's approach, therefore, makes a strong case for Levitical צרעת to have been a construct within the priestly *Weltanschauung* which had the properties of *contagiousness* and causing *major defilement*. The evidence for her view that non-Levitical צרעת reprsented a congeries of symptoms and signs of a host of major or minor diseases is more difficult to accept. Whatever צרעת might have been, it imperilled wholeness and thereby the ritual purity that was necessary for the holiness required for Yahweh's continued presence in the sanctuary and in the land.

Chapter 12

צרעת AND UN-HOLINESS

In previous chapters, a linguistic and medical approach to the way in which wholeness and purity may have been compromised by צרעת and זוב and perhaps even by מום. A majority of authors has avoided a medical approach preferring to be concerned with the theological effects of צרעת (or perhaps more often, "leprosy"), and זוב as factors in the causation of impurity and especially in the relationship [or not] of this defiling mechanism with sin. If we accept from the previous chapter that צרעת (and זוב), in the worldview of the Levitical priesthood, begat un-wholeness, it now becomes necessary to investigate how that situation extended into un-holiness. First, the relationship of צרעת and sin as seen by Baden and Moss; this will be followed by a consideration of the work of Regev who extends the understanding of the *wholeness↔holiness* relationship by comparing Leviticus with Deuteronomy. Finally, how this may have fitted into the priestly, ritual-dominated milieu of ancient Israel and the Hebrew Bible will be considered.

BADEN'S AND MOSS'S VIEW — צרעת AND SIN

In chapter 5, it was seen that Klawans generally dismisses the idea that צרעת is the fruit of sin although he tends to sit on the fence by accepting that there are some biblical textual examples that, nevertheless, may imply this (e.g. Num 12; 2 Chron 26). Klawans attempts to circumvent this difficulty by suggesting that the problem is less about moral sin *per se* than about reducing the probability of the מצרע's inadvertently defiling holy objects whilst in a state of personal pollution.

Klawans sees two occasions on which ritual impurity does lead to sin. If an individual voluntarily omits to purify himself after defilement by a corpse (Num 19:13; 19:20), this causes remote defilement of the sanctuary and the punishment is כרת. Klawans justifies this proposition by suggesting that the dynamic *ritual-impurity↔moral-impurity↔sin* is in operation here, because any voluntary decision not to purify must surely be the product of sinful thinking. The second case, afforded the same penalty of כרת, is defilement of the sanctuary by contact with holy foods while knowingly in a state of ritual impurity (Lev 7:20–21; 15:31; 22:3–7).

This viewpoint is at odds with that recently posited by Baden and Moss.[769] These authors believe that, from the very start, it is necessary to postulate different

---

[769] J. S. Baden and Candida R. Moss, "The Origin and Interpretation of Sara'at in Leviticus 13–14," *JBL* 130, no. 4 (2011): 643–62.

kinds of sin↔צרעת relationship in Levitical and non-Levitical material in the Hebrew Bible and also, within the P and H material of Leviticus. The latter distinction must be made because Levitical H quite clearly lumps צרעת together with sin and so is closer to the non-Levitical examples. Baden and Moss indicate that nowhere in Leviticus chapters 13 and 14—the two P chapters dealing specifically with צרעת—is it implied that צרעת is caused by sin(fullness). Although Baden and Moss do not specifically address the possibility that their ideas operate also for זוב it seems entirely probable that this differential may apply to both conditions. In the following "equations" one should therefore read צרעת (and זוב) for each occurrence of צרעת.

Baden and Moss's thesis is based upon the proposition that if:

צרעת ≡ direct result of sin

This thinking would entail an intrinsic problem because:

- צרעת (and זוב) has been widely defined and accepted as ritual impurity which defiles by contagion but cannot defile the land.
- Sin has been widely defined and accepted as moral impurity which is not contagious but can defile the land.

The solution to this problem proposed by Klawans and others has been to suppose that צרעת can remain a ritual impurity because it is not sin in itself that causes צרעת but certain corollaries of sin such as sinful thinking. So:

צרעת ≠ sin (*per se*)

And therefore, we may suppose that, for Klawans, צרעת (and זוב± מום) is the *divine consequence of*, but not necessarily the *divine punishment for*, sin—this seems rather tendentious and difficult to accept as logical.

Baden and Moss are completely in agreement that צרעת is associated with sin in the following textual examples: Num 12:10, 11 (E); Deut 24:8 (D); 2 Sam 3:29 (DtrH); 2 Kgs 5:3, 6, 7, 27; 15:5 (DtrH); 2 Chron 26:19, 20, 21 (Chlr). The letters in brackets after each reference denote the supposed origins of these texts according to the *Documentary Hypothesis* and these are also the categories accepted by Baden and Moss.[770] It is interesting to note there is no J example.[771] They also find two examples from Leviticus (14:34 and 26:16, 25). The second of these examples has always been viewed as H text and the former is peculiar in that it is claimed to be the only suggestion of a divine origin for צרעת in Leviticus. Baden and Moss share with Knohl and Milgrom the view that this verse is a late interpolation of H material into what is otherwise undiluted P

---

[770] Baden and Moss, "The Origin and Interpretation of Sara'at," 644.
[771] See scheme in chapter 2.

text.⁷⁷² In contrast to this, Baden and Moss point out that everywhere else in Leviticus—and particularly in chapters 13 and 14—the context makes it clear that undoubtedly:

צרעת ≠ sin

In support of this hypothesis, they note that in Leviticus (P) where:

- צרעת affects fabrics; this may be thought of as having a divine causation but this does not necessarily imply divine punishment for the owner's sin.

And where:

- In non-P narrative texts ([J], E, D, DtrH, Chlr, H), when צרעת affects a human, it is *always* as divine punishment for sin.

But since:

- Both of these sources entail the same dermatological/mycological signs and symptoms, (i.e. platydysmorphism), and so are pathologically identical.

It must follow that in Leviticus P, for the same condition:

צרעת ≠ sin

Baden and Moss have lamented, "Scholars continue to try to understand the priestly concept of צרעת as if it is not only related to the non-priestly texts but, in fact, identical to it." They postulate that there has been a clear and continuing confusion which has operated to bring about an artificial distinction of ritual and moral impurity and the specific involvement of sin in the causation of both of these states.

In summary, the Baden and Moss view is in Leviticus P:

צרעת ≠ sin

But, in Leviticus H and elsewhere:

צרעת ≡ sin

It is, of course, as one becomes used to reading and writing about or speaking of Levitical P material, easy to forget that this is an expression of the viewpoint of the priests operating within their particular *Weltanschauung*⁷⁷³ and so it is, therefore, in literary terms, a *priestly genre*. The equation above is a behavioural formula by which the priests operated ritually in their dealings with other members of society as diagnosticians of צרעת and protectors of sacred things. In

---

772 Baden and Moss, "The Origin and Interpretation of Sara'at," 652. Knohl, *The Sanctuary of Silence*, 95 N119. Milgrom, *Leviticus: A New Translation*, Vol. 1, 886–887.
773 See chapter 4.

their world of ritual there was no need for this affliction to bear any religious or moral stigma or to invoke guilt. It was, quite simply (and like זוב and מום), a fact of everyday life.

When viewed against authors such as Milgrom and Klawans, Baden and Moss's view demands clarification of the nature of חטאת. This term is to be found both in relation to Levitical and non-Levitical צרעת but in particular in Lev 14 relating to the latter. They note that חטאת is has traditionally been seen as (atonement by) a *sin offering*—in most English translations of the Hebrew Bible—but this cannot, in fact, be the case if we believe their hypothesis. Milgrom has considered חטאת in minute detail and written at length on the subject. He too concludes that חטאת cannot be a *sin-offering* but must be a *purification-offering* and the requirement is placed (in a priest-dominated environment) upon the מצרע to provide חטאת.[774] Baden and Moss entirely support this viewpoint as far as the priestly Levitical P-textual material is concerned. Wherever מצרעים are to be found, there follows the remote pollution of the sanctuary. If it is צרעת that causes this, the polluting ritual impurity is necessarily requiring to be purged by the provision of a purificatory offering and not by a sin offering.

The nature of the sacrifice known as אשם also prescribed by the priests (Lev 14:12), must be addressed in addition. This is usually referred to as a *guilt-offering* but if we accept that צרעת is not a sin, this cannot logically be an accurate definition as, in the biblical world, it is sin that begets guilt. Baden and Moss agree with Milgrom that *reparation offering* would be more appropriate. This view is based upon the fact that the אשם is offered only *after* the subject has already been cleansed. This arrangement would make no sense if it were a *guilt-offering* because in that case, one would expect healing not to have begun, nor the guilt to have been assuaged, until *after* the sacrificial dues of אשם had been paid.

Baden and Moss consider their viewpoint to be supported by what they call the "theological singularity of the priestly writings", but add that by focussing unduly upon this, scholars may have failed to regard and appreciate the significance of the dichotomy between priestly and non-priestly צרעת, each of which is representative of a different worldview and ideology. Baden and Moss argue that perhaps also, a failure adequately to appreciate the significance of monotheism in Israelite culture may have led to over-extrapolation from the cultures of polytheistic societies; for example, Mesopotamia. Much of Baden and Moss's paper is of necessity directed at recounting and refuting specific examples of the pre-existing counter-viewpoint that they regard as traditional and even entrenched. They have something of an exegetical hill to climb, given the

---

[774] Milgrom, *Leviticus: A New Translation*, Vol. 1, 253–292; 822–857.

authorship involved, but their novel view seems entirely logical and makes considerable sense.⁷⁷⁵

If we accept the views of Baden and Moss, we see a fundamental difference between the priest and the physician that impinges upon the central hypothesis of the present work. Priests and physicians initially had in common the job of being diagnosticians but thereafter their job-descriptions divaricated. The physician's role after making a diagnosis is, as far as possible, to cure, or at least treat, the individual: his patient. For the priest, the objective that followed diagnosis was not to treat a patient but rather to protect sacred objects and places from further contamination. The object of a priest's duties was *contagion* whereas a physician's was *disease*. Priests were obliged to achieve the decontamination of sacred places by organizing purification offerings on the part of the carrier of the צרעת. There was no obligation upon the part of the priests themselves to care, in any way, for the health or well-being of their "parishioners" or for any individual מצרע.

IMPURITY AND HOLINESS: THE INFLUENCE OF DEUTERONOMY

Concerning the Torah we may observe that because Leviticus and Deuteronomy share a legalistic viewpoint and approach to purity and to sin and צרעת, but not a priestly worldview, it may be profitable to consider their similarities and differences in some detail.

The word צרעת occurs only once in the book of Deuteronomy, where the author advises that the well-known Levitical rules and interdictions should be followed.

השמר בנגע־הצרעת לשמר מאד ולעשות ככל אשר־יורו אתכם הכהנים הלוים כאשר צויתם תשמרו לעשות

> Take heed in the plague of leprosy, that thou observe diligently, and do according to all that the priests the Levites shall teach you: as I commanded them, so ye shall observe to do. (Deut 24:8)

---

775 The final part of Baden's and Moss's paper is concerned with Disability Studies that embody the idea that disability in biblical times was thought to have been engendered by sin. Caveats relating to disability studies have been raised already in chapter 9; tendentious arguments must always be avoided and strict validity in the strict philosophical sense established in arguments used to support the point of view of any special-interest group. See: Julian Baggini and Peter S. Fosl, *The Philosopher's Toolkit: A Compendium of Philosophical Concepts and Methods* (Malden, MA; Oxford: Blackwell, 2003). Baden and Moss cite an example worthy of this criticism of the view of צרעת taken in many biblical disability studies. This is Melcher's likening of צרעת to the Greek στίγμα as a sign of moral failure deserving of and receiving divine punishment. See, S. J. Melcher, "Visualizing the Perfect Cult," in *Human Disability and the Service of God: Reassessing Religious Practice*, ed. Nancy L. Eiesland and Don E. Saliers (Nashville: Abingdon, 1998). They point out that Melcher is widely using non-P data to support her argument about levitical P-matters. Olyan too, may be guilty of transposition and conflation of textual sources when he works from a generalized definition of צרעת which he applies throughout the entire gamut of texts. See, Olyan, "Honor, Shame, and Covenant Relations in Ancient Israel and Its Environment."; Olyan, "The Exegetical Dimensions of Restrictions on the Blind and the Lame in Texts from Qumran."; Olyan, *Disability in the Hebrew Bible*; Olyan, "The Ascription of Physical Disability as a Stigmatizing Strategy in Biblical iconic Polemics."

Despite this, however, there is an important difference in the ideas of (im)purity and holiness in the book of Deuteronomy compared with Leviticus. It is likely that the writing of the book of Deuteronomy and the beginning of the redaction of Leviticus took place at roughly the same time. Further redaction of either or both went on through the exile and into the Second Temple period. There were thus manifold opportunities for conflation of the two viewpoints to satisfy the needs of the *Zeitgeist*, the changing influence of the priesthood and the centralization required by deuteronomic doctrine and dogma. Such changes might be expected to have involved the *wholeness↔holiness* relationship.

Levitical Dynamic-Holiness and Deuteronomic Static-Holiness

An extensive and detailed comparison of Levitical and Deuteronomic impurity and holiness has been made by Regev.[776] This impinges significantly upon the *wholeness↔holiness* tension and secondarily upon the relationship of disease/medicine with priestly activity. Regev's argument reduces to the idea that if *P-impurity* and *D-impurity* can be shown to be different, it follows that *P-wholeness* and *D-wholeness* must also be different and so there *must* be a corresponding difference between *P-holiness* and *D-holiness*. Of course, this association can also be argued in the reverse direction and it is specifically in the dynamics of holiness that the differences are perceived by Regev. He considers the priestly/Levitical concept of holiness to be dynamic, hence *Dynamic-P-holiness*, whereas the Deuteronomic concept is static, hence *Static-D-holiness*.[777] Regev's argument does not specifically include mention of צרעת but it is tacitly implicated in *impurity*, when he draws a distinction between the P-stated and the D-stated attitudes applied to the *purity/impurity↔wholeness↔holiness* relationship. As a result of his study, Regev identifies three major and six minor areas of difference:[778]

1. Cultic differences (6 subsections):

   i. Centrality of the temple/tabernacle P≫D.[779]
   ii. Sacrifice, P → חטאת and אשם, and Day of Atonement; D → protection of sacredness and sanctuary not implied: sacrifices reflect personal gratitude.
   iii. Priests and priestly dues P≫D. D emphasizes holiness of people of Israel.
   iv. P-impurity, D-abomination, see below.

---

776 Regev, "Priestly Dynamic Holiness." See also, Poorthuis and Schwartz, *Purity and Holiness*.
777 Regev avoids the P/H distinction in Leviticus by regarding them as "one school". The present author does not regard this distinction as safe but accepts Regev's view where the comparison is strictly P with D.
778 For details see: Regev, "Priestly Dynamic Holiness," 245–253.
779 The ≫ signs indicate which textual form gives greater or lesser weight to the matter in question.

v. P → heavenly glory (כבוד) dwells in temple/tabernacle; D → the divine presence cannot be localized.

vi. P → people are sanctified in a continual process by the observance of given commands. D → holiness of the people is de facto consequence of Yahweh's election of Israel.

2. Typology of holiness: P= theocentric, D = anthropocentric.

3. P → worldview presupposes a divine order with emphasis on creating orderliness by ritual and assigning individuals to their status in the holiness spectrum. D → Yahweh has already created a permanent cosmic system of holiness and so there is no need for ritual.

Regev's holiness models therefore suppose distinct differences in the way in which the P and D authors viewed impurity and how this impinged upon the P and D typology of holiness.

Dynamic and Static Impurity: P-impurity (טמא) and D-abomination (תועבה)

In chapter 5, it was seen that Levitical impurity/defilement/pollution was everywhere characterized by its intensely destructive force which was able to imperil the sanctuary, even at a distance, by violating its holiness. As Milgrom and most of the authors who have considered the Levitical purity laws have noted, the primary purpose of the Levitical interdictions was to protect the sacred places, people, and objects from such defilement and so ultimately to prevent the desecration and desolation of the land of Israel itself and the departure of the deity. As far as possible, this was policed through ritual by the priests whose methods involved principally *identification*, *segregation*, and *isolation* followed by *cleansing* and *sacrifice*.

In contrast, we find that Deuteronomy has a less strict interpretation of impurity/defilement/pollution than that found in Leviticus; in particular the emphasis on ritual is not present and the terminology, significantly, is different also. Whereas Leviticus uses טמא to imply impurity, the preferred term in Deuteronomy is תועבה, (√תעב) which is traditionally translated into English as "abomination".[780] This is identified by Regev who describes it as, "Intolerable filth, both physically repulsive and morally disgraceful. It is an obligation which holiness imposes upon the people of Israel." The word occurs in Deuteronomy sixteen times in relation to five categories of abomination.[781]

These are:

i. Idolatry, Molech-worship, sorcery, and magic.

---

780 Clines, ed., *Dictionary of Classical Hebrew*, 607–609. TDOT, 591–604.
781 Deut 7:25, 26; 12:31; 13:15; 14:3; 17:1, 4; 18:9, 12; 20:18; 22:25; 23:19; 24:4; 25:16; 27:15; 32:16.

ii. Animals unfit to be eaten; unworthy sacrifice; payment of sanctuary dues with tainted money.
iii. Bigamy; inappropriate (re-)marriage.
iv. Cross-dressing.
v. Dishonesty applied to weights and measures.

In Deuteronomy, תועבה clearly always implies something flawed, faulty, and undesirable. The noun either appears alone or in construct with a subjective or objective genitive or with a preposition (before/unto), or prepositional clause indicating by whom it is found to be abominable or to whom it is abominable. This last is most commonly תועבת יהוה אלהיך ("The Lord your God"), as might be expected.

What is perhaps a more important distinction to be drawn between P-impurity and D-impurity is that nowhere in Deuteronomy are any strictly forensic consequences enumerated. This is in stark contrast to the lengthy and exhaustive Levitical legalistic discourses on such matters. Deuteronomical תועבה is much less specific and defined and everywhere remains a generalization and an abstraction.

The word תועבה does not appear in P-Leviticus; it does appear in H-Leviticus six times (18:22, 26, 27, 29, 30 and 20:13), but its usage here is quite different from that in Deuteronomy. It was noted above that Regev specifically chose not to include H as a separate sub-category when he made a distinction between *P-dynamic* and *D-static* holiness. This may be seen as mildly advantageable when he then elects to differentiate Levitical *P-impurity* from *H-impurity* by their respective exclusion and inclusion of the Deuteronomic word תועבה. It is very obvious, even to the casual reader, that תועבה enjoys a very much more specific usage throughout H-Leviticus than it does in Deuteronomy. H-תועבה is used to refer to *sexual sins*, such as homosexuality, sodomy, buggery, and incest. Moreover, unlike D-תועבה, H-תועבה can, if sufficiently intensive, defile the land and it demands, for the transgressor, the ultimate punishment of כרת. H-תועבה therefore, is not an abstraction but has the destructive force and consequences of P-טמא (i.e. ritual impurity). It is, however, engendered not by צרעת or זוב but by what Klawans and others have classified as *moral impurity*.[782]

Typology of Holiness: P-dynamic and D-static Holiness

According to Regev, *P-impurity* (טמא) and *D-abomination* (תועבה) each entail an equivalent form of holiness. Regev bases his argument for this correspondence on Durkheim's view that *holiness* is the foundation of every religion and cult.[783] It therefore becomes crucial to any discourse on holiness

---

782 See chapter 5.
783 E. Durkheim, *Les Formes Élémentaires de la Vie Religieuse* (Paris: Presses Universitaire de France, 1979); Moshe Weinfeld, *Deuteronomy and the Deuteronomic School* (Oxford: Clarendon, 1972).

and its relationship to wholeness, to establish its definition and scope and to enumerate those things that may obtrude into it and cause compromise.[784] Regev's model makes some headway into doing this by seeing P-holiness as "Dynamic, sensitive and dangerous with limited access to the sacred", where in contrast, D-holiness is "Static, not dangerous or threatening and with less restriction of access to the sacred."

This division of holiness into dynamic or static forms is not envisaged, either by Regev or other authors, simply to depend upon ideas of impurity/abomination. The initial binary division entails two further sub-classifications. These sub-classifications themselves entail the nature of the being around whom the holiness centres and the origins of the holiness itself.

P-theocentricity and D-anthropocentricity

Regev's model envisages dynamic holiness as essentially theocentric whereas static holiness is anthropocentric.[785] Because, for the reasons considered in the preceding paragraph, P-impurity imperils P-holiness, their dynamic *must* be shared. This is not the case with תועבה and D-anthropocentric holiness.

In the P worldview, the requirements upon the person that the attainment of holiness demands are particularly obedience to Yahweh, and the performance of certain highly-specified and priest-mediated rituals such as those involved in the relationship to priests and the sanctuary, sacrifices, and observance of the Day of Atonement. These observances are treated even more rigorously when the subject is not an ordinary individual but a priest. Dynamic holiness, therefore, fits into the priestly divine cosmic order and it may be violated by its anti-type, dynamic impurity, but may be protected and preserved by the adoption of ritual anti-impurity countermeasures.[786]

In contrast, D-impurity and D-holiness reflect an anthropocentric weighting by implicating and emphasizing the role of the ordinary Israelite operating in all things, *under the will of Yahweh*. Static D-holiness must be seen as a permanent fixture affecting the Israelites in much the same way as the Law itself. It therefore does not change from day to day and so does not reflect behaviour and failures of obedience. Static holiness depends entirely on the relationship between Yahweh and the people who make up the nation of Israel: it is essentially a defining statement of what is allowed or prohibited, proper or improper. Because Yahweh has created a permanent system of holiness, any ritual practised under this system can and must only happen if so ordered by Yahweh: ritual is not necessary to create or preserve what Yahweh has ordained. Static holiness, being

---

784 Jeffrey Stackert, *Rewriting the Torah: Literary Revision in Deuteronomy and the Holiness Legislation* (Tubingen: Mohr Siebeck, 2007).
785 This distinction perhaps calls to mind the similar, later parallel of katabatic and anabatic Christology.
786 See chapter 3.

derived solely from Yahweh's will and representing a *legal status* has, therefore, no dependence upon worldview and cosmic order or any other form of orderliness and so it is not directly imperilled by static impurity which is, quite simply, a statement of the fact that rules have been broken. Static holiness and static impurity, while co-existing in the Deuteronomic milieu, may not be regarded as type and anti-type like their P-counterparts.

P-ontological (Dynamic) Holiness and D-deontological (Static) Holiness

The priests' inclination to grade holiness has been discussed in relation to Jenson's ideas.[787] However, as Regev points out, it is important to recognize that only dynamic holiness can be graded. Static holiness requires that everything must be one of either of two polar opposites, *sacred* or *not sacred*, where "sacred" means ordained by Yahweh's will, embodied in Yahweh's law and destined specifically for the Israelites. With only two absolute categories, grading is impossible.

Regev speculates upon how the perceptions of what he has classified as dynamic and static holiness may have come about.[788] He supposes that they each reflect a different *Weltanschauung*, derived from different socially and temporally defined *mores* of Israelite society and so formulating historical patterns for the relationship between Yahweh and mankind. He classifies these patterns as *ontological* and *deontological*.

In the priestly *Weltanschauung*, all holiness was derivative save only the holiness of Yahweh; but unclean things were intrinsically unclean so this quality had to be primary and not derivative. Dynamic holiness was, therefore, seen by the priests and so in P-Leviticus, as *ontological* because it relates to nature, both human nature and that which makes up the natural world around. The inter-relationship between man's nature and the universe[789]—in other words his behaviour—is *de facto* a dynamic process because the behaviour of humans affects the nature of the environment and thereby ontology.

In Regev's *deontological* model, which corresponds to static-holiness, there are only two behavioural options: *obedience* and *reward* (and both relate directly to Yahweh). These qualities may be existent or non-existent but they do not have specifiable anti-types. Disciplined behaviour in obedience to the will of Yahweh is the deontological pattern for the relationship between Yahweh and mankind and, therefore, is static and has no effect upon nature or the environment.

Stackert, working from a literary starting-point, has emphasized the difference between P-holiness on the one hand and D-holiness along with H-holiness on

---

[787] Jenson, *Graded Holiness*.
[788] Regev, "Priestly Dynamic Holiness."
[789] See chapter 4.

the other. He sees considerable overlap in a shared legalistic component in D-holiness and H-holiness.[790]

Stackert identifies areas of correspondence in D and H textual sources both in overall structure and in details, along with similarities in the treatment of legal topics and the sequence of law-making over time. He also identifies areas of lexical, grammatical, and syntactical congruence. Stackert does not specifically concern himself with the matter of impurity but bases his argument around the laws on asylum, manumission, and (especially) tithes. Nevertheless, the identification of such similarities opens up the way for speculation that the undoubtedly observed correspondences between D-holiness/abomination and H-holiness/moral-impurity may signify, if not common authorship, a common hortatory purpose such that the H material may be an update of aspects of D-Torah. Stackert suggests that legislation for holiness practices, as documented in H specifically though not entirely, depended on prior knowledge of Deuteronomy. He postulates that "Holiness legislators ... employ a method of literary revision in which they reconceptualize source material according to their own ideological biases." In other words, as suggested in chapter 2, the H-code in Leviticus may be seen as paraenetic for the people: effectively re-writing the P-material, to include all of the people within its scope. Stackert calls this "super law" and supposes that the intention of the H authors was to supersede P-law by something more universal and possibly more appealing and up-to-date. This task involved using a multi-source approach where the importing of D material in particular allowed for a reformulation which better fitted the currently perceived best objectives.

When considering all of these differences between Leviticus and Deuteronomy, it is important to bear in mind the mechanisms that have taken place in their transmission. Significant difficulty must have presented itself to redactors in the form of the tradition demanding that sacred texts may not be altered. We know from examples such as the story of the creation or that of Noah, that the remedy for this was generally the simplistic ploy of interdigitating new material with old in a way that sometimes defied logic.

צרעת IN BIBLICAL PASSAGES BEYOND THE TORAH

A search for the lexeme *lep** in the Hebrew Bible beyond the Torah produces only fourteen "hits" in the נביאים and the כתובים. Of these, 10 "hits" are in the Deuteronomic History (the canonical books of Deuteronomy, Joshua, Judges, Samuel, and Kings/Former Prophets) and 4 "hits" are in Chronicles. These are the narrative examples of צרעת that Lieber considers to be case-histories of psoriasis and Baden and Moss consider to be associated with sin. Mention

---

790 Stackert, *Rewriting the Torah*.

Job's Illness: Was it צרעת?

Many authors have written on Job and some have suggested that Job's illness may have been צרעת or even "leprosy" [*sic*] even though the word צרעת is nowhere to be found in that biblical book.[791] The most often cited reasoning for this proposition is the presence, in the Book of Job (2:7), of the word שחין, which also appears in Lev 13:23. The two instances may be compared:

ויצא השטן מאת פני יהוה ויך את־איוב בִּשְׁחִין רע מכף רגלו (עד) [וְעַד] קדקדו

ἐξῆλθεν δὲ ὁ διάβολος ἀπὸ τοῦ κυρίου καὶ ἔπαισεν τὸν Ιωβ ἕλκει πονηρῷ ἀπὸ ποδῶν ἕως κεφαλῆς

> So Satan went forth from the presence of the Lord, and smote Job with sore boils from the sole of his foot unto his crown. (Job 2:7)

ואם־תחתיה תעמד הבהרת לא פשתה צָרֶבֶת הַשְּׁחִין הוא וטהרו הכהן

ἐὰν δὲ κατὰ χώραν μείνῃ τὸ τηλαύγημα καὶ μὴ διαχέηται οὐλὴ τοῦ ἕλκους ἐστίν καὶ καθαριεῖ αὐτὸν ὁ ἱερεύς

> But if the bright spot stay in its place, and be not spread, it is the scar of the boil; and the priest shall pronounce him clean. (Lev 13:23)

In the case of Leviticus, the word צרבת is usually translated as "scar" and is a quite different word from צרעת.[792] It is a noun in the construct state and is used in the expression צרבת השחין which quite clearly refers to a *physical sign and not a disease*. The term refers to the scarring left behind in the aftermath of an abscess—a boil—which has completely or partially healed, probably after spontaneous disemburthening of pus or as the result of surgical drainage by lancing. This abscess is likely originally to have been the consequence of a bacterial infection, but there is nothing to suggest any direct causative association with צרעת particularly in Job's case. Boils themselves were very common in pre-antibiotic days[793] and were often seen as being associated with misfortune and as a divine consequence of misdeeds.[794] There are two notable non-Levitical biblical references to boils besides those affecting Job (2:7). Both of these (Exod 9:11; Deut 28:27), use the word שחין which is almost universally translated as "boils" or "ulcers" (LXX = ἕλκος -εος, τό; Vulgate = *ulcus -eris, n*).

---

791 See variatim: D. J. A. Clines, *Job 1–20*, WBC Vol. 17 (Dallas, TX: Word Books, 1989); D. J. A. Clines, *Job 21–37*, WBC Vol. 18a (Nashville, TN: Thomas Nelson, 2006); D. J. A. Clines, *Job 38–42*, WBC Vol. 18b (Nashville, TN: Thomas Nelson, 2011). E. P. Dhorme, *A Commentary on the Book of Job*; [Le livre de Job], trans. Harold Knight (London: Nelson, 1967). C. L. Seow, *Job 1–21: Interpretation and Commentary* (Grand Rapids, MI: Eerdmans, 2013).
792 For more details see chapter 6 and also TDOT and Clines, ed., *Dictionary of Classical Hebrew*.
793 Hippocrates et al., *Hippocrates*.
794 Avalos, *Illness and Health Care in the Ancient Near East*; Prioreschi, *A History of Medicine*.

Both boils and ulcers[795] would be expected to heal by scarring and the phrase צרבת השחין would seem a very proper and accurate way of describing the endpoint of this sequence of events. In none of these cases is there any implication or suggestion of צרעת or "leprosy".

While boils appear to occupy a central place in the constellation of misfortunes afflicting Job, a psychiatric diagnosis seems more appropriate given the symptomatology and such was suggested by Jung[796] and more recently by Kahn.[797] Given the dearth of evidence relating to psychiatric illness in the Hebrew Bible, this singular example is worth considering in respect of the biblical *healthcare↔wholeness↔holiness* relationship.

The clue to a psychiatric diagnosis first appears at the beginning of the Book when Job's premorbid personality is described (Job 1:1), as "perfect/whole/integrated" but clearly also obsessional and therefore fragile. As Job's misfortunes accrue, his symptomatology progresses through *psychosomatic → psychoneurotic → psychotic* phases to which *obsessional neurosis, reactive-depression* and *paranoia* become super-added. These states represent different and deepening expressions of the same underlying morbidity. Job's decline accords with Freud's (and Melanie Klein's) view that the *ego*, under pressure, gives way to overwhelming doubt and uncertainty. This manifests itself as Job's forceful and repeated questioning of accepted viewpoints.

While the evidence for dermatological and systemic disease reported from the Land of Uz is so non-specific as to be baffling to the present-day physician (or surgeon), the modern psychiatrist could easily identify Job's mental state from the biblical account. Job's obsessional personality is a case in point: his total identification by himself and others as תם means that he has an impossible task in living up to expectations. In an attempt to achieve this, he becomes obsessional even in the smallest thing. Such a fragile personality under pressure easily succumbs to neurosis and ultimately to psychosis.

A rudimentary form of psychotherapy is instituted when the "friends"—scarcely psychotherapists—seek to end Job's isolation on the ash-heap; but the actual cure comes from within Job himself. As in all psychoanalysis, the crucial factor is the development of *insight*. There are clues in the text as to how this is acquired but the result is quite different from the simple picture of the old Job restored to health. A new Job-description reveals that his obsessional insistence on exact measure ("skin for skin") in his dealings with man and Yahweh has given way to a new, integrated personality. The new Job is willing to settle for less than his due or graciously to accept more than his due.

---

795 Which, of course, are completely different in respect of causation and pathological presentation.
796 C. G. Jung, *Answer to Job* [Antwort auf Hiob] trans. R. F. C. Hull (London: Routledge and Kegan Paul, 1979).
797 Kahn and Solomon, *Job's Illness*.

Job's "cure" appears to have been effected through a sort of DIY-psychotherapy in which he derives insight by talking to a variety of people: notably the "friends", Elihu, and God. There is no clear strategy for directing the patient to acquire his own insight so this is not good psychotherapy. Eventually it seems the tit-for-tat, "skin-for-skin" obligations of a perfect man and his God no longer obsess him and he has renewed his mental integrity. This is clear from the story, but if we are to accept this as treatment we must be able to see a progression-in-reverse of Job's symptoms. Such a progression is not to be found from evidence in the text. A mortal psychiatrist may understand and quantify Job's mental decline, but to comprehend the *auto-psychotherapy* behind his recovery is beyond the power of men.

While a psychiatric diagnosis for Job seems to be well supported by the Hebrew text, we may be tempted, nevertheless, to ask, "Do we need a psychiatric view of Job?" The question parallels that for a medical/pathological view of צרעת and provides endless opportunity for speculation and argument. In the end it must depend upon whether or not we favour a naturalistic, analytical, deductive approach to biblical medical conundrums or not. We must ask, bearing in mind earlier caveats about *hyperdiagnosis*, "Is the 'medical' approach at variance with the literary and theological aspects?" In the case of Job the answer "Probably not" has been very effectively argued by Kahn,[798] and this argument has been re-stated effectively by Howard,[799] who sets out to diagnose and to de-mythologize biblical medical events—albeit in the New Testament. Howard's central observation is that malignant disease, tuberculosis, neuro-degenerative disorders, and conditions requiring surgery *never* appear in biblical narratives. The conditions that *do* figure are mainly chronic and functional; the majority comprising (*quondam*, "hysterical"), psychogenic or psychosomatic, *dissociation* or *conversion disorders* treatable by *abreaction therapy*. Additionally, minor organic conditions were known to have been treated, at the time, by acquired practical techniques such as *manual couching*.[800] More often than not, it was *symptoms* that were treated rather than the underlying disease process. Such treatments were well-established (and still are), within the repertoire of contemporary faith healers. Of these, there were many, and Jesus and the disciples were examples.

Because of the pious exaggeration afforded to these New Testament medical reportings, especially where speed and extent of recovery was concerned, Howard believes their role in biblical texts to have been primarily hortatory. This New Testament material is mentioned here particularly to stress its contrast with Old Testament and Apocryphal textual material. Given that a comparable role

---

798 Kahn and Solomon, *Job's Illness*.
799 Howard, *Medicine, Miracle and Myth in the New Testament*.
800 Dislocation of the lens by manual pressure upon the eyeball. By forcibly dislocating the opacified lens out of the visual axis, some degree of vision might be recovered albeit such that people might appear as "trees, walking". See (Mark 8:23–24).

for physicians is nowhere evident in the Hebrew Bible, its emergence in New Testament writings must reflect a significant change in attitude towards healthcare and possibly the emergence of a medical profession. This change perhaps had roots in Ben Sira but more probably was the result of Babylonian influence during the exile, together with a concomitant decline in priestly influence. The eventual most likely influence of all was, of course, *Hellenization*. It is to be hoped that these observations justify this brief *excursus* from Leviticus to Job and back; the clear inference being that Job's psychiatric history could never have been compiled under the priestly worldview P-Leviticus.

THE CASE OF ANCIENT ISRAEL

יהוה נתן ויהוה לקח

the Lord gave, and the Lord hath taken away. (Job 1:21)

This famous quotation from Job 1:21 effectively, though unintentionally, summarizes any concept of *healthcare* that ancient Israel might have had. This understanding entails certain potential difficulties for all three of the Abrahamic faiths, especially where there is a tendency to fundamentalism. This difficulty pertains even to the present time and has been well summed-up by Lord Sacks, the recently retired Chief Rabbi of the United Hebrew Congregations of the Commonwealth, who has said, "The historic danger in monotheism has been the willingness of believers to divide humanity into the redeemed against the infidel."[801] The important dogmatic statement known as the *Shema,*

שמע ישראל יהוה אלהינו יהוה אחד

Hear, O Israel: The Lord our God is one Lord (Deut 6:4)

does not differentiate between, for example, monotheism and monolatry.[802] It is probably unhelpful, therefore, to invoke the notion of monotheism in its modern sense, in relation to the subject-matter under consideration here. We are obliged, nevertheless, to consider the view—perhaps employing the less controversial umbrella of *Yahwism*—that God both dispenses and alleviates disease, as having been essential to the development of any interrelationship between priestly activities and inchoate healthcare.[803] The development of Yahwism and its

---

801 Jonathan Sacks writing in The Times 16th August 2014. It is important, however to be clear about what is meant by monotheism. It should not, in particular, be confused with monolatry or henotheism and, in the case of Ancient Israel, we must be particularly judicious with regard to any assertions made in either context with respect to era. Although by Second Temple times the religion of Israel was embracing monotheism, it is not entirely clear that this process had, by any means, reached the end-point of present day Judaism: there is no doubt that the process was a gradual one. The difficulties we have in dating the book of Leviticus, immediately call into question any associated comments we might choose to make on the evolution of monotheism out of polytheism in Israelite/Jewish religion. While today we recognize and describe the three Abrahamic faiths as monotheistic, applying a particular meaning to the word, practices in pre-exilic times may not have permitted such a clear-cut definition.
802 We must look to Deutero-Isaiah for the textual roots of true monotheism.
803 Of all the major religions and cultures both monotheistic and polytheistic, Christianity is the only one that does not concern itself with ritual defilement and its alleviation. Sunni Islam is also unique in that its

priesthood undoubtedly must be implicated in the genesis of attitudes to both priestly ritual and the development or failure of development of any kind of healthcare profession(s).[804]

If we believe that the Levitical purity laws, at least in seminal form, go back to the pre-exilic *Vorlage(n)* of Leviticus, and that they include the oldest interdictions relating to צרעת and זוב, we may *not* suppose them to have had a purely Yahwistic origin.[805]

We are obliged to suppose, then, that the *Vorlage* of Leviticus was likely to have been written in a polytheistic hierarchical milieu where other, lesser gods or godlets were undoubtedly recognized and in some sense worshipped, perhaps, in some cases, specifically in relation to medical matters. Yahweh, nevertheless, became increasingly seen as יהוה צבאות and may eventually have come to occupy a presidential role so as in time to become considerably more than simply *primus inter pares*.

Over the time of the evolution of the book of Leviticus from *Vorlage* to redacted final text in exilic or post-exilic times, the priestly worldview had been instituted and its influence established, but having reached its peak of efficacy was latterly on the wane. It seems likely that during such a period of evolution, the priesthood moved more quickly towards the idea of a single, or at least presidential god, than the population at large; but it is unclear when and how far this viewpoint became incorporated into priestly texts. Coincidentally, the activities of the priests gradually took on a more pyramidal shape with an

---

purity/impurity regulations do not recognize—let alone emphasize—ceremonially contagious contamination of human beings: Ze'ev Maghen, "Close Encounters: Some Preliminary Observations on the Transmission of Impurity in Early Sunnī Jurisprudence," *IL&S* 6, no. 3 (1999): 348–92. See also, M S. Smith, *The Origins of Biblical Monotheism: Israel's Polytheistic Background and the Ugaritic Texts* (Oxford: Oxford University Press, 2001), 167–178. See also, F. L. Cross and Elizabeth A. Livingstone, *The Oxford Dictionary of the Christian Church* (Oxford: Oxford University Press, 2005).

804 Smith and others have written at length on the evolutionary processes necessary to of establish an Israelite godhead and Judaism. He postulates a gradual development from early ideas of royal gods through an Israelite national god (or gods) into three models deriving from earlier myths and re-using these myths for specific new purposes. Smith believes that the three models for the functional nature of an otherwise indeterminate godhead evolved. These were: (1) a priestly model, where the cosmos was seen as a holy place analogous to the sanctuary. This is the model that best fits in with ideas of priestly ritual purity/impurity and it has the particular advantage in being independent of number where god(s) are involved. (2) A wisdom model where wisdom takes on a female persona as in Proverbs, and (3) an apocalyptic model. See: Smith, *The Origins of Biblical Monotheism*, 167–178. See also, Cross and Livingstone, The Oxford Dictionary of the Christian Church.

805 Yahwism presumably came about by degrees so that the establishment of genuine monotheism in Judaism has a terminus a quo generally accepted as no earlier than the Second Temple period. There it came to occupy as important a place in worship as it did in doctrine. In the pre-exilic period, however, other deities besides Yahweh undoubtedly persisted and were worshipped to a variable degree both in Israel and Judah. Biblical evidence for this is traditionally held to be the expression יהוה צבאות, "Lord of Hosts". It is entirely possible that now forgotten deities, specifically involved with medical matters, may have been included in any such pantheon, just as they were in Egypt or Mesopotamia and, much later, in Greece. It is likely that the social circumstances of the exile may have been the stimulus which triggered a gradual consolidation of such ideas about worship towards strict monotheistic Yahwism. Equally, it has been suggested that members of a pre-existing purely Yahwistic sub-group among the exiled Israelites may have selectively prospered by either actively or passively ingratiating themselves with their captors. There is, however, no doubt that a pre-exilic minority of Yahweh-worshippers had become a powerful and active majority by the Hellenic period. Consolidation of monotheism was undoubtedly further brought about by the Maccabean reaction against the Seleucid king Antiochus Epiphanes and by the time of the Roman period, Jewish monotheism was firmly established. See, L. W. Hurtado, "Monotheism," in *The Eerdmans Dictionary of Early Judaism*, ed. John Joseph Collins and Daniel C. Harlow (Grand Rapids, MI: Eerdmans, 2010).

increasing concentration of power in the Jerusalem temple and a decline in the number of the individual sanctuaries throughout the land. Priestly activity and ritual were thus significantly changed by the Second Temple period, and such a change would have reduced the opportunity for the priest to be involved in diagnostic activities and so increased the need for some form of written regulations containing advice about צרעת and זוב that could be readily available for the indoctrination of the the masses. One might, therefore, imagine that in a Levitical *Vorlage*, צרעת and זוב could have had an early association with medical deities and so appeared in a context less directly associated with Yahweh. However, for the late redactors who operated in an environment where a single god was preeminent and who were faced with the indefeasible nature of Scripture, the tolerance—even encouragement—of pietic licence, and a geographical concentration of the priesthood, the specifics of the aetiology of these conditions almost certainly needed adjustment to fit in with the *Zeitgeist*.[806]

An exponent of what might be called the traditional view of the relationship between attribution of the genesis and cure of disease to a single deity and the evolution of medical thinking is that of W. A. Mason.[807] Mason believes that in ancient civilizations there operated variously mantic, animist, demonological, metaphysical, and theurgic attitudes to, and interpretations of, sickness and death.[808] He believes the theurgic approach to have been central in Hebrew medicine and asserts, "The theocratic principle dominated the moral, social and political life of the Jewish people. ... There [was seen to be] but one God the source of all goodness and health, but also of all sickness and imperfection of body and mind. Such concepts and religious ideals submerge, though they do not entirely eradicate the animistic and demonic concepts and the magic medicine that followed in their wake." As evidence for the retention of at least

---

806 The late Cuthbert Simpson is one of a few writers who have tackled, from a textual standpoint, the progression of polytheism into Yahwism in earliest Israel. His extensive book of 675 pages deals primarily with the emergence of the Jahvist [sic] tradition and so tends to dwell particularly on J and E material. Its being based around and so championing the Documentary Hypothesis makes it rather unfashionable today. Although Simpson makes relatively few comments about the priesthood, one of these offers some insight. Regarding the origins of the levitical priesthood, Simpson states, "It seems likely that many local priesthoods, later regarded as levitical, were levitical only by a kind of legal fiction; that is, they had been admitted into the priestly caste of Levi, and so had come to be reckoned as members of the 'tribe'. In view of the fact, indicated by Josh 24:1–25, 8:30–34, that as late as the date of the compilation of the E document one of the salient features of the cult of the Oak of Moreh seems to have been a ceremony which had originated in the pre-Jahvist days of the sanctuary, it is by no means impossible that its priesthood was originally a non-Jahvist priesthood which, like the Levites at Kadesh, had identified themselves with Jahvism." Was this an early example of social climbing as a career move? If the priests had had to enter Israelite society as if intruders from outside, they would undoubtedly have had first to operate a system of give-and-take in order to become absorbed into the genius loci and to establish themselves as credible and ultimately eiusdem generis. See, Simpson, *The Early Traditions of Israel*, 456 FN 3.
807 W. A. Mason, "The Monotheistic Concept and the Evolution of Medical Thought," *Phylon* 12, no. 3 (1951): 255–63. Today, Mason's paper might be considered to be euphuistic and overly florid in its use of language and thought rather tendentious. It is certainly dogmatic in its approach but, unlike much that has been written on Israelite religious practices, Mason, at least, considers the medical implications as more than an "aside".
808 See also, M. J. Geller, "Taboo in Mesopotamia: A Review Article," *JCS* 42, no. 1 (1990): 105–17; also Geller, *Ancient Babylonian Medicine*. These two articles offer a direct comparison between Mesopotamia and Israel as regards the inter-reactions between religion and medicine.

some of the old magic and manticism by the Hebrews, Mason cites the following passage from Isa 47:13,

> נלאית ברב עצתיך יעמדו־נא ויושיעך (הברו) [הברי] שמים החזים בכוכבים מודיעם לחדשים מאשר יבאו עליך

> Thou art wearied in the multitude of thy counsels: let now the astrologers, the stargazers, the monthly prognosticators, stand up, and save thee from the things that shall come upon thee. (Isa 47:13)

It is perhaps because of the indefeasibility of sacred texts that this message persists; it was clearly countermanded by the time of H-Leviticus (19:26).

> לא תאכלו על־הדם לא תנחשו ולא תעוננו

> Ye shall not eat any thing with the blood: neither shall ye use enchantments, nor practise augury. (Lev 19:26)

It is important to realize that Mason is not postulating Yahwism as specifically having brought about the Hebrews' attitudes to medical matters: given the sparsity of evidence, that would be a step too far. After all, he argues that although, for the Hebrews, these effects were held to be the result of direct divine or spiritual action, this explanation was, in fact, no different from that held by certain polytheistic societies. Such is suggested *prima facie* to the reader of Homer, Virgil, and other such authors. However, according to Mason, the difference between what he calls the Greek, "Universe of natural law" and the Hebrew "Universe of moral law" was that only the latter embodied a strong element of ritual. It was for the priests to codify and administer the operation of this ritual as they were effectively God's representatives on earth and symbols of his power. From them the entire structure of Jewish social and political culture was to develop and it follows logically that if health and disease were controlled by God in the cosmic, universal sphere, then in the local sphere these processes and everything to do with them should devolve upon the priests. By its very nature of clinging to a worldview embodying cosmic, social, and cultic elements, priestly doctrine became rigid and ritualized with little or no regard for any aetiological or pathophysiological ideas that might have entailed. In such a situation it is easy to suppose that those diseases that appeared to violate categories of cleanliness, appearance, and reproductive capacity of the body—i.e. those physiological aspects of life that most obviously (and visibly) interacted with religion—should have been given priority in the daily dealings of the priests around the sanctuary. Minor ailments, because they did not impinge upon priestly activities and worldview, were simply not important enough for the priests to be bothered with.

A similar, if rather simplistic, viewpoint was expressed by Barton, writing in 1930[809] where he attributes (somehow) to Yahwism that, "All savages have fixed traditions and taboos about foods". Because of this viewpoint, which Barton extends to other taboos, all that he believes to be necessary are two verses, Exod 15:26:

ויאמר אם־שמוע תשמע לקול יהוה אלהיך והישר בעיניו תעשה והאזנת למצותיו ושמרת כל־חקיו כל־המחלה אשר־שמתי במצרים לא־אשים עליך כי אני יהוה רפאך

and he said, If thou wilt diligently hearken to the voice of the Lord thy God, and wilt do that which is right in his eyes, and wilt give ear to his commandments, and keep all his statutes, I will put none of the diseases upon thee, which I have put upon the Egyptians: for I am the Lord that healeth thee. (Exod 15:26)

and Deuteronomy 32:39:

ראו עתה כי אני אני הוא ואין אלהים עמדי אני אמית ואחיה מחצתי ואני ארפא ואין מידי מציל

See now that I, even I, am he, And there is no god with me: I kill, and I make alive; I have wounded, and I heal: And there is none that can deliver out of my hand. (Deut 32:39)

God alone dispenses and heals all diseases: there is no need, as in other cultures, for physicians—or perhaps even priests—to practise medicine.[810]

Since on the evidence that is available, we cannot comment with authority on whether the Levitical purity laws and rituals presented in the Hebrew Bible were devised and formulated to operate in a wholly Yahwistic society or were inherited from their polytheistic antecedents. We must accept that, it would be a great mistake to draw any factitious distinction between natural phenomena and the work of Yahweh.[811]

Whatever conclusions we may draw about the relationships between *healthcare* and the Levitical purity laws, the influence of Yahwism is unavoidable but *not* overwhelming. Equally important may have been gradual changes in the priestly worldview through the Second Temple period into the period of Persian and Hellenic influence. Another possible effect was the evolution of priestly rituals

---

809 George Aaron Barton, *A History of the Hebrew People from the Earliest Times to the Year 70 A.D., Largely in the Language of the Bible* (New York; London: Century Co., 1930).
810 In a civilization where death was not uncommon, even at an early age, it is unlikely that mortality statistics would have been collected to measure the success of any healthcare regimen.
811 Josephus, with the eye of retrospection clearly believed that monotheism was the essential ingredient of Judaism and of the Israelite people. Θεὸς γὰρ εἷς καὶ τὸ Ἑβραίων γένος ἕν. But such a view is now known to be hopelessly oversimplified and indeed, historically innaccurate, not least because Josephus is unclear about what he means by monotheism in the contest of Yahwism. (Josephus, *Antiquities*, 4:201).

from the essentially parochial, taking place in a multitude of sanctuaries, to centralization in the Temple of Jerusalem.[812]

We remain totally ignorant of how far those aspects of healthcare with which the priests elected not to concern themselves flourished or perished in Israelite society with changing *mores* and the passage of time.

The priests concerned themselves intently with events that appeared to interfere with their rituals and practices; they ignored anything that did not. It may therefore be concluded that if they had any concept of *hygiene* it was purely *sacramental hygiene*.

---

[812] Nevertheless, it is not unreasonable to suppose that the priests felt empowered to operate and even modify the simple idea of divine influence insofar as the social and political aspects of their work demanded it and it was with such modifications that the levitical laws were formulated and the levitical texts written. The practices relating to contagion and isolation were probably of priestly origin and contingent upon the obligations imposed upon them by their perception of divine law in the conduct of their everyday duties. This is, in effect, the principle of precedence at law which has a distinguished pedigree in underpinning the better legal systems even up to the present day.

Chapter 13

HEALTHCARE, WHOLENESS, AND HOLINESS: SYNERGY OR TENSION?

The foregoing chapters have contained separate investigations into aspects of the relationship between wholeness and holiness. These were seen in terms of the interaction of, on the one hand nosology and practical medicine, and on the other hand the priestly worldview and ideology of ritual underlying the Levitical purity laws, their formulation, transmission, doctrinal purpose, and day-to-day application. It is now appropriate to ask how far this relationship was one of synergy or one of tension.

HEALTHCARE ↔ WHOLENESS ↔ HOLINESS

In order to discuss the conclusions of this study, one must return to and reconsider the working hypothesis stated in chapter 1:

1. That in the worldview of the Levitical priesthood, holiness was established and maintained through ritual purity.
2. That ritual purity in individuals depended upon their organic integrity—wholeness.
3. That wholeness was manifested in terms of bodily appearance and reproductive capacity and, to a lesser extent, by the absence of blemish.
4. That wholeness, and therefore ritual purity, was compromised by violation of these categories.
5. That the most serious of these violations, צרעת and זוב were characterized by their being contagious.
6. That both צרעת and זוב had features in common with, but were not wholly identifiable as, diseases known today.
7. That the priestly countermeasures—sacramental hygiene—taken against these infractions of wholeness were aimed solely at the preservation of holiness and should not be interpreted as rudimentary public health medicine.
8. That their later adoption into the field of medical care was fortunate but unintentional.

This can be considered in three stages:

Healthcare ↔ Wholeness

This interaction has been investigated in chapter 3. Rudimentary practices of medical care such as those of Egypt and Mesopotamia *may* have been passed on. However, almost nothing has been handed down to indicate if this was the case and how it operated in Israel. This failure was probably due to the following factors:

1. Medical care, such as it was, may have variously involved magicians, diviners, mantics, sorcerers, and the priests.
2. The magicians, diviners, mantics and sorcerers had no tradition of producing written texts so that no account of their practices has survived for scrutiny.
3. The priests, who did leave a textual heritage, may have wished to preserve for themselves the business of dealing with צרעת and זוב for reasons discussed above (passim) and/or never made the connection that these conditions were in the nature of organic disease or injury.

In fact, it seems there was no formalized practice of *healthcare* in ancient Israel. What the magicians and mantics did was unlikely to effect anything curative unless by chance. Rudimentary first-aid, perhaps even to the extent of encompassing bone-setting, was presumably available in the domestic sphere. All of this was probably *ad hoc* and unrefined.

Wholeness ↔ *Holiness*

Two models for wholeness necessary for the establishment and maintenance of ritual purity within the worldview of the Levitical priesthood have been postulated:

1. Sociological model (Turner, Douglas)—ritual purity entails the absence of any antitypicality of appearance (visible body parts) or compromise of reproductive function.
2. Taxonomical model (various authors)—ritual purity is a maintained state of sacramental hygiene

There is no evidence to support one of these models over the other, but what is important is that in either model it is the same conditions that ultimately trigger impurity. In the first case it is the presence of antitypicality *per se* that sets the individual apart in a state of impurity. In the second case the antitypicality is seen less as an affection of the individual and more as a potential for upsetting directly the priest-mediated state of sacramental hygiene.

As far back as early Mesopotamian civilization, there appears to have been a perceived association between *holiness* and *cleanliness*.[813] In Akkadian, the word *ellu* (Ideogram = KUG = 𒆪),[814] denoted both of these states with *cleanliness* implying not only the absence of dirt but also the positive attribute of brilliance or luminosity. Smith has seen this dualistic idea continued through Ugaritic

---

[813] Geller, *Ancient Babylonian Medicine*; Geller, "Taboo in Mesopotamia."
[814] Oppenheim and Reiner, eds., *The Assyrian Dictionary*, Vol. 4, 102–106. Borger, *Mesopotamisches Zeichenlexikon*, 194.

where the same meaning is given to the word *ṭhr* (𐤈𐤄𐤓 = adj = pure, sparkling),⁸¹⁵ into Aramaic (טהר = verb = be ritually clean),⁸¹⁶ and eventually into Hebrew to appear in the Hebrew Bible as טהור in the verse:

ויראו את אלהי ישראל ותחת רגליו כמעשה לבנת הספיר וכעצם השמים לטהר:

and they saw the God of Israel; and there was under his feet as it were a paved work of sapphire stone, and as it were the very heaven for clearness. (Exod 24:10)

Smith's conclusion is that the idea of purity—which is cultic holiness—is "Based analogically upon the profane notion of cleanliness both in its negative connotation as free of dirt and in its positive connotation of brilliance."⁸¹⁷

If, like Mary Douglas, we suppose "free of dirt" to mean "all matter in the right place", this idea seems not too far removed from Douglas's and Turner's appreciation of the *wholeness↔holiness* interrelationship and its primarily sociological undertones. However, as a notion it sits less harmoniously with the interaction of the *wholeness↔holiness* tension and the טהור↔טמא relationship as seen by authors such as Milgrom, Neusner, Frymer-Kensky, and Klawans. This is, surely, because their appreciation of and approach to the situation has been largely quantitative and taxonomical whilst that of Mary Douglas's has been qualitative and aetiological.⁸¹⁸ In all cases, however, the relationship of un-cleanness (≡ *un-wholeness* ≡ *antitypicality*) to holiness is one of reciprocal exclusion and so holiness cannot exist where there is un-wholeness.

In the Levitical writings of the Hebrew Bible, all holiness apart from the holiness of God is seen to be derivative, but unclean things are regarded as intrinsically unclean and not derivatively unclean. Uncleanliness is, therefore, a primary quality of intrinsically unclean things that offend the eye or compromise the life-force. Examples of each might be צרעת, *(dermopathic) platydysmorphism*—which was seen as being defiling like the flesh of the dead—and זב which was seen as jeopardizing the future of Israel. They confer the sort of social antitypicality Mary Douglas recognized and so they probably functioned in the priests' minds, not as indicators of illness or disease, but as *delible marks of impurity*. Both of these infractions of holiness have persisted into later Christianity, though their importance became altered with the geographical spread of religion(s) and with measures to control disease. Over time, and particularly after the crusades, צרעת became confused with true leprosy and thereby served the church well, providing ecclesial power by means of the

---

815 Smith, *The Origins of Biblical Monotheism*, 888.
816 Sokoloff, *A Dictionary of Jewish Babylonian Aramaic*, 494.
817 For an interesting, semi-mathematical and highly informative discourse on analogy see: Mascall, *Existence and Analogy*.
818 See chapter 5.

induction and control of religious fear and obedience in a climate of *oderint dum metuant*.

Equally widespread but more persistent in reaching into present-day religious practices, was the influence of זוב which fitted so well into the near universal obsession of religious thinkers—ancient and modern—with sexual sin. The reasoning behind the persistence of the unholy consequences of זוב has been well summed-up by MacCulloch: "A man's semen contained the entire foetus in embryo: so anything which stopped male seed doing its job was an act of murder—anything, from masturbation to contraception to same-sex sexual relations. The idea was taken up by the second-century Christian teacher Clement of Alexandria, and it has become deeply embedded in the Christian moral tradition."[819] Holiness, therefore, everywhere apart from the holiness of God, was derived as a direct consequence of the wholeness ($\equiv$ cleanliness) of the subject-matter. The priests held themselves to be the arbiters and guardians of wholeness/cleanliness among their own kind and among the population at large. As such their role was diagnostic and preventive but never therapeutic. The text of Leviticus is the priests' formal statement—strictly contained within their worldview—of the doctrine of the *wholeness↔holiness* relationship and of any dogma to be derived therefrom.

Healthcare ↔ Holiness

Smith has defined holiness in the West Semitic world as, "A general characteristic adhering to material realia and social processes in shrines, including theophany."[820] The question that faces us here is how far, if at all, the priests considered *healthcare* as one of those *realia*. This in turn, leads to a pair of opposing propositions as to whether the priests:

1. Formulated the purity laws by applying prior knowledge of diseases and their management.

Or

2. Formulated the purity laws de novo and incidentally incorporated practices nowadays associated with preventive medicine.

It has been suggested in that features of disease might have been applied to curses and that the *contagion of misfortune* might have arisen and become associated with interdictions already applied to impurity. Working along these lines, Kaplan has suggested, on the grounds that isolation for צרעת was required only for what he calls "moral contagion", that the symptoms and signs described in Leviticus were intentionally contrived to fit no known disease. This idea seems

---

819 D. MacCulloch, *Reformation, Europe's House Divided 1490–1700*, Vol. 2 (London: Folio Society, 2013), 650–651.
820 Smith, *The Origins of Biblical Monotheism*, 93.

highly tendentious and it is most unlikely that the priesthood of the time would have had the knowledge and experience, or even the deviousness, to think up such a ploy. This arrangement would, theoretically, exclude those whose only sin was to be affected by an obvious cutaneous disease. In any case, it is virtually impossible to accept this view when, from the dearth of evidential material from secular sources, we can have no possible idea of what, if any, diseases were known at the times of both the Levitical *Vorlage* and its later redaction(s).[821] This viewpoint, like that of many other authors, credits the priests with more technical knowledge than they can possibly have had.

A more difficult question is whether those—later-to-become medical—principles such as diagnosis, contagion, and quarantine arose purely out of the priestly ethos of purity legislation and practices or whether they were observed by the priests as coming from earlier civilizations, like Mesopotamia, where there was a relatively well-developed medical tradition. Equally, the priests could have observed them in a developing secular healthcare milieu of which no evidence remains. If either was the case, we have to find a reason why the Israelite priesthood chose to concern itself with medical matters in the first place. On balance, it seems unlikely that they would see any purpose or virtue in this. It does not, however, rule out the possibility that they identified principles and practices from these other sources as offering useful tools for the management of ritual impurity.

Historically, in any society, ancient and modern, it has been the priests' job to maintain holiness and the physicians' job to maintain wholeness (in the anatomical, physiological, and psychological sense). If a particular society chooses to adopt the duality of the *wholeness↔holiness/type↔antitype* arrangement and physicians do not really exist in any powerful or effective way, the entire *wholeness↔holiness* problem might fall to the priests. It does not really matter whether the practices relating to diagnosis, contagion, and quarantine, as applied to ritual impurity, were formulated by the priests *de novo* or borrowed from other more medically competent societies. In either case, it is easy to see how they might have become embodied in an existing intellectual framework, with which the priests were already familiar, to end up as a *wholeness↔holiness* paradigm for incorporation into the Levitical (im)purity laws.

It was noted above, that there appear to be several possible explanations as to why we have so little material concerned with *healthcare* in ancient Israel. It may now be possible to expand that reasoning a little further by suggesting that passive and active elements may have been in operation in formulating the (im)purity laws to include צרעת and זוב and quasi-medical practices such as

---

[821] D. L. Kaplan, "Biblical Leprosy: An Anachronism Whose Time has Come," *J Am Ac Derm* 28, no. 3 (1993): 507–10.

diagnosis, contagion and isolation without coincidentally requiring the parallel development of true medical practices. Important influences might have been:

A. Passive

1. Bias in transmission—where, out of religious or pietic zeal or for other reasons, it has been seen by later redactors as necessary either to boost the role of the priesthood or to play down the role of secular healthcare workers. An example might be the Essenes at Qumran.

2. Literary—it is possible that if a physician class existed, it may not have been sufficiently educated to leave behind textual evidence.

3. Geographical—The majority of textual material is from Judah the Southern Kingdom. We have little information about practices in the Northern Kingdom.

B. Active

1. There was an active suppression by the priesthood of either medical practices or medical reporting.

Nevertheless, whether or not the priests thought of צרעת and זוב specifically as afflictions/diseases as we would think of them today, they invariably attributed to them a divine aetiology. It seems unlikely that they were operating in such a way as to try specifically to control disease, public health or the general hygiene of the population as they almost certainly had no notion of these concepts or any idea of therapeutic methods or the principles of preventive medicine. Rather, they were operating a preventive policy designed *only* to control the incidence and spread of (non-physical) ritual impurity and so protect individuals, society and the Israelite homeland from its defiling effects. As such they were operating within the framework of the cosmic, social, and cultic principles demanded by their established worldview, so as both to vouchsafe and safeguard *sacramental hygiene*. It follows that they were not in any way, concerned with *hygiene* as it is understood today.

A system of *sacramental hygiene* first requires a means of recognizing and measuring ritual impurity within the individual and within the population. It is easy to see, in the light of such reasoning, how failure of the reproductive process and so how זוב might have been used to explain infertility and a dearth of progeny or how visible disfigurement, as manifested by a class of major and/or minor afflictions of the (dermopathic) platydysmorphic type, might have become mentally associated and thereafter identified as צרעת. Because priests operated in the sphere of the holy, their actions would have been seen, above all, as tending to preserve holy dogma embodying the ultimate requirement that *life and death should not and must not be mixed*. Those things that the priests worked to prevent, would most likely have been seen as unholy and so the sufferers from צרעת and זוב would have been readily identifiable as antitypes of holiness.

Although it seems to have been with the diagnosis and treatment of ritual impurity, and not with medical matters that the priests were concerned, their activities must have overlapped with certain practices that were inchoate at that time but which we see today as central to and routine within medical care. In their zeal to preserve טהור and to protect against טמא and תועבה, they, perhaps unconsciously, developed the concepts of contagion and quarantine and instituted what they perceived as cleansing measures—usually sacrificial—to combat these violations of purity. Incidentally these measures may have proved, ultimately, to be advantageous in the field of public health.

Because of the signal imbalance of evidence, when we compare the copious formal hortative Levitical texts, other purely narrative writings from the Hebrew Bible, and also later Jewish sources with the exiguous measure of material from equivalent secular sources, it is almost impossible to be convinced that a fair appraisal of the entire evidential mass can ever be arrived at. Even if the secular data are boosted by extrapolation from the recorded practices of other cultures, it can never be more than hypothesis—and hypotheses are never without their limitations. Newton's advice about hypotheses and the handling of evidence in general should never be forgotten:

> Hypotheſes non fingo. Quicquid enim ex phaenomenis non deducitur, hypotheſis vocanda eſt; et hypotheſes ſeu metaphyſicae, ſeu, phyſicae, ſeu qualitatem occultarum, ſeu mechanicae, in philoſophia experimentali locum non habent. In hac philoſophia propoſitiones deducuntur ex phaenomenis, et redduntur generales per inductionem.[822]

Or Pliny the Elder's pithier reminder in more elegant Latin—*Ne supra crepidam sutor iudicaret*—that we should not draw conclusions beyond the available evidence.[823] With such caveats in operation, it is impossible to apply deductive logic in an even-handed way. So, as far as can be seen from this imbalance of evidence, where *tension* existed between any putative medical establishment of ancient Israel and the substantive priesthood, it was unlikely to have been a result of disagreement over the management of צרעת or זוב or even about the

---

[822] "I feign no hypotheses. For whatever is not deduced from the phenomena must be called a hypothesis; and hypotheses, whether metaphysical or physical, or based on occult qualities, or mechanical, have no place in experimental philosophy. In this philosophy particular propositions are inferred from the phenomena, and afterwards rendered general by induction." (Isaac Newton, *Scholium Generale*, Philosophiae Naturalis Principia Mathematica, 1713.)

[823] "Let a shoemaker not judge above his last" (Pliny the Elder, *Naturalis Historiae* XXXV, xxxvi, 85).

conflict of טמא and טהור: they were simply cultures apart and had no reason to interact either additively or subtractively. As for *synergy*, this happened, but was probably unintended. Its effect was to impinge passively, as a consequence of priestly measures envisaged solely for the preservation of ritual purity, by generating an ethic and operating practical measures for *sacramental hygiene*. These concepts, nevertheless, eventually percolated into the world of ordinary people and there, being applied at a different time, under a different worldview, and in a different place and society, gave rise to the immensely important and practically valuable modern hygienic principles of *contagion* and *isolation*.[824] It would be wrong to suppose, as many authors have, that in the Levitical context, these should be thought of as hygienic measures in the modern, medical, sense because they were not; nor were they ever envisaged to be. That they subsequently found a significant place in preventive medicine appears to have been both fortuitous and fortunate.

---

[824] It is thought-provoking to note that, at the time of writing, there is a near pandemic of Ebola haemorrhagic fever in Western Africa. This disease has a >>90% mortality rate and there is currently no specific treatment or way of contriving immunity. In Western countries a very few cases have survived after maintenance with costly and highly specialized intensive barrier nursing. The only practical way, therefore, to deal with this disease in Africa is identical to that practised in the 1348 Black Death and the 1664 Great Plague of London—a clear understanding of the principles of contagion and isolation, and their rigorous application.

BIBLIOGRAPHY

Abegg, M., P. Flint and E. Ulrich. *The Dead Sea Scrolls Bible*. Edinburgh: T&T Clark, 1999.

Accordance. "Bible Software." Altamonte Springs, FL 32701 USA: Oaktree Software, 2013.

Ackerman, S. "The Blind, the Lame and the Barren Shall Not Come into the House." Pages 29–45 in *Disability Studies and Biblical Literature*. Edited by Candida R. Moss and Jeremy Schipper. New York: Palgrave Macmillan, 2011.

Adamson, P. B. "Schistosomiasis in Antiquity." *Medical History* 20, no. 2 (1976): 176–88.

Adolphs, Ralph, James A. Russell, and Daniel Tranel. "A Role for the Human Amygdala in Recognizing Emotional Arousal from Unpleasant Stimuli." *Psychological Science*, no. 2 (1999): 167–71.

Ahituv, Shmuel. *Echoes from the Past: Hebrew and Cognate Inscriptions from the Biblical Period.* Jerusalem: Carta, 2008.

Alexander, Patrick H. *The SBL Handbook of Style: for Ancient Near Eastern, Biblical, and Early Christian Studies*. Peabody, Mass.: Hendrickson Publishers, 1999.

Ali, Abdullah Yusuf. *The Holy Qur'an (text and translation)*. Birmingham: IPCI Islamic Vision, 1999.

Andersen, Johs G. "Leprosy in Translations of the Bible." *Bible Translator (Ap, O Practical Papers)* 31, no. 2 (1980): 207–12.

Anderson, Adam K. and Elizabeth A. Phelps. "Expression without Recognition: Contributions of the Human Amygdala to Emotional Communication." *Psychological Science*, no. 2 (2000): 106–11.

Anderson, Gary A. *Sin: A History*. New Haven, CT; London: Yale University Press, 2009.

Aristotle. *The Complete Works of Aristotle*. Edited by J Barnes. 2 vols. Princeton, NJ: Princeton University Press, 1984.

Arrian, F. A. X. *The Anabasis of Alexander*. Loeb Classical Library. Cambridge, MA; London: Harvard University Press, 1989.

Avalos, Hector. *Illness and Health Care in the Ancient Near East: the Role of the Temple in Greece, Mesopotamia, and Israel*. Atlanta: Scholars Press, 1995.

Baden, J. S. "The Nature of Barrenness in the Hebrew Bible." Pages 13–25 in *Disability Studies and Biblical Literature*. Edited by Candida R. Moss and Jeremy Schipper. New York: Palgrave Macmillan, 2011.

Baden, J. S. and Candida R. Moss. "The Origin and Interpretation of saraʿat in Leviticus 13–14." *Journal of Biblical Literature* 130, no. 4 (2011): 643–62.

Bafverstedt, B. "Dermatological and Venereal Diseases Told About in the Bible." *Lakartidningen* 68, no. 34 (1971): 3793–802.

Baggini, Julian and Peter S. Fosl. *The Philosopher's Toolkit: A Compendium of Philosophical Concepts and Methods.* Malden, MA; Oxford: Blackwell Publishers, 2003.

Baillie, R. A. and E. E. Baillie. "Biblical Leprosy as Compared to Present-day Leprosy." *South. Med. J.* 75, no. 7 (1982): 855–57.

Barr, J. *Semantics and Biblical Theology: A Contribution to the Discussion.* Congress Volume, Uppsala 1971. Vetus Testamentum Supplement 22. Leiden: Brill, 1972.

Barr, J. *History and Ideology in the Old Testament.* Oxford: Oxford University Press, 2000.

Barr, James, John Barton, and Ernest W. Nicholson. *Bible and Interpretation: The Collected Essays of James Barr.* 3 vols. Oxford: Oxford University Press, 2013.

Barton, George Aaron. *A History of the Hebrew People from the Earliest Times to the Year 70 A.D., Largely in the Language of the Bible.* Prepared by George A. Barton. New York; London: Century Co., 1930.

Bauer, Walter, William Arndt, F. Wilbur Gingrich, and Frederick W. Danker. *A Greek-English Lexicon of the New Testament and Other Early Christian Literature.* 2nd ed. Chicago: University of Chicago Press, 1979.

Baumann, Bill B. "The Botanical Aspects of Ancient Egyptian Embalming and Burial." *Economic Botany* 14, no. 1 (1960): 84–104.

Beeston, A. F. L. *The Arabic Language Today.* London: Hutchinson University Library, 1970.

Beeston, A. F. L. *Written Arabic: An Approach to the Basic Structures.* Cambridge: Cambridge University Press, 1968.

Bennahum, D. A. "Psoriasis, Leprosy and the Dead Sea Valley." *Korot.* 9; 1–2 (1985): 86–89.

Bennett, R. *Diseases of the Bible.* Oxford: Oxford University Press, 1891.

Bevan, V. "Gonorrhoea: An Unlikely Love Affair." *Microbiologist* December (2004): 30–31.

Bibleworks. "Software for Biblical Exegesis and Research." Norfolk, VA: BibleWorks LLC, 2011.

Bienkowski, P. and A. Millard. *Dictionary of the Ancient Near East*. Philadelphia, PA: University of Pennsylvania Press, 2000.

Blackman, Philip, ed. *Mishnayoth* 3rd ed. 6 vols. New York: Judaica Press, 1965.

Bloomfield, M. *Hymns of the Atharva Veda*. Whitefish, MT: Kessinger, 2004.

Blunt, Wilfrid and Sandra Raphael. *The Illustrated Herbal*. Rev. ed. New York: Thames and Hudson, 1994.

Blythin, Islwyn. "Magic and Methodology." *Numen* 17, no. 1 (1970): 45–59.

Borger, R. *Mesopotamisches Zeichenlexikon*. Münster: Ugarit-Verlag, 2004.

Botterweck, G. J., H. Ringgren, and H. J. Fabry. *Theological Dictionary of the Old Testament*. 15 vols. Grand Rapids, MI: Eerdmans, 1995.

Boyd, R. H. "Origin of Gonorrhoea and Non-specific Urethritis." *British Journal of Venereal Diseases* 31 (1955): 246–48.

Brandes, S. B. and J. W. McAninch. "Surgical Methods of Restoring the Prepuce: A Critical Review." *British Journal of Urology* 83, Suppl 1 (1999): 109–13.

Breasted, J. H. *The Edwin Smith Surgical Papyrus: Facsimile, Hieroglyphic Transliteration and Translation*. Chicago, IL: University of Chicago Press, 1930.

Brenner, Athalya. *The Intercourse of Knowledge: On Gendering Desire and 'Sexuality' in the Hebrew Bible*. Biblical Interpretation Series. Vol. 26. Leiden: Brill, 1997.

Brenner, Athalya. The Israelite Woman: Social Role and Literary Type in Biblical Narrative. 2nd ed. New York: Bloomsbury T&T Clark, 2015.

Brodal, A. *Neurological Anatomy: In Relation to Clinical Medicine*. 2nd ed. Oxford: Oxford University Press, 1972.

Brown, F., S. R. Driver, and C. A. Briggs. *A Hebrew and English Lexicon of the Old Testament*. Oxford: Clarendon, 1960.

Browne, S. G. "Some Aspects of the History of Leprosy: The Leprosie of Yesterday." *Proc.R.Soc.Med.* 68, no. 8 (1975): 485–93.

Browne, S. G. "Was Leprosy Common in Palestine in New Testament Times?" *Zambia Nurse J.* 4, no. 3 (1970): 10–11.

Browne, S. G. *Leprosy in the Bible*. London: Christian Medical Fellowship Publications, 1970.

Browne, Stanley G. "'Leprosy' in the New English Bible." *Bible Translator (Ja, Jl Technical Papers)* 22, no. 1 (1971): 45–46.

Bryan, C. P. *The Papyrus Ebers*. African Heritage Classical Research Studies Series. Chesapeake, NY: E.C.A. Associates, 1990.

Buchler, A. *Studies in Sin and Atonement in the Rabbinic Literature of the First Century*. London: Oxford University Press, 1928.

Budge, E. A. Wallis. *Egyptian Hieroglyphic Dictionary*. 2 vols. New York: Dover, 1920.

Budge, E. A. Wallis. *Egyptian Language: Easy Lessons in Egyptian Hieroglyphics with Sign List*. London: Routledge and Kegan Paul, 1910.

Butterfield, Jeremy. *Fowler's Dictionary of Modern English Usage*. 4th ed. Oxford: Oxford University Press, 2015.

Campbell, Antony F. and Mark A. O'Brien. *Sources of the Pentateuch: Texts, Introductions, Annotations*. Minneapolis: Fortress, 1993.

Carroll, Lewis. *Through the Looking Glass*. London: The Folio Society, 1962.

Ceccarelli, G. "Leprosy in the Bible." *Minerva Med.* 85, no. 4 (1994): 197–201.

Celsus, Aulus Cornelius. *De medicina. With an English translation by W. G. Spencer*, Loeb Classical Library. London; Cambridge: William Heinemann, 1935.

Clines, D. J. A., ed. *Dictionary of Classical Hebrew*. 9 vols. Sheffield: Phoenix, 2010.

Clines, D. J. A. *Job 1–20*. Word Biblical Commentary. Vol. 17. Dallas, TX: Word Books, 1989.

Clines, D. J. A. *Job 21–37*. Word Biblical Commentary. Vol. 18a. Nashville, TN: Thomas Nelson, 2006.

Clines, D. J. A. *Job 38–42*. Word Biblical Commentary. Vol 18b. Nashville, TN: Thomas Nelson, 2011.

Cochrane, R. G. "Biblical Leprosy." *Bible Translator (Ap, O Practical Papers)* 12, no. 4 (1961): 202–03.

Cochrane, R. G. "In Defense of the Name 'leprosy'." *Int.J.Lepr.Other Mycobact.Dis.* 38, no. 2 (1970): 207–09.

Cohen, Shaye J. D. *Why Aren't Jewish Women Circumcised? Gender and Covenant in Judaism*. Berkeley; London: University of California Press, 2005.

Collins, John Joseph. "Ecclesiasticus, or the Wisdom of Jesus Son of Sirach." Pages 667–98 in *The Oxford Bible Commentary*. Edited by John Barton and John Muddiman. Oxford: Oxford University Press, 2001.

Collins, John Joseph, and Daniel C. Harlow. *The Eerdmans Dictionary of Early Judaism*. Grand Rapids, MI: Eerdmans, 2010.

Conrad, L. I., and D Wujastyk. *Contagion, Perspectives in Pre-modern Societies*, Aldershot: Ashgate, 2000.

Conrad, L. I. "A Ninth-Century Muslim Scholar's Discussion of Contagion." Pages 137–77 in *Contagion, Perspectives in Pre-modern Societies*. Edited by L. I. Wujastyk and D. Conrad. Aldershot: Ashgate, 2000.

Contineau, J. "Racines et Schèmes dans les Langues Sémitiques." *Actes du XXIe Congrès International des Orientalistes*; Paris 23–24 Juillet 1948 (1949): 93–95.

Coogan, Michael David. *The Oxford Encyclopedia of the Books of the Bible*. 2 vols. New York: Oxford University Press, 2011.

Cowley, A. "Some Remarks on Samaritan Literature and Religion." *The Jewish Quarterly Review* 8, no. 4 (1896): 562–75.

Cross, F. L. and Elizabeth A. Livingstone. *The Oxford Dictionary of the Christian Church*. 3rd ed. Oxford: Oxford University Press, 2005.

Csonka, G. W. "Gonorrhoea." Pages 5.409–5.15 in *Oxford Textbook of Medicine*. Edited by D. J. Weatherall, J. G. G. Ledingham and D. A. Warrell. Oxford: Oxford University Press, 1989.

Danby, H. *The Mishnah*. Oxford: Oxford University Press, 1933.

Dauphin, Claudine. "Leprosy, Lust and Lice : Health and Hygiene in Byzantine Palestine." *Bulletin of the Anglo-Israel Archaeological Society* 15 (1996): 55–80.

Davies, M. L. and T. A. Davies. "Biblical Leprosy: A Comedy of Errors." *J.R.Soc.Med.* 82, no. 10 (1989): 622–23.

Davies, Thomas Witton. *Magic, Divination, and Demonology Among the Hebrews and their Neighbours: Including an Examination of Biblical References and of the Biblical Terms*. London; Leipzig: James Clarke & Co.; M. Spirgatis: 1898.

Davies, Thomas Witton. *Old Testament Words for Magic or in Relation to it*. London; Leipzig: James Clarke & Co; M. Spirgatis, 1898.

Dhorme, E. P. *A Commentary on the Book of Job*. Translated by H. D. Knight. London: Nelson, 1967.

Diamond, James Arthur. "Maimonides on Leprosy: Illness as Contemplative Metaphor." *Jewish Quarterly Review* 96, no. 1 (2006): 95–122.

Dimant, Devorah and Lawrence H. Schiffman. *Time to Prepare the Way in the Wilderness: Papers on the Qumran Scrolls*. Studies on the Texts of the Desert of Judah. Vol. 16. Leiden: Brill, 1995.

Dols, M. W. "Leprosy in Medieval Arabic Medicine." *Journal of the History of Medicine & Allied Sciences* 34 (1979): 314–33.

Doolan Heins, Barbara. "From Leprosy to Shalom and Back Again: A Discourse Analysis of 2 Kings 5." *OPTAT* 2, no. 1 (1988): 20–33.

Douglas, M. *Purity and Danger: An Analysis of Concepts of Pollution and Taboo.* London: Routledge and Keegan Paul, 1966.

Douglas, Mary. "The Forbidden Animals in Leviticus." *Journal for the Study of the Old Testament*, no. 59 (1993): 3–23.

Douglas, Mary. *Leviticus as Literature.* Oxford: Oxford University Press, 1999.

Driver, S. R. *An Introduction to the Literature of the Old Testament.* International Theological Library. New York: Charles Scribner's Sons, 1916.

Durkheim, E. *Les Formes Élémentaires de la Vie Religieuse. French text.* Paris: Presses Universitaire de France, 1979.

Dzierzykray-Rogalski, T. "Paleopathology of the Ptolemaic Inhabitants of the Dakhleh Oasis (Egypt)." *Journal of Human Evolution* 9 (1980): 71–74.

Eimer M, Gosling A., and Duchaine B. "Electrophysiological Markers of Covert Face Recognition in Developmental Prosopagnosia." *Brain* 135 (2012): 542–54.

Elliger, Karl, Rudolf Kittel, Wilhelm Rudolph, and Adrian Schenker. *Biblia Hebraica Stuttgartensia.* 5th rev. ed. Stuttgart: Deutsche Bibelgesellschaft, 2007.

Euripides. *Bacchae; with an English Translation by D. Kovacs.* Loeb Classical Library. Cambridge, MA: Harvard University Press, 2002.

Feder, Y. "Contagion and Cognition: Bodily Experience and the Conceptualization of Pollution (ṭumah) in the Hebrew Bible." *Journal of Near Eastern Studies* 72, no. 2 (2013): 151–67.

Feder, Y. "The Polemic Regarding Skin Diseases in 4QMMT." *Dead Sea Discoveries* 19 (2012): 55–70.

Feinbrun, Naomi and Michael Zohary. *Flora of the Land of Israel.* Jerusalem: Weizmann Science Press, 1956.

Feinbrun-Dothan, Naomi and Michael Zohary. *Flora Palaestina.* Jerusalem: Israel Academy of Sciences and Humanities, 1981.

Fitzmyer, Joseph A. *The Genesis Apocryphon of Qumran Cave I.* 2nd rev. ed. Biblica et Orientalia 18a. Rome: Biblical Institute, 1971.

Fonrobert, Charlotte Elisheva and Martin S. Jaffee. *The Cambridge Companion to the Talmud and Rabbinic Literature.* Cambridge Companions to Religion. Cambridge; New York: Cambridge University Press, 2007.

Fox, C.J., H. M. Hanif, G. Iaria, B. Duchaine and J. J. S. Barton. "Perceptual and Anatomic Patterns of Selective Deficits in Facial Identity and Expression Processing." *Neuropsychologia* 49, no. 12 (2011): 3188–200.

Freilich, A. R. "Tzaraat: 'Biblical Leprosy'." *J.Am.Acad.Dermatol.* 6, no. 1 (1982): 131–34.

Freud, Sigmund, Angela Richards, and James Strachey. *Introductory Lectures on Psychoanalysis.* Pelican Freud Library. Vol. 1. Harmondsworth: Penguin, 1973.

Freud, Sigmund, Angela Richards, James Strachey, and Alan Tyson. *The Psychopathology of Everyday Life.* Pelican Freud Library. Vol. 5. Harmondsworth: Penguin, 1975.

Freud, Sigmund, James Strachey, and Angela Richards. *On Sexuality: Three Essays on the Theory of Sexuality and Other Works.* Pelican Freud Library. Vol. 7. Harmondsworth: Penguin, 1977.

Friedman, R. E. *The Bible with Sources Revealed.* San Francisco: Harper Collins, 2003.

Frymer-Kensky, Tikva. "Pollution, Purification and Purgation in Biblical Israel: Major and Minor Pollutions." Pages 400–14 in *The Word of the Lord Shall go Forth: Essays in Honor of David Noel Freedman in Celebration of his Sixtieth Birthday.* Special Volume Series. American Schools of Oriental Research. Edited by Carol L. Meyers and Michael Patrick O'Connor. Winona Lake, IN: Eisenbrauns, 1983.

Gagarin, M. *The Oxford Encyclopaedia of Ancient Greece and Rome.* 7 vols. Oxford: Oxford University Press, 2010.

Galen, Ian Johnston, and G. H. R. Horsley. *Method of Medicine.* 3 vols. The Loeb Classical Library. Cambridge, MA; London: Harvard University Press, 2011.

Gardiner, A. *Egyptian Grammar.* Oxford: Griffith Institute, 1927.

Gascoyen, G. G. "On Spermatorrhoea and its Treatment." *British Medical Journal* 1 (577), January 20th (1871): 67–69.

Gejrot, T. "Leprosy in the Bible: Incorrect Translation." *Lakartidningen* 96, no. 12 (1999): 1463.

Gelb, Ignace J. *Assyrian Dictionary.* Chicago: University of Chicago Press, 1956.

Geller, M. J. *Ancient Babylonian Medicine: Theory and Practice.* Oxford: Wiley-Blackwell, 2010.

Geller, M. J. "Taboo in Mesopotamia: A Review Article." *Journal of Cuneiform Studies* 42, no. 1 (1990): 105–17.

Gesenius, Wilhelm, A. E. Cowley, E. Kautzsch, Julius Euting, and Mark Lidzbarski. *Gesenius' Hebrew Grammar: With a Facsimile of the Siloam*

Inscription by J. Euting and a Table of Alphabets by M. Lidzbarski. 2nd English ed. Oxford: Clarendon, 1910.

Gibson, John C. L. *Textbook of Syrian Semitic Inscriptions*: Oxford: Clarendon, 1971.

Gildersleeve, Basil L. and Gonzalez Lodge. *Latin Grammar*. London: Bristol Classical Press, 1997.

Glare, P. G. W. *Oxford Latin Dictionary*. 2nd ed. 2 vols. Oxford: Oxford University Press, 2012.

Glasby, M. A. "New Testament Diagnoses." *Expository Times* 122, no. 2 (2010): 98.

Glasby, M. A. "The Control of Posture and Movement." Pages 549–63 in *Applied Physiology for Surgery and Critical Care*. Edited by M. A. Glasby and C. L. H. Huang. Oxford: Butterworth-Heinemann, 1995.

Glasby, M. A., S. Evans, and C. L. H. Huang. "Nerve Regeneration Through Treated Muscle Grafts During Experimental Treatment with Antileprotic Drugs." *Neuro-Orthopedics* 8 (1989): 1–7.

Glasby, Michael A. "An Assessment of the Predictive Value of Laboratory Studies in the Management of Peripheral Nerve Injuries." MD thesis, University of Edinburgh, 2005.

Glasby, Michael A. "What was Biblical Leprosy?" MTh thesis, University of Edinburgh, 2011.

Glickman, F. S. "Lepra, Psora, Psoriasis." *J.Am.Acad.Dermatol.* 14, no. 5 Pt 1 (1986): 863–66.

Goldman, L., R. S. Moraites, and K. W. Kitzmiller. "White Spots in Biblical Times: A Background for the Dermatologist for Participation in Discussions of Current Revisions of the Bible." *Arch.Dermatol.* 93, no. 6 (1966): 744–53.

Good, Edwin M. "Capital Punishment and its Alternatives in Ancient near Eastern Law." *Stanford Law Review* 19, no. 5 (1967): 947–77.

Gordon, Maurice Bear. "Medicine Among the Ancient Hebrews." *Isis* 33, no. 4 (1941): 454–85.

Gorman, Frank H. *The Ideology of Ritual: Space, Time and Status in the Priestly Theology*. Journal for the Study of the Old Testament. Supplement Series. Sheffield: JSOT Press, 1990.

Goshen-Gottstein, M. "Philologische Miszellen zu den Qumrantexten." *Revue de Qumran* 2 (1959-60): 43–51.

Gray, Henry and Susan Standring. *Gray's Anatomy: The Anatomical Basis of Clinical Practice*. 40th ed. Edinburgh: Churchill Livingstone, 2008.

Greenfield, J. C. "Early Aramaic Poetry." *Journal of the Ancient Near Eastern Society* 11 (Bravmann Memorial Volume) (1979): 45–51.

Greer, D. M., P. C. Mohl, and K. A. Sheley. "A Technique for Foreskin Reconstruction and Some Preliminary Results." *Journal of Sex Research* 18, no. 4 (1982): 324–30.

Grieve, Maud and C. F. Leyel. *A Modern Herbal: The Medicinal, Culinary, Cosmetic and Economic Properties, Cultivation and Folklore of Herbs, Grasses, Fungi, Shrubs and Trees with all their Modern Scientific Uses*. London: Tiger Books International, 1998.

Haas, C. J., A. Zink, G. Palfi, U. Szeimies, and A. G. Nerlich. "Detection of Leprosy in Ancient Human Skeletal Remains by Molecular Identification of Mycobacterium Leprae." *American Journal of Clinical Pathology* 114 (2000): 428–36.

Haber, Susan and Adele Reinhartz. *"They Shall Purify Themselves": Essays on Purity in Early Judaism*. Early Judaism and its Literature. Vol. 24. Atlanta, GA: Society of Biblical Literature, 2008.

David Weiss Halivni. *The Formation of the Babylonian Talmud*. Translated by Jeffrey L. Rubenstein. New York: Oxford University Press, 2013.

Hanhart, Robert, Udo Quast, Alfred Rahlfs, John William Wevers, and Joseph Ziegler. *Septuaginta: Vetus Testamentum Graecum*: Göttingen: Vandenhoeck & Ruprecht, 1931.

Hansen, G. H. A. "Undersøgelser Angående Spedalskhedens Årsager (Investigations Concerning the Etiology of Leprosy)." *Norsk Mag. Laegervidenskaben* 4 (1874): 1–88.

Haran, Mehahem. "Behind the Scenes of History: Determining the Date of the Priestly Source." *Journal of Biblical Literature* 100, no. 3 (1981): 321–33.

Hatch, Edwin and Henry A. Redpath. *A Concordance to the Septuagint and the Other Greek Versions of the Old Testament (Including the Apocryphal Books)*. Grand Rapids, MI: Baker, 1983.

Heimpel, W. *Letters to the King of Mari*. Winona Lake, IN: Eisenbrauns, 2003.

Heller, R. M., T. W. Heller, and J. M. Sasson. "Mold: 'tsara'at,' Leviticus, and the History of a Confusion." *Perspect.Biol.Med.* 46, no. 4 (2003): 588–91.

Herodotus. *The Persian Wars*. Translated by A. D. Godley. 4 vols. Loeb Classical Library. Vols 117–120. Cambridge, MA: Harvard University Press, 1999.

Hess, R. S. "A Reassessment of the Priestly and Cultic and Legal Texts." *Journal of Law and Religion* 17, no. 1/2 (2002): 375–91.

Hillers, D. R. "A Difficult Curse in Aqht (19[1 Aqht] 3.152–154" in *Biblical and Related Studies Presented to Samuel Iwry*. Edited by A. Morschauser and S. Kort. Winona Lake, IN: Eisenbrauns, 1985.

Hobart, W. K. *The Medical Language of St Luke*. London: Longmans, 1882.

Hodges, F M. "The Ideal Prepuce in Ancient Greece and Rome: Male Genital Aesthetics and Their Relation to Lipodermos, Circumcision, Foreskin Restoration, and the Kynodesme." *Bulletin of the History of Medicine* 75 (2001): 375–405.

Hoffmann, David, Tsevi Har-Shefer, and Aharon Liberman. *Sefer va-Yikra Meforash*. 2 vols. Jakob Michael Library. Translations and Collections in Jewish Studies. Yerushalayim: Mosad ha-Rav Kook, 1963.

Homer, George Dimock, and A. T. Murray. *The Odyssey*. Revised ed. 2 vols. Loeb Classical Library. Cambridge, MA: Harvard University Press, 2002.

Hourani, A. *A History of the Arab Peoples*. London: Folio Society, 2009.

Howard, J. K. *Medicine, Miracle and Myth in the New Testament*. Eugene, OR: Wipf and Stock, 2010.

Huehnergard, John. *A Grammar of Akkadian*. 2nd ed. Winona Lake, IN: Eisenbrauns, 2005.

Hulse, E V. "Joshua's Curse and the Abandonment of Ancient Jericho: Schistosomiasis as a Possible Medical Explanation." *Medical History* 15, no. 4 (1971): 376–86.

Hulse, E. V. "Nature of Biblical Leprosy and the Use of Alternative Medical Terms in Modern Translations of the Bible." *Palestine Exploration Quarterly* 107 (1975): 87–105.

Hurtado, L. W. "Monotheism." Pages 961–64 in *The Eerdmans Dictionary of Early Judaism*. Edited by John Joseph Collins and Daniel C. Harlow. Grand Rapids, MI: Eerdmans, 2010.

Hurwitz, A. "Dating the Priestly Source in Light of the Historical Study of Biblical Hebrew a Century after Wellhausen." *Zeitschrift für die Alttestamentliche Wissenschaft* 100 (1988): 88–99.

Hurwitz, A. *A Linguistic Study of the Relationship between the Priestly Source and the Book of Ezekiel*. Vol. 20. Cahiers de la Revue Biblique. Paris: J. Gabala, 1982.

Impey, S. P. *Handbook on Leprosy*. Philadelphia: Blakiston, Son & Co, 1896.

Isaacs, H. D. *Medical and Para-medical Manuscripts in the Cambridge Genizah Collections.* Edited by S. C. Reif. Vol. 11. Cambridge University Library Genizah Series. Cambridge: Cambridge University Press, 1994.

Ivanov, S. A. *Holy Fools in Byzantium and Beyond.* Oxford: Oxford University Press, 2006.

Jastrow, M. *Dictionary of the Targumim, the Talmud Babli and Yerushalmi and the Midrashic Literature.* Peabody, MA: Hendrickson, 2006.

Jauss, Hans Robert and Timothy Bahti. *Toward an Aesthetic of Reception.* Minneapolis: University of Minnesota Press, 1982.

Jauss, Hans Robert. *Aesthetic Experience and Literary Hermeneutics.* Minneapolis: University of Minnesota Press, 1982.

Jeffers, Ann. *Magic and Divination in Ancient Palestine and Syria.* Studies in the History of the Ancient Near East. Leiden: Brill, 1996.

Jenson, Philip Peter. *Graded Holiness: a Key to the Priestly Conception of the World.* Journal for the Study of the Old Testament Supplement Series no. 106. Sheffield: JSOT, 1992.

Johnston, I. *Galen: On Diseases and Symptoms.* Cambridge: Cambridge University Press, 2006.

Jones, W. H. S., E. T. Withinton, Paul Potter, Wesley D. Smith, and Heraclitus. *Hippocrates.* 10 vols. Loeb Classical Library. Cambridge, MA; London: Harvard University Press; William Heinemann, 1923–2012.

Josephus, Titus Flavius. *Josephus (Joseph ben Matityahu). Collected Works: with English Translations.* Translated by H. ST. J. Thackeray and L. Feldman. 13 vols. Loeb Classical Library. Cambridge, MA: Harvard University Press, 2004.

Joüon, P and T Muraoka. *A Grammar of Biblical Hebrew.* 2 vols. Rome: Editrice Pontifico Instituto Biblico, 2005.

Jung, C. G. and R. F. C. Hull. *Answer to Job.* London: Routledge and Kegan Paul, 1979.

Kahn, J. and H. Solomon. *Job's Illness: Loss, Grief and Integration. A Psychological Interpretation.* 2nd ed. London: Gaskell/Royal College of Psychiatrists, 1986.

Kaplan, D. L. "Biblical Leprosy: An Anachronism Whose Time has Come." *J.Am.Acad.Dermatol.* 28, no. 3 (1993): 507–10.

Kaufmann, Y. *The Religion of Israel.* London: George Allen & Unwin Ltd, 1961.

Kawabata, Hideaki and Semir Zeki. "Neural Correlates of Beauty." *Journal of Neurophysiology* 91, no. 4 (2004): 1699–705.

King, L. W. *First Steps in Assyrian*. London: Kegan Paul, Trench, Trübner & Co, Ltd, 1898.

Kinnier-Wilson, J. V. "Medicine in the Land and Times of the Old Testament." Pages 337–65 in *Studies in the Period of David and Solomon and Other Essays*. Edited by T Ishida. Winona, IN: Eisenbrauns, 1982.

Kinnier-Wilson, J. V. "Diseases of Babylon: An Examination of Selected Texts." *Journal of the Royal Society of Medicine* 89 (1996): 135–40.

Kittel, G., G. Friedrich, and R. Pitkin. *Theological Dictionary of the New Testament*. 10 vols. Grand Rapids, MI: Eerdmans, 1976.

Klawans, Jonathan. "Notions of Gentile Impurity in Ancient Judaism." *Association of Jewish Studies Review* 20, no. 2 (1995): 285–312.

Klawans, Jonathan. "Pure Violence: Sacrifice and Defilement in Ancient Israel." *The Harvard Theological Review* 94, no 2 (2001): 133–55.

Klawans, Jonathan. *Impurity and Sin in Ancient Judaism*. Oxford: Oxford University Press, 2000.

Klawans, Jonathan. *Purity, Sacrifice, and the Temple: Symbolism and Supersessionism in the Study of Ancient Judaism*. New York; Oxford: Oxford University Press, 2010.

Knohl, I. *The Sanctuary of Silence*. Minneapolis: Fortress, 1995.

Köcher, F. and A. L. Oppenheim. "The Old Babylonian Omen Text VAT 7525." *Archiv für Orientforschung* 18 (1957): 62–77.

Köhler, Ludwig, Walter Baumgartner, Johann Jakob Stamm, and M. E. J. Richardson. *The Hebrew and Aramaic Lexicon of the Old Testament*. Study ed. Leiden: Brill, 2001.

Kratz, R. G. "The Growth of the Old Testament." Pages 459–88 in *The Oxford Handbook of Biblical Studies*. Edited by J. W. Rogerson and Judith Lieu. Oxford: Oxford University Press, 2008.

Labat, R. and F. Malbran-Labat. *Manuel d'Épigraphie Akkadienne: Signes Syllabaire Idéogrammes*. Edited by Librairie Orientaliste Paul Geuthner. Paris: Geuthner S.A., 1988.

Lampe, G. W. H. *A Patristic Greek Lexicon*. Oxford: Oxford University Press, 1961.

Lane, D. J. "The Best Words in the Best Order: Some Comments on the 'Syriacing' of Leviticus." *Vetus Testamentum* 39, no. 4 (1989): 468–79.

Lane, Edward William. *Arabic-English Lexicon*. Cambridge: Islamic Texts Society, 1863, repr 2003.

Lemos, T. M. "Shame and Mutilation of Enemies in the Hebrew Bible." *Journal of Biblical Literature* 125, no. 2 (2006): 225–41.

Lemos, T. M. "The Universal and the Particular: Mary Douglas and the Politics of Impurity." *Journal of Religion* 89, no. 2 (2009): 236–51.

Levias, Caspar. *A Grammar of the Aramaic Idiom Contained in the Babylonian Talmud: With Constant Reference to Gaonic Literature.* Cincinnati: Bloch Publishing & Printing Co., 1896.

Lewis, Charlton Thomas, Charles Short, and William Freund. *A Latin Dictionary: Founded on Andrews' Edition of Freund's Latin Dictionary.* Oxford: Clarendon, 1975.

Lewis, Gilbert. "A Lesson from Leviticus: Leprosy." *Man* 22, no. 4 (1987): 593–612.

Liddell, H. G. and R. Scott. *Greek English Lexicon.* Oxford: Oxford University Press, 1940.

Liddell, K. "Skin Disease in Antiquity." *Clin.Med.* 6, no. 1 (2006): 81–86.

Lieber, E. "Cleansing the Leper in the Old and New Testaments." *Korot.* 13 (1998): 77–101.

Lieber, E. "Leprosy in the Lands of the Bible, and the Demons Bes and Pazuzu. Part I: Ancient Egypt and the Bes-image." *Korot.* 10 (1993): 25–43.

Lieber, E. "Old Testament 'Leprosy', Contagion and Sin." Pages 99–136 in *Contagion, Perspectives in Pre-modern Societies.* Edited by L. I. Wujastyk and D. Conrad. Aldershot: Ashgate, 2000.

Lieber, Elinor. "Asaf's 'Book of Medicines': A Hebrew Encyclopedia of Greek and Jewish Medicine, Possibly Compiled in Byzantium on an Indian Model." *Dumbarton Oaks Papers* 38 (1984): 233–49.

Lim, T. H. "The Defilement of the Hands as a Principle Determining the Holiness of Scriptures." *Journal of Theological Studies* 61, no. Pr 2 (2010): 501–15.

Liveing, R. *Elephantiasis Graecorum or True leprosy.* London: Spottiswoode & Co., 1872.

Lutz, H. F. "A Contribution to the Knowledge of Assyro-Babylonian Medicine." *The American Journal of Semitic Languages and Literatures* 36, no. 1 (1919): 67–83.

MacCulloch, D. *Reformation, Europe's House Divided 1490–1700.* 2 vols. London: Folio Society, 2013.

Maghen, Ze'ev. "Close Encounters: Some Preliminary Observations on the Transmission of Impurity in Early Sunnī Jurisprudence." *Islamic Law and Society* 6, no. 3 (1999): 348–92.

Maimonides, Moses and Gerrit Bos. *Medical Aphorisms. Treatises 1-5: A Parallel Arabic-English Edition*. 2 vols. Provo, UT: Brigham Young University Press, 2004.

Maimonides, Moses and Gerrit Bos. *Medical Aphorisms. Treatises 6-9: A Parallel Arabic-English Edition*. 2 vols. Provo, UT: Brigham Young University Press, 2007.

Maimonides, Moses and Gerrit Bos. *Medical Aphorisms. Treatises 10-15: A Parallel Arabic-English Edition*. Provo, UT: Brigham Young University Press, 2010.

Mandelkern, S. *Veteris Testamenti Concordantiae Hebraicae atque Chaldaicae*. Editio Altera Locupletissime Aucta et Emendata Cura. F. Margolin ed. 2 vols. Gratz: Akademische Druck U. Verlagsanstalt, 1896.

Margolis, Howard and Arthur Shapiro. "Countering Negative Images of Disability in Classical Literature." *The English Journal* 76, no. 3 (1987): 18–22.

Martinez, F. G. and E. J. C. Tigchelaar. *The Dead Sea Scrolls. Study Edition* 2. Leiden; Boston, MA: Brill, 1998.

Mascall, E. L. *Existence and Analogy*. London: Longmans, Green and Co., 1949.

Mason, W. A. "The Monotheistic Concept and the Evolution of Medical Thought." *Phylon (1940-1956)* 12, no. 3 (1951): 255–63.

Massey, E. W. "Leprosy: Biblical Opprobrium?" *South.Med.J.* 71, no. 10 (1978): 1294–95.

Matheson, C. D., K. K. Vernon, A. Lahti, R. Fratpietro, M. Spigelman, S. Gibson, C. L. Greenblatt, and H. D. Donoghue. "Molecular Exploration of the First Century Tomb of the Shroud in Akeldama, Jerusalem." *PLoS ONE* 4, no. 12 (2009).

McCaughey, J. D. "The Leper." *Med.J.Aust.* 1, no. 13 (1975): 425–26.

McCutchan, J. Allen. "Epidemiology of Venereal Urethritis: Comparison of Gonorrhea and Nongonococcal Urethritis." *Reviews of Infectious Diseases* 6, no. 5 (1984): 669–88.

Meigs, A. S. "A Papuan Perspective on Pollution." *Man* 13 (1978): 304–18.

Melcher, S J. "Visualizing the Perfect Cult." Pages 55–71 in *Human Disability and the Service of God: Reassessing Religious Practice*. Edited by Nancy L. Eiesland and Don E. Saliers. Nashville, TN: Abingdon, 1998.

Milgrom, Jacob. *Leviticus: A Continental Commentary.* Minneapolis: Fortress, 2004.

Milgrom, Jacob. "Two Kinds of hattā't." *Vetus Testamentum* 26, no. 3 (1976): 333-37.

Milgrom, Jacob. *Leviticus: A New Translation with Introduction and Commentary.* Anchor Bible 3 vols. New York: Doubleday, 1991.

Miller, Douglas B. and R. Mark Shipp. *An Akkadian Handbook: Paradigms, Helps, Glossary, Logograms, and Sign List.* Winona Lake, IN: Eisenbrauns, 1996.

Monier-Williams, M. *A Sanskrit - English Dictionary.* Oxford: Oxford University Press, 1899.

Moran, W. L. "Review of ARMTX." *Journal of the American Oriental Society* 100 (1980): 186–89.

Morton, R. S. "The Sibbens of Scotland." *Medical History* 11, no. 4 (1967): 374–80.

Mull, Kenneth V. and Carolyn Sandquist Mull. "Biblical Leprosy: Is it Really?" *Bible Review* 8, no. 2 (1992): 32.

Muraoka, T. *A Grammar of Qumran Aramaic.* Ancient Near Eastern Studies. Supplement 38. Leuven; Walpole, MA: Peeters, 2011.

Muraoka, T. *A Greek-English Lexicon of the Septuagint.* Louvain: Peeters, 2009.

Muraoka, T., M. F. J. Baasten, and W. Th van Peursen. *Hamlet on a Hill: Semitic and Greek Studies Presented to Professor T. Muraoka on the Occasion of his Sixty-fifth Birthday.* Orientalia Lovaniensia Analecta 118. Leuven; Dudley, MA: Peeters, 2003.

Mykytiuk, Lawrence J. *Identifying Biblical Persons in Northwest Semitic Inscriptions of 1200–539 BCE.* Society of Biblical Literature Academia Biblica no 12. Atlanta: Society of Biblical Literature, 2004.

Nestle, E. and B. Aland. *Novum Testamentum Graece.* Na28 ed. Münster: Institute For New Testament Textual Research, 2014.

Neufeld, Edward. "Hygiene Conditions in Ancient Israel (Iron Age)." *The Biblical Archaeologist* 34, no. 2 (1971): 42–66.

Neufeld, Edward. "The Earliest Document of a Case of Contagious Disease in Mesopotamia, (Mari Tablet ARM X, 129)." *Journal of Ancient near Eastern Studies* 18 (1986): 53–66.

Neusner, Jacob and Alan J. Avery-Peck. *Encyclopaedia of Midrash: Biblical Interpretation in Formative Judaism.* 2 vols. Leiden: Brill, 2005.

Neusner, Jacob. "Studying Synoptic Texts Synoptically, the Case of Leviticus Rabbah." *Proceedings of the American Academy for Jewish Research* 53 (1986): 111–45.

Neusner, Jacob. "The Idea of Purity in Ancient Judaism." *Journal of the American Academy of Religion* 43, no. 1 (1975): 15–26.

Neusner, Jacob. *The Idea of Purity in Ancient Judaism.* Studies in Judaism in Late Antiquity. Vol. 1. Leiden: Brill, 1973.

Nida, Eugene Albert. "The Translation of 'leprosy': A Brief Contribution to the Discussion." *Bible Translator (Ap, O Practical Papers)* 11, no. 2 (1960): 80–81.

Noth, Martin. *A History of Pentateuchal Traditions.* Scholars Press Reprint Series no.5. Chico, CA: Scholars Press, 1981.

Noth, Martin. *The History of Israel.* 2nd ed. London: Xpress Reprints, 1996.

Nuchtern, M. "'And the Skin Turned White as Snow...' On Skin Diseases and Leprosy in the Bible." *Dtsch.Krankenpflegez.* 42, no. 7 (1989): 425–29.

Nutton, V. "Did the Greeks Have a Word for It? Contagion and Contagion Theory in Classical Antiquity." Pages 137–62 in *Contagion, Perspectives in Pre-modern Societies.* Edited by L. I. Wujastyk and D. Conrad. Aldershot: Ashgate, 2000.

Olmo Lete, Gregorio del, Joaquín Sanmartín, and Wilfred G. E. Watson. *A Dictionary of the Ugaritic Language in the Alphabetic Tradition.* 2nd rev. ed. 2 vols. Leiden; Boston: Brill, 2004.

Olyan, S. M. "The Ascription of Physical Disability as a Stigmatizing Strategy in Biblical iconic Polemics." Pages 89–102 in *Disability Studies and Biblical Literature.* Edited by Candida R. Moss and Jeremy Schipper. New York: Palgrave Macmillan, 2011.

Olyan, Saul M. "Honor, Shame, and Covenant Relations in Ancient Israel and Its Environment." *Journal of Biblical Literature* 115, no. 2 (1996): 201–18.

Olyan, Saul M. "The Exegetical Dimensions of Restrictions on the Blind and the Lame in Texts from Qumran." *Dead Sea Discoveries* 8, no. 1 (2001): 38–50.

Olyan, Saul M. "What Do Shaving Rites Accomplish and What Do They Signal in Biblical Ritual Contexts?" *Journal of Biblical Literature* 117, no. 4 (1998): 611–22.

Olyan, Saul M. *Disability in the Hebrew Bible: Interpreting Mental and Physical Differences.* Cambridge: Cambridge University Press, 2008.

Olyan, Saul M. *Rites and Rank: Hierarchy in Biblical Representations of Cult.* Princeton, NJ; Chichester: Princeton University Press, 2000.

Oppenheim, A. L. and E. Reiner, eds. *The Assyrian Dictionary of the Oriental Institute of the University of Chicago.* Vol. 4. Chicago, IL: Oriental Institute, 1958.

Ostrer, B. S. "Leprosy: Medical Views of Leviticus Rabba." *Early Science and Medicine* 7, no. 2 (2002): 138–54.

Parker, Robert. *Miasma: Pollution and Purification in Early Greek Religion.* Oxford: Clarendon, 1983.

Paton, L. B. "The Original Form of Leviticus xvii.-xix." *Journal of Biblical Literature* 16, no. 1/2 (1897): 31–77.

Paton, L. B. "The Original Form of Leviticus xxi., xxii." *Journal of Biblical Literature* 17, no. 2 (1898): 149–75.

Paton, L. B. "The Original Form of Leviticus xxiii., xxv." *Journal of Biblical Literature* 18, no. 1/2 (1899): 35–60.

Paton, Lewis B. "Notes on Driver's Leviticus." *Journal of Biblical Literature* 14, no. 1/2 (1895): 48–56.

Pelling, C. B. R. *Plutarch and History.* Swansea: Classical Press of Wales, 2002.

Pereira, J. H., D. D. Palande, T. S. Narayanakumar, A. S. Subramanian, S. Gschmeissner, and M. Wilkinson. "Nerve Repair by Denatured Muscle Autografts Promotes Sustained Sensory Recovery in Leprosy." *Journal of Bone and Joint Surgery* 90-B (2007): 220–24.

Perez Fernandez, Miguel. *An Introductory Grammar of Rabbinic Hebrew.* Leiden; New York: Brill, 1997.

Peters, J. P. "The Hebrew Idea of Holiness." *The Biblical World* 14, no. 5 (1899): 344–55.

Phipps, William E. "The Menstrual Taboo in the Judeo-Christian Tradition." *Journal of Religion and Health* 19, no. 4 (1980): 298–303.

Pietersma, Albert and Benjamin G. Wright. *A New English Translation of the Septuagint: and the Other Greek Translations Traditionally Included Under that Title.* New York; Oxford: Oxford University Press, 2007.

Pilch, John J. "Biblical Leprosy and Body Symbolism." *Biblical Theology Bulletin* 11 (1981): 108–13.

Pliny the Elder. *Naturalis Historia.* Translated by H. Rackham. 10 vols. Loeb Classical Library. Cambridge, MA: Harvard University Press, 1938.

Plutarch. *Lives.* 11 vols. Translated by B. Perrin. Loeb Classical Library. Cambridge, MA; London: Harvard University Press, 1989.

Poorthuis, Marcel and Joshua Schwartz. *Purity and Holiness: the Heritage of Leviticus.* Jewish and Christian Perspectives Series. Leiden; Boston: Brill, 2000.

Porten, B. and A. Yardeni. *Textbook of Aramaic Documents from Ancient Egypt.* Jerusalem: Hebrew University, 1986.

Porten, B. *The Elephantine Papyri in English.* Edited by P. M. M. G. Akkermans, C. H. J. de Geus Haerinck, P. J. Hout, M. Stol, and D. Van der Plas. Documenta et Monumenta Orientis Antiqui. Leiden; New York; Koln: Brill, 1996.

Porter, J. R. "The Legal Aspects of the Concept of 'Corporate Personality' in the Old Testament." *Vetus Testamentum* 15, no. 3 (1965): 361–80.

Prioreschi, Plinio. *A History of Medicine* 2 vols. Omaha, NE: Horatius Press, 1996.

Pritchard, J. B., ed. *Ancient Near Eastern Texts Relating to the Old Testament.* 3rd ed. Princeton, NJ: Princeton University Press, 1969.

Propp, William H. C. "The Priestly Source Recovered Intact?" *Vetus Testamentum* 46, no. 4 (1996): 458–78.

Rafi, A., M. Spigelman, J. Stanford, E. Lemma, and H. D. Donoghue. "Mycobacterium Leprae DNA from Ancient Bone Detected by PCR." *Lancet* 343 (1994): 1360–61.

Rahlfs, Alfred, and Robert Hanhart, eds. *Septuaginta.* Stuttgart: Deutsche Bibelgesellschaft, 2007.

Ranson, Stephen Walter and Sam Lillard Clark. *The Anatomy of the Nervous System. Revised by Sam Lillard Clark.* 10th ed. Philadelphia; London: W. B. Saunders Co., 1959.

Regev, Eyal. "Priestly Dynamic Holiness and Deuteronomic Static Holiness." *Vetus Testamentum* 51, no. 2 (2001): 243–61.

Ricœur, Paul. *The Symbolism of Evil.* Translated by E Buchanan. Boston: Beacon, 1969.

Robbins, G., V. M. Tripathy, V. N. Misra, R. K. Mohanty, V. S. Shinde, K. M. Gray, and M. D. Schug. *Ancient Skeletal Evidence for Leprosy in India (2000BC)* (5) www.plosone.org, 2009

Rosenthal, Franz. *A Grammar of Biblical Aramaic.* 6th rev. ed. Porta Linguarum Orientalium Neue Serie. Bd. 5. Wiesbaden: Harrassowitz, 1995.

Rosner, F. *Encyclopaedia of Medicine in the Bible and the Talmud.* Northvale, NJ: Jason Aronson, 2000.

Rubin, J. P. "Celsus' Decircumcision Operation. Medical and Historical Implications." *Urology* 16, no. 1 (1980): 121–24.

Sáenz-Badillos, Angel. *A History of the Hebrew Language*. 1st paperback ed. New York: Cambridge University Press, 1996.

Sanders, E. P. *Judaism: Practice and Belief 63 BCE–66 CE*. 2nd impr. with corr. ed. London; Philadelphia: SCM; Trinity Press International, 1994.

Sanders, E. P. *Paul and Palestinian Judaism: A Comparison of Patterns of Religion*. London: SCM, 1977.

Sawyer, J. F. A. "A Note on the Etymology of sara'at." *Vetus Testamentum* 26, no. 2 (1976): 241–45.

Saxey, Roderick. "A Physician's Reflections on Old Testament Medicine." *Dialogue* 17, no. 3 (1984): 122–28.

Schattner-Rieser, Ursula. *L' Araméen des Manuscrits de la mer Morte*, Instruments pour l'Étude des Langues de l'Orient Ancien 5. Lausanne: Editions du Zèbre, 2004.

Scrolls, Dead Sea. "Dead Sea Scrolls Electronic Library." Provo, UT: Brigham Young University, 2006.

Segal, M. H. *A Grammar of Mishnaic Hebrew*. Oxford: Clarendon, 1927.

Seow, C. L. *Job 1–21: Interpretation and Commentary*. Grand Rapids, MI: Eerdmans, 2013.

Shivtiel, A. and F. Niessen, eds. *Arabic and Judaeo-arabic Manuscripts in the Cambridge Genizah Collections*. Edited by S. C. Reif. Vol. 14 of Cambridge University Library Genizah Series. Cambridge: Cambridge University Press, 2006.

Shoulson, Mark. *The Torah: Jewish and Samaritan versions compared*. 2nd ed. Leac an Anfa, Co. Mhaigh Eo: Evertype, 2008.

Simpson, C. A. *The Early Traditions of Israel*. 1st ed. Oxford: Oxford University Press, 1948.

Simpson, J. A. and E. S. C. Weiner. *The Oxford English Dictionary*. 2nd ed. 20 vols. Oxford: Clarendon, 1989.

Skinsnes, O. K. "Leprosy and the New English Bible." *Int.J.Lepr.Other Mycobact.Dis.* 38, no. 3 (1970): 310–12.

Smith, M. S. *The Origins of Biblical Monotheism: Israel's Polytheistic Background and the Ugaritic Texts*. Oxford: Oxford University Press, 2001.

Smith, Virginia. *Clean: A History of Personal Hygiene and Purity*. Oxford: Oxford University Press, 2007.

Smyth, Herbert Weir and Gordon M. Messing. *Greek Grammar*. Rev ed. Cambridge, MA: Harvard University Press, 1984.

Snaith, N. H. "The Cult of Molech." *Vetus Testamentum* 16, no. 1 (1966): 123–24.

Snaith, N. H. *Leviticus and Numbers.* London: Nelson, 1967.

Soden, W. von and B. Meissner. *Akkadisches Handwörterbuch. 3 vols.* Wiesbaden: Otto Harrassowitz, 1965.

Sokoloff, M. *A Dictionary of Jewish Babylonian Aramaic of the Talmudic and Geonic Periods.* Ramat-Gan, Israel; Baltimore, MA; London: Bar Ilan University Press; Johns Hopkins Press, 2002.

Sokoloff, M. *A Dictionary of Jewish Palestinian Aramaic of the Byzantine Period.* 2nd ed. Ramat-Gat, Israel; Baltimore; London: Bar Ilan University Press; Johns Hopkins University Press, 2002.

Sokoloff, M. *A Dictionary of Judean Aramaic.* Ramat-Gat, Israel: Bar Ilan University Press, 2003.

Soncino. *The Soncino Classics Collection: Judaic Texts; Talmud, Mishnah, Midrash Rabbah and Zohar in Hebrew, Aramaic and English.* Chicago, IL: Davka Corporation and Soncino Press, 2009.

Sperber, A., ed. *The Bible in Aramaic Based on Old Manuscripts and Printed Texts.* 5 vols. Leiden: Brill, 1973.

Stackert, Jeffrey. *Rewriting the Torah: Literary Revision in Deuteronomy and the Holiness Legislation.* Forschungen zum Alten Testament 52. Tubingen: Mohr Siebeck, 2007.

Stern, M., ed. *Greek and Latin Authors on Jews and Judaism.* 3 vols. Jerusalem: Israel Academy of Sciences and Humanities, 1974.

Stevenson, W. B. *Grammar of Palestinian Jewish Aramaic.* Vol. 2. Oxford: Clarendon, 1962.

Stewart, D. T. "Sexual Disabilities in the Hebrew Bible." Pages 67–87 in *Disability Studies and Biblical Literature.* Edited by Candida R. Moss and Jeremy Schipper. New York: Palgrave Macmillan, 2011.

Sticht-Groh, V. and G. Bretzel. "Leprosy: Current Aspects of a Disease from Biblical Times." *Immun.Infekt.* 23, no. 6 (1995): 216–21.

Stolberg, Michael. "Self-Pollution, Moral Reform, and the Venereal Trade: Notes on the Sources and Historical Context of Onania (1716)." *Journal of the History of Sexuality* JHS 9, no. 1/2 (2000): 37–61.

Strack, H. L., Gunter Stemberger, and Markus N. A. Bockmuehl. *Introduction to the Talmud and Midrash.* 2nd ed. Minneapolis: Fortress Press, 1996.

Sullivan, R. "Deformity: A Modern Western Prejudice with Ancient Origins." *Proceedings of the Royal College of Physicians of Edinburgh* 31 (2001): 262–66.

Swellengrebel, J. L. "'Leprosy' and the Bible: The Translation of tsara'ath and lepra." *Bible Translator (Ap, O Practical Papers)* 11, no. 2 (1960): 69–80.

Swift, T. R. and T. D. Sabin. "Leprous Neuritis." Pages 1236–43 in *Clinical Neurology*. Edited by M. Swash and J. Oxbury. Edinburgh: Churchill Livingstone, 1991.

Tal, A. *A Dictionary of Samaritan Aramaic*. 2 vols. Leiden: Brill, 2000.

Tawil, Hayim ben Yosef. *An Akkadian Lexical Companion for Biblical Hebrew*. Jersey City, NJ: KTAV Publishing House, 2009.

Thompson, R. Campbell. *A Dictionary of Assyrian Botany*. London: British Academy, 1949.

Todd, John. "Leprosy, Biblical and Mediaeval." *Modern Churchman* 34; 4–6 (1944): 129–37.

Toorn, K. van der, Bob Becking, and Pieter Willem van der Horst. *Dictionary of Deities and dDmons in the Bible (DDD)*. Leiden: Brill, 1995.

Touati, F. O. "Contagion and Leprosy: Myth, Ideas and Evolution in Medieval Minds and Societies." Pages 179–202 in *Contagion, Perspectives in Pre-modern Societies*. Edited by L. I. Wujastyk and D. Conrad. Aldershot: Ashgate, 2000.

Trevaskis, Leigh M. *Holiness, Ethics and Ritual in Leviticus*. Hebrew Bible Monographs. Sheffield: Sheffield Phoenix 2010.

Trible, Phyllis. "The Israelite Woman: Social Role and Literary Type in Biblical Narrative by Athalya Brenner Review." *Journal of Biblical Literature* 106, no. 4 (1987): 700–01.

Tupper, Kerr B. "The Samaritan Pentateuch." *The Hebrew Studen*, 1, no. 2 (1882): 7–8.

Turner, V. *The Ritual Process: Structure and Anti-structure*. Picataway, NJ: Transaction Rutgers, 1969.

Turner, Victor W. and Richard Schechner. *The Anthropology of Performance*. New York: PAJ Publications, 1986.

Tyndale, W. *The New Testament; Tyndale's 1526 Edition with Original Spelling*. London: British Library, 2003.

Ullendorff, Edward. "The Bawdy Bible." Bulletin of the School of Oriental and African Studies, University of London, 42, no. 3 (1979): 425–56.

Ulrich, E. *The Biblical Qumran Scrolls*. Edited by H. M. Barstad, R. P. Gordon, A. Hurvitz, G. N. Knoppers, A. Van Der Kooij, A. Lemaire, C. A. Newsom, H.

Spieckermann, J. Trebolle Barrera, and H. G. M. Williamson. Supplements to Vetus Testamentum 134. Leiden; Boston, MA: Brill, 2010.

Van de Mieroop, Marc. *A History of the Ancient Near East, ca. 3000–323 BC*. 2nd ed. Blackwell History of the Ancient World. Oxford: Blackwell, 2007.

Visotzky, Burton L. *Golden Bells and Pomegranates: Studies in Midrash Leviticus Rabbah*. Tübingen: Mohr Siebeck, 2003.

Waters, M. F. R. "Leprosy (Hansen's Disease)." Pages 5.305–5.13 in *Oxford Textbook of Medicine*. Edited by D. J. Weatherall, J. G. G. Ledingham, and D. A. Warrell. Oxford: Oxford University Press, 1989.

Weed, W. W. "Biblical Leprosy." *J.Am.Acad.Dermatol.* 29, no. 6 (1993): 1058–59.

Weinfeld, Moshe. *Deuteronomy and the Deuteronomic School*. Oxford: Clarendon Press, 1972.

Weiss, Charles. "Medicine in the Bible." *The Scientific Monthly* 50, no. 3 (1940): 266–71.

Wellhausen, Julius. *Prolegomena To the History of Israel*. Edinburgh: Black, 1885.

Wenham, G. J. "The Priority of P." *Vetus Testamentum* 19, no. 2 (1999): 240–58.

Wenham, G. "Why does Sexual Intercourse Defile? (Lev 15:18)." *Zeitschrift für die Alttestamentliche Wissenschaft* 95 (1983): 432–34.

Wenham, Gordon J. *The Book of Leviticus*. Grand Rapids, MI: Eerdmans, 1979.

Wevers, John William, Robert Hanhart, Werner Kappler, Alfred Rahlfs, and Joseph Ziegler, eds. *Septuaginta-Unternehmen*. Akademie der Wissenschaften in Göttingen. *Septuaginta: Vetus Testamentum Graecum*. Göttingen: Vandenhoeck & Ruprecht, 1931.

Wevers, John William. *Notes on the Greek Text of Leviticus*. Edited by Bernard A. Taylor. Society of Biblical Literature Septuagint and Cognate Studies Series 44. Atlanta: Scholars' Press, 1997.

Whitekettle, Richard. "Leviticus 15:18 Reconsidered: Chiasm, Spatial Structure and the Body." *Journal for the Study of the Old Testament*, no. 49 (1991): 31–5.

Wise, Michael Owen, Martin G. Abegg, and Edward M. Cook. *The Dead Sea Scrolls: A New Translation*. London: Harper Collins, 1996.

Wiseman, D. J. "The Vassal-Treaties of Esarhaddon." *Iraq* 20, no. 1 (1958): i–99.

Wootton, David. *Bad Medicine: Doctors Doing Harm since Hippocrates.* Oxford: Oxford University Press, 2006.

World Health Organization. *Eliminating Female Genital Mutilation: An Interagency Statement.* W.H.O., 2008.

Wright, D. P. "The Spectrum of Priestly Impurity." Pages 150–165 in *Priesthood and Cult in Ancient Israel.* Edited by G. A. Anderson and S. M. Olyan. Sheffield: JSOT Press, 1991.

Wright, D. P. "Holiness in Leviticus and Beyond." *Interpretation* 53, no. 4 (1999): 351–64.

Wright, D. P. "Two Types of Impurity in the Priestly Writings of the Bible." *Koroth* 9 (1988): 180–93.

Wytton Davies, T. "Bible Leprosy." *The Old and New Testament Student* 11, no. 3 (1890): 142–52.

Young, Ian, Robert Rezetko, and Martin Ehrensvärd. *Linguistic Dating of Biblical Texts.* 2 vols. BibleWorld. London; Oakville, CT: Equinox, 2008.

Zadoks, Annie Nicolette. *Ancestral Portraiture in Rome and the Art of the Last Century of the Republic.* Allard Pierson Stichting Deel 1. Archaeolische-historische Bijdragen. Amsterdam: N. v. Noord-Hollandsche uitgevers-mij., 1932.

Ziegler, Joseph, Werner Kappler, Robert Hanhart, Alfred Rahlfs, and Septuaginta-Unternehmen. Akademie der Wissenschaften in Göttingen. *Septuaginta: Vetus Testamentum Graecum Auctoritate Academiae Litterarum Göttingensis ditum.* 2. durchgesehene Aufl. ed. Göttingen: Vandenhoeck & Ruprecht, 1967.

Zohary, Daniel and Maria Hopf. *Domestication of Plants in the Old World.* 3rd ed. Oxford: Oxford University Press, 1999.

Zohary, M. *Plants of the Bible.* Cambridge: Cambridge University Press, 1982.

Zohary, Michael. *The Flora of Iraq and its Phytogeographical Subdivision:* Baghdad. Iraq Ministry of Economics. Directorate-General of Agriculture. Bulletin. no. 31. 1946.

Zysk, K. G. *Religious Medicine: The History and Evolution of Indian Medicine.* Edison, NJ: Transaction, 1992.

SELECTED INDEX

Affliction(s) 23, 34, 46, 73, 87, 95, 119, 136, 162, 2104, 234, 262

Aanalytical 59, 88, 96, 100, 246, 278

Apothecaries 53, 55, 62-5, 251

Bacterial 127-8, 151, 153-4, 179-80, 260, 262, 276

Benign 148, 156, 178, 226, 258

Bilharzia 180-2

Biological 38-9, 49, 207

Bladder 48, 181-3

Blemish(es) 9-10, 14, 94-6, 102, 111, 119-20, 199-228, 285

Blennorrhoea 179-80

Blind(ness) 81, 178, 181, 183, 213-4, 216, 219-20, 224, 226, 235

Blood 36, 78, 101, 162, 182, 223

Boil 80, 138, 153

Burn 22, 103, 154, 218

Causation 39, 95, 120, 265, 267

Cells 127-8, 152-4, 259

Chronic 121, 124, 128, 132, 151, 160, 175, 180, 259-63, 278

Cleansing 43, 107, 155, 167, 185-6, 195, 239, 242, 244, 271, 291

Cognate(s) 64, 73, 86, 129, 134, 136, 145, 175, 234, 240, 243, 254

Copulation 172, 186-7, 189-91, 193

Corpses 85, 98, 113, 141, 186

Cure 42, 49, 56, 73, 80, 126, 179, 233, 258, 269, 277-8, 281

Cutaneous 80, 258-9, 263, 289

Deaf 219, 228

Deformity 130, 201, 216

Dermatological 42, 46, 79, 144, 157, 162, 267, 277

Dermopathic 106, 159, 216, 228, 254, 287

Disabilities 199, 202-3, 227

Doctors 41, 44, 55, 178, 249

Drugs 155, 250

Dysfunction 81, 202, 208, 216, 220, 227

Effluxions 166, 170-1, 183

Elephantiasis graecorum/arabum 121, 140, 234, 255

Emissions 105, 171, 192

Endemic 47, 81, 127, 182, 261

Faeces 106, 182, 198, 241

Fomites 192, 231, 233-4

Fractures 42-3

Fungal 155, 157, 185, 258, 260

Genitals/genitalia 119, 176, 204, 211, 216, 227

Gonorrhoea 81, 172, 176, 184

Schistosoma haematobium/mansoni 181, 183

Hansen's disease 76, 81, 121-4, 133, 159, 233, 255, 258-9, 261-3

Hippocrates 40, 49, 131, 146-7, 236, 251

Hyperdiagnosis 12-3, 76, 161, 257, 264, 278

Identification 48, 64, 68, 141, 143, 177, 244, 271, 275, 277, 301

Infection(s)/infectious 72, 81, 123, 177, 179-81, 184-5, 234, 240-2, 259

Inflammatory 124, 128, 137, 146-7, 153-6, 177, 180

Insanity 81, 225-6

Intercourse 58, 164-5, 167-8, 172-3, 186-9, 193, 198

Leishmaniasis 80, 259, 263

Lepers 71, 81, 121, 130, 166-7

Leprae 122, 124-5, 141

Lepromatous 124-5, 127, 130, 136

Madness 74, 81, 224-6

Medicinal 51, 64

Medicines 41, 54, 63, 74

Menstruation 85, 105, 162, 171, 191, 221, 253

Mutilation 201, 203-4, 217-223

Mycobacterial 126-7, 130, 132

Mycobacterium leprae 122, 124-5

Nerve(s) 78, 124-5, 127-8, 259

Neurosis 224-5, 277

Ophthalmia neonatorum 81, 179

Organism 180-1, 189

Pachydermatous 125, 128, 136, 155, 258-9

Pathognomonic 48, 130, 132, 148, 154-6, 169, 259

Pathological/pathology 42, 144, 153, 159, 169, 182, 217, 229, 238, 255, 259

Physician(s) 12, 41, 49-57, 74, 249, 251, 269, 279, 283, 289

Plague 36, 135-9, 147, 161, 182, 229, 231, 237, 243, 269

Platydysmorphism/-ic 157, 159, 169-70, 213, 216, 228, 254-5, 263, 267, 287

Psoriasis 80, 131-3, 148, 259, 263, 275

Psychological 74, 256, 260, 289

Purgation 43, 101-3, 110

Quarantine 72, 81, 146-58, 167, 186, 195, 233-4, 289

Remedies 42-3, 56, 64-5, 251

Rubor 132, 144-6, 153, 156

Scabies 80, 155, 258

Scale 14, 124, 134-6, 152, 159, 162, 175, 241, 259, 261

Scarring 146, 150, 154, 157, 159, 259, 261, 263, 276-7

Schistosomiasis 43, 47, 180-2, 198

Scutula 155, 259, 263

Semen 24, 105, 172-6, 186, 193, 203, 206, 288

Sensorimotor 220, 227

Sensory 202, 207-8, 220, 255

Sexually transmitted 183

Stigmata 204, 227, 229, 252

Stigma 126, 142, 216, 223, 268

Surgery 42-3, 52, 278

Swelling 129, 132, 136, 145-6, 150, 153

Symptomatology 39, 122, 124, 133, 159, 180-1, 197, 256-9, 263-4, 277

Therapeutic 12, 33, 49, 52, 63, 81, 180, 288-90

Thickening 124-5, 128, 130, 132, 155, 259

Tissue 125, 150, 154, 177

Trachoma 43, 51, 81, 180-1

Transmission 66, 126, 177, 184, 187, 196, 198, 229, 231, 236-7, 243, 275, 285, 290

Treponematoses 160, 260-1

Tuberculosis 125-7, 130-2, 141, 278

Tumor 146, 153, 156

Ulceration 145, 148, 151, 153-5, 261

Urethritis 180, 182, 197-8

Urinary 171, 177, 181-3

Venereal disease 178, 183, 197, 223

Whiteness 121, 123, 128, 131, 135, 137, 140, 146, 150, 152-3, 159-60, 259

Wounds 43, 73-4, 78-9

www.ingramcontent.com/pod-product-compliance
Lightning Source LLC
Chambersburg PA
CBHW070232230426
43664CB00014B/2279